Advanced
PRACTICAL
COOKERY

Victor Ceserani, MBE, CPA, MBA, FHCIMA
Formerly Head of The School of Hotel Keeping and Catering,
Ealing College of Higher Education (now Thames Valley University)

Ronald Kinton, BEd (Hons), FHCIMA
Formerly of Garnett College, College of Education for Teachers
in Further and Higher Education

David Foskett, BEd (Hons), FHCIMA
Head of Programmes, School of Hospitality Studies,
Thames Valley University

Hodder & Stoughton

A MEMBER OF THE HODDER HEADLINE GROUP

Photos by J. Gerard Smith from *Advanced Professional Cooking* by Wayne Gisslen (John Wiley & Sons Inc, 1992).

The publishers are very grateful to John Wiley & Sons for giving permission to reprint the photographs featured in this book.

54074

British Library Cataloguing in Publication Data

Ceserani, Victor
  Advanced Practical Cookery
  I. Title
  641.5

ISBN 0–340–61153–7

First published 1995
Impression number   10 9 8 7 6 5 4 3 2 1
Year   1999 1998 1997 1996 1995
Copyright © 1995 Victor Ceserani, Ronald Kinton and David Foskett

Typeset by Wearset, Boldon, Tyne and Wear.
Printed in Great Britain for Hodder & Stoughton Educational, a division of Hodder Headline Plc, 338 Euston Road, London NW1 3BH by St Edmundsbury Press Ltd, Bury St Edmunds, Suffolk.

CONTENTS

FOREWORD

Forte is delighted to sponsor the nutritional analysis of the recipes for such a practical and valuable publication.

In the light of the recent publication of the government White Paper, *The Health of the Nation*, and the increasing public awareness of the importance of healthy eating together with the demand for vegetarian dishes, our industry has a key role to play in monitoring the nutritional content of the food we serve.

Forte is strongly committed to promoting healthy eating, and teaching our staff to prepare healthy food is an essential part of the training programme. As the largest hotel and catering company in the UK, we have always placed great emphasis on the importance of training our staff, and it is a key element in our commitment to provide quality service to our guests throughout the world.

With over 50,000 employees worldwide, Forte also believes that training must continue in the workplace, and we invest over £30 million every year towards training and developing the people within our company. One example of this policy is demonstrated by Forte putting 13,000 UK staff through our food hygiene programme in two years as a result of the Food Safety Act which brought a renewed emphasis to food hygiene training. In 1994 we were especially proud to be awarded a National Training Award for one of these programmes.

We hope that *Advanced Practical Cookery* will provide an invaluable source of information for catering students, suggesting dishes that are not only delicious and attractively presented, but also nutritionally sound.

INTRODUCTION

The content of this book encompasses the requirements of those taking Food Preparation and Cooking, Kitchen and Larder, and Patisserie and Confectionery units at NVQ/SVQ levels 3 and 4. The qualification is awarded by City and Guilds, SCOTVEC and the HCTC, and is intended for those already working in industry, as well as those taking full- and part-time courses. Taken with the accompanying workbook, *NVQ/SVQ Workbook, Level 3 – Food Preparation and Cooking*, this book will be useful for those engaged in supported self-study and open learning programmes, and for those wanting to increase their qualifications in the workplace. Reference to *The Theory of Catering* may also be helpful.

However, having acquired the basic culinary knowledge and skills, all students taking courses which include practical cookery or gastronomy will find this book helpful. The content will also be useful therefore for those taking GNVQ courses in Hospitality and Catering, as well as those seeking qualifications from the HCIMA.

The aim is to extend the repertoire of catering students and professionals. To gain an advanced craft qualification, the chef should be able to adapt and extend existing recipes, to develop their own variations, and have a broad awareness of a wide variety of ingredients and cuisines. Where appropriate, we suggest variations for recipes, with the intention of stimulating further ways of adapting and creating different dishes. Adaptability is essential when producing dishes which at first glance appear impractical and expensive. By using common sense and with practical application, almost all recipes can be adapted to meet budgetary or any other restrictions.

KEY TO SYMBOLS

T	Recipe from the trade (hotels and restaurant sector).
I	Recipe from the industrial and institutional sector.
V	Recipe suitable for vegans.

CONTRIBUTIONS FROM THE TRADE

Over the past two decades, a number of British chefs have emerged who have developed individual styles of cooking and serving food. Their success has led to many now being in charge of their own kitchens, having established enviable reputations not only for the food, but as personalities within the industry. We have included a number of recipes which were willingly contributed by more than 40 top chefs.

CONTRIBUTIONS FROM THE INDUSTRIAL AND INSTITUTIONAL SECTOR

This sector is one of the largest and most important in the industry as it caters for a large segment of the population in a variety of ways.

Staff dining rooms are provided in many forms offering meals and snacks throughout the working period for manual, clerical and managerial staff. In some cases, smaller dining rooms have to be serviced and these are frequently used for working business breakfasts, lunches or dinners.

A large proportion of industrial catering is undertaken by contract caterers, such as Gardner Merchant, Sutcliffe, Compass, and Catering and Allied Catering and many others. Their clients include almost every type of catering, for example, schools, colleges, halls of residence, hospitals, the armed forces and a wide variety of industrial and business companies.

We feature a selection of recipes kindly supplied by a number of industrial caterers as examples of the type of food prepared and served which, in many cases, is superior to many commercial establishments.

USE AND EASE OF REFERENCE

Most recipes give quantities for four and ten portions, the most useful combinations for those working in an operating kitchen, or realistic working environment.

A selection of recipes have been analysed for nutritional value, giving the student the essential underpinning knowledge now required in this area.

Both metric and imperial measurements are given; the latter is still in common use within the industry, both for purchasing of ingredients and in the kitchen itself.

CURRENT TRENDS AND HEALTHY EATING

We have included separate chapters for ethnic and vegetarian recipes, since there is a great and growing emphasis on these sorts of cuisine. Some recipes are suitable for vegans, and these have also been highlighted in the text.

For those wishing to reduce fat and cholesterol levels in the diet, the following suggestions may be useful.

Consideration where suitable can be given to using:

- oils and fats high in monosaturates and polyunsaturates in place of hard fats;
- the minimum of salt or low-sodium salt;
- wholemeal flour in place of, or partly in place of, white flour;
- natural yoghurt, quark or fromage frais (all lower in fat) in place of cream;
- skimmed milk, or semi-skimmed, instead of full-cream milk;
- minimum use of sugar or, in some cases, reduced calorie sweeteners;
- low-fat cheese instead of full-fat cheese.

Many of the recipes in this book have been adjusted, incorporating some of these principles as alternatives to be used as and when required. Where we state oil, sunflower oil is recommended other than for fierce heat, when olive oil is more suitable. When yoghurt is stated, we mean natural yoghurt with a low-fat content.

The following table is an example of how traditional recipe ingredients may be replaced by healthier ones.

INSTEAD OF	CHOOSE
Whole milk	Skimmed milk (or semi-skimmed)
Butter or hard margarine	Polyunsaturated margarine
Lard, hard vegetable fats	Pure vegetable oils, e.g. corn oil, sunflower oil
Full-fat cheeses, e.g. Cheddar	Low-fat cheeses, e.g. low-fat Cheddar has half the fat
Fatty meats	Lean meats (smaller portion) or chicken or fish
Cream	Plain yoghurt, quark, smetana, fromage frais

A number of non-dairy creamers are available now. Some are produced specifically for pastry work and, being sweetened, are unsuitable for savoury recipes. However, there are also various unsweetened products which may be used in place of fresh cream for soups, sauces, etc. It is important to determine the heat stability of these products before use, i.e. by testing whether they will withstand boiling without detriment to the product.

The following chart indicates which cooking oils, fats and margarines are healthiest, i.e. those with the smallest percentage of saturated fats.

OIL/FAT	SATURATED	MONO-UNSATURATED	POLY-UNSATURATED
	%	%	%
Coconut oil	85	7	2
Butter	60	32	3
Palm oil	45	42	8
Lard	43	42	9
Beef dripping	40	49	4
Margarine, hard (vegetable oil only)	37	47	12
Margarine, hard (mixed oils)	37	43	17
Margarine, soft	32	42	22
Margarine, soft (mixed oils)	30	45	19
Low-fat spread	27	38	30
Margarine, polyunsaturated	24	22	54
Ground nut oil	19	48	28
Maize oil	16	29	49
Wheatgerm oil	14	11	45
Soya bean oil	14	24	57
Olive oil	14	70	11
Sunflower seed oil	13	32	50
Safflower seed oil	10	13	72
Rape seed oil	7	64	32

Receipt, storage and issue of resources

Control the receipt, storage and issue of resources

1   Understand the preparation of the receiving area and staff use available to take receipt of deliveries.
2   Identify the goods and match these against all documentation, including specification, noting any discrepancies.
3   Demonstrate prompt action in dealing with discrepancies and deviations.
4   Understand the storage and legislation appertaining to goods.
5   Maintain all security procedures.
6   Demonstrate the correct handling of stock in accordance with product instructions, organisational policy and current legislation.
7   Specify and identify the opportunities for the improvement of the stock system.
8   Articulate all the main principles of managing stock with an establishment.

MONITOR AND CONTROL RECEIPT OF GOODS

Staff responsible for receiving goods should be trained to recognise the items being delivered and to know if the quality, quantity and specific sizes, etc., are those ordered. This skill is acquired by experience and by guidance from the departmental head, e.g. Head chef, who will use the items.

Purchasing specifications detailing the standards of the goods to be delivered assist in this matter. However, the chef, supervisor, storekeeper, food and beverage manager, or whoever is responsible for controlling receipt of goods, needs to check that the specification is adhered to. If the system of the establishment does not have specifications, the expected standards of goods delivered must still be checked. In the event of goods being unsatisfactory, they should not be accepted.

Receipt of goods

Receipt of deliveries must be monitored to ensure that goods delivered correspond with the delivery note and there are no discrepancies. It is essential that items are of the stipulated size or weight since this could affect portion control and costing, for example 100 g (4 oz) fillets of plaice will need to be that weight, melons to be used for four portions should be of the appropriate size.

It is necessary to ensure that effective control can be practised. This means that delivery access and adequate checking and storage space are available, that these areas are clean, tidy and free from obstruction, and that staff are available to receive goods. It is important that the standard of cleanliness and temperature of the delivery vehicles is also satisfactory. If this is not up to the required standard, the supplier must be informed at once.

Temperatures

Vehicles over 7.5 tonnes must have a temperature of 5°C or below when delivering food outside their locality. Vehicles under 7.5 tonnes making local deliveries of food should be 8°C or under.

On receipt of goods they should be transferred as soon as possible to the correct storage area. Frozen items should be stored at these optimum temperatures.

Meat	−20°C
Vegetable	−15°C
Ice-cream	−18°C to −20°C

Refrigerator temperature should be 3–4°C and larders provided for cooling of food should be no higher than 8°C.

It is essential that a system of reporting non-compliance with the procedures of the establishment are known. Every place of work will have a security procedure to ensure that goods are safely stored. It is important that staff are aware of the system and to whom they should report any deviation.

CONTROL THE STORAGE OF GOODS

If control of stock is to be effective, ample storage space with adequate shelving bins, etc., must be available to enable the correct storage of goods. The premises must be clean and easy to keep clean, well lit and well ventilated, dry, secure and safe. Space should be available for easy access to all items which should not be too high, and heavy items should be stored low down.

Stock rotation is essential so as to reduce waste – the last items in are the last items to be issued. Any deterioration of stock should be identified and action taken and reported. To keep a check on stock a system of documentation is necessary which states the amount in the stores, the amounts issued, to whom and when, and the amounts below which stock should not fall.

Shelf life and justification on 'use by' date information should be complied with. As a guide to storage, consider these points.

Canned goods	Store up to 9 months. Discard damaged rusted, swollen tins.
Bottles and jars	Store at room temperature. Store in refrigerator once opened.
Dry foods	Dry room temperature. Humid atmosphere causes deterioration.
Milk and cream	Refrigerate and use within 3 days.
Butter	Up to two months, refrigerated.
Cheese	According to manufacturers instruction. Soft cheese should be used as soon as possible.
Salads	They keep longer if refrigerated or in a dark well-ventilated area.

Meat and poultry	Up to one week in refrigerator.
Meat products	For example, sausages and pies, refrigerated up to 3 days.
Fish	Use on day of purchase ideally or up to 12 hours if refrigerated.
Ice-cream	Deep frozen for a week.
Frozen foods	Six months: meat −18°C, fruit and vegetables −12°C.

Persons responsible for controlling the storage of stock, in addition to checking the personnel using the stores and working as storekeepers, must also check the correct storage temperatures of storerooms, refrigerators, deep freezers, etc. The policy of the establishment may expect records of temperature checks to be recorded.

Storage temperatures

TEMPERATURE	FOOD ITEM
8°C or below	Soft cheese whole
5°C or below	Cut cheese
5°C	Cooked foods Smoked and cured fish Smoked and cured meat Sandwiches and rolls containing meat, fish, eggs (or substitutes), soft cheeses, or vegetables
8°C or below	Desserts containing milk or milk substitutes (with pH value of 4.5 or more) Vegetable and fruit salads Pies and pastries containing meat, fish, or substitute, or vegetables into which nothing has been added after cooking. Cooked sausage rolls. Uncooked or partly cooked pastries and dough products containing meat or fish or substitutes. Cream cakes

Checking stock

An essential aspect of the supervisory role is the full stock audit and spot check of goods in the stores, to assess deterioration and losses from other causes. Spot checks by their very nature are random, stock audits will occur at specified times during the year. Some establishments have a system of daily records of stock-in-hand. This procedure assists in security since there is no time lapse between checks. This is particularly important when dealing with expensive items.

Particular attention must be paid to items of a hazardous nature, e.g. bleach and other cleaning items. They should be stored away from foods. All items of cleaning should have a record or bin card stating amount in stock and to whom issues are made.

CONTROL THE ISSUE OF STOCK AND GOODS

To supervise the issuing of stock a system of control is needed so that a record of each item – how much, to whom and when – is kept. This enables a check to be made so that only authorised persons can obtain goods, the amount of items issued can be controlled, and it is known how much of each item is used over a period of time.

This should help avoid over-ordering and thus having too much stock on the premises. It should also diminish the risk of pilfering.

Having documentation enables accurate records to be available so that action can be taken to control the issues of goods.

To be effective the requisition document should include the date, the amount of the item or items required and the department, section or person to whom they are to be issued. Usually a signature of the superior, e.g. chef, chef de partie or supervisor is required. It may be desirable to draw a line under the last listed item so that unauthorised items are not then added.

IMPLEMENT THE PHYSICAL STOCK-TAKE

The purpose of a physical stock-taking procedure is to check that the documentation of existing stock tallies with the actual stock held on the premises. The reason for this exercise is to prevent capital being tied up by having too much stock in hand. It also provides information regarding the accuracy of the system and thus indicates where modifications could be made.

At the same time as the physical stock-take, details of discrepancies may become apparent which would then be investigated. Items such as returned empties, damaged stock, credit claims, etc., will be reconciled so that an accurate record is made for use by appropriate staff. This may mean that both the storekeeper and the manager responsible will take action on the stock-take details. It is for this reason that records must be accurate, legible and carefully retained in order to achieve the aim of the exercise.

To be effective every item should be recorded indicating the appropriate detail such as weight, size, etc., and the number of items in stock.

Health, safety and security

> ## Monitor and maintain the health, safety and security of workers, customers and other members of the public

1   Understand the procedures for maintaining operations in accordance with relevant legislation.
2   Demonstrate that the premises and equipment are regularly checked.
3   Report all breaches of security and faults with safety equipment.
4   Identify potential problems and recommend improvements to security and safety.
5   Specify cleaning standards and routines in line with current legislation.
6   Understand that all accidents should be dealt with, reported and recorded accurately in the accident book and that the appropriate people are notified.
7   Appreciate that ongoing training and instruction is made available to enable staff to perform their work safely and efficiently.

MAINTAIN SECURITY AND SAFETY PROCEDURES IN OWN AREAS OF RESPONSIBILITY

To ensure that legislation regarding safety and security is implemented, it is necessary:

1 for the legislation to be known;
2 that the requirements are carried out;
3 that a system of checks makes certain that the legislation is complied with.

Firstly, all people involved in an establishment must be made aware of the need for safety and security and their legal responsibilities towards themselves, their colleagues, their employers and other members of the public.

A system of checks, both spot checks and regular inspections at frequent intervals, needs to be set up and the observations and recommendations resulting from these inspections should be recorded and passed to superiors for action. The details would include time and date of inspection, exact site and a clear description of the breach of security or fault of safety equipment. This information would be acted upon promptly according to the policy of the organisation.

It is the responsibility of everyone at the workplace to be conscious of safety and security and to pass on to the appropriate people recommendations for improving the procedures for maintaining safety and security.

Inspections of equipment to make certain that they are available and ready for use include security equipment, first-aid and fire-fighting equipment. The supervisor or person responsible for these items needs to regularly check and record that they are in working condition and that, if they have been used, they are restored ready for further use. Security systems and fire-fighting equipment are usually checked by the makers. It is the responsibility of the management of the establishment to ensure that this equipment is correctly maintained. First-aid equipment is usually the responsibility of the designated first-aider, whose function includes replenishing first-aid boxes. However, a chef de parti or supervisor will be aware that if fire extinguishers and first-aid equipment are used, they have a responsibility to take action to maintain the equipment by reporting to the appropriate person.

MONITOR AND MAINTAIN THE HEALTH, SAFETY AND SECURITY OF WORKERS, CUSTOMERS AND OTHER MEMBERS OF THE PUBLIC

Routine checks or inspections need to be carried out in any establishment to see that standards of hygiene and safety are maintained for the benefit of workers, customers and other members of the public. Visitors, suppliers and contractors are also entitled to expect the premises to be safe when they enter. Particular attention needs to be paid to exits and entrances, passageways and the provision of adequate lighting. Floors need to be sound, uncluttered and well lit. Disposal of rubbish and bin areas need particular care regarding cleanliness and safety. Toilets, staff rooms and changing rooms need to be checked regularly. All staff must adopt hygienic and safe work practices – they should be conscious at all times and in all places of work of the health and safety of the premises. Failure to do so may result in the spread of infections and accidents. Any discrepancies and damage should be reported as well as any unsafe or unhealthy features.

Checks or inspections would usually be carried out by a person responsible for the health and safety within the organisation, with authority to take action to remedy faults and discrepancies, and to implement improvements.

Monitoring of inspections and the recording of evidence is an important aspect of the supervisor's role. Even more important is that any short-comings are remedied at once. Inspections should be regular, and particular attention paid to hazards, security, safety equipment and cleanliness.

Records, which should be accurate and legible, should include date and time of inspection, by whom and what has been checked. Any hazards, faults, lack of cleanliness, damage or discrepancies should be recorded.

Unhygienic and unsafe practices observed can best be remedied by training and giving constructive explanations as to why they are unhygienic and unsafe. Persons with infections or notifiable diseases must be made aware of their responsibility to inform their employer.

MAINTAIN A HEALTHY AND SAFE WORKING ENVIRONMENT

It is necessary to be aware of the policy and procedures of the organisation in relation to health and safety legislation. Every individual at work anywhere on the premises needs to develop an attitude towards possible hazardous situations so as to prevent accidents to themselves or others. Training is also essential to develop good practice and would include information on what hazards to look for, hygienic methods of working and the procedures to follow in the event of an incident. Records of staff training in these areas would be kept.

Checks are essential to maintain high standards of health and safety at work and to comply with the law so that employees, employers and members of the public remain safe and healthy.

Every organisation will have procedures to follow in the event of a fire, accident, flood or bomb alert; every employee needs to be acquainted with the procedures.

Every establishment must have a book to record accidents. It is also desirable to have a book to record items needing maintenance due to wear and tear or damage so that these faults can be remedied. Details of incidents, such as power failure, flooding, infestation, contamination, etc., which do not result in an accident should be recorded in an incident book.

Items lost, damaged or discarded should be recorded, giving details of why and how it happened and what subsequent steps have been taken.

The responsibility of chefs, supervisors and others concerned with health and safety is to ensure that training and instruction is given so as to prevent accidents and to help staff work efficiently and safely. Problems with any staff failing to comply with health and safety standards should be identified and appropriate action taken.

Measurement tables and oven temperatures

—— Approximate equivalents of weights and measures ——

IMPERIAL WEIGHT	METRIC WEIGHT	IMPERIAL MEASURE	METRIC MEASURE
$\frac{1}{4}$oz	5g		5ml
$\frac{1}{2}$oz	10g		10ml
1oz	25g	1floz	25ml
2oz	50g	2floz	50ml
2$\frac{1}{2}$oz	60g	2$\frac{1}{2}$floz ($\frac{1}{8}$pt)	60ml
3oz	75g	3floz	75ml
4oz ($\frac{1}{4}$lb)	100g	4floz	100ml
5oz	125g	5floz ($\frac{1}{4}$pt)	125ml
6oz	150g	6floz	150ml
7oz	175g	7floz	175ml
8oz ($\frac{1}{2}$lb)	200g	8floz	200ml
9oz	225g	9floz	225ml
10oz	250g	10floz ($\frac{1}{2}$pt)	250ml ($\frac{1}{4}$ litre)
11oz	275g	11floz	275ml
12oz	300g	12floz	300ml
13oz	325g	13floz	325ml
14oz	350g	14floz	350ml
15oz	375g	15floz ($\frac{3}{4}$pt)	375ml
16oz (1lb)	400g	16floz	400ml
		20floz	500ml ($\frac{1}{2}$ litre)
		2pt (1qt)	1000ml (1 litre)

IMPERIAL	METRIC	IMPERIAL	METRIC
$\frac{1}{4}$in	$\frac{1}{2}$cm	4in	10cm
$\frac{1}{2}$in	1cm	5in	12cm
1in	2cm	6in	15cm
$1\frac{1}{2}$in	4cm	$6\frac{1}{2}$in	16cm
2in	5cm	7in	18cm
$2\frac{1}{2}$in	6cm	12in	30cm
3in	8cm	18in	45cm

Oven temperatures

	CELSIUS	REGULO	FAHRENHEIT
cool	110	$\frac{1}{4}$	225
	130	$\frac{1}{2}$	250
	140	1	275
	150	2	300
	160	3	325
moderate	180	4	350
	190	5	375
	200	6	400
hot	220	7	425
	230	8	450
very hot	250	9	500

Assessing taste and quality of dishes

It is important for chefs to continue to assess the quality of dishes by tasting. In this way they learn about flavour and are able to become skilled in blending and mixing different flavour components.

Organoleptic assessment simply means using our senses to evaluate food. We detect the flavour of food through the senses of taste and smell. The overall taste of food is made up of one or more primary tastes of which there are four. These are:

- sweet
- sour
- salt
- bitter

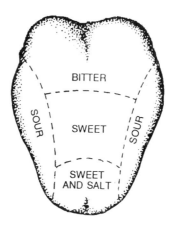

The sensation of taste is detected by taste buds in the mouth, mostly on the upper surface of the tongue. Different parts of the tongue are particularly sensitive to different primary tastes.

Our sensitivity to different primary tastes varies greatly.

The colour of food is extremely important to our enjoyment of it. People are sensitive to the colour of the food they eat and will reject food that is not considered to have the accepted colour. Colouring matter is sometimes added to food to enhance its attractiveness. There is a strong link between the colour and the flavour of food. Our ability to detect the flavour of food is very much connected with its colour, for if the colour is unusual our sense of taste is confused. For example, if a fruit jelly is red it is likely that the flavour detected will be that of a red-coloured fruit, such as raspberry or strawberry, even if the flavour is lemon or banana.

The depth of colour in food also affects our sense of taste. We associate strong colours with strong flavours. For example, if a series of jellies all contain the same amount of given flavour, but are of different shades of the same colour, then those having a stronger colour will appear also to have a stronger flavour.

Because the nose shares an airway, the pharynx, with the mouth, we smell and taste our food simultaneously, and what we call the flavour or the 'taste' of the food is really a combination of these two sensations. To quote Brillat-Savarin:

> **Smell and taste form a single sense, of which the mouth is the laboratory and the nose is the chimney, or to speak more exactly, of which one serves for the tasting of actual bodies and the other for the savouring of their gases.**

With taste and smell, then, we first decide whether a particular food is edible and then go on to sample its chemistry simply to enjoy it.

Foods are chemical mixtures, so that we seldom encounter any of the basic taste sensations in isolation. The temperature of food also affects our sensitivity to its taste. Low temperatures decrease the rate of detection. Maximum taste sensitivity ranges from 22 to 44°C (72–105°F). Sweet and sour are enhanced at the upper end, salt and bitter at the lower end. At any given temperature, however, we are much more sensitive to bitter substances than we are to sweet, sour or salty ones, by a factor of about 10,000. Synthetic sweeteners are effective at concentrations nearer to bitter substances than to table sugar.

Our sensitivity to the flavour of food in our mouth is greatest when we breath out with the mouth closed; air from the lungs passes along the back of the mouth on its way to the nose and brings some food vapours with it.

It is important when assessing food to remember that taste, smell and colour are closely linked and contribute to the overall assessment of the dish. Training and knowledge are therefore essential if one is to develop a discriminating palate and to acquire the ability to identify individual flavours.

Food must be presented in such a way that it can be fully appreciated by the customer. This will vary according to the culture and customs of the various groups in society. It may vary in the different sectors of the industry. For example, airline catering will be different in presentation from a Michelin Star restaurant. School meals will differ from staff feeding. In all cases, the food should look appetising, colourful and easily identifiable. Particular attention must be paid to colour, presentation, size, nutritional balance, texture, flavour and consistency of the various components that make up the dish. The garnish must also be in harmony with the dish.

Hors-d'oeuvre and buffet items

Prepare, cook and present cold buffet items

1 Select type, quantity and quality of ingredients in accordance with recipe specifications.
2 Demonstrate appropriate adjustments to the recipe in order to meet customers' expressed requirements
3 Demonstrate that prepared products meet recipe specifications.
4 Comply with relevant hygiene legislation.

— *Cold preparations* —

The preparation of hors-d'oeuvre and salads offers wide scope for ingenuity and creativity.

Almost all foods can be used, raw or cooked, which if carefully selected and blended and mixed where necessary with suitable dressings can produce attractively appetising and highly popular dishes.

INGREDIENTS

The following are just some of the ingredients which can be used.

Leaves

round lettuce
cos (romaine) lettuce
iceberg lettuce
oak leaf lettuce
radicchio
curly endive
chicory
cress
watercress
rocket

corn salad (lamb's lettuce)
sorrel
dandelion
escarole (broad-leafed endive, Batavian lettuce)
nasturtium
red cabbage
white cabbage
spinach
Chinese leaves

Vegetables (raw)

celery	radishes
carrots	tomatoes
onions	mushrooms
spring onions	cucumber
pimentos (peppers)	celeriac

Vegetables (cooked)

sweetcorn	peas
baby sweetcorn	beans – French, broad, runner
beetroot	artichokes
potatoes	Jerusalem artichokes
carrots	asparagus
turnips	broccoli

Herbs

chives	thyme
parsley	lovage
basil	sweet cicely
mint	marjoram
coriander leaves	tarragon
fennel leaves	bay leaves
dill	chervil

Pulses

black-eyed beans	chick peas
flageolets	mung beans
borlotti beans	red kidney beans
haricot beans	

Pasta

macaroni, spaghetti, etc.	noodles

Fruits

grapefruit	guava
orange	kiwi
apples	bananas
grapes	melon
dates	pineapples
mango	cherries
avocado	

Nuts

walnuts	peanuts
hazelnuts	Brazil nuts
almonds	cashew nuts

Miscellaneous

hard-boiled eggs	olives
cheese	gherkins
rice	capers
poppyseeds	mung bean sprouts
sunflower seeds	bamboo shoots
sesame seeds	water chestnuts

Meats

cooked meats – beef/lamb/pork	duck
sausages, salamis	ham
chicken	bacon
turkey	tongue

Fish

anchovies	crab
tuna	lobster
salmon	shrimps
sardines	prawns
white fish	mussels
mackerel	cockles
herring	

COLD DRESSINGS AND SAUCES

Vinaigrette and mayonnaise are used extensively for salads, but sour cream, tofu and yoghurt may also be used.

Oils	*Vinegars*	*Vinaigrettes*
olive	cider	With the addition of:
corn	red wine	garlic
sunflower	white wine	capers
peanut	malt	curry paste
sesame	herb	eggs
safflower	lemon	blue cheese
walnut	raspberry	herbs
soya	balsamic	

Seasonings	*Herbs*	*Mayonnaise*
English mustard	chervil	with the addition of:
French mustard	tarragon	tomato ketchup
Dijon mustard	thyme	horseradish
German mustard	mint	lemon juice
salt	basil	herbs
pepper	marjoram	capers
spices	coriander	gherkins
herb salt	fennel	curry powder
	dill	herbs

Also		*Fruit or vegetable*
soured cream	smetana	*sauces*
tofu	crème fraîche	see pages 105–9
yoghurt	quark	

1 ‒ Vinaigrette

		4 portions	10 portions
olive oil		3–6 tbsp	6–12 tbsp
French mustard	combine	1 tsp	2 tsp
vinegar		1 tbsp	2 tbsp
salt, mill pepper			

Variations to vinaigrette:

(a) English mustard in place of French mustard;
(b) chopped herbs (e.g. chives, parsley, tarragon);
(c) chopped hard-boiled egg;
(d) lemon juice in place of vinegar (lemon dressing);
(e) vary the type of oil.

Note The ratio of vinegar to oil can vary considerably according to individual taste.

> Using 3 tbsp oil
> This recipe provides:
>
> 415 kcals/1740 kJ
> 45.5 g fat
> (of which 6.3 g saturated)
> 0.5 g carbohydrate
> (of which 0.1 g sugars)
> 0.6 g protein
> 0.0 g fibre
>
> Using 6 tbsp oil
> This recipe provides:
>
> 819 kcals/3439 kJ
> 90.5 g fat
> (of which 12.6 g saturated)
> 0.5 g carbohydrate
> (of which 0.1 g sugars)
> 0.6 g protein
> 0.0 g fibre

2 – Acidulated cream

	4 portions	10 portions
lemon juice	$\frac{1}{4}$	$\frac{3}{4}$
cream	4 tbsp	12 tsp

This recipe provides:

200 kcals/838 kJ
21.0 g fat
(of which 13.3 g saturated)
1.6 g carbohydrate
(of which 1.6 g sugars)
1.2 g protein
0.0 g fibre

Gently stir the juice into the cream at the last moment before serving.

3 – Mayonnaise sauce

This is a basic cold sauce and has a wide variety of uses, particularly in hors-d'oeuvre dishes. It should always be available on any cold buffet.

If during the making of the sauce, it should become too thick, then a little vinegar or water may be added. Mayonnaise will turn or curdle for several reasons:

1 If the oil is added too quickly.
2 If the oil is too cold.
3 If the sauce is insufficiently whisked.
4 If the yolk is stale and therefore weak.

	4 portions	10 portions
egg yolks	2	5
vinegar	2 tsp	5 tsp
salt, ground white pepper		
English or Continental mustard	$\frac{1}{8}$ tsp	$\frac{1}{2}$ tsp
olive or other good quality oil	250 ml ($\frac{1}{2}$ pt)	625 ml ($1\frac{1}{4}$ pt)
boiling water	1 tsp (approx)	2 tsp

This recipe provides:

2388 kcals/10 030 kJ
262.2 g fat
(of which 38.9 g saturated)
0.3 g carbohydrate
(of which 0.1 g sugars)
6.8 g protein
0.0 g fibre

1 Place yolks, vinegar and seasoning in a bowl and whisk well.
2 Gradually pour on the oil very slowly, whisking continuously.
3 Add the boiling water whisking well.
4 Correct the seasoning.

The method of rethickening a turned mayonnaise is either

(a) by taking a clean basin, adding 1 teaspoon boiling water and gradually whisking in the curdled sauce, or
(b) by taking another yolk thinned with $\frac{1}{2}$ teaspoon cold water whisked well, then gradually whisking in the curdled sauce.

Note It is recommended that pasteurised egg yolks be used.

4 – Garlic-flavoured mayonnaise

	4 portions	10 portions
egg yolks	2	5
vinegar or lemon or lime juice	2 tsp	5 tsp
salt, ground white pepper		
mustard	$\frac{1}{8}$ tsp	$\frac{3}{8}$ tsp
cloves of garlic (juice or chopped)	2	5
olive oil or vegetable oil	250 ml ($\frac{1}{2}$pt)	625 ml (1$\frac{1}{4}$pt)
boiling water	1 tsp	2 tsp

1 Place the yolks, vinegar, seasoning and garlic in a bowl and mix well.
2 Gradually pour on the oil very slowly, whisking continuously.
3 Add the boiling water, whisking well.
4 Correct the seasoning.

Other suggested additions:
(a) tomato ketchup;
(b) anchovy essence;
(c) tomato and anchovy essence;
(d) horseradish, finely grated.

5 – Green or herb sauce

	4 portions	10 portions
spinach, tarragon, chervil, chives, watercress	50 g (2 oz)	125 g (5 oz)
mayonnaise	250 ml ($\frac{1}{2}$pt)	625 ml (1$\frac{1}{4}$pt)

1 Pick, wash, blanch and refresh the green leaves.
2 Squeeze dry.
3 Pass through a very fine sieve.
4 Mix with the mayonnaise.

May be served with cold salmon or salmon trout.

6 – Cumberland sauce

	4 portions	10 portions
redcurrant jelly	100 ml ($\frac{3}{16}$ pt)	250 ml ($\frac{1}{2}$ pt)
chopped shallots	5 g ($\frac{1}{4}$ oz)	12 g ($\frac{1}{2}$ oz)
lemon juice	$\frac{1}{4}$	$\frac{1}{2}$
port	2 tbsp	5 tbsp
juice of orange	1	2
English mustard	$\frac{1}{4}$ level tsp	$\frac{1}{2}$ tsp

This recipe provides:

336 kcals/1410 kJ
0.3 g fat
(of which 0.0 g saturated)
78.8 g carbohydrate
(of which 78.6 g sugars)
1.1 g protein
1.2 g fibre

1 Warm and melt the jelly.
2 Blanch the shallots well and refresh.
3 Add the shallots to the jelly with the remainder of the ingredients.
4 Cut a little fine julienne of orange zest, blanch, refresh and add to the sauce.

May be served with cold ham.

7 – Fresh tomato sauce (raw)

	4 portions	10 portions
tomatoes, skinned and pips removed	400 g (1 lb)	1$\frac{1}{4}$ kg (2$\frac{1}{2}$ lb)
vinegar	$\frac{1}{2}$ tbsp	1$\frac{1}{2}$ tbsp
oil	3 tbsp	8 tbsp
salt and mill pepper		
chopped parsley and tarragon	1 tbsp	3 tbsp

1 Squeeze the tomatoes to remove excess juice and liquidise the flesh.

2 Place in a bowl and gradually whisk in the vinegar and oil.
3 Season and mix in the herbs.

Note A recipe for a cooked tomato sauce can be found on page 107.

8 – Tofu salad dressing

This soya bean curd can be used as a salad dressing. As tofu is tasteless it can be flavoured with garlic, lemon, mint, etc. Tofu has to be mixed to a creamy consistency before use with skimmed milk, lemon juice, etc.

Quark, crème fraîche, fromage frais and yoghurt may also be used.

SALADS AND COLD HORS-D'OEUVRE

9 – Smoked salmon, avocado and walnut salad

	4 portions	10 portions
smoked salmon	100 g (4 oz)	250 g (10 oz)
avocado pears	2	5
walnuts	50 g (2 oz)	125 g (5 oz)
fennel or parsley		
vinaigrette		
radicchio		
curly endive		

I portion provides:
calculated with 2 tbsp vinaigrette

341 kcals/1413 kJ
32 g fat
(of which 4.8 g saturated)
2.7 g carbohydrate
(of which 1.4 g sugars)
10.7 g protein
4.2 g fibre

1 Cut the smoked salmon in strips and neatly dice the peeled avocado.
2 Carefully mix together with the walnuts, chopped fennel or parsley and vinaigrette.
3 Neatly pile on a base of radicchio and curly endive leaves.

Note Flaked cooked fresh salmon or flaked smoked mackerel can be used to create a variation of this salad.

▣ 10 ~ Salmon and asparagus salad with a rose petal dressing and shiso

(ANTHONY MARSHALL)

	4 portions	10 portions
red tomatoes (skinned)	4	10
yellow·tomatoes (skinned)	4	10
Scotch smoked salmon	200 g (8 oz)	500 g (1¼ lb)
asparagus sticks (spears)	20	50
thyme	20 g (1 oz)	50 g (2 oz)
shiso	100 g (4 oz)	250 g (10 oz)
curly endive (spider lettuce)	100 g (4 oz)	250 g (10 oz)
oakleaf	40 g (2 oz)	100 g (4 oz)
lollo rosso	2	5
rose head	4	10
rose petal vinegar	1 tsp	2½ tsp
virgin oil	1 tbsp	2½ tbsp

1 Peel and clean the asparagus and place into boiled salted water with thyme to add some flavour. Leave until the tips are cooked.
2 Remove and place into a bowl of iced water to refresh.
3 Cut the smoked salmon into fine slivers.
4 Wash and mix the salads together and cut the rose petals into fine strips.
5 Make a crown of salmon and place five tips of asparagus in the centre, with yellow and red tomato quarters in between.
6 Add the dressing to the salad, drain and place into the middle of the salmon and sprinkle with shiso.

Note Shiso is a small leaf purple-coloured herb similar to mustard and cress with a basil-like flavour.

~ Rose petal dressing

	4 portions	10 portions
rose petal vinegar	1 tsp	2½ tsp
virgin oil	1 tsp	2½ tsp
shallot finely cut	30 g (1⅓ oz)	75 g (3 oz)

Mix the oil and vinegar together, then add the shallots and finely cut rose petals (yellow and reds preferable).

11 – Salmon and tomato salad

	4 portions	10 portions
salmon or other very fresh white fish	200 g (8 oz)	500 g (1¼ lb)
juice of lemon or lime	1	2
shallots	50 g (2 oz)	125 g (5 oz)
chopped basil, chervil or parsley		
tofu	25 g (1 oz)	60 g (2½ oz)
seasoning		
skinned tomatoes, deseeded and lids removed	8	20

1 Remove the bones and skin from the fish.
2 Chop the fish and mix with half the lemon juice and allow to stand for 20 minutes.
3 Finely chop the shallots, mix with the rest of the lemon juice, the herbs and the tofu, and beat well.
4 Add the drained fish, season and use to fill the tomato shells.

Note   The fish must be very fresh as it is eaten raw. However, as an alternative, the fish may be slightly steamed or poached.

12 – Herring, apple and potato salad

	4 portions	10 portions
smoked herrings	2	5
cooked potato	100 g (4 oz)	250 g (10 oz)
eating apple	100 g (4 oz)	250 g (10 oz)
chopped parsley, chervil and fennel		
vinaigrette		

1 Fillet and skin the herrings and cut the flesh into dice.
2 Mix with the diced potato and diced apple.
3 Add the herbs and vinaigrette. Correct seasoning.

Note   As a variation smoked mackerel, eel or trout could be used.

13 – Smoked fish platter

	4 portions	10 portions
fillets of smoked mackerel	2	5
fillet of smoked trout	1	2–3
smoked eel or halibut	200 g (8 oz)	500 g (1¼ lb)
smoked salmon	100 g (4 oz)	250 g (10 oz)
lemon	1	2
mayonnaise with horseradish	60 ml ($\frac{1}{8}$ pt)	150 ml ($\frac{1}{3}$ pt)

1 Carefully remove the skin from the mackerel, trout and eel fillets, and divide into four pieces.
2 Arrange with a cornet of salmon on each plate.
3 Garnish with quarter of lemon.
4 Serve separately, mayonnaise sauce containing finely grated horseradish.

14 – Shellfish platter

A selection of shellfish, e.g. lobster, crab, prawns and shrimps, neatly arranged and garnished with heart of lettuce, tomato quarters, and quarters of hard-boiled eggs; served with mayonnaise sauce separately.

15 – Medallion of grilled goats cheese served on a garlic infused mushroom stool with a crisp asparagus salad and a tomato salsa

(CARLOS DIAZ)

	4 portions	10 portions
St Christopher goat's cheese	1	2½
large grilling mushrooms	4	10
cloves of garlic crushed	1	3
olive oil	2 tbsp	5 tbsp
butter	25 g (1 oz)	60 g (2½ oz)
freshly ground black pepper		
salt		

1 Remove the straw from the centre of the cheese and cut into 10 cm (4 in) rounds.

2 Lightly heat heat the oil and butter, add the garlic and cook gently and add seasoned mushrooms cooking for 4 minutes turning. Remove and keep warm.

~ *Tomato salsa*

	4 portions	10 portions
Finely chopped red onion	50 g (2 oz)	125 g (5 oz)
cloves of garlic crushed	1	3
small red capsicum cut into fine dice	1	3
virgin olive oil	2 tbsp	5 tbsp
tarragon vinegar	2 tbsp	5 tbsp
tomatoes skinned and deseeded and finely diced	2	5
tomato juice	70 ml (3 fl oz)	170 ml (7 fl oz)
bunches of chopped chives	$\frac{1}{2}$	$1\frac{1}{2}$

1 Heat the oil and gently fry the garlic and onion for 2 minutes.
2 Add the red capsicum and cook for a further 2 minutes.
3 Add the vinegar and boil rapidly until reduced by half; remove from heat and add the remaining ingredients.

~ *Asparagus salad garnish*

	4 portions	10 portions
Equal sliced pieces of trimmed and prepared		
curly endive		
lollo rosso		
radicchio		
little gem		
thin tips of asparagus	16	40

1 Place a round of cheese on each mushroom and grill under a fierce heat until golden brown.
2 Transfer on to four warm plates. Cook the asparagus in simmering salt water for 1 minute.
3 Place four small bunches of salad around the mushroom and top with a cross of warm asparagus tips.
4 Gently heat the salsa and spoon into the remaining gaps.

T 16 – Cornish crab salad with lime and pimentoes, grilled scallops and a warm potato and chive salad on a red pepper coulis

(RON MAXFIELD)

	4 portions	10 portions
scallops	12	30
white crab meat	200 g (8 oz)	500 g (1¼ lb)
mixed lettuce – oak leaf, lollo rosso, radicchio, frisee		
small new potatoes	200 g (8 oz)	500 g (1¼ lb)
sprigs of dill	5	12
sprigs of chervil	12	30
mayonnaise	100 g (4 fl oz)	250 ml (½ pt)
finely diced pimento (red, yellow, green)	2 tbsp	5 tbsp
pepper coulis	12 tbsp	30 tbsp
chopped chives	2 tbsp	5 tbsp
sprig of thyme		
Coulis		
red peppers	2	5
fish stock	250 ml (½ pt)	600 ml (1¼ pt)
shallots	2	5
Salad dressing		
walnut oil	100 ml (3 fl oz)	250 ml (½ pt)
white wine vinegar	2 tsp	5 tsp
Dijon mustard	1 tsp	2–3 tsp
lime, juice of	1	2–3

1 To make the coulis: remove seeds from red pepper and chop roughly.
2 Sweat off pepper with finely sliced shallots, add small sprig of thyme.
3 Add fish stock and reduce stock by three-quarters.
4 Put the contents into a liquidiser and blitz until smooth in consistency.
5 Season with salt and pepper.
6 To make the salad dressing: whisk together the vinegar, honey and mustard.
7 Slowly whisk in the oil.
8 Season with salt and pepper.
9 Add the finely diced pimento and lime juice.
10 Cook the potatoes and slice into 6 mm (¼ in) discs.

11 Take the crab meat and add some of the dressing with plenty of diced pimento and check seasoning.
12 Place salad into a 7.5 cm (3 in) pastry ring into the middle of your plate. Place crab meat on top of salad and remove pastry cutter.
13 Place the dill around the top of the salad.
14 Take out the warm potatoes and place in the mayonnaise with the chives and season.
15 Place the warm coulis at 3 intervals on the plate and place the cooked scallops on to the coulis.
16 Place the warm potato salad in between the scallops and garnish with the sprigs of chervil.

17 – Palm hearts salad

	4 portions	10 portions
tinned palm hearts	400 g (1 lb)	1¼ kg (2½ lb)
lime or lemon juice dressing	1 dsp	2–3 dsp
French mustard	1 tsp	2–3 tsp
salt and mill pepper		
oil	4 dsp	10 dsp

1 Drain palm hearts thoroughly and cut into even-shaped pieces.
2 Mix dressing ingredients, pour over palm hearts, toss well and serve.

18 – Rice, tomato and pepper salad

	4 portions	10 portions
tomatoes, skinned, deseeded and diced	50 g (2 oz)	125 g (5 oz)
red peppers in julienne	50 g (2 oz)	125 g (5 oz)
cooked rice	100 g (4 oz)	250 g (10 oz)
clove garlic, crushed and chopped	1	2–3
chopped onion	25 g (1 oz)	60 g (2½ oz)
chopped basil, tarragon or parsley		
vinaigrette		

1 portion provides: calculated with 2 tbsp vinaigrette

372 kcals/1533 kJ
23.7 g fat
(of which 3.2 g saturated)
38.1 g carbohydrate
(of which 6.1 g sugars)
4 g protein
1.8 g fibre

Mix all the ingredients together lightly. If required, more garlic can be added.

19 ~ Avocado stuffed with cream cheese, walnuts and chives

	4 portions	10 portions	
avocados	2	5	I portion provides: calculated with 25 g (I oz) mayonnaise
lemon	1	2–3	
cream cheese	100 g (4 oz)	250 g (10 oz)	406 kcals/I 673 kJ
mayonnaise			41.9 g fat
			(of which I I.9 g saturated)
chives	50 g (2 oz)	125 g (5 oz)	2.5 g carbohydrate
walnuts	50 g (2 oz)	125 g (5 oz)	(of which I.2 g sugars)
			4.9 g protein
			3.6 g fibre

1 Halve and remove the stone from the avocados.
2 Scoop out some of the flesh to slightly enlarge the cavity and sprinkle with lemon juice.
3 Mix this pulp with the cream cheese, mayonnaise, chopped chives and nuts, and season.
4 Use to fill the avocado halves and dress on lettuce leaves.

Note   Alternative fillings can include shellfish, cheese and ham, tuna fish, etc.

20 ~ Avocado mousse

	4 portions	10 portions
large avocado	1	2–3
lemon, juice of	1	2–3
seasoning		
mayonnaise	60 ml ($\frac{1}{8}$ pt)	150 ml ($\frac{1}{3}$ pt)
aspic jelly	60 ml ($\frac{1}{8}$ pt)	150 ml ($\frac{1}{3}$ pt)
or sheets gelatine	1–2	2–3
double cream or	60 ml ($\frac{1}{8}$ pt)	150 ml ($\frac{1}{3}$ pt)
unsweetened vegetable		
creamer		
salad vegetables for garnish		

1 Cut the avocado in half, remove the stone and peel.
2 Pass through a sieve or liquidise in a food processor.
3 Add the lemon juice and seasoning and place in a bowl.
4 Stir in the mayonnaise and aspic jelly or the soaked, melted gelatine.

5 Place on ice and stir until setting point, then carefully fold in the beaten cream.
6 Pour into individual china serving dishes or dariole moulds.
7 When set, unmould the darioles on to plates and decorate with lettuce, tomatoes, radish and cucumber.

21 – Fruit and nut salad

	4 portions	10 portions
red eating apples	4	10
banana, diced	50 g (2 oz)	125 g (5 oz)
pineapple, diced	50 g (2 oz)	125 g (5 oz)
walnuts	25 g (1 oz)	60 g (2½ oz)
lemon	1	2–3
salt		
cream or natural yoghurt	60 ml (⅛ pt)	150 ml (⅓ pt)
lettuce	1	2½

1 Slice off the stalk end of the top of each apple to act as a lid.
2 With a parisienne cutter remove the centre, leaving only a thin layer by the skin. Rub the inside with lemon juice.
3 Mix the neatly diced apple flesh, banana, pineapple and walnuts together with lemon juice.
4 Add a little salt and cream to bind, refill the apples and replace the lid.
5 Serve with the heart of lettuce cut into quarters.

Note Variations can include fruits such as redcurrants, grapes, etc. and peeled almonds or mixed nuts.

22 – Apple, banana and celery salad

	4 portions	10 portions
apples, diced	4	10
bananas, sliced	2	5
celery, diced	200 g (8 oz)	500 g (1¼ lb)
mayonnaise		
few drops of lemon juice		

Mix all the ingredients together. Serve on a bed of lettuce, curly endive or radicchio.

23 – Tropical salad

	4 portions	10 portions
melon (depending on type and size)	$\frac{1}{2}$	1–2
avocado, skinned, stoned and diced	1	2–3
kiwi fruit, peeled and sliced	1	2–3
lemon, juice of	1	2–3
olive or vegetable oil	2 tbsp	5 tbsp
salt and pepper		
mint		
Chinese leaves		

1 Remove the skin and seeds from the melon and dice.
2 Place with the avocado and kiwi fruit.
3 Add the lemon juice and carefully mix with oil, seasoning and chopped mint.
4 Dress on a bed of Chinese leaves.

Note Other fruits, such as fresh figs and paw paw, can also be used. In place of oil, bind with tofu, natural yoghurt or mayonnaise. If tofu is used it must be mixed to a creamy consistency with skimmed milk or lemon juice.

24 – Salmon marinaded in dill (Gravlax)

	4 portions	10 portions
middle-cut, fresh, descaled raw salmon	$\frac{3}{4}$ kg (1$\frac{1}{2}$ lb)	1$\frac{3}{4}$ kg (3$\frac{3}{4}$ lb)
bunch dill, washed and chopped	1	2
castor sugar	25 g (1 oz)	60 g (2$\frac{1}{2}$ oz)
salt	25 g (1 oz)	60 g (2$\frac{1}{2}$ oz)
peppercorns, crushed	1 tbsp	2 tbsp

1 Cut the salmon lengthwise and remove all the bones.
2 Place one half, skin-side down, in a deep dish.
3 Add the dill, sugar, salt and peppercorns.
4 Cover with the other piece of salmon, skin-side up.

5 Cover with foil, lay a tray or dish on top, and evenly distribute weights on the foil.
6 Refrigerate for 48 hours, turning the fish every 12 hours and basting with the liquid produced by the ingredients. Separate the halves of salmon and baste between them.
7 Replace the foil, tray and weights between basting.
8 Lift the fish from the marinade, remove the dill and seasoning.
9 Place the halves of salmon on a board, skin-side down.
10 Slice thinly, detaching the slice from the skin.
11 Garnish gravlax with lemon and serve with mustard and dill sauce.

25 – Mustard and dill sauce

	4 portions	10 portions
mayonnaise	125 ml ($\frac{3}{4}$ pt)	300 ml ($1\frac{3}{4}$ pt)
white wine	60 ml ($\frac{1}{8}$ pt)	150 ml ($\frac{1}{3}$ pt)
castor sugar	12 g ($\frac{1}{2}$ oz)	60 g ($2\frac{1}{2}$ oz)
coarse mustard	1 dsp	$2\frac{1}{2}$ dsp
fresh chopped dill	$\frac{1}{2}$ tsp	1 tsp
salt and pepper		

Mix into the mayonnaise the rest of the ingredients; correct the seasoning with salt and pepper.

Note There are many variations to this recipe: 60 ml ($\frac{1}{8}$ pt) double cream (150 ml, $\frac{1}{3}$ pt for 10 portions) or natural yoghurt may be added; alternatively a French dressing base may be used in place of mayonnaise.

26 – Tomatoes stuffed with tuna fish, egg and herbs

	4 portions	10 portions
tomatoes, depending on size (skinned if required)	4–8	10–20
salt and pepper		
tuna fish	100 g (4 oz)	250 g (10 oz)
eggs, hard-boiled	2	5
onion, diced (optional)	25 g (1 oz)	60 g ($2\frac{1}{2}$ oz)
chopped parsley, tarragon, and chervil		
mayonnaise		

1 Slice the tops of the tomatoes to form a lid.
2 Remove the seeds from the inside, season.
3 Fill with a mixture of tuna fish, chopped hard-boiled egg, onion and herbs, bound with mayonnaise.
4 Replace the lid.

Note A variety of fillings can be used, e.g. white fish with capers and gherkins; smoked salmon and avocado; mixed vegetables in vinaigrette; chicken and ham in sour cream; mushrooms and peas in yoghurt; sweetcorn, rice and flageolet beans.

Cucumber can also be stuffed with such fillings. The cucumber should be cut in 5 cm (2 in) lengths, the centres removed with a parisienne cutter, the shells blanched if required and then stuffed with the required filling.

—— *Buffet items* ——

The preparation and presentation of attractive, inviting cold buffets should give pleasure to customers and help stimulate their appetites. When preparing and decorating dishes it must always be borne in mind that they are to be presented and served in front of customers; therefore, *ease* of service is important and should be considered when choosing the method of decoration. A cold buffet should not look a wreck after a handful of customers or one or two portions have been served.

Sound standards of personal, kitchen and food hygiene are essential as cold foods if not hygienically prepared, cooked, handled, stored and displayed can be easily infected and lead to food poisoning.

PREPARING A COLD BUFFET

An example of the sequence of events prior to preparation of a cold buffet:

1 Agree the required dishes for the buffet and the amount of each.
2 Compile lists of ingredients.
3 Order food sufficiently in advance to allow time for preparation, cooking, cooling and decorating.

There are numerous variations to a cold buffet depending on:

1 The time of year, which can affect choice of seasonal foods.
2 The time of day – breakfast, lunch, dinner, supper.
3 The occasion and number of guests, e.g.:
   - 8.30 am meeting of EEC Ministers in March, 50 guests
   - 1 o'clock wedding reception in June, 250 guests.
   - Gathering of 1,000 international lawyers in October at 8 pm.
   - Midnight supper in February for 500 following a gala performance of an opera.
4 Any special requests by the host/hostess.

Once all requirements are known, then a sensibly varied, colourful and appetising range of dishes can be prepared. It is not necessarily the number of dishes that give a cold buffet customer appeal, but rather the choice of foods, their quality and the way that they are displayed, e.g.:

smoked salmon	York ham	green salad
potted shrimps	roast beef	tomato and cucumber
		potato salad
		vegetable salad

On the other hand, for a large, special occasion the following may be prepared:

fresh prawns	roast turkey	whole chicken	stuffed eggs
lobster	roast venison	in chaudfroid	stuffed tomatoes
dressed crab	roast saddle of	whole duck in	green salad
dressed crawfish	lamb	chaudfroid	potato salad
eel terrine	York ham	whole pheasant	vegetable salad
dressed salmon	ox tongue	in chaudfroid	minted carrot
		chicken pie	salad
		game pie	

As the chef has prepared all these dishes, he/she should be involved in their display and the following points borne in mind:

1 Display food under refrigeration if possible. If not then keep in cool/cold storage until the last possible moment bearing in mind that cold buffet food is a favourite target for bacteria. (Refer to Guidelines for the Catering Industry on the Food Hygiene Regulations Amendments 1990 and 1991, HMSO.)
2 Select the most outstanding dish as the centrepiece.

3 Consider carefully how the food is to be served or even self-served by the customers when placing all dishes in position. The satisfactory service of many excellent cold buffets is often spoiled because insufficient thought has been given to the *way* in which they are to be served.
4 If the customers are to help themselves then see that all dishes are within reach.
5 Ensure that the various complementing dressings and salads are by the appropriate dishes, otherwise customers will be moving backwards and forwards unnecessarily and causing hold-ups.
6 On self-service buffets, dishes quickly become untidy. Have staff on hand to remove and replace or tidy up dishes as required.

27 – Light buffet items

These are small items of food, hot or cold, which are served at cocktail parties, buffet receptions and may be offered as an accompaniment to drinks before any meal (luncheon, dinner or supper). Typical items for cocktail parties and light buffets are:

1 Hot savoury pastry patties of lobster, chicken, crab, salmon, mushroom, ham, etc., small pizzas, quiches, brochettes, hamburgers.
2 Hot sausages (chipolatas), various fillings, such as chicken livers, prunes, mushrooms, tomatoes, gherkins, etc., wrapped in bacon and skewered and cooked under the salamander. Fried goujons of fish.
3 Savoury finger toasts to include any of the cold canapés. These may also be prepared on biscuits or shaped pieces of pastry. On the bases the following may be used: salami, ham, tongue, thinly sliced cooked meats, smoked salmon, caviar, mock caviar, sardine, eggs, etc.
4 Game chips, gaufrette potatoes, fried fish balls, celery stalks spread with cheese.
5 Sandwiches, bridge rolls – open or closed but always small.
6 Sweets such as trifles, charlottes, jellies, bavarois, fruit salad, gâteaux, strawberries and raspberries with fresh cream, ice creams, pastries.
7 Beverages, coffee, tea, fruit-cup, punch-bowl, iced coffee.

Canapés are served on neat pieces of buttered toast or puff or short pastry. A variety of foods may be used – slices of hard-boiled egg, thin slices of cooked meats, smoked sausages, fish, anchovies, prawns, etc. They may be left plain, or decorated with piped butter and coated with aspic jelly. The size of a canapé should be suitable for a mouthful.

28 – Bouchées

Bouchée fillings are numerous as bouchées are served both hot and cold. They may be served as cocktail savouries, or as a first course, a fish course or as a savoury. All fillings should be bound with a suitable sauce, for example:

Mushroom – chicken velouté or béchamel.
Shrimp – fish velouté or béchamel or curry.
Prawn – fish velouté or béchamel or curry.
Chicken – chicken velouté.
Ham – chicken velouté or béchamel or curry.
Lobster – fish velouté or béchamel or mayonnaise.
Vegetable – mayonnaise, natural yoghurt, fromage frais, quark or béchamel.

29 – Savouries using barquettes and tartlets

There are a variety of savouries which may be served either as hot appetisers (at a cocktail reception) or as the last course of an evening meal. The tartlet or barquette may be made from thinly rolled short paste and cooked blind.

Examples of fillings
Shrimps in curry sauce.
Chicken livers in demi-glace or devilled sauce.
Mushrooms in béchamel, suprême or aurora sauce.
Poached soft roes with devilled sauce.
Poached soft roes covered with cheese soufflé mixture and baked.

The cooked tartlets or barquettes should be warmed through before service, the filling prepared separately and neatly placed in them, garnished with a sprig of parsley.

30 – Aspic jelly and chaudfroid

Chaud-froid sauces and aspic jelly are basic larder preparations. Chaud-froid sauces are derived from béchamel, velouté or demi-glace to which aspic jelly or gelatine is added so as to help them to set when cold. They are used to mask fish, meat, poultry and game, either whole or cut in pieces, for cold buffets, which are then usually decorated and finally coated with aspic.

Aspic is a savoury jelly which may be used on cold egg, fish, meat, poultry, game and vegetable dishes that are prepared for cold buffets so as to give them an attractive appearance. For meat dishes a beef or veal stock is made; for fowl, chicken stock; and for fish, fish stock.

Aspic jelly is produced from fish, poultry, game or meat stock with the addition of gelatine. Vegetarian aspic jelly is produced from vegetable stock with the addition of agar-agar as a setting agent.

Great care must be taken when using aspic jelly as it is an ideal medium for the growth of micro-organisms. Therefore the following procedures should be observed:

1 Always use fresh aspic, bring to the boil and simmer for 10 minutes. Cool quickly and use sparingly.
2 Avoid using warm aspic, especially over long periods.
3 Do not store aspic for long periods at room temperature.
4 If required for further use, chill rapidly and store in the refrigerator.
5 If stored in refrigerator, simmer for 10 minutes before further use. Discard after 24 hours storage.
6 Once a dish has been glazed with aspic, keep refrigerated and consume within 8 hours.
7 It is advisable, if possible, to make only the quantity required for use and so avoid storage. Where possible, display in refrigerated units.

Uses
- As a glaze for cold preparations.
- To prevent food from losing moisture.
- As a garnish for certain dishes.
- To aid presentation and appearance.

31 – Points to observe when using aspic jelly or chaudfroid

1 Always work with one basin of aspic at coating consistency and another of hot jelly, so that when the jelly being used becomes too thick a little hot may be added to bring it back to coating consistency. The same applies when using fairly large quantities of chaudfroid.
2 It is best to let jelly set naturally. It remains at coating consistency much longer than when 'forced' on ice because the container is the temperature of the jelly, whereas if it has been on ice it will continue to reduce the temperature of the jelly.

3 Always work with two trays: one to glaze on and one for any surplus jelly or sauce to drip on while your work is setting in the fridge.

4 Use plenty of sauce or jelly so that the object to be coated may be completely covered in one steady sweep of the ladle. For larger objects, such as galantines or tongues, aim first at the top of the curve nearest to you so that the sauce or jelly runs both forwards and backwards. This should be followed immediately by two or more ladles in quick succession, so that a smooth surface completely free of ridges is formed. When saucing whole poultry, start by coating the tail end under the legs, from the rear, then coat the rest of the bird from the front. Two or even three coats of chaudfroid will be needed and each coat should be allowed to set in the fridge before applying the next, unless you are already working in a very cold temperature.

5 All decorations should be fastened in place with a little jelly so that they are not washed off when the final glaze of jelly is applied.

6 To chemise or glaze a dish it is best to use hot jelly. This reduces the risk of forming bubbles, which should be avoided at all times as they detract from the appearance of the dish. Allow to set on a level surface, preferably in a refrigerator. If the dish is such that it is necessary to apply the jelly after it has been dressed, the jelly must be applied carefully and quickly – almost at setting point.

7 When the weather is warm, or if the jelly is likely to be in a warm room for some time, it should have extra gelatine added. Jelly for chopping or cutting in shapes should also be firmer.

32 – Aspic jelly

	4 portions	10 portions	
whites of egg	2–3	5	This recipe provides:
strong, fat-free, seasoned stock (as required poultry, meat, game or fish)	1 litre (1 qt)	2½ litre (2½ qt)	397 kcals/1668 kJ 0.0 g fat (of which 0.0 g saturated) 7.4 g carbohydrate
vinegar	1 tbsp	2½ tbsp	(of which 0.1 g sugars)
sprigs tarragon	2	5	91.3 g protein
leaf gelatine	75 g (3 oz)	190 g (7 oz)	0.0 g fibre

1 Whisk the whites in a thick-bottomed pan with $\frac{1}{4}$ litre ($\frac{1}{2}$ pt) of the cold stock and the vinegar and tarragon.

2 Heat the rest of the stock, add the gelatine (previously soaked for 10

minutes in cold water) and whisk till dissolved.

3 Add the stock and dissolved gelatine into the thick-bottomed pan. Whisk well.
4 Place on the stove and allow to come gently to the boil until clarified.
5 Strain through a muslin.
6 If the jelly is not clear, repeat the whole procedure using egg whites only.

33 – Aspic jelly flavoured with wine

When an aspic is flavoured with wine the following quantities may be used but the wine must only be added when the aspic is almost cold. If wine is added earlier it can spoil the clarification process giving a cloudy rather than a sparkling clear aspic.

- White or red wines: 125 ml ($\frac{1}{4}$ pt) to 1 litre (2 pt)
- Sherry or port: 60 ml ($\frac{1}{8}$ pt) to 1 litre (2 pt)

In all cases the liquid quantity of stock should be reduced by the quantity of wine to be added *or* extra gelatine used.

34 – White chaudfroid

	4 portions	10 portions
leaf gelatine	50 g (2 oz)	125 g (5 oz)
béchamel or velouté	1 litre (2 pt)	2$\frac{1}{2}$ litre (5 pt)
cream (if necessary to improve the colour of the sauce)	125 ml ($\frac{1}{4}$ pt)	300 ml ($\frac{5}{8}$ pt)

1 Soak the gelatine in cold water.
2 Bring the sauce to the boil.
3 Remove from the heat.
4 Add the well-squeezed gelatine and stir until dissolved, and correct the seasoning.
5 Pass through a tammy cloth.
6 When the sauce is half cooled mix in the cream.

35 – Brown chaudfroid

This is a light demi-glace with the addition of gelatine; use 25 g (1 oz) to 500 ml (1 pt) of sauce. For a game chaudfroid, brown game stock should be used in the making of the demi-glace.

36 – Pale pink chaudfroid

This is normal chaudfroid to which a little sweated paprika has been added to give a pale pink colour.

37 – Materials which may be used for decorating

The decoration of various cold dishes provides great scope for the chef's artistic talents, and a wide variety of materials may be used. The designs should be neat and accurately cut; a good effect may be obtained not only by fine intricate designs but also by bold, uncomplicated ideas. In these days, when speed is so important, bold effective designs which can be produced quickly are very necessary; but when the occasion arises, and time permits, a great impression may be made by fine decoration. It is appreciated by the customer if the decoration of a buffet takes its theme from something topical or from the occasion of the party.

Among the materials suitable for decoration, the following may be used: tomato flesh, with or without skin, pimento, cucumber skin (scraped clean of any adhering flesh), green of leek (blanched), white of egg (which may also be tinted to give a two-tone effect), radishes, carrots, truffle, black and green olives, mint leaves (for lamb), watercress and cressonette, chervil, parsley, and celery leaves.

Materials which have a shiny surface, such as tomato skin or cucumber peel, should always be put on shiny side down. All pieces should be dipped in cool jelly before placing in position to ensure they remain in place.

To make pimento easier to work with, and to economise with truffles, make a purée of each of them, add a little strong jelly and run out thinly on to plates or trays to allow to set.

Piping is another method of decoration which, if used sparingly and carefully, can be effective. Butter is the usual medium and can for example be used from a fine paper cornet on canapés. The butter can be coloured or/and flavoured to give variation. Meat glaze used very sparingly can also be used to give simple artistic effects.

38 – Methods of cutting decorations

The principal tool used is a small sharp knife, preferably with a fine sharp point. If the design is to be floral, care must be taken to make it look natural. It is not necessary to copy exactly a particular type of flower, but take care to avoid obvious faults. Do not mix natural and geometrical designs of flowers, but designs of flowers may have geometrical borders, etc., or patterns may be made entirely of geometrical shapes.

Leaves and petals should have a natural shape.

Petals may be cut from tomatoes or eggs by cutting round a selected point and continuing all round, thus forming the points for a second line of petals. By cutting in the same way, but with a sawing movement, egg or coloured chaudfroid may be formed into carnation-type petals. Flowers may also be formed by fluting carrots or radishes down the four quarters and then cutting in thin slices.

Squares and triangles or diamonds are cut with a small knife also and may be 'mass produced' by cutting several parallel lines at once. Circles or dots may be cut by using the appropriate sized plain tubes. Fancy cutters of all shapes and sizes are used to form parts of decorative schemes. Large cuts make pieces which may be cut into smaller ones.

39 – Decoration of whole hams

When the ham is cooked and cold remove the aitch-bone, rind and all the brown flesh from the underside. Remove surplus fat from the upperside and scrape the surface with a knife until it is smooth. Place in the refrigerator to get thoroughly cold and firm.

Place on a wire tray and coat with aspic jelly which is almost at setting point. Decorate. Glaze with aspic jelly.

Allow to set thoroughly and place on a ham stand with a paper frill around the bone.

Hams may be coated with chaudfroid before decorating.

Two simple methods of preparation where decoration is not required are as follows:

1 The ham is trimmed as above then coated in brown breadcrumbs.
2 The ham is parboiled, skinned, studded with cloves, dusted with brown sugar, baked and glazed.

40 – Cold ox tongue

Tongues for cold buffet use should be soaked in brine for 8–10 days before cooking, but this is usually done by the supplier. The tongue is then placed in plenty of cold water, brought to the boil and simmered for $2\frac{1}{2}$–3 hours according to size. When cooked it should be easy to remove the skin. This should be done while hot, the small bones and gristle removed and the underneath trimmed. The tongues should be pressed in a specially constructed box, giving them an arched 'slipper' shape, and covered with a damp cloth.

When cold and set, the tongue is coated with a strong red-brown aspic. If a number of tongues are to be coated they may be dipped in the jelly, drained on a wire tray and the jelly ladled over, taking care to coat smoothly. When cold, trim off any 'tears' of jelly and dress on an oval dish with bunches of watercress under the arch of the tongue.

41 – The serving of cold cooked meats

Cold cooked meat should be sliced as near to serving time as possible, and arranged neatly on a dish with finely diced or chopped aspic around the edge. It may be decorated with a bunch of picked watercress or presented in the piece with 3 or 4 slices cut.

Whole joints, particularly ribs of beef, are often placed on a buffet table. They should either be boned or have any bones that may hinder carving removed before being cooked, They should be trimmed if necessary, strings removed and, after glazing with aspic jelly or brushing with oil, dressed on a dish garnished with watercress; lettuce leaves and fancy-cut pieces of tomato may also be used to garnish the dish.

Fillet of beef Wellington (page 260) and roast suckling pig (page 284) are popular cold buffet dishes.

42 – The serving of cold roast chicken

If the chicken is to be displayed whole at a buffet it may be brushed with aspic, or oil. It is then dressed on a suitably-sized oval dish with watercress and a little diced aspic jelly.

To keep roast suckling pig and roast chicken moist and succulent, roast 2–3 hours before being required and do not refrigerate.

When serving individual portions it is usual to serve either a whole wing of chicken neatly trimmed, or a half chicken. If a half is served, the leg is removed, the wing trimmed, and the surplus bone removed from the leg, which is then placed in the wing ($1\frac{1}{2}$ kg/3 lb chickens). Larger chickens may be cut into four portions, the wings in two lengthwise and the legs in two joints. Sometimes the chicken may be requested sliced; it is usual to slice the breast only and then reform it on the dish in its original shape.

43 – The serving of cold duck

Use the same methods as for chicken.

44 – The serving of cold turkey or goose

For display, cold turkey or goose may be brushed with jelly or oil, but otherwise it is normally served sliced, with dark meat under the white, chopped jelly and watercress.

45 – The serving of cold game

Larger birds, such as pheasant, may be sliced or served in halves or quarters; small birds, whole or in halves. The birds are served with watercress and game chips. Most of the smaller birds are served on a fried bread croûte spread with a little of the corresponding pâté, farce au gratin, or pâté maison.

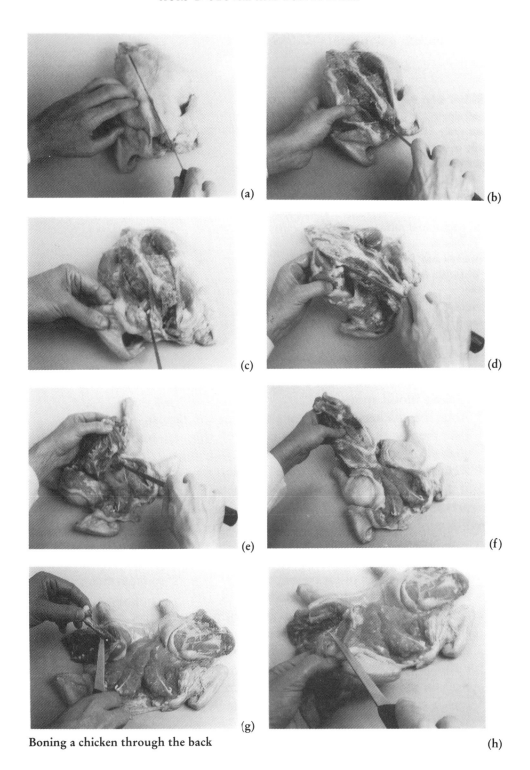

Boning a chicken through the back

53

46 – Chicken galantine

8 portions

chicken meat free from all sinew	200 g (8 oz)
lean veal	100 g (4 oz)
belly of pork	100 g (4 oz)
bread soaked in 125 ml ($\frac{1}{4}$ pt) of milk	75 g (3 oz)
double cream	250 ml ($\frac{1}{2}$ pt)
egg	1
salt, pepper and nutmeg to season	
blanched and skinned pistachio nuts	12 g ($\frac{1}{2}$ oz)
ham ⎫ cut into $\frac{1}{2}$ cm	25 g (1 oz)
tongue ⎬ ($\frac{1}{4}$ in) batons	25 g (1 oz)
bacon ⎭	25 g (1 oz)
thin slices of fat bacon or lardons	

> 1 portion provides:
>
> 390 kcals/1636 kJ
> 33.3 g fat
> (of which 16.6 g saturated)
> 6.3 g carbohydrate
> (of which 1.6 g sugars)
> 16.6 g protein
> 0.4 g fibre

1 Clean and carefully skin a chicken, place the skin in cold water to remove blood spots.
2 Bone the chicken and save one suprême for garnish.
3 Pass the rest through a fine mincer with the veal, pork and squeezed soaked breadcrumbs.
4 Remove into a basin, mix in the egg and pass through a sieve.
5 If using a food processor, add the egg while the mixture is in the processor and continue to chop until very fine.
6 Place into a basin over a bowl of ice, add the cream slowly, mixing well between each addition.
7 Place a damp cloth on a table, arrange the chicken skin on the cloth. Cover with slices of fat bacon, to about 5 cm (2 in) from the edge.
8 Spread on one-third of the mixture.
9 Garnish with alternative strips of ham, tongue, bacon, pistachio nuts and the chicken suprême also cut in $\frac{1}{2}$ cm ($\frac{1}{4}$ in) batons.
10 Place another layer of mixture on top and repeat the process.
11 Finish with a one-third layer of the mixture.
12 Roll the galantine up carefully. Tie both ends tightly.
13 Poach in chicken stock for approximately $1\frac{1}{2}$ hours.
14 When thoroughly cold remove cloth.
15 Cut in slices, serve garnished with salad.

Galantines may be coated with a white chaudfroid sauce, decorated and then masked with aspic jelly and served with a suitable salad.

Note   To enhance the flavour of the mixture, some fresh chopped herbs, such as tarragon and chervil, may be added.

Making a chicken galantine

Boned out chicken through the back

Adding prepared mixture

Rolling

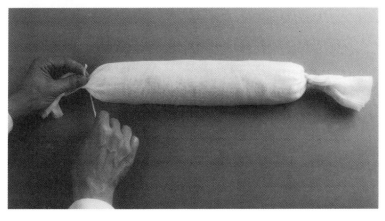
Tying in cloth

55

I 47 ~ Smoked breast of chicken and mango wrapped in lime fromage frais with tarragon, topped with roasted cashew nuts and warm sesame seed croûtons

(SIMON TEMPLE)

	4 portions	10 portions
smoked chicken breasts	2	10
fromage frais	125 g (5 oz)	310 g (12½ oz)
roasted cashew nuts	75 g (3 oz)	190 g (7½ oz)
sesame seeds	25 g (1 oz)	60 g (2¼ oz)
olive oil	2 tsp	5 tsp
mixed lettuce leaves	150 g (6 oz)	375 g (15 oz)
ripe mango	1	10
lime	1	10
chopped tarragon	pinch	pinch
slices wholemeal bread	4	40
sunflower margarine	1 tsp	30 ml ($\frac{1}{16}$ pt)
light vinaigrette	4 tsp	62 ml ($\frac{1}{8}$ pt)

1 Remove skin from chicken breasts and any bone.
2 Cut chicken into 1 cm ($\frac{1}{2}$ in) dice.
3 Remove skin from mango and dice the flesh the same size as chicken and lightly mix together.
4 In a large bowl mix fromage frais, juice from one lime and the tarragon. Add chicken and mango, carefully bind together, cover bowl and chill.
5 Wash lettuce leaves and drain. Toss in vinaigrette, cover and keep in fridge.
6 Remove crusts from bread, lightly spread slices with margarine and then sprinkle sesame seeds over both sides firmly pressing in. Cut into small dice.
7 Arrange lettuce on the chilled plates.
8 Carefully spoon chicken on, mixing into neat, even mounds.
9 Share cashew nuts out evenly on top of chicken.
10 Heat olive oil and fry sesame croûtons till golden and crisp. Sprinkle over salad and serve immediately.

*Use cherry tomatoes and sprigs of mint for extra garnish.

48 – Ballottines

A ballottine is a boned-out stuffed leg of poultry, usually chicken, duck or turkey, which can be prepared, stuffed with a variety of forcemeat stuffings, cooked, cooled and prepared for service cold.

It can be served:

- Simply, garnished with a suitable salad.
- Decorated and coated with aspic.
- Coated with a white or brown chaudfroid and decorated.

Note When preparing ballottines, keep the skin long as it can then help to give a good shape which can be long, round or like a small ham.

49 – Preparation of chicken in cold white sauce or chaudfroid

Select a large, well-shaped chicken; it must not be damaged, particularly the legs. Remove all the toes except the longest one on each foot, from these just clip off the claws. In order for the chicken to have a good shape it should be cleaned entirely through the neck. Truss the chicken firmly, as for roasting, so that the wings and back are as flat as possible.

Poach the chicken, taking care not to damage the legs, which may be loosely tied together to prevent splaying. When cooked, remove from the stock and allow to cool. If the legs have pulled down towards the tail during cooking, hang the feet over some suitable object so that the weight of the chicken gradually drops – pulling the legs back into an almost upright position.

When the chicken is cold, carefully remove the suprêmes and pull out the breast bone. The breast is replaced by the required mousse (foie gras, ham, tomato, page 72) and moulded nicely to a rounded shape. Allow to cool thoroughly in a cold room. Meanwhile cut the suprêmes into two or three neat pieces each, maintaining the original shape as much as possible. When dealing with large numbers, whole suprêmes from smaller chickens are often used.

When thoroughly cooled, coat the chicken and suprêmes with chaudfroid, taking care that all is covered completely and smoothly, leaving no 'tears' around the tail of the chicken. Decorate, glaze and dress with the appropriate garnish.

50 – Cold poached chicken with tomato mousse

Poach the chicken prepared as in previous recipe. When cold, skin and remove the suprêmes and breastbone. Reform the breast with a tomato mousse (page 73), refrigerate until set and chaudfroid the rest of the carcass. Decorate. The pattern may include truffle and, if possible, roses of tomato or egg. Cut the suprêmes into escalopes and chaudfroid. Decorate to match the poularde and glaze with aspic.

There are various methods of garnishing, for example:

1 Dress the escalopes on small pastry barquettes filled with tomato mousse.
2 Pipe a little mousse part way or right round each escalope. Dress on a glazed dish, with the poularde on a socle of rice, stearine or semolina.

51 – Cold poached chicken with ham mousse

Prepare the chickens as for previous recipe, but use a ham mousse (page 74).

Cover the suprêmes with white chaudfroid. Mould all barquettes or pads of ham mousse to fit each piece of chicken. Mask the poularde with pale pink chaudfroid, decorate and glaze with aspic. (The breast may also be left unsauced.)

Dress the chicken on a socle on a glazed dish with the decorated suprêmes on the pads of mousse. Decorate the edge of the dish with neatly cut pieces of jelly.

52 – Socles

Socles are bases, usually of rice, wax (stearine) or semolina, on which decorated chickens etc. are mounted. Stearine has the advantage that once it has been moulded and carved it can be used many times without deterioration. It may also be remoulded. Stearine with the addition of mutton fat and bee's wax may be worked by hand to make flowers, animals etc. Socles are also made from ice for certain dishes.

The simplest method of making a socle is to make a very thick semolina pudding from milk and semolina with the addition of soaked gelatine, pour into a lightly oiled dish and allow to set in the refrigerator. For example, 500 ml (1 pt) milk, 150 g (6 oz) semolina, 50 g (2 oz) gelatine.

53 – Cold suprêmes of chicken in white sauce with foie gras or chicken liver pâté (Jeanette)

Use cooked poached chickens, allow to cool and remove the skin. Cut off the suprêmes and carefully trim. Cut into two or leave whole.

Cover each suprême with purée of foie gras or chicken liver pâté, approximately $\frac{1}{4}$ cm ($\frac{1}{8}$ in) thick. Cover with chaudfroid sauce. Decorate with blanched tarragon leaves and finish with aspic jelly.

Serve on a base of aspic flavoured with tarragon. Garnish with small bouquets of asparagus tips which have been glazed. Finish with chopped jelly around the base of the suprêmes.

54 – Cold wild duck with cherries (Montmorency)

The duck is roasted, but kept lightly underdone. When it is cold remove the breasts and take out the breast bone. Reform the breast with a mousse made from the debris of the flesh, the liver of the duck and foie gras (proceed as for chicken liver mousse, page 74). Slice the breasts thinly. Arrange a few slices to cover the mousse and arrange the rest neatly on the dish on which the duck is to be served. A border of the mousse may be piped all round the slices and decorated with stoned cherries (tinned or fresh, poached in red wine). Glaze the dish and the duck with port wine or red wine jelly.

When set, place a croûte of fried bread or a socle on the dish and dress the duck on top. Decorate with tiny points of parsley. Alternatively, the duck may be cut in aiguillettes and coated with brown chaudfroid before reforming on the mousse. The cherries may then be served set in small darioles of aspic.

55 – Cold duck with orange in aspic

This may be made using either Aylesbury or wild duck. Prepare the duck in the same way as for Montmorency, a little of the mousse being piped around the slices of meat on the breast only. The remaining slices are arranged neatly on the dish.

Glaze with aspic jelly containing a little Curaçao and fine julienne of blanched orange peel. Decorate the dish with glazed segments of orange, or fancy cut slices, or small darioles of orange. Place a line of chopped jelly around the sliced duck on the dish, and place a bunch of picked watercress at either side of the duck's tail.

56 – Pheasant in aspic

This dish can be prepared in the same way as duck Montmorency using a foie gras mousse, decorating with neatly cut truffle and garnishing with small tartlets of game mousse and chestnut purée. Finally, coating with port or red wine aspic.

57 – Pheasant medallions

Allow one cooked pheasant breast per portion. Cut the breasts to an equal size and thickness.

1 Decorate using a star tube with foie gras and/or game purée, add a cooked chestnut and glaze with port flavoured aspic.
2 Lightly coat the pheasant breasts with a game chaudfroid, decorate simply, glaze with port or red wine aspic and garnish with small croûtes of foie gras, game purée and chestnuts.

58 – Pâtés and terrines

The composition of these two preparations is similar, the difference being the actual cooking and the receptacle in which they are cooked.

The filling consists of a forcemeat prepared from the required meat, poultry or game well seasoned with herbs, spices and any other garnish that may be relevant to the particular pâté or terrine.

To make a pâté a raised pie mould is lined with pie pastry, then with thin slices of larding bacon. The forcemeat is then added with the garnish in between layers until the mould is full, the last layer being forcemeat. The top is covered with larding bacon and pie pastry, neatly decorated and then one or more holes 1 cm ($\frac{1}{2}$in) are made in the top into which are inserted short, oiled, stiff-paper funnels to enable steam to escape during cooking. The top is then egg washed 2–3 times and baked for $1\frac{1}{4}$–$1\frac{1}{2}$ hours at 190°C (375°F). When cold, the pie is filled through the holes in the top with a well-flavoured aspic jelly or a flavour to suit the pie.

Making a pâté en croûte (continued overleaf)

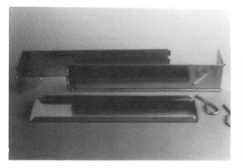

Collapsible mould so that pâté can be removed without damage

Rolling pastry

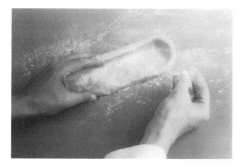

Shaping pastry

Folding pastry

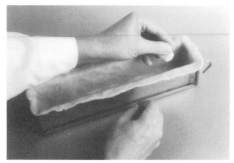

Lining mould

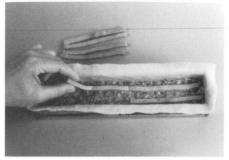

Adding filling

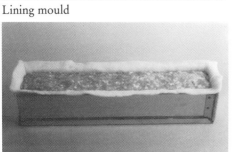

Filled mould

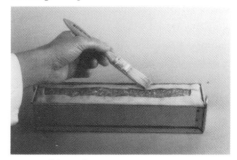

Eggwashing edges

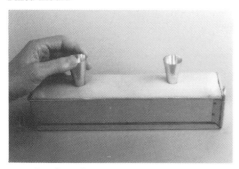

Inserting funnels

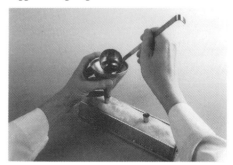

Adding aspic jelly after cooking and cooling of the pâté

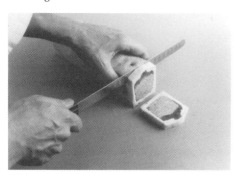

Slicing

59 – Pie pastry

	4 portions	10 portions
flour	400 g (1 lb)	1¼ kg (2½ lb)
butter or margarine	100 g (4 oz)	250 g (10 oz)
lard	100 g (4 oz)	250 g (10 oz)
egg	1	2–3
water	125 ml (¼ pt)	300 ml (⅝ pt)
salt		

1 Sieve the flour and salt.
2 Rub in the fat.
3 Add beaten egg and water.
4 Mix well and allow to rest before using.

60 – Veal and ham pie

	4 portions	10 portions
Forcemeat		
lean veal	100 g (4 oz)	250 g (10 oz)
lean pork	100 g (4 oz)	250 g (10 oz)
fat bacon	200 g (8 oz)	500 g (1¼ lb)
egg (beaten)	1	2–3
salt	10 g (½ oz)	25 g (1 oz)
Spice, seasoning, e.g., nutmeg, mace, allspice		

Pass the meats through a fine mincer then mix with the egg, salt and spice.

	4 portions	10 portions
Filling		
veal fillet	300 g (12 oz)	750 g (1¾ lb)
pork fillet	300 g (12 oz)	750 g (1¾ lb)
lean ham or gammon	200 g (8 oz)	500 g (1¼ lb)
larding bacon	200 g (8 oz)	500 g (1¼ lb)
salt	15 g (¾ oz)	35 g (1½ oz)
spices, e.g. nutmeg, cinnamon, allspice		
brandy, sherry or Madeira (optional)	60 ml (⅛ pt)	150 ml (⅓ pt)
pie pastry	200 g (½ lb)	500 g (1¼ lb)

Marinade the meats in the brandy and spices for 1–2 hours.

61 – Chicken pie

	4 portions	10 portions
Forcemeat		
chicken flesh	100 g (4 oz)	250 g (10 oz)
lean veal	50 g (2 oz)	125 g (5 oz)
lean pork	50 g (2 oz)	125 g (5 oz)
fat bacon	200 g (8 oz)	500 g (1¼ lb)
egg beaten	1	2
salt	10 g (½ oz)	25 g (1 oz)
spices		
Filling		
chicken fillets	300 g (12 oz)	750 g (1¾ lb)
larding bacon	200 g (8 oz)	500 g (¼ lb)
brandy	60 ml (⅛ pt)	150 ml (⅝ pt)
salt	15 g (¾ oz)	37 g (1½ oz)
spices		
Optional:		
foie gras	100 g (4 oz)	250 g (10 oz)
truffle	100 g (4 oz)	250 g (10 oz)
pistachio nuts	50 g (2 oz)	125 g (5 oz)

Marinade the meats in the brandy and spices for 1–2 hours.

62 – Raised pork pie

Certain pies are not cooked in moulds but are hand raised in which a hot water pastry is used.

	4 portions	10 portions
Hot water paste		
lard or margarine (alternatively use 4 parts lard and 1 part butter or margarine)	125 g (5 oz)	300 g (12 oz)
strong plain flour	250 g (10 oz)	625 g (1½ lb)
water	125 ml (¼ pt)	312 ml (⅝ pt)
salt		

> 1 portion provides:
>
> 683 kcals/2867 kJ
> 41.8 fat
> (of which 17.1 g saturated)
> 54.1 g carbohydrate
> (of which 1.5 g sugars)
> 26.1 g protein
> 3.2 g fibre

1 Sift the flour and salt into a basin.
2 Make a well in the centre.
3 Boil the fat with the water and pour immediately into the flour.
4 Mix with a wooden spoon until cool.
5 Mix to a smooth paste and use while still warm.

	4 portions	10 portions
Filling		
shoulder of pork (without bone)	300 g (12 oz)	750 g (1¾ lb)
bacon	100 g (4 oz)	250 g (10 oz)
allspice, or mixed spice, and chopped sage	½ tsp	1¼ tsp
salt and pepper		
bread soaked in milk	50 g (2 oz)	125 g (5 oz)
stock or water	2 tbsp	5 tbsp

1 Cut the pork and bacon into small even pieces and combine with the rest of the ingredients.
2 Keep one-quarter of the paste warm and covered.
3 Roll out the remaining three-quarters and carefully line a well-greased raised pie mould.
4 Add the filling and press down firmly.
5 Roll out the remaining pastry for the lid.
6 Eggwash the edges of the pie.
7 Add the lid, seal firmly, neaten the edges, cut off any surplus paste.
8 Decorate if desired.
9 Make a hole 1 cm (½ in) in diameter in the centre of the pie.
10 Brush all over with eggwash.
11 Bake in a hot oven 230–250°C (446–482°F) for approximately 20 minutes.
12 Reduce the heat to moderate 150–200°C (302–392°F) and cook for 1½–2 hours in all.
13 If the pie colours too quickly, cover with greaseproof paper. Remove from the oven and carefully remove tin. Eggwash the pie all over and return to the oven for a few minutes.
14 Remove from the oven and fill with approximately 125 ml (¼ pt) of good hot stock in which 5 g (¼ oz) of gelatine has been dissolved.
15 Serve when cold, garnished with picked watercress and offer a suitable salad.

63 – Game pies

These can be made from hare, rabbit or any of the game birds. The filling should be marinaded in the liquor, salt and spices for 1–2 hours.

	4 portions	10 portions
Forcemeat		
game flesh	200 g (8 oz)	500 g (1¼ lb)
fat bacon	200 g (8 oz)	500 g (1¼ lb)
beaten egg	1	2–3
salt	10 g (½ oz)	25 g (1 oz)
spices		
Filling		
game fillets	300 g (12 oz)	750 g (1¾ lb)
larding bacon	200 g (8 oz)	500 g (1¼ lb)
brandy or Madeira	60 ml (⅛ pt)	150 ml (⅓ pt)
salt	15 g (¾ oz)	35 g (1½ oz)
spices		

64 – Terrines

These are cooked in ovenproof dishes fitted with a lid. Once the mixture is in the dish the lid may be replaced and sealed with a plain flour and water paste to prevent the steam escaping. Terrines can be made from chicken, duck, veal, hare, rabbit, turkey and chicken livers, etc.

1 The forcemeat is made in the same way as for a pâté, as is the filling which is marinaded in the liquor and spices.
2 Line the bottom and sides of the terrine with thin slices of larding bacon.
3 Add half of the forcemeat (if this is too dry, moisten with a little good stock).
4 Neatly lay in the marinaded garnish.
5 Add the remainder of forcemeat and spread it evenly.
6 Cover the top with larding bacon and add a bay leaf and a sprig of thyme.
7 Put a thin layer of flour and water paste around the rim of the terrine and press the lid down firmly to seal it.
8 Place the terrine in a bain-marie and cook it in a moderate oven 190°C (375°F) for approximately 1¼ hours.
9 If the fat which rises to the top of the terrine is perfectly clear (shows

no signs of blood) when lightly pressed with the fingers, this indicates that it is cooked.

10 When cooked, remove from the bain-marie, remove the lid and add a piece of clean wood which will fit inside the dish and place a weight of 2–3 lb to press the meat down evenly. Allow to cool.

11 When cool, remove the weight and board and all the fat from the surface.

12 To remove the terrine from the dish, place it into boiling water for a few seconds.

13 Turn the terrine out, trim and clean it and cut it into slices as required.

Note   If the terrine is to be served in its cooking dish then wash and thoroughly dry the dish before returning the terrine to the dish.

If the terrine is then to be covered with a layer of aspic jelly, all fat must be removed from the top beforehand.

I 65 – Chicken, spinach and almond terrine

(IAN MURRAY)

	4 portions	10 portions	1 portion will provide:
diced cooked chicken breast	200 g (8 oz)	500 g (1¼ lb)	456 kcals
whipping cream	250 ml (½ pt)	750 ml (1¼ pt)	42.4 g fat
egg whites	3	8	(of which 20.1 g saturated)
salt	¼ tsp	¾ tsp	2.9 g carbohydrate
nutmeg, grated	pinch	pinch	(of which 1.5 g sugars)
toasted flaked almonds	100 g (4 oz)	250 g (10 oz)	16.1 g protein
smoked bacon	200 g (8 oz)	500 g (1¼ lb)	1.8 g fibre
cooked and squeezed dry spinach	400 g (1 lb)	1 kg (2¼ lb)	
soft full-fat cream cheese	200 g (½ lb)	500 g (1¼ lb)	

1 In a blender mix the chicken for 3 minutes until a fine purée is obtained, add the egg whites and salt, mix in, scrape down the sides and chill for 30 minutes.

2 Mix in the cream and nutmeg (*do not overmix or the cream will curdle*) and chill for 20 minutes.

3 Line a terrine mould with the bacon so as to cover the sides and bottom evenly leaving the ends hanging over the sides.

4 Cover the base of the mould and bacon with half the mousseline mixture.
5 Cover the mousseline with the spinach and sprinkle the almonds on top.
6 Cover the the spinach and almonds with the cream cheese and then the rest of the mousseline.
7 Cover with a lid.
8 Cook in a bain-marie in the oven at 200°C (400°F). Cooking time will alter according to thickness (you are only cooking the outside thirds). Cooking time approximatly 30 minutes. The terrine should be firm to the touch.

66 – Liver pâté

This is a home-made preparation often seen on the menu as pâté maison. A typical recipe is:

	4 portions	10 portions
liver (chicken, pigs, calves, lambs, etc.)	100 g (4 oz)	250 g (10 oz)
butter, oil or margarine	25 g (1 oz)	60 g (2½ oz)
chopped onion	10 g (½ oz)	25 g (1¼ oz)
clove garlic	½	1–2
sprig of thyme, parsley, chervil		
fat pork	50 g (2 oz)	125 g (5 oz)
lean pork	50 g (2 oz)	125 g (5 oz)
salt, pepper		
fat bacon	25 g (1 oz)	60 g (2½ oz)

1 portion provides:

213 kcals/896 kJ
19.1 g fat
(of which 8.5 g saturated)
0.7 g carbohydrate
(of which 0.1 g sugars)
9.8 g protein

1 Cut the liver in 2 cm (1 in) pieces.
2 Toss quickly in the butter in a frying-pan over a fierce heat for a few seconds with the onion, garlic and herbs.
3 Allow to cool.
4 Pass with the pork, twice through a mincer. Season.
5 Line an earthenware terrine with wafer-thin slices of fat bacon.
6 Place in the mixture. Cover with fat bacon.
7 Stand in a tray half full of water and bring to simmering point.
8 Cook in a moderate oven for 1 hour.

When quite cold cut in ½cm (¼in) slices and serve on lettuce leaves on a plate or dish.

Usually accompanied with freshly made toast.

67 – Cold salmon

Clean, scale and remove the fins from the salmon, and wash it. Prepare a court bouillon, cook it for 15 minutes and allow to cool completely. Place in the whole salmon, bring to the boil, and poach gently on the side of the stove for about 20 minutes, according to size. Allow to stand in the liquor until cold and then remove all the skin and blood.

Garnish with, for example, overlapping slices of hard-boiled egg and peeled tomatoes round the sides, alternately with lettuce quarters. Serve mayonnaise separately.

68 – Decorated cold salmon

Cook as for above and remove the skin. Decorate with prawns from which the tails have been removed, leaving the carapace. The prawns are placed along the middle of the salmon with the points into the fish. Place a trellis of blanched tarragon leaves on each side of the prawns, and glaze with a clear fish jelly.

Dress on a dish with a jelly base and garnish with, for example, boats of cucumber, which have been blanched and stuffed with prawns, bound with mayonnaise and flavoured with horseradish.

69 – Salmon mayonnaise

Dress flaked salmon free from skin and bone on to shredded lettuce. Coat with mayonnaise sauce and decorate with quarters of tomato and hard-boiled egg, slices of cucumber, thin fillets of anchovies, capers, olives and chopped parsley.

Salmon salad
Proceed as for salmon mayonnaise, omitting the mayonnaise sauce which may be served separately.

70 – Dressed crab

When buying crabs, care should be taken to see that they have both claws and that they are heavy in comparison to their size. When possible they should be bought alive to ensure freshness.

Place the crabs in boiling salted water with a little vinegar added. Allow to boil for approximately 15–30 minutes according to size; these times apply to crabs weighing from $\frac{1}{2}$–$2\frac{1}{2}$ kg (1–5 lb). Allow to cool in the cooling liquor.

To dress
1 Remove large claws and sever at the joints.
2 Remove the flexible pincer from the claw.
3 Crack or saw carefully and remove all flesh.
4 Remove flesh from two remaining joints with handle of spoon.
5 Carefully remove the soft under-shell.
6 Discard the gills (dead man's fingers) and the sac behind the eyes.
7 Scrape out all the inside of the shell and pass through sieve.
8 Season with salt, pepper, Worcester sauce and a little mayonnaise sauce, thicken lightly with fresh white breadcrumbs.
9 Trim the shell by tapping carefully along the natural line.
10 Scrub the shell thoroughly and leave to dry.
11 Dress the brown meat down the centre of the shell.
12 Shred the white meat, taking care to remove any small pieces of shell.
13 Dress neatly on either side of the brown meat.
14 Decorate as desired, using any of the following; chopped parsley, hard-boiled white and yolk of egg, anchovies, capers, olives.
15 Serve the crab on a flat dish, garnish with lettuce leaves, quarters of tomato and the legs.

Serve a vinaigrette or mayonnaise sauce separately.

Allow 200–300 g (8–12 oz) unprepared crab per portion.

71 – Cooking a lobster

Lobsters are usually bought in sizes from $\frac{1}{4}$–1 kg ($\frac{1}{2}$–2 lb). They should be bought alive to ensure freshness. They should be washed, then plunged into a pan of boiling salted water containing 60 ml ($\frac{1}{8}$ pt) vinegar to 1 litre (1 qt) water. Cover with a lid, bring to the boil and allow to simmer for

15–25 minutes according to size. Do not over-cook otherwise the tail-flesh can become tough and the claws hard and fibrous. When possible allow to cool in the cooking liquor.

72 – Cleaning of cooked lobster

1 Remove the claws and the pincers.
2 Crack the claws and joints and remove the meat in one piece.
3 Cut the lobster in half with a large knife, by inserting the point of the knife 2 cm (1 in) above the tail on the natural centre line.
4 Cut through the centre of the tail firmly.
5 Turn the lobster round the other way and cut through the carapace.
6 Remove the halves of the sac from each half (this is situated at the top of the head).
7 With a small knife remove the trail. Wash if necessary.

73 – Lobster mayonnaise

As for salmon mayonnaise (recipe 69), using 1 kg (2 lb) lobster cut in escalopes, in place of salmon.

Decorate with the lobster's head, tail, legs and chopped coral.

74 – Lobster salad

As for salmon salad (recipe 69) using one 1 kg (2 lb) cooked lobster, cut in escalopes in place of the salmon.

Decorate as for lobster mayonnaise.

75 – Cold lobster, mayonnaise sauce

Half a $\frac{1}{2}$ kg (1 lb) cooked lobster per portion.

Clean the halves, remove the trail and sac, remove the meat from the claws and place in the sac aperture. Serve garnished with quarters of lettuce and quarters of tomato accompanied by a sauceboat of sauce mayonnaise.

76 – Cold mousses

A mousse is basically a purée of the bulk ingredient from which it takes its name, with the addition of a suitable non-dairy or cream sauce, cream and aspic jelly. The result should be a light creamy mixture, just sufficiently set to stand when removed from a mould.

Care must be taken when mixing not to curdle the mixture, which will produce a 'bitty' appearance with small white grains of cream showing. The cream should only be half whipped as a rubbery texture will otherwise be obtained; also, if fresh cream is over-whipped the mixture will curdle.

Various types of mousse are used as part of other dishes as well as dishes on their own. A mould of a particular substance may be filled with a mousse of the same basic ingredient. Whole decorated chickens may have the breast reformed with a mousse such as ham, tomato or foie gras. Mousse may be piped to fill cornets of ham, borders for chicken suprêmes or cold egg dishes.

Although most recipes quote a lined mould for the mousse to be placed in when being served as an individual dish, mousses may often be poured into a glass bowl (or even smaller dishes for individual portions) to be decorated on top when set, then glazed. Although truffle is frequently quoted, garnishing paste or other materials are now used.

Note Convenience aspic jelly granules may be used for all mousse recipes.

T 77 – Stilton and port mousse with walnuts

(Murdo Macsween)

	4 portions	10 portions
leaves gelatine	5	13
aspic and garnish as needed		
Stilton	100 g (4 oz)	250 g (10 oz)
port	50 ml (2 fl oz)	125 ml (5 fl oz)
walnuts, chopped	25 g (1 oz)	60 g (2½ oz)
double cream	125 ml (¼ pt)	300 ml (⅝ pt)
egg whites	4	10
seasoning		

1 Soak gelatine in cold water.
2 Line individual moulds with a little aspic and garnish, e.g. slices of stuffed olives.
3 Liquidise Stilton and port together, adding a little single cream if necessary, and add walnuts.
4 Half-whip double cream and fold into Stilton mixture.
5 Whip up egg whites.
6 Squeeze all the water from gelatine and melt over a low heat, then add to egg whites while still whipping.
7 Fold egg whites into Stilton mixture and season.
8 Place mousse into moulds and allow to set for 2 hours.

This is served as a first course.

78 – Tomato mousse

	4 portions	10 portions
finely chopped onion	50 g (2 oz)	125 g (5 oz)
butter or margarine	50 g (2 oz)	125 g (5 oz)
white stock or consommé	500 ml (1 pt)	$2\frac{1}{2}$ litre ($2\frac{1}{2}$ pt)
tomatoes, skinned, deseeded and diced	250 g (10 oz)	600 g ($1\frac{1}{2}$ lb)
tomato purée	25 g (1 oz)	60 g ($2\frac{1}{2}$ oz)
salt and pepper		
pinch of paprika		
velouté	125 ml ($\frac{1}{4}$ pt)	600 ml ($1\frac{1}{4}$ pt)
aspic jelly	125 ml ($\frac{1}{4}$ pt)	600 ml ($1\frac{1}{4}$ pt)
whipping cream, half beaten	125 ml ($\frac{1}{4}$ pt)	600 ml ($1\frac{1}{4}$ pt)

1 Sweat the onion in the butter or margarine without colour.
2 Moisten with the stock or consommé, reduce by half.
3 Add the tomatoes and tomato purée. Simmer for approximately 20 minutes, season and add paprika.
4 Add the velouté and aspic, simmer for 2 minutes, then liquidise.
5 Place in a basin on ice, stir till setting point, and fold in the half-whipped cream.
6 Use as required: either place in individual moulds, allow to set, turn out on to individual plates, decorate and serve as a first course; or use as part of a cold dish.

79 – Chicken liver pâté mousse

	4 portions	10 portions
chicken liver pâté	100 g (4 oz)	250 g (10 oz)
aspic jelly	125 ml ($\frac{1}{4}$ pt)	300 ml ($\frac{5}{8}$ pt)
velouté	125 ml ($\frac{1}{4}$ pt)	300 ml ($\frac{5}{8}$ pt)
sheets of soaked gelatine	2	5
salt and pepper		
whipping cream, half beaten	125 ml ($\frac{1}{4}$ pt)	300 ml ($\frac{5}{8}$ pt)

1 Cream the liver pâté well; add the hot aspic and velouté, mix well.
2 Pass through a sieve or liquidise.
3 Add the gelatine, place in a basin on ice and season.
4 Allow to cool until setting point.
5 Fold in the half-whipped cream.
6 Place in individual moulds to use as a starter or use as required as part of a cold dish.

Note   The mousse may also be turned out on to individual plates, decorated with salad items and served.

80 – Ham mousse

	4 portions	10 portions
minced cooked ham	400 g (1 lb)	1$\frac{1}{4}$ kg (2$\frac{1}{2}$ lb)
velouté	125 ml ($\frac{1}{4}$ pt)	300 ml ($\frac{5}{8}$ pt)
aspic jelly	125 ml ($\frac{1}{4}$ pt)	300 ml ($\frac{5}{8}$ pt)
salt and pepper		
whipping cream	250 ml ($\frac{1}{2}$ pt)	600 ml (1$\frac{1}{4}$ pt)

1 Place the minced ham into a basin, add the velouté and aspic jelly. Season with salt and pepper.
2 Place into a saucepan and boil for approximately 2 minutes.
3 Purée in a food processor, then pour into a basin over ice.
4 Stir until setting point and fold in the half-whipped cream. Use as required.

Note   25 g (1 oz) finely chopped onion sweated in 10 g ($\frac{1}{2}$ oz) butter or margarine with 10 g ($\frac{1}{2}$ oz) paprika may be added at stage 2 if desired (increase proportions by 2$\frac{1}{2}$ for 10 portions).

81 – Chicken mousse

As for previous recipe, using minced cooked chicken, omitting any paprika.

82 – Salmon mousse

	4 portions	10 portions
cooked salmon, free from skin and bone	400 g (1 lb)	1¼ kg (2½ lb)
velouté	125 ml (¼ pt)	300 g (⅝ pt)
fish aspic jelly	125 ml (¼ pt)	300 ml (⅝ pt)
little sweated paprika if desired		
salt and pepper		
whipping cream	250 ml (½ pt)	600 ml (1¼ pt)

1 Purée the salmon, place in a saucepan with the velouté and aspic and boil for 2 minutes.
2 Pass through a sieve, add the sweated paprika, and mix well. Season.
3 Place in a basin over a bowl of ice, stir until setting point, then fold in the half-whipped cream.
4 Pour into a glass bowl or individual moulds. Decorate and use as required.

⊤ 83 – Scotch salmon terrine layered with scallops, served on a lime yoghurt dressing

(STEPHEN GOODLAD)

	4 portions	10 portions
scallops, cleaned out of shell	400 g (12 oz)	1 kg (2 lb)
sole flesh	80 g (3 oz)	200 g (8 oz)
egg whites	1	3
double cream	250 ml (½ pt)	625 ml (1¼ pt)
brunoise vegetables (carrot, leek, celery)	40 g (1½ oz)	100 g (4 oz)
soft butter	20 g (¾ oz)	50 g (2 oz)
fine herbs	2½ tbsp	1 tbsp
dry sherry	10 ml (2 tsp)	25 ml (1 fl oz)

side fresh salmon (from 4 kg (8 lb) wild salmon)*	$\frac{1}{2}$	1
cooked leaf spinach	160 g (6$\frac{1}{2}$ oz)	400 g (1 lb)
single cream	40 ml (1$\frac{1}{2}$ fl oz)	100 ml ($\frac{1}{4}$ pt)
lime, juice of	$\frac{1}{2}$	1
natural yoghurt	50 ml (1$\frac{1}{2}$ fl oz)	125 ml ($\frac{1}{4}$ pt)
sprigs of picked chervil	1	3

* A 1$\frac{1}{2}$ kg (3 lbs) side yields 1 kg (2 lb) salmon to line terrine after trimming.

1 Purée 200 g (8 oz) scallops and the sole flesh in a food-processor, add the egg whites and seasoning, then slowly blend in 125 ml ($\frac{1}{4}$ pt) double cream.
2 Remove the purée and push it through a fine drum sieve.
3 Beat the remaining double cream into the purée, and leave the bowl to rest on ice for 30 minutes.
4 Add the brunoise of vegetables, which have been sweated down in the butter and herbs and deglazed with the dry sherry. Cool and add to the purée.
5 Fillet the salmon, remove the skin, bones and the brown pieces of flesh. Cut into the same size as the terrine and butterfly.
6 Place the salmon between a piece of lightly greased clingfilm (with oil) and gently tap it out using a cutlet bat. This will lubricate the salmon and make flattening it easier.
7 Grease the terrine with clarified butter and silicone paper, then line the salmon into the mould.
8 Cover with spinach, lay the spinach out flat and place fresh scallops down the middle. Spread a thin layer of mousse over the scallops to hold them in place.
9 Roll the spinach into a sausage shape the same length as the terrine.,
10 Place a layer of mousse half-way up the lined terrine, lay the spinach sausage into the mousse, cover with the remaining mousse, then fold the overlapping salmon.
11 Cover with greaseproof paper, place the lid on and poach in a bain-marie for 1 hour in a low oven (160°C, 325°F).
12 Remove from the oven and allow to cool. Leave overnight in the terrine to set.
13 Stir the single cream and lime juice into the yoghurt. Use to sauce medium-sized plates.
14 Remove the terrine from the mould. Slice with a warm thin bladed knife and lay on top of the sauce on a 30 cm (12 in) plate. Place a sprig of chervil at the top of the plate and serve.

Note   It is advisable to use wild salmon when available and in season at its cheapest, but farmed salmon or salmon trout can also be used. It is a good idea to lay the salmon on to greased silicone paper. This will make it easier to line the terrine and to turn it out when set.

84 – Dressed crawfish

1 Tie a live crawfish to a board with the tail out flat.
2 Cook in a pan of boiling salted water containing 60 ml ($\frac{1}{8}$ pt) vinegar to 1 litre (1 qt) of water (the crawfish must be covered in liquid). Cooking time depends on size – 2 kg (4 lb) crawfish will require approximately 25–30 minutes.
3 Allow to cool in the cooking liquid.
4 When completely cold, remove from the board. Remove the tail flesh in one piece by cutting with fish scissors two parallel lines about 4 cm ($1\frac{1}{2}$ in) apart down the tail and remove the piece of shell.
5 Carefully remove the tail meat in one piece.
6 Cut into thick even slices, decorate simply, e.g. small diamonds of blanched cucumber skin and tomato skin, and coat with fish aspic jelly (if required).
7 Remove the flesh and creamy parts from the carapace, cut the flesh into small dice and add to a diced vegetable salad, e.g. carrot, turnip, French beans, peas.
8 Pan the creamy parts through a sieve, add to a mayonnaise and mix with the vegetable salad.
9 Fill the empty shell of the crawfish with the vegetable salad and place it with this head pointing upwards on a wedge-shaped base of deep-fried bread or a socle.
10 Neatly place the prepared slices of crawfish overlapping on to the back of the filled shell starting with the largest at the head.
11 The dish can then be garnished simply with lettuce hearts and segments of tomatoes and mayonnaise sauce accompaniment.

85 – Cold stuffed fish

When preparing cold stuffed fish, the aim should be to remove the bones so that the customer can enjoy the fish without having to worry about these.

86 – Stuffed round fish

Trout, red mullet and sea bass should have the back bone removed leaving the head and tail intact on the skin. The cavity can then be filled with a suitable stuffing, for example:

- Trout with a salmon or lobster forcemeat with diced mushrooms.
- Red mullet with a white fish forcemeat with chopped fennel.
- Sea bass with a crayfish forcemeat with diced crayfish.

The fish is then reshaped (held in shape with greased greaseproof paper if necessary) and gently poached in a little stock or stock and wine in the oven.

When cooled the fish may be served:

- Plain with a suitable accompanying cold sauce.
- The skin removed, the fish cleaned, garnished with salad.
- Decorated and coated with a fish aspic or fish wine aspic.

87 – Red mullet with tomatoes, garlic and saffron

	4 portions	10 portions
red mullet	4 × 150 g (6 oz)	10 × 150 g (6 oz)
salt and pepper		
dry white wine	125 ml ($\frac{1}{4}$ pt)	300 ml ($\frac{5}{8}$ pt)
vegetable oil	60 ml ($\frac{1}{8}$ pt)	150 ml ($\frac{1}{3}$ pt)
tomatoes, skinned, deseeded and diced	150 g (6 oz)	375 g (15 oz)
clove of garlic (crushed)	1	2–3
sprig of thyme, bayleaf		
pinch of saffron		
peeled lemon	4 slices	10 slices

> 1 portion provides:
>
> 298 kcals/1228 kJ
> 18.7 g fat
> (of which 2 g saturated)
> 1.4 g carbohydrate
> (of which 1.4 g sugars)
> 26.8 g protein
> 0.4 g fibre

1 Clean, prepare and dry the fish.
2 Place in a suitable oiled dish. Season with salt and pepper.
3 Add the white wine, oil, tomatoes, garlic, herbs and saffron.
4 Cover with aluminium foil and bake in the oven at 220°C (425°F) for approximately 10 minutes. Allow to cool in dish.
5 Serve on individual plates with a little of the cooking liquor, garnished with a slice of peeled lemon.

88 – Stuffed fillets of sole

Flatten the fillets of sole and roll each one round a buttered wooden cylinder approximately 2 cm (1 in) diameter. Poach gently in a buttered pan in fish stock and white wine. When cooled and the pieces of wood are removed, the fillets should now be in short tube shapes ready for stuffing or filling, for example:

- Dice of cooked lobster and mushrooms in a lobster cream sauce.
- Peeled and pipped grapes, diced bananas and tomato in a lightly soured cream sauce.
- Mousse of crayfish or salmon and an asparagus sauce.
- Flaked white crab meat in a light mayonnaise.

—— *Hot hors-d'oeuvre* ——

Customers may request snacks and hors-d'oeuvre at almost any time of the day or night. An interesting variety should be offered and in order to give an appetising presentation, they should be prepared as near to service time as possible in which case they need not be refrigerated. Items to be baked should be served warm but not too hot as guests may have to eat them with their fingers. As at most receptions the guests remain standing, items should not be larger than a comfortable mouthful.

Although an attractive display should always be provided, in the interests of hygiene cold snacks, canapés, etc., should not be allowed to go into the reception until the last possible moment.

Hot snacks are normally offered after the guests have arrived, during the reception, and sent out from the kitchen in small quantities.

When to be served as reception snacks all the following items should be made to a size suitable for one bite.

89 – Anchovy sticks

	4 portions	10 portions
puff pastry	150 g (6 oz)	375 g (15 oz)
anchovy fillets	100 g (4 oz)	250 g (10 oz)
egg wash		

1 Roll out half the puff pastry in a rectangle 7 cm × 12 cm (3 in × 5 in).
2 Place on to a lightly greased baking sheet.
3 Lay on the anchovy fillets; egg wash the edges.
4 Roll out remaining puff pastry slightly larger than the first half.
5 Cover the anchovies with this pastry, seal down the edges well.
6 Egg wash all over, mark edges with the back of a small knife. Cut into sticks $\frac{1}{2}$ cm ($\frac{1}{4}$ in) wide.
7 Bake in a moderate oven (220°C, 425°F) for approximately 10 minutes until golden brown.
8 May be served hot or cold.

90 – Spinach and cheese sticks

As for anchovy sticks; in place of anchovies use chopped, cooked spinach bound with béchamel and sprinkled with grated Parmesan cheese.

91 – Garlic and pimento sticks

Proceed as for anchovy sticks; in place of the anchovies, spread the pastry with a mixture of garlic butter, finely chopped red pimento and ham.

92 – Dartois

These savoury puff pastry slices are made and cooked in a long strip, then cut after cooking.

Fillings include:

smoked haddock	tuna	chicken and mushroom
anchovies	chicken	ratatouille
sardines	mushroom	

93 – Attereaux

These are small pieces of cooked food, which are coated with a thick sauce, allowed to cool, passed through flour, egg and breadcrumbs and then deep fried. They are served on cocktail sticks.

Meat
chicken – coated with suprême sauce
pork – coated with tomato sauce
veal – coated with a mustard sauce
beef – coated with a red wine sauce

Fish
scampi
mussels   } white wine, curry or tomato sauce
goujons of plaice or sole

Vegetables
cauliflower
courgettes   } curry, cream or tomato sauce
broccoli

94 – Brioches

Small bite-sized brioches may be made for appetisers using the recipe on page 505. The centre is scooped out and various fillings may be used, for example:

Fish
creamed smoked haddock
lobster in lobster sauce
prawns in curry sauce
mussels in cream or curry sauce etc.

Meat
diced cooked beef or lamb in red wine or tomato sauce
diced cooked chicken, veal or rabbit in cream or white wine sauce

Vegetables
finely diced ratatouille
mushrooms in cream sauce
courgettes in tomato sauce

95 – Deep-fried savoury pancakes

These are very small pancakes which may be stuffed with a variety of fillings, as for brioche, folded over or rolled. They are passed through flour, egg and breadcrumbs and deep fried.

96 – Savoury fritters

These are small pieces of marinaded meat, fish or vegetables, which are dipped in batter, deep fried and served on cocktail sticks.

97 – Lamb, peach and cashew bitoks

	4 portions	10 portions
dried peaches	100 g (4 oz)	250 g (10 oz)
minced lamb	450 g (1 lb)	1¼ kg (2½ lb)
clove of garlic, crushed and chopped	1	2–3
salt and pepper		
egg	1	2–3
breadcrumbs	50 g (2 oz)	125 g (5 oz)
cashew nuts	50 g (2 oz)	125 g (5 oz)

1 Reconstitute the peaches in boiling water for 5 minutes; drain well. Chop finely and add to the lamb.
2 Add the garlic and season. Bind with egg and breadcrumbs.
3 Form into small cocktail pieces, insert a cashew nut into each and mould into balls. Flatten slightly.
4 Fry the bitoks in a shallow pan in vegetable oil, drain.
5 Place on a dish with a cocktail stick in each. Serve a yoghurt and cucumber dressing separately (see below).

Note Pine kernels may be used in place of cashew nuts and beef or chicken used in place of lamb.

98 – Yoghurt and cucumber dressing

	4 portions	10 portions
cucumber	100 g (4 oz)	250 g (10 oz)
natural yoghurt	125 ml (¼ pt)	300 ml (⅝ pt)
salt/pepper		
chopped mint	¼ tsp	¾ tsp

1 Peel the cucumber, blanch in boiling water for 5 minutes, refresh and drain.
2 Purée the cucumber in a food processor.

3 Add the cucumber to the natural yoghurt, season and finish with freshly chopped mint.

99 – Puff pastry slice with spinach

	4 portions	10 portions
chopped spinach	200 g (8 oz)	500 g (1¼ lb)
butter or margarine	25 g (1 oz)	60 g (2½ oz)
Mornay sauce	125 ml (¼ pt)	300 ml ($\frac{5}{8}$ pt)
Parmesan	10 g (½ oz)	25 g (1¼ oz)
salt, pepper, nutmeg		
puff pastry	150 g (6 oz)	375 g (15 oz)

1 Prepare the filling by sweating the spinach in the butter or margarine, mix with a little Mornay sauce, add the Parmesan and season, then allow to cool.
2 Roll out pastry into a rectangle 15 cm × 24 cm (6 in × 10 in) long.
3 Cut into half lengthwise, slightly off centre.
4 Lay the narrower half on to a lightly greased baking sheet.
5 Spread spinach over the band of pastry, and egg wash the edges.
6 Fold the remaining half of pastry into half lengthwise and, with a sharp knife, cut slits across the fold about 1½ cm (¾ in) apart to within approximately 1 cm (½ in) up the edge.
7 Lay this over the spinach, seal the edges with egg wash.
8 Brush all over with egg wash and bake at 220°C (425°F) for approximately 10 minutes.
9 When cooked cut into fingers 1½–2 cm (¾ in–1 in) wide.
10 Serve on a flat dish paper.

Note   Low-fat yoghurt or fromage frais may be used in place of Mornay sauce.

100 – Spinach, egg and smoked salmon slice

	4 portions	10 portions
short pastry	150 g (6 oz)	375 g (15 oz)
puff pastry	100 g (4 oz)	250 g (10 oz)
cooked leaf spinach	150 g (6 oz)	375 g (15 oz)
butter or margarine	25 g (1 oz)	60 g (2½ oz)
salt and pepper		
hard-boiled eggs	2	5
Mornay sauce	125 ml (¼ pt)	300 ml (⅝ pt)
smoked salmon trimmings	100 g (4 oz)	250 g (10 oz)
Parmesan cheese	25 g (1 oz)	60 g (2½ oz)

1 Roll out short pastry into a rectangle 15×24 cm (6×10 in).
2 Place on to a lightly greased baking sheet. Dock* the base, egg wash the edges.
3 Roll out 2 strips of puff pastry 24 cm (10 in) long, 2 cm (1 in) wide. Lay these strips on top of the short pastry to form two edges.
4 Press down firmly, with the back of a small knife, scallop the edge. Egg wash lightly.
5 Bake in a moderately hot oven (220°C, 425°F) for approximately 10 minutes.
6 Reheat the spinach in butter or margarine, season. Spread the spinach on the pastry base.
7 Dice the hard-boiled eggs, bind with Mornay sauce. Add the chopped smoked salmon trimmings.
8 Lay the mixture over the spinach and sprinkle with grated Parmesan cheese.
9 Glaze under the salamander or in the oven.
10 Cut into fingers approximately 2 cm (1 in) wide, and serve on a dish garnished with picked parsley.

*Dock: to perforate pastry with numerous small holes.

101 – Spring rolls

	4 portions	10 portions
Batter		
eggs	2	5
milk	125 ml ($\frac{1}{4}$ pt)	312 ml ($\frac{2}{3}$ pt)
flour	50 g (2 oz)	125 g (5 oz)
salt		
Filling		
butter or margarine	50 g (2 oz)	125 g (5 oz)
finely chopped onion	25 g (1 oz)	60 g (2$\frac{1}{2}$ oz)
sliced bamboo shoots	50 g (2 oz)	125 g (5 oz)
cooked diced pork	50 g (2 oz)	125 g (5oz)
finely diced celery	25 g (1 oz)	60 g (2$\frac{1}{2}$ oz)
ground nut oil	1 tbsp	2$\frac{1}{2}$ tbsp
ve-tsin*	$\frac{1}{2}$ tbsp	1$\frac{1}{4}$ tbsp
peeled shrimps	100 g (4 oz)	250 g (10 oz)

1 Make the batter by, first, beating the eggs and milk together.
2 Gradually add the flour, season and strain.
3 Lightly oil a small shallow pan, diameter approximately 8 cm (3 in). Heat over a fierce heat.
4 Gently pour in a thin layer of batter. Cook for 1 minute on one side only. Turn out and allow to cool.
5 Prepare the filling: heat the butter or margarine in a suitable pan, add the finely chopped onion, sweat without colour for 2 minutes.
6 Add all other ingredients except the shrimps, mix well. Simmer for 3 minutes.
7 Turn out into a clean basin and leave to cool. Add the shrimps.
8 Put a small spoonful of filling on to the cooked side of each pancake, roll up, tucking in and sealing the edges with egg wash. Place on a tray and chill well for 20 minutes approximately.
9 Deep fry in hot oil, approximately 190°C (375°F), until golden brown; drain well and serve immediately on a dish on dish paper.

* Ve-tsin is a flavour enhancer, similar to monosodium glutamate.

Stocks, gravies and hot sauces

Prepare, cook and finish hot sauces, soups and cold dressings

1 Select the type, quantity and quality of ingredients in accordance with recipe specifications.
2 Identify that the products not for immediate consumption are stored in accordance with recipe specification and current legislation.
3 Demonstrate that the nutritional value of the ingredients is adequately retained during the preparation and cooking.

Also refer to cold dressings in chapter 1.

—— *Stocks* ——

As stocks are the foundation of many kitchen preparations, great care must be taken in their preparation. The function of stock is to add flavour and give body, e.g. the gelatinous consistency of a well-produced veal stock.

The following ground rules should always be observed:

1 Unsound meat or bones and decaying vegetables will give stock an unpleasant flavour and cause it to deteriorate quickly.
2 Scum should be removed, otherwise it will boil into the stock and spoil the colour and flavour.
3 Fat should be skimmed, otherwise the stock will taste greasy.
4 Stock should always simmer gently, for if it is allowed to boil quickly, it will evaporate and go cloudy.
5 It should not be allowed to go off the boil, otherwise, in hot weather, there is a danger of its going sour.
6 Salt should not be added to stock.
7 When making chicken stock, if raw bones are not available, then a boiling fowl can be used.
8 If stock is to be kept, strain, reboil, cool quickly and place in the refrigerator.

1 – White meat stock

4 litres (1 gallon)

meaty raw bones	2 kg (4 lbs)
water	4 litres (1 gal)
vegetables (onion, carrot, celery, leek)	½ kg (1 lb)
bouquet garni (thyme, bay leaf, parsley)	

1 Chop bones into small pieces, remove any fat or marrow.
2 Place in a clean stock pot, add cold water, bring to the boil.
3 When boiling point is almost reached a dirty scum will have floated to the surface.
4 Wash off the bones, clean the stock pot, add the cleaned bones, cover with water and reboil.
5 Allow to simmer gently and skim frequently.
6 After 1–2 hours, add peeled whole vegetables and bouquet garni.
7 Simmer for 6–8 hours, skim and strain.

2 – Brown meat stock

Proceed as above, browning the bones well in an oven; pour off any fat. Place bones in a stock pot and deglaze the tray pouring this also into the pot. Brown the vegetables before adding. Mushroom trimmings and squashed tomatoes (as long as they are sound) may be added.

3 – Chicken stock

White or brown stock are made in the same way using either raw chicken bones or an old boiling fowl. The cleaned necks, gizzards and hearts can also be used. Two to three hours cooking time is sufficient.

4 – Game stock

This is made in the same way as brown stock using trimmings, bones and tough pieces from venison and hare or/and raw game bird carcasses or old tough game birds.

5 – Vegetable stock

See page 396.

6 – Fish stock

5 litres (1 gallon)

margarine or butter	50 g (2 oz)	
onions	200 g (8 oz)	
white fish bones (preferably sole, whiting, or turbot)	2 kg (4 lb)	
juice of lemon	$\frac{1}{2}$	
peppercorns	6	
bay leaf	1	
parsley stalks		
water	5 litres (1 gal)	

> Using hard margarine
> This recipe provides:
>
> 366 kcals/1536 kJ
> 40.1 g fat
> (of which 17.6 g saturated)
> 0.2 g carbohydrate
> (of which 0.2 g sugars)
> 0.1 g protein
> 0.0 g fibre

1 Melt the margarine or butter in a thick-bottomed pan.
2 Add the sliced onions, the well-washed fish bones and remainder of the ingredients except the water.
3 Cover with greaseproof paper and a lid and sweat (cook gently without colouring) for 5 minutes.
4 Add the water, bring to the boil, skim and simmer for 20 minutes then strain.

7 – Shellfish stock

This can be made from the well-crushed soft shells of some shellfish, e.g. shrimp, prawn, crayfish, lobster, crawfish and crab. This stock is used for soups and sauces.

1¼ litres (2½ pints)

shell and trimmings	1 kg (2 lb)
butter or oil	75 g (3 oz)
onion ⎫	100 g (4 oz)
carrot ⎬ roughly cut	100 g (4 oz)
celery ⎭	50 g (2 oz)
tomato purée	100 g (4 oz)
fish stock or water	1¼ litres (2½ pt)
bouquet garni	

90

1 Melt butter or oil in a thick-bottomed pan.
2 Add the well-pounded or crushed shells and sweat steadily for 5 minutes stirring frequently.
3 Add the vegetables, sweat for a further 5 minutes.
4 Mix in the tomato purée and add the stock or water.
5 Bring to the boil, add bouquet garni, simmer for 45 minutes and strain.

Note Added optional ingredients: 60 ml ($\frac{1}{8}$ pt) brandy added after the sweating process, then ignite; 125–250 ml ($\frac{1}{4}$–$\frac{1}{2}$ pt) white wine; $\frac{1}{2}$ garlic clove crushed.

—— *Gravies* ——

A fat free, well-flavoured, appetising coloured gravy should always be made and offered with any roast joint of meat, poultry or game.

1 After the joint is roasted, it should be removed from the roasting pan.
2 Carefully pour off all fat, leaving the sediment and meat juices in the pan.
3 Return pan to the stove, add the required measure of the specific brown stock, i.e. beef stock for beef, game stock for game, and allow to simmer gently so that all the meat juices and sediment are incorporated into the stock (which is now the gravy).
4 Strain, skim, correct seasoning and serve.

Note If a joint is not being roasted, roast gravy can be made by the same method as brown stock, in which case the bones should be in small pieces to lessen the cooking time.

8 – Roast gravy

	$\frac{1}{4}$ litre ($\frac{1}{2}$ pint)	
raw meaty bones	200 g (8 oz)	
stock or water	250 ml (1 pt)	
onion	50 g (2 oz)	
celery	25 g (1 oz)	mirepoix
carrot	50 g (2 oz)	

Using sunflower oil
This recipe provides:

120 kcals/504 kJ
10.0 g fat
(of which 1.3 g saturated)
1.8 g carbohydrate
(of which 0.0 g sugars)
5.6 g protein
0.0 g fibre

For preference use beef bones for roast beef gravy and the appropriate bones for lamb, veal, mutton and pork.

1 Chop bones and brown in the oven or brown in a little fat on top of the stove in a frying-pan.
2 Drain off all fat.
3 Place in a saucepan with the stock or water.
4 Bring to the boil, skim and allow to simmer.
5 Add the lightly browned mirepoix which may be fried in a little fat in a frying-pan, or added to the bones when partly browned.
6 Simmer for 1½–2 hours.
7 Remove the joint from the roasting tin when cooked.
8 Return the tray to a low heat to allow the sediment to settle.
9 Carefully strain off the fat, leaving the sediment in the tin.
10 Return to the stove and brown carefully, deglaze with the brown stock.
11 Allow to simmer for a few minutes.
12 Correct the colour and seasoning. Strain and skim.

9 – Thickened gravy (jus-lié)

¼ litre (½ pint)

			Using sunflower oil This recipe provides:
raw meaty veal or chicken bones		200 g (8 oz)	
celery	⎫	25 g (1 oz)	189 kcals/793 kJ
onion		50 g (2 oz)	10.0 g fat
carrot	⎬ mirepoix	50 g (2 oz)	(of which 1.3 g saturated)
bay leaf		½	13.6 g carbohydrate
sprig of thyme	⎭		(of which 0.6 g sugars)
tomato purée		5 g (¼ oz)	11.4 g protein
stock or water		500 ml (1 pt)	0.3 g fibre
mushroom trimmings		50 g (2 oz)	
arrowroot or cornflour		10 g (½ oz)	

1 Chop the bones and brown in the oven or in a little fat in a sauteuse on top of the stove.
2 Add mirepoix, brown well.
3 Mix in the tomato purée and stock.
4 Simmer for 2 hours. Add mushroom trimmings.
5 Dilute the arrowroot in a little cold water.

6 Pour into the boiling stock, stirring continuously until it reboils.
7 Simmer for 10–15 minutes. Correct the seasoning.
8 Pass through a fine strainer.

If thickened gravy is required for specific dishes or sauce, the thickening is best done by incorporating diluted arrowroot (in cold water) or cornflour to the boiling gravy and allowing it to reboil. Thickened gravy should only have the lightest possible consistency.

Note Thickened gravy may be replaced by a stock-reduced sauce.

—— *Hot sauces* ——

10 – Stock-reduced base sauce

Many establishments have discontinued using espagnole and demi-glace as the basis for brown sauces and use instead rich, well-flavoured brown stocks of veal, chicken, etc., reduced until the lightest form of natural thickening from the ingredients is achieved.

No flour is used in the thickening process and consequently a lighter textured sauce is produced. Care needs to be taken when reducing this type of sauce so that the end product is not too strong or bitter. The following recipe is for reduced veal stock.

4 litres (1 gallon)

veal bones, chopped	4 kg (8 lbs)
calves' feet, split lengthways	2
carrots	400 g (1 lb)
onions	200 g ($\frac{1}{2}$ lb)
celery	100 g ($\frac{1}{4}$ lb)
tomatoes, quartered	1 kg (2 lb)
mushrooms, chopped	200 g ($\frac{1}{2}$ lb)
large bouquet garni	1
unpeeled cloves of garlic (optional)	4

1 Brown the bones and calves' feet in a roasting tray in the oven.
2 Place the browned bones in a stock pot, cover with cold water and bring to simmering point.

3 Using the same roasting tray and the fat from the bones, brown off the carrots, onions and celery.
4 Drain off the fat, add vegetables to the stock and deglaze the tray.
5 Add remainder of the ingredients, simmer gently for 4–5 hours. Skim frequently.
6 Strain the stock into a clean pan and reduce until a light consistency is achieved.

11 – Glazes

Meat, poultry, game or fish glazes are made by steadily reducing a stock to a light sticky gelatinous consistency. Glazes can be cooled, stored in jars and when cold, refrigerated for up to one week.

If required deep frozen, place into preserving jars which have been sterilised for 1 hour. The glaze can then be kept for several months.

Glazes are used to improve the flavour of a prepared sauce or dish which may taste bland or lacking in strength.

Fish sauces are frequently made from a base made by reducing the strained cooking liquor.

12 – Crayfish coulis sauce

live freshwater crayfish or Dublin Bay prawns	2 kg (4 lb)
butter or oil	75 g (3 oz)
onion	100 g (4 oz)
carrot } finely cut	100 g (4 oz)
celery	50 g (2 oz)
tomato purée	100 g (4 oz)
brandy	30 ml ($\frac{1}{16}$ pt)
dry white wine	250 ml ($\frac{1}{2}$ pt)
double cream	500 ml (1 pt)
bouquet garni	
salt and cayenne pepper	

1 Heat the butter or oil in a thick bottomed pan.
2 Add the crayfish, cover with a lid and cook for 5–6 minutes.
3 Remove the pan from heat, remove the crayfish, detach and shell the tails and reserve.

4 Pound or crush all the shells.
5 Return pan to the heat, add a little more butter or oil if necessary.
6 Add the vegetables, cover with a lid and sweat for 2–5 minutes.
7 Add the crushed shells, sweat well, but do not allow them to brown.
8 Add brandy and ignite, mix in the tomato purée.
9 Add white wine and bouquet garni, bring to the boil, simmer for 10 minutes.
10 Add the cream and simmer for 10 minutes.
11 Correct seasoning and strain firmly to extract all juices and flavour.

Note   This sauce can also be made using the crushed soft shell of cooked crayfish, crab, crawfish, shrimps, prawns and lobster, but obviously the sauce will not have the same flavour or quality as when the whole live shellfish are used.

Lobster sauce or coulis can be made from the following recipe omitting the flour and finishing with 250 ml ($\frac{1}{2}$pt) double cream.

13 – Lobster sauce

1 litre (2 pints)

live hen lobster	$\frac{3}{4}$–1 kg (1$\frac{1}{2}$–2 lb)
butter or oil	75 g (3 oz)
onion ⎫	100 g (4 oz)
carrot ⎬ roughly cut (mirepoix)	100 g (4 oz)
celery ⎭	50 g (2 oz)
brandy	60 ml ($\frac{1}{8}$pt)
flour	75 g (3 oz)
tomato purée	100 g (4 oz)
fish stock	1$\frac{1}{4}$ litres (2$\frac{1}{2}$pt)
dry white wine	120 ml ($\frac{1}{4}$pt)
bouquet garni	
crushed clove garlic	$\frac{1}{2}$
salt	

1 Well wash the lobster.
2 Cut in half lengthwise tail first, then the carapace.
3 Discard the sac from the carapace, clean the trail from the tail, remove any spawn into a basin.
4 Wash the lobster pieces.
5 Crack the claws and the four claw joints.

6 Melt the butter or oil in a thick-bottomed pan.
7 Add the lobster pieces and the onion, carrot and celery.
8 Allow to cook steadily without colouring the butter for a few minutes, stirring continuously with a wooden spoon.
9 Add the brandy and allow it to ignite.
10 Remove from the heat, mix in the flour and tomato purée.
11 Return to a gentle heat and cook out the roux.
12 Cool slightly, gradually add the fish stock and white wine.
13 Stir to the boil.
14 Add bouquet garni, garlic and season lightly with salt.
15 Simmer for 15–20 minutes.
16 Remove the lobster pieces.
17 Remove the lobster meat from the pieces.
18 Crush the lobster shells, return them to the sauce and continue simmering for $\frac{1}{4}$–$\frac{3}{4}$ hour.
19 Crush the lobster spawn, stir in to the sauce, reboil and pass through a coarse strainer.

This sauce may be made in a less expensive way by substituting cooked lobster shell (not shell from the claws) which should be well crushed in place of the live lobster.

14 – Butter sauce (beurre blanc)

	4 portions	10 portions
water	125 ml ($\frac{1}{4}$ pt)	300 ml ($\frac{5}{8}$ pt)
wine vinegar	125 ml ($\frac{1}{4}$ pt)	300 ml ($\frac{5}{8}$ pt)
finely chopped shallot	50 g (2 oz)	125 g (5 oz)
unsalted butter	200 g (8 oz)	500 g (1$\frac{1}{4}$ lb)
lemon juice	1 tsp	2$\frac{1}{2}$ tsp
salt and pepper		

1 Reduce the water, vinegar and shallots in a thick bottomed pan to approximately $\frac{1}{6}$ pint (2 tablespoons).
2 Allow to cool slightly.
3 Gradually whisk in the butter in small amounts, whisking continually until the mixture becomes creamy.
4 Whisk in lemon juice, season lightly and keep warm in a bain-marie.

Note   The sauce may be strained if desired. It can be varied by adding, for example, freshly shredded sorrel or spinach or blanched fine julienne of lemon or lime. It is suitable for serving with fish dishes.

15 – Blood-thickened sauce

This is done by mixing blood from the animal with some cold stock from that to be thickened, mixing thoroughly and gradually mixing in to the hot sauce at the last moment. After adding the blood the stock must not be allowed to reboil otherwise it will curdle. (See recipe 77, page 343.)

16 – White sauce (Béchamel)

This is a basic white sauce made from milk and a white roux.

1 litre (2 pints)

margarine or butter	100 g (4 oz)
flour	100 g (4 oz)
milk	1 litre (2 pt)
studded onion	1

1 Melt the margarine or butter in a thick-bottomed pan.
2 Add the flour and mix in.
3 Cook for a few minutes over a gentle heat without colouring.
4 Remove from heat to cool the roux.
5 Gradually add the warmed milk and stir till smooth.
6 Add the onion studded with a clove.
7 Allow to simmer for 30 minutes.
8 Remove the onion, pass the sauce through a conical strainer.
9 Cover with a film of butter or margarine to prevent a skin forming.

Using whole milk/hard margarine
This recipe provides:

1721 kcals/7228 kJ
120.3 g fat
(of which 59.5 g saturated)
124.8 g carbohydrated
(of which 48.6 g sugars)
42.5 g protein
3.6 g fibre

Using skimmed milk/hard margarine
This recipe provides:

1401 kcals/5884 kJ
83.3 g fat
(of which 36.1 g saturated)
127.8 g carbohydrate
(of which 51.6 g sugars)
43.5 g protein
3.6 g fibre

17 – Velouté (chicken, veal, mutton, fish)

This is a basic white sauce made from white stock and a blond roux.

1 litre (2 pints)

margarine, butter or oil	100 g (4 oz)
flour	100 g (4 oz)
stock (chicken, veal, mutton, fish) as required	1 litre (2 pt)

1 Melt the fat or oil in a thick-bottomed pan.
2 Add the flour and mix in.
3 Cook out to a sandy texture over gentle heat without colour.
4 Allow the roux to cool.
5 Gradually add the boiling stock.
6 Stir until smooth and boiling.
7 Allow to simmer for approximately 1 hour.
8 Pass through a fine conical strainer.

A velouté sauce for chicken, veal or fish dishes is usually finished with cream and, in some cases, also egg yolks.

Using hard margarine
This recipe provides:

1094 kcals/4594 kJ
82.6 g fat
(of which 35.4 g saturated)
79.0 g carbohydrate
(of which 1.6 g sugars)
13.3 g protein
3.6 g fibre

Using sunflower oil
This recipe provides:

1263 kcals/5304 kJ
101.5 g fat
(of which 13.3 g saturated)
78.9 g carbohydrate
(of which 1.5 g sugars)
13.2 g protein
3.6 g fibre

18 – Brown sauce

1 litre (1 quart)

good dripping or oil	50 g (2 oz)
flour	60 g (2½ oz)
tomato purée	25 g (1 oz)
brown stock	1 litre (2 pt)
carrot	100 g (4 oz)
onion	100 g (4 oz)
celery	50 g (2 oz)

Using hard margarine
This recipe provides:

686 kcals/288 kJ
42.0 g fat
(of which 17.8 g saturated)
67.2 g carbohydrate
(of which 20.2 g sugars)
14.0 g protein
8.6 g fibre

1 Heat the dripping or oil in a thick-bottomed pan.
2 Add the flour, cook out slowly to a light brown colour, stirring frequently.

3 Cool and mix in the tomato purée.
4 Gradually mix in the boiling stock. Bring
  to the boil.
5 Wash, peel and roughly cut the vegetables.
6 Lightly brown in a little fat or oil in a frying-
  pan.
7 Drain off the fat and add to the sauce.
8 Simmer gently for 4–6 hours. Skim when
  necessary. Strain.

Using sunflower oil
This recipe provides:
771 kcals/3236 kJ
51.5 g fat
(of which 6.8 g saturated)
67.1 g carbohydrate
(of which 20.2 g sugars)
13.9 g protein
8.6 g fibre

Care should be taken when making the brown roux not to allow it to cook too quickly, otherwise the starch in the flour (which is the thickening agent) will burn, and its thickening properties weaken. Over-browning should also be avoided as this tends to make the sauce taste bitter.

19 – Demi-glace sauce

This is a refined espagnole and is made by simmering 1 litre (2 pt) espagnole and 1 litre (2 pt) brown stock and reducing by a half. Skim off all impurities as they rise to the surface during cooking. Pass through a fine chinois (conical strainer), reboil, correct the seasoning. A stock-reduced sauce may be used in place of demi-glace (see page 93).

CREAM THICKENED SAUCES

These are used mainly in poached fish, veal and chicken dishes.

20 – Suprême of chicken in cream sauce

	4 portions	10 portions
butter or margarine	50 g (2 oz)	125 g (5 oz)
seasoned flour	25 g (1 oz)	60 g (2½ oz)
suprêmes of chicken	4	10
sherry or white wine	30 ml ($\frac{1}{16}$ pt)	75 mm ($\frac{1}{8}$ pt)
double cream or non-dairy cream	125 ml ($\frac{1}{4}$ pt)	312 ml ($\frac{6}{10}$ pt)
salt, cayenne		

1 Heat the butter or margarine in a sauté pan.

99

2 Lightly flour the suprêmes.
3 Cook the suprêmes gently on both sides (7–9 minutes) with the minimum of colour.
4 Place the suprêmes in an earthenware serving dish, cover to keep warm.
5 Drain off the fat from the pan.
6 Deglaze the pan with the sherry or white wine.
7 Add the cream, bring to the boil and season.
8 Allow to reduce to a lightly thickened consistency. Correct the seasoning.
9 Pass through a fine chinois on to the suprêmes and serve.

An alternative method of preparing the sauce is to use half the amount of cream (fresh or non-dairy) and an equal amount of chicken velouté.

21 – Veal escalope with cream sauce

	4 portions	10 portions
butter or margarine	50 g (2 oz)	125 g (5 oz)
seasoned flour	25 g (1 oz)	60 g ($2\frac{1}{2}$ oz)
veal escalopes (slightly battened)	4	10
sherry or white wine	30 ml ($\frac{1}{16}$ pt)	75 ml ($\frac{1}{8}$ pt)
double cream	125 ml ($\frac{1}{4}$ pt)	250 ml ($\frac{1}{2}$ pt)
salt, cayenne		

1 Heat the butter in a sauté pan.
2 Lightly flour the escalopes.
3 Cook the escalopes gently on both sides with the minimum of colour. They should be a delicate light brown.
4 Place the escalopes in an earthenware serving dish, cover and keep warm.
5 Drain off all fat from the pan.
6 Deglaze the pan with the sherry.
7 Add the cream, bring to the boil and season.
8 Allow to reduce to a lightly thickened consistency, correct the seasoning.
9 Pass through a fine chinois over the escalopes and serve.

An alternative method of preparing the sauce is to use half the amount of cream and an equal amount of chicken velouté.

Fish sauces: after a dish of fish is poached the stock can be strained off, reduced, double cream added and reboiled to the required consistency.

Certain vegetables, e.g. carrots and broad beans, when almost cooked can have double cream added and cooking completed to form a cream sauce. Cream sauces may also be produced from a béchamel or velouté base.

22 – Supreme sauce

Uses   served hot with boiled chicken, vol-au-vent, etc., and also for white chaud-froid sauce.

This is a velouté made from chicken stock flavoured with well-washed mushroom trimmings.

	$\frac{1}{2}$ litre (1 pint) 8–12 portions
chicken velouté	$\frac{1}{2}$ litre (1 pt)
mushroom trimmings (white)	25 g (1 oz)
cream	60 ml ($\frac{1}{8}$ pt)
yolk	1
lemon juice	2–3 drops

1 Allow the velouté to cook out with the mushroom trimmings.
2 Pass through a fine strainer. Reboil.
3 Mix the cream and yolk in a basin (liaison).
4 Add a little of the boiling sauce to the liaison.
5 Return all to the sauce – do not reboil.
6 Mix, finish with lemon juice and correct the seasoning.

23 – Smitaine sauce

butter or margarine	25 g (1 oz)
finely chopped onion	50 g (2 oz)
white wine	60 ml ($\frac{1}{8}$ pt)
sour cream	$\frac{1}{2}$ litre (1 pt)
seasoning	
lemon juice	$\frac{1}{4}$

1 Melt butter or margarine in a sauteuse and cook onion without colour.
2 Add the white wine and reduce by half.
3 Add sour cream and season lightly, reduce by one-third.
4 Pass through a fine strainer and finish with lemon juice.

24 – Yoghurt/fromage frais thickened sauces

Natural yoghurt or fromage frais can be used in place of cream in any sauce. This considerably reduces the fat content of the sauce and is therefore a major consideration with regard to healthy eating.

Care must be taken when adding natural yoghurt; excessive heat will give a curdled appearance.

EGG-BASED SAUCES

Note   To reduce the risk of salmonella infection, use pasteurised egg yolks. Once made, egg-based sauces should not be kept warm for more than 2 hours, they should then be discarded.

25 – Hollandaise sauce

$\frac{1}{4}$ litre ($\frac{1}{2}$ pint)
4–6 portions

crushed peppercorns	6	
vinegar	1 tbsp	
egg yolks	2	
butter	200 g (8 oz)	
salt, cayenne		

This recipe provides:

1616 kcals/6789 kJ
176.2 g fat
(of which 107.9 g saturated)
0.1 g carbohydrate
(of which 0.1 g sugars)
7.3 g protein
0.0 g fibre

1 Place the peppercorns and vinegar in a small sauteuse or stainless steel pan and reduce to one-third.
2 Add 1 tablespoon cold water, allow to cool.
3 Mix in the yolks with a whisk.
4 Return to a gentle heat and whisking continuously cook to a sabayon (this is the cooking of the yolks to a thickened consistency, like cream, sufficient to show the mark of the whisk).

5 Remove from the heat and cool slightly.
6 Gradually whisk in the melted warm butter until thoroughly combined.
7 Correct the seasoning. If a reduction is not used, add a few drops of lemon juice.
8 Pass through a muslin, tammy cloth, or fine strainer.
9 The sauce should be kept at only a slightly warm temperature until served.
10 Serve in a slightly warm sauceboat.

The cause of hollandaise sauce curdling is either because the butter has been added too quickly, or because of excess heat which will cause the albumen in the eggs to harden, shrink and separate from the liquid.

Should the sauce curdle, place a teaspoon of boiling water in a clean sauteuse and gradually whisk in the curdled sauce. If this fails to reconstitute the sauce then place an egg yolk in a clean sauteuse with a dessertspoon of water. Whisk lightly over gentle heat until slightly thickened. Remove from heat and gradually add the curdled sauce whisking continuously. To stabilise the sauce during service, 60 ml ($\frac{1}{8}$ pt) thick béchamel may be added before straining.

Served with hot fish (salmon, trout, turbot), and vegetables (asparagus, cauliflower, broccoli).

Variations can include the following additions to $\frac{1}{2}$ litre (1 pt) of hollandaise:

Mousseline sauce
125 ml ($\frac{1}{4}$ pt) of lightly whipped sauce.

Maltaise sauce
The lightly grated zest and juice of one blood orange.

26 – Sabayon sauce

	8 portions
egg yolks	4
castor or unrefined sugar	100 g (4 oz)
dry white wine	$\frac{1}{4}$ litre ($\frac{1}{2}$ pt)

1 Whisk egg yolks and sugar in a 1 litre (2 pt) pan or basin until white.
2 Dilute with the wine.
3 Place pan or basin in a bain-marie of warm water.
4 Whisk mixture continuously until it increases to 4 times its bulk and is firm and frothy.

Sauce sabayon may be offered as an accompaniment to any suitable hot sweet, e.g. pudding soufflé.

A sauce sabayon may also be made using milk in place of wine which can be flavoured according to taste, e.g. vanilla, nutmeg, cinnamon.

27 – Sabayon with olive oil (which may be used as an alternative to sauce hollandaise)

	4–6 portions	8–12 portions
crushed peppercorns	6	15
vinegar	1 tbsp	2½ tbsp
egg yolks	3	8
olive oil	250 ml (½ pt)	625 ml (1¼ pt)
salt, cayenne pepper		

1 Place the peppercorns and vinegar in a small sauteuse or stainless-steel pan and reduce to one-third.
2 Add 1 tablespoon of cold water and allow to cool.
3 Add the egg yolks and whisk over a gentle heat in a sabayon.
4 Remove from heat. Cool.
5 Whisk in gradually the tepid olive oil.
6 Correct the seasoning.
7 Pass through a muslin or fine strainer.
8 Serve warm.

If the sauce curdles, the same principles apply to rectify as with hollandaise.

This sauce is healthier in that it does not contain the cholesterol that hollandaise made with butter does.

28 – Béarnaise sauce

$\frac{1}{4}$ litre ($\frac{1}{2}$ pt)
4–6 portions

chopped shallots	10 g ($\frac{1}{2}$ oz)
crushed peppercorns	6
tarragon	5 g ($\frac{1}{4}$ oz)
tarragon vinegar	1 tbsp
egg yolks	3
butter	200 g (8 oz)
sprig chopped chervil	

1 Make a reduction with the shallots, peppercorns, tarragon stalks and vinegar.
2 Proceed as for hollandaise sauce.
3 After passing, add the chopped tarragon leaves and chervil.

Usually served with grilled meat and fish, e.g. Chateaubriand grillé, sauce béarnaise. This sauce should be twice as thick as hollandaise.

Variations can include the following additions to $\frac{1}{2}$ litre (1 pt) béarnaise:

Choron sauce
200 g ($\frac{1}{2}$ lb) tomato concassé, well dried and sieved. The chopped tarragon and chervil leaves are omitted.

Foyot or valois sauce
25 g (1 oz) of warm meat glaze.

Paloise sauce
This sauce is made as for béarnaise using chopped mint stalks in place of tarragon and chervil and adding chopped mint at the end.

VEGETABLE AND FRUIT PURÉES

Used as sauces, they are known as a cullis or coulis.

Some vegetables and fruits are suitable for making into purées which can then be thinned into a sauce consistency. In certain dishes where vegetables are cooked in with fish or meat, once the dish is cooked the vegetables can be puréed and thinned with the dish cooking liquor to make the sauce.

29 – Avocado sauce

Ripe, peeled, chopped avocados processed to a purée, seasoned with salt and pepper, and thinned with oil, cream or natural yoghurt and stirred.

30 – Avocado and fennel sauce

400 g (1 lb) cooked fennel well processed to a purée with 2 ripe avocados.

31 – Avocado and celery sauce

As above using 400 g (1 lb) cooked celery or celeriac.

These sauces are suitable for serving hot or cold with many vegetarian dishes.

32 – Beetroot sauce

400 g (1 lb) cooked, peeled beetroot puréed in a food blender with sufficient red wine to give a light consistency, then strained. When heated, finish with 50 g (2 oz) butter, 2 teaspoons castor sugar, salt and pepper. Can be served with roast fish and cuts of venison.

33 – Broccoli sauce

cooked broccoli	400 g (1 lb)
sunflower seeds	75 g (3 oz)
smetana *or*	250 ml ($\frac{1}{2}$ pt)
silken tofu *or*	
natural yoghurt or cream	
lemon juice	1
seasoning	

Liquidise the ingredients with $\frac{1}{2}$ litre (1 pt) of water and strain through a coarse strainer.

34 – Fresh tomato sauce (cooked)

4 portions

tomatoes	1 kg (2 lb)
onion	50 g (2 oz)
clove garlic	1
butter	25 g (1 oz)
salt and pepper	
pinch of sugar	

1 Skin, halve, remove the seeds and chop the tomatoes.
2 Sweat the chopped onion and garlic in the butter.
3 Add the tomatoes and season.
4 Simmer for 15 minutes.
5 Purée in a liquidiser or food processor.
6 Bring to the boil and correct the seasoning.

Note Herbs, such as rosemary, thyme or bay leaf, may be added and shallots used in place of onion.

Fully, ripe, well-flavoured tomatoes are needed for a good fresh tomato sauce. Italian plum tomatoes are also suitable and it is sometimes advisable to use tinned plum tomatoes if the fresh tomatoes which are available lack flavour and colour.

Asparagus, celery, fennel, mushroom, onion, salsify, spinach, tomato, watercress and yellow pepper are other vegetables which can be seasoned with herbs or spices, then processed, strained and thinned to the suitable consistency for a sauce, or enriched with butter and/or cream.

Some pulse vegetables, e.g. lentils, peas and beans, are suitable for cooking and processing into sauces.

Fruit purées, used as sauces, fall into two categories:

First, fruits, e.g. apple, cranberry and gooseberry, which are cooked with the minimum of sugar so as to retain a degree of sharpness and which are used for serving with fish, meat or poultry dishes.

Secondly, fruits which are puréed and used for sweet dishes, e.g. apricot, blackcurrant, blackberry, damson, plum and rhubarb, which are lightly cooked in a little water with sufficient sugar to sweeten then liquidised and strained.

35 – Gooseberry sauce

gooseberries, trimmed and washed	400 g (1 lb)
sugar	50 g (2 oz)
water	60–100 ml ($\frac{1}{8}$–$\frac{1}{4}$ pt)

Boil together all ingredients and liquidise and strain if required. May be served with grilled mackerel, roast goose, grilled pork chops.

OIL-BASED SAUCES

These fall roughly into two categories:

1 Cold: mayonnaise and derivatives
               vinaigrette and variations.
2 Hot: vinaigrette and variations.
  vinaigrettes used with some fish and vegetable dishes.

When preparing hot vinaigrettes, various flavoured oils and vinegars can be used to give variety of taste. Oils, such as olive, walnut, sesame seed, sunflower, grape seed, peanut and safflower, can be flavoured by marinating herbs, e.g. basil, thyme, oregano, rosemary, garlic or onions, in them in one of two ways.

1 Place a bunch of the chosen herb/s into a bottle of oil, cork tightly and keep on a cool shelf.
2 Warm the oil with herb/s for 15–20 minutes.

There is scope here for experimentation with various herbs, spices and vegetables, e.g. onion, garlic, shallots, so that a mise-en-place of several flavoured oils can be produced.

Red or white vinegars can be flavoured with herbs such as thyme, tarragon, dill, mint, rosemary, etc.

- Fruit vinegars include raspberry, strawberry, blackberry, peach, plum, apple, cherry.
- Floral vinegars, e.g. elderflower, rose.
- Sharp vinegars, e.g. chilli, garlic, horseradish.

When making vinaigrettes for use in hot dishes, there is obviously considerable room for experimentation, and the skill lies in the blending of the ingredients and flavours of both oils and vinegars to complement the dishes with which they are to be used and ensuring that they do not dominate. For example, red mullet fillets or skate, lightly steamed, grilled or fried and lightly masked with a hot vinaigrette is a basic recipe to which many variations can be applied, such as

- a lightly cooked small brunoise of vegetables added;
- finish with chopped fennel or dill.

Many vegetables simply cooked either by boiling or steaming can be given additional flavours by finishing with a light dribble of a suitably flavoured hot vinaigrette, for example:

- sliced or diced beetroot, carrots, turnips, swedes;
- a mixture of cooked vegetables;
- crisply cooked shredded cabbage.

I 36 ‑ Garlic, red onion and ginger oil

(MARK McCANN)

olive oil	500 ml (1 pt)
onions (roast one for 10 minutes)	3 large
root ginger	150 g (6 oz)
garlic (one bulb roasted)	1½ bulbs
mirepox	200 g (8 oz)
bayleaves	2
black peppercorn	8
sea salt	12 g (½ oz)
cinnamon	1 stick
lemon grass (split and roasted for 5 minutes)	1 stick
olive oil	1 tsp
white wine vinegar	1 tsp

1 Heat 1 teaspoon of olive oil in a pan.
2 Sweat mirepox, the two onions that have not been roasted, 75 g (3 oz) of the ginger and the ½ bulb of garlic that has not been roasted. Fry until golden brown
3 Add one of the bayleaves, peppercorns and sea salt and cook for 3–4 minutes.
4 Add half of the olive oil and bring up to boiling point.

5 Take from the heat and allow to cool.
6 When completely cold, pass through a chinoise into a kilner jar.
7 Add the lemon grass, cinnamon and remaining ingredients.
8 For the best flavour, leave for one month.

I 37 – Roasted pepper oil

(MARK McCANN)

virgin olive oil		500 ml (1 pt)
red pepper	⎫ one of each	2
yellow pepper	⎬ to be cleaned	2
green pepper	⎭ and roasted	2
mirepoix		200 g (8 oz)
cloves garlic		2
bayleaves		2
black peppercorns		8
sea salt		$\frac{1}{2}$ tsp
virgin olive oil		1 tsp
white wine vinegar		1 tsp

1 Heat 1 teaspoon of olive oil in a pan.
2 Sweat the mirepox and one of each of the peppers until golden brown.
3 Add 1 bayleaf, the black peppercorns, one clove of garlic and the sea salt, and cook for a further 3–4 minutes.
4 Add half of the olive oil and bring to the simmering point.
5 Take off the heat and allow to cool.
6 When completely cool, pass through a chinoise into a clean kilner jar.
7 Add the white wine vinegar and the remaining olive oil, roasted garlic, roasted peppers and remaining bayleaf.
8 For full flavour, leave for at least one month before use.

SOUPS

Prepare, cook and finish hot sauces, soups and cold dressings

1   Select the type, quantity and quality of ingredients in accordance with recipe specifications.
2   Identify that the products not for immediate consumption are stored in accordance with recipe specification and current legislation.
3   Demonstrate that the nutritional value of the ingredients is adequately retained during the preparation and cooking.

— *Introduction* —

In keeping with healthy eating practices these points can be considered when making soup:

1 Purée soups may be thickened by vegetables and require no flour.
2 Wholemeal flour can be used for thickened soups.
3 Cream and velouté soups may be made with skimmed milk and finished with non-dairy cream, low-fat natural yoghurt, quark or fromage frais.
4 Velouté soups may be finished with non-dairy cream, natural yoghurt or fromage frais.

Variations can be created, for example, by:

1 Combining finished soups, e.g. adding a watercress soup to a tomato soup.
2 Using the main ingredients together, e.g. tomatoes and watercress in the initial preparation.
3 Careful use of different herbs to introduce a subtle flavour, e.g. basil, rosemary, chervil.
4 Using a garnish which is varied, e.g. blanched watercress leaves, chopped chives and tomato concassée and finishing with non-dairy cream or yoghurt.

The following are some examples of 'combination' soups:

watercress with lettuce	tomato with courgette
watercress and spinach	potato and spinach
watercress and courgettes	tomato and mushroom
leek and onion	tomato and celery
leek and broccoli	tomato and cauliflower
leek and tomato	tomato and cucumber
leek and cucumber	chicken and mushroom
potato and endive	chicken and leek

An essential ingredient for soup is the liquid and only the best quality stock of the appropriate flavour should be used to enhance the soup. Care should be taken, however, to preserve the flavour of the main ingredient, for example, mushroom and lettuce should not be overpowered by an over-strong stock.

The following table indicates the variety of stocks, finishes, accompaniments and garnishes which can be used in the making and serving of soups.

STOCKS	FINISHES	ACCOMPANIMENTS	GARNISHES	
bacon	cream	toasted flutes	julienne or brunoise of:	
ham	milk	bread sticks	beetroot	celery
chicken	yolks	Melba toast	celeriac	peppers
beef	yoghurt	toast spread with paté	carrots	beans
veal	quark	cheese straws	turnips	leeks
game	fromage frais	grated cheese	mushrooms	game
mutton	non-dairy cream	profiteroles	poultry	meat
vegetable	port	croûtons	also savoury pancakes	
fish	Madeira		meat balls, quenelles	
	white wine		chopped or leaves of:	
			parsley	mint
			sorrel	chervil etc.

1 ~ Clear soup (consommé)

	4 portions	10 portions
minced beef	200 g (8 oz)	500 g (1¼ lb)
egg whites	1–2	3–5
salt		
white or brown beef stock or beef and chicken stock	1 litre (2 pt)	2½ litre (5 pt)
mixed vegetables (onion celery, leek, carrot)	100 g (4 oz)	250 g (10 oz)
bouquet garni		
peppercorns	3–4	7–10

1 Mix the beef, egg white and salt with 250 ml (½ pt) cold stock in a thick-bottomed pan.
2 Add the finely chopped vegetables, remainder of the stock, bouquet garni and peppercorns.
3 Bring slowly to the boil, stirring frequently.
4 Boil rapidly for 5–10 seconds, give a final stir.
5 Simmer very gently for 1½–2 hours without stirring.
6 Strain through a double muslin, removing all fat.
7 Correct the seasoning and colour.

Note   It is essential to have a good, well-flavoured stock to produce a consommé of quality. Possible variations include:

(a) Use minced veal and veal stock in place of minced beef and beef stock and follow recipe above.
(b) Proceed as for beef clear soup, using brown chicken or game stock in place of beef stock and add chopped giblets with the minced beef.
(c) Proceed as for recipe 1; when adding the vegetables, add 300–400 g (12 oz–1 lb) of chopped tomato, mushroom or celery.
(d) Garnish the clear chicken soup with piped, pea-sized quenelles, gently poached in clear soup.
(e) Proceed as for beef clear soup; for the final 15 minutes of simmering, infuse the soup with a sprig of tarragon, then remove the tarragon before serving.

2 – Clear vegetable soup

	4 portions	10 portions
chopped mixed vegetables – onion, leek, carrot, celery	400 g (1 lb)	1¼ kg (2½ lb)
vegetable oil	60 ml (⅛ pt)	150 ml (⅓ pt)
egg whites	1–2	4–5
water	1 litre (2 pt)	2½ litre (5 pt)
tomatoes	100 g (4 oz)	250 g (10 oz)
mushroom trimmings	50 g (2 oz)	125 g (5 g)
peppercorns	6	18
bouquet garni		
yeast extract	5 g (¼ oz)	12 g (⅝ oz)
salt		

1 Fry the vegetables in the oil until golden brown.
2 Drain off all the oil, place vegetables in a saucepan.
3 Deglaze the frying pan with a little water and add the fried vegetables.
4 Lightly beat the egg whites with the remaining water and add to the pan.
5 Add the remainder of the ingredients and bring to the boil stirring occasionally.
6 Allow to simmer without stirring for 45 minutes to 1 hour.
7 Strain through a double muslin, skim off all the fat, correct the seasoning and serve.

3 – Clear fish soup

	4 portions	10 portions
white fish fillet	200 g (8 oz)	500 g (1¼ lb)
egg whites	1–2	3–4
dry white wine	125 ml (¼ pt)	300 ml (⅝ pt)
well-flavoured fish stock	1 litre (2 pt)	2½ litre (5 pt)

1 Process or pound the fish flesh with the egg whites.
2 Place in a thick-bottomed pan.
3 Add white wine, stock and a little salt.
4 Place over a gentle heat, stir occasionally and bring to the boil.
5 Allow it to boil for 5–10 seconds and give a final stir.
6 Lower the heat, allow the soup to simmer gently for 15 minutes.
7 Strain carefully through a double muslin and correct the seasoning.

Note   This soup can be made using any type of fish or shellfish in which case the name of the fish would be given to the soup, e.g. clear pike soup, lobster consommé.

Obviously, the quality of the soup will depend on the freshness and quality of the fish stock. Other optional flavours can be added, e.g. white mushroom trimmings and herbs such as tarragon, chervil and fennel. Garnishes can include fish quenelles.

4 – Purée soups

As well as the pulses listed, others such as borlotti beans, red kidney beans, black beans, pinto beans, chick peas and green lentils may also be used.

The following soups can be made by using the named pulse in the basic pulse soup recipe below.

Red lentil soup
Brown lentil soup
Red kidney bean soup
Flageolet bean soup
Flageolet and haricot bean soup

5 – Basic pulse soup recipe

	4 portions	10 portions
pulse	200 g (8 oz)	500 g (1¼ lb)
white stock or water	1½ litre (3 pt)	3¾ litre (7½ pt)
carrot	50 g (2 oz)	125 g (5 oz)
onion	50 g (2 oz)	125 g (5 oz)
knuckle of ham or bacon (optional)	50 g (2 oz)	125 g (5 oz)
bouquet garni		
salt, pepper		
Croûtons		
slices stale bread	1	2–3
butter	50 g (2 oz)	125 g (5 oz)

1 Pick over and wash the pulses, then place in a thick-bottomed pan with stock or water.
2 Bring to the boil, skim and add all other ingredients except salt (which will toughen the pulse).
3 Simmer until the pulse is very soft, skim and season lightly with salt.
4 Remove the bouquet garni (and the carrot if making flageolet bean soup) and the ham.
5 Pass through a sieve and fine strainer or liquidise.
6 Correct the seasoning and consistency.
7 Serve with fried or toasted croûtons separately.

Note Combinations of beans, lentils or peas can be considered and, instead of frying the croûtons in butter, use bacon fat or vegetable oil.

6 – Mutton broth

	4 portions	10 portions
scrag end of mutton	200 g (8 oz)	500 g (1¼ lb)
water or mutton or lamb stock	1 litre (2 pt)	2½ litre (5 pt)
barley	25 g (1 oz)	60 g (2½ oz)
vegetables (carrot, turnip, leek, celery, onion)	200 g (8 oz)	500 g (1¼ lb)
bouquet garni		
salt, pepper		
chopped parsley		

1 Place the mutton in a saucepan and cover with cold water.
2 Bring to the boil, immediately wash off under running water.
3 Clean the pan, replace the meat, cover with cold water, bring to the boil, skim.
4 Add the washed barley, simmer for 1 hour.
5 Add the vegetables, cut as for Scotch broth, bouquet garni and season.
6 Skim when necessary, simmer till tender, approximately 30 minutes.
7 Remove the meat, allow to cool and cut from the bone, remove all fat, and cut the meat into neat dice the same size as the vegetables, add to the broth.
8 Correct the seasoning, skim, add the chopped parsley and serve.

7 – Scotch broth

	4 portions	10 portions
barley	25 g (1 oz)	60 g (2½ oz)
white beef stock	1 litre (2 pt)	2½ litre (5 pt)
vegetables (carrot, turnip, leek, celery, onion)	200 g (8 oz)	500 g (1¼ lb)
bouquet garni		
salt, pepper		
chopped parsley		

> 1 portion provides:
>
> 48 kcals/204 kJ
> 0.2 g fat
> 9.7 g carbohydrate
> (of which 4.2 g sugars)
> 2.5 g protein
> 2.4 g fibre

1 Wash the barley. Simmer in the stock for approximately 1 hour.
2 Peel and wash the vegetables and cut into neat 3 mm (⅛ in) dice.
3 Add to the stock with a bouquet garni and season.
4 Bring to the boil, skim and simmer until tender, approximately 30 minutes.
5 Correct the seasoning, skim, remove the bouquet garni, add the chopped parsley and serve.

8 – Chicken broth

	4 portions	10 portions
boiling fowl	¼	¾
water	1 litre (2 pt)	2½ litre (5 pt)
vegetables (celery, turnip, carrot, leek)	200 g (8 oz)	500 g (1¼ lb)
bouquet garni		
salt, pepper		
rice	25 g (1 oz)	60 g (2½ oz)
chopped parsley		

1 Place the fowl in a saucepan, add the cold water, bring to the boil and skim. Simmer for 1 hour.
2 Add the vegetables, prepared as for Scotch broth, bouquet garni and season. Simmer until almost cooked.
3 Add the washed rice and continue cooking.
4 Remove all skin and bone from the chicken and cut into neat dice the same size as the vegetables, add to the broth.
6 Skim, correct the seasoning, add the chopped parsley and serve.

9 – Chicken soup with mushrooms and tongue

	4 portions	10 portions	
chicken velouté	1 litre (2 pt)	2½ litre (5 pt)	I portion provides:
mushroom trimmings	200 g (8 oz)	500 g (1¼ lb)	calculated with double cream
yolks of egg ⎫ liaison	2	5	469 kcals/1948 kJ
cream ⎭	125 ml (¼ pt)	312 g (⅝ pt)	20.7 g carbohydrate
salt and pepper			(of which sugars 1.6 g)
mushrooms ⎫	25 g (1 oz)	60 g (2½ oz)	40 g fat
chicken ⎬ julienne garnish	25 g (1 oz)	60 g (2½ oz)	(of which 10.7 g saturates)
tongue ⎭	25 g (1 oz)	60 g (2½ oz)	7.8 g protein
			1.4 g fibre

1 Prepare a chicken velouté, adding the chopped mushroom trimmings at the initial stage.
2 Liquidise and add the liaison by adding some soup to the liaison of yolks and cream and returning all to the pan.
3 Bring almost to the boil, stirring continuously, then strain into a clean pan.
4 Correct the seasoning and consistency, add the garnish and serve.

Note 100 g (4 oz) raw minced chicken may be cooked in the velouté then liquidised with the soup to give a stronger chicken flavour (for 10 portions, increase the proportion 2½ times).

10 – Kidney soup

	4 portions	10 portions
good dripping or oil	50 g (2 oz)	125 g (5 oz)
flour, white or wholemeal	50 g (2 oz)	125 g (5 oz)
tomato purée	10 g (½ oz)	25 g (1¼ oz)
brown stock	1½ litre (3 pt)	3¾ litre (7 pt)
kidney (usually ox)	200 g (8 oz)	500 g (1¼ lb)
carrot ⎫ diced	100 g (4 oz)	250 g (10 oz)
onion ⎭	100 g (4 oz)	250 g (10 oz)
bouquet garni		
salt, pepper		

1 Melt the fat in a thick-bottomed pan, mix in the flour.
2 Cook slowly to a brown roux. Cool slightly.
3 Mix in the tomato purée.

4 Gradually mix in the hot stock. Stir to the boil.

5 Remove the skin and gristle from the kidney and cut into $\frac{1}{2}$ cm ($\frac{1}{4}$ in) dice.

6 Quickly fry the kidney in a little hot fat in a frying-pan for a minute, then add the carrot and onion and lightly brown together. Drain off all fat and add to the soup.

7 Add the bouquet garni and seasoning.

8 Simmer for $1\frac{1}{2}$–2 hours, skim when necessary.

9 Remove bouquet garni, pass the soup through a fine strainer or liquidise.

10 Return to a clean pan, reboil.

11 Correct the seasoning and consistency and serve.

12 This soup may be garnished with a little of the diced kidney.

11 – Thick oxtail soup

	4 portions	10 portions	Using sunflower oil 1 portion provides:
oxtail	200 g (8 oz)	500 g (1¼ lb)	
oil or fat	50 g (2 oz)	125 g (5 oz)	238 kcals/1001 kJ
onion	100 g (4 oz)	250 g (10 oz)	16.6 g fat
clove garlic (optional)	$\frac{1}{2}$	1	(of which 3.2 g saturated)
carrot and turnip	100 g (4 oz)	250 g (10 oz)	13.7 g carbohydrate
flour, white or wholemeal	50 g (2 oz)	125 g (5 oz)	(of which 4.1 g sugars)
tomato purée	10 g (½ oz)	25 g (1¼ oz)	9.4 g protein
brown stock	1½ litre (3 pt)	3¾ litre (7 pt)	2.2 g fibre
bouquet garni			
salt and mill pepper			
carrot and turnip for garnish	100 g (4 oz)	250 g (10 oz)	

1 Cut the oxtail into pieces through the natural joints.

2 Quickly fry in the hot oil or fat till lightly brown.

3 Add the diced onion, garlic (if using) and carrot and turnip and brown well together.

4 Mix in the flour and cook to a brown roux over gentle heat or in the oven.

5 Cool slightly. Mix in the tomato purée.

6 Gradually mix in the hot stock. Stir to the boil and skim.

7 Add the bouquet garni and seasoning. Simmer for 3–4 hours.

8 Remove the bouquet garni and pieces of oxtail.

9 Pass the soup through a fine strainer.
10 Remove flesh from the oxtail and liquidise with the soup.
11 Return to a clean pan, reboil, correct the seasoning and consistency.
12 Garnish with the extreme tip of the tail cut into rounds, and a little carrot and turnip turned in small balls with a solferino spoon, or cut into 2 mm ($\frac{1}{12}$ in) dice and cooked in salted water.
13 This soup may be finished with 2 tablespoons sherry.

12 – Clear oxtail soup

1 As for previous recipe without using any flour.
2 Drain off all the fat before adding to the stock.
3 Before adding the garnish add 25 g (1 oz) diluted arrowroot to the soup, reboil until clear, and strain.
4 Finish and serve for thick oxtail soup.

13 – Petite marmite

This is a double-strength consommé garnished with neat pieces of chicken winglet, cubes of beef, turned carrots and turnips and squares of celery, leek and cabbage. The traditional method of preparation is for the marmites to be cooked in special earthenware or porcelain pots ranging in size from 1–6 portions. Petite marmite should be accompanied by thin toasted slices of flute, grated Parmesan cheese and a slice or two of poached beef marrow.

	4 portions	10 portions
chicken winglets	4	10
lean beef (cut in 1 cm dice)	50 g (2 oz)	125 g (5 oz)
good strength beef consommé	1 litre (2 pt)	2½ litre (5 pt)
carrots	100 g (4 oz)	250 g (10 oz)
celery	50 g (2 oz)	125 g (5 oz)
leeks	100 g (4 oz)	250 g (10 oz)
cabbage	25 g (1 oz)	60 g (2½ oz)
turnips	100 g (4 oz)	250 g (10 oz)
slices of beef-bone marrow	8	20
toasted slices of flute	50 g (2 oz)	125 g (5 oz)
Parmesan cheese (grated)	25 g (1 oz)	60 g (2½ oz)

I portion provides:

261 kcals/1098 kJ
16.2 g fat
(of which 7.1 g saturated)
13.0 g carbohydrate
(of which 4.4 g sugars)
16.5 g protein
3.2 g fibre

1 Trim chicken winglets and cut in halves.
2 Blanch and refresh chicken winglets and the squares of beef.
3 Place the consommé into the marmite or marmites.
4 Add the squares of beef. Allow to simmer for 1 hour.
5 Add the winglet pieces, turned carrots and squares of celery.
6 Allow to simmer for 15 minutes.
7 Add the leek, cabbage and turned turnips, allow to simmer gently until all the ingredients are tender. Correct seasoning.
8 Degrease thoroughly using both sides of 8 cm (3 in) square pieces of kitchen paper.
9 Add the slices of beef bone marrow just before serving.
10 Serve the marmite on a dish paper or a round flat dish accompanied by the toasted flutes and grated cheese.

14 – Country style French vegetable soup

	4 portions	10 portions
dried haricot beans	50 g (2 oz)	125 g (5 oz)
olive oil	2 tbsp	5 tbsp
white of leek, finely shredded	100 g (4 oz)	250 g (10 oz)
carrot	100 g (4 oz)	250 g (10 oz)
turnip	50 g (2 oz)	125 g (5 oz)
French beans, cut into 2.5 cm (1 in) lengths	50 g (2 oz)	125 g (5 oz)
courgettes	100 g (4 oz)	250 g (10 oz)
broad beans	100 g (4 oz)	250 g (10 oz)
tomatoes skinned, deseeded and chopped	4	10
tomato purée	50 g (2 oz)	125 g (5 oz)
macaroni	50 g (2 oz)	125 g (5 oz)
vegetable stock	1 litre (2 pts)	$2\frac{1}{2}$ litre (5 pt)
seasoning		
basil	25 g (1 oz)	60 g ($2\frac{1}{2}$ oz)
clove garlic	1	$2\frac{1}{2}$
Gruyère cheese	50 g (2 oz)	125 g (5 oz)
olive oil	6 tbsp	15 tbsp

(basil, clove garlic, Gruyère cheese, olive oil grouped as pistou)

1 Soak the haricot beans for approximately 8 hours.
2 Place the beans in a pan of cold water, bring to the boil and gently simmer for approximately 20 minutes Refresh and drain.

3 Heat 2 tablespoons of oil in a suitable pan, add the white of leek and sweat for 5 minutes.
4 Add the carrot and turnip (both cut into brunoise) and cook for a further 2 minutes.
5 Add the haricot beans. Cover with the vegetable stock and add the remaining ingredients. Cook until everything is tender.
6 Make the pistou by puréeing the basil, garlic and cheese in a food processor. Gradually add the oil until well mixed and emulsified.
7 Correct the seasoning and consistency of the soup and serve with the pistou separately.

15 – Cock-a-leekie

½ litre (1 pt) good chicken stock and ½ litre (1 pt) good veal stock garnished with a julienne of prunes, white of chicken and leek.

16 – Cream of green pea soup with rice, sorrel and lettuce

	4 portions	10 portions	Béchamel made with skimmed milk I portion provides:
shelled peas	400 g (1 lb)	1¼ kg (2½ lb)	
sprig of mint			
onion	25 g (1 oz)	60 g (2½ oz)	376 kcals/1569 kJ
bouquet garni			21.7 g fat
thin béchamel	500 ml (1 pt)	1¼ litre (2½ pt)	(of which 13.7 g saturated)
cream	60 ml (⅛ pt)	150 ml (⅕ pt)	33.7 g carbohydrate
lettuce	¼	¾	(of which 11.1 g sugars)
sorrel	25 g (1 oz)	60 ml (2½ oz)	14 g protein
rice, cooked	50 g (2 oz)	125 g (5 oz)	4.9 g fibre

1 Cook the peas in water with a little salt, mint, onion and bouquet garni.
2 Remove the mint, onion and bouquet garni.
3 Purée the peas in a food processor or liquidiser and add to the béchamel.
4 Bring to the boil and simmer for 5 minutes.
5 Correct the seasoning; pass through a medium strainer.
6 Correct the consistency and add the cream.
7 Garnish with shredded lettuce, sorrel, cooked in butter, and cooked rice, and serve.

17 – Cream of asparagus soup

	4 portions	10 portions
onions or white of leek	50 g (2 oz)	125 g (5 oz)
celery	50 g (2 oz)	125 g (5 oz)
butter	50 g (2 oz)	125 g (5 oz)
flour	50 g (2 oz)	125 g (5 oz)
chicken stock	1 litre (2 pt)	2½ litre (5 pt)
asparagus trimmings	400 g (1 lb)	1¼ kg (2½ lb)
bouquet garni		
salt and pepper		
milk *or*	250 ml (½ pt)	600 ml (1¼ pt)
cream	125 ml (¼ pt)	300 ml (⅝ pt)

1 Sweat the sliced onion and celery in the butter without colour.
2 Remove from heat, add flour, return to heat and cook for a few minutes without colour.
3 Cool, gradually add the hot stock, stir to the boil.
4 Add the washed asparagus trimmings, the bouquet garni and season.
5 Simmer for 30 minutes. Remove the bouquet garni.
6 Purée in a food processor or liquidise and pass through a conical strainer.
7 Return to a clean pan, reboil, add the milk or cream.
8 Correct the seasoning and consistency and serve.

Variations on recipe
(a) Add 25 g (1 oz) sprigs of mint with the asparagus. Garnish with blanched mint leaves, using 2 or 3 per portion.
(b) Add the flesh of 1½ avocado pears added with the asparagus trimmings. The remaining half of avocado pear is neatly diced and used as garnish. This may be served cold.
(c) Use 200 g (8 oz) asparagus trimmings and 200 g (8 oz) mushrooms. Slice 150 g (6 oz) mushrooms and sweat them with the onion and celery. Garnish with the remaining 50 g (2 oz) sliced mushrooms cooked in a little butter.

18 – Cream of celery and cheese soup

	4 portions	10 portions
celery	200 g (8 oz)	500 g (1¼ lb)
onions } chopped	50 g (2 oz)	125 g (5 oz)
leeks	50 g (2 oz)	125 g (5 oz)
butter or margarine	50 g (2 oz)	125 g (5 oz)
flour	50 g (2 oz)	125 g (5 oz)
white stock	750 ml (1½ pt)	2¼ litre (4½ pt)
bouquet garni		
salt and pepper		
cheese (Stilton or strong Cheddar), grated	100 g (4 oz)	250 g (10 oz)
milk or	250 ml (½ pt)	600 ml (1¼ pt)
cream	125 ml (¼ pt)	300 ml (⅝ pt)

> Using 125 ml single cream
> I portion provides:
>
> 311 kcals/1293 kJ
> 25.1 g fat
> (of which 15.9 g saturated)
> 12.9 g carbohydrate
> (of which 2.9 g sugars)
> 9.2 g protein
> I g fibre

1 Sweat the vegetables in the fat without colour.
2 Mix in the flour, cook for a few minutes and cool.
3 Gradually add the hot stock, stir to the boil.
4 Add the bouquet garni, season and simmer for approximately 45 minutes.
5 Skim, remove the bouquet garni and pass or liquidise.
6 Return to a clean pan, bring to the boil, add the cheese and stir until incorporated into the soup.
7 Correct the seasoning and consistency, add the milk or cream and serve.

19 – Brown onion soup

	4 portions	10 portions
onions	600 g (1½ lb)	1½ kg (3¾ lb)
butter or margarine	25 g (1 oz)	60 g (2½ oz)
clove of garlic, chopped (optional)	1	2–3
flour, white or wholemeal	10 g (½ oz)	25 g (1 oz)
brown stock	1 litre (2 pt)	2½ litre (5 pt)
salt, mill pepper		
flute	¼	¾
grated cheese	50 g (2 oz)	125 g (5 oz)

> Using butter
> I portion provides:
>
> 197 kcals/827 kJ
> 9.7 g fat
> (of which 5.8 g saturated)
> 20.4 g carbohydrate
> (of which 8.1 g sugars)
> 8.3 g protein
> 3.1 g fibre

1 Peel the onions, halve and slice finely.

2 Melt the butter in a thick-bottomed pan, add the onions and garlic and cook steadily over a good heat until cooked and well browned.

3 Mix in the flour and cook over a gentle heat, browning slightly.

4 Gradually mix in the stock, bring to the boil, skim and season.

5 Simmer for approximately 10 minutes until the onion is soft. Correct the seasoning.

6 Pour into an earthenware tureen or casserole or individual dishes.

7 Cut the flute (French loaf, 2 cm (1 in) diameter) into slices and toast on both sides.

8 Sprinkle the toasted slices of bread liberally on the soup.

9 Sprinkle with grated cheese and brown under the salamander.

10 Place on a dish and serve.

20 – Mulligatawny

	4 portions	10 portions	Using sunflower oil 1 portion provides:
chopped onion	100 g (4 oz)	250 g (10 oz)	
clove of garlic (chopped)	$\frac{1}{2}$	1–2	227 kcals/952 kJ
butter, margarine or oil	50 g (2 oz)	125 g (5 oz)	17.1 g fat
flour, white or wholemeal	50 g (2 oz)	125 g (5 oz)	(of which 5.0 g saturated)
curry powder	1 dsp	$2\frac{1}{2}$ dsp	16.3 g carbohydrate
tomato purée	1 dsp	$2\frac{1}{2}$ dsp	(of which 4.1 g sugars)
brown stock	1 litre (2 pt)	$2\frac{1}{2}$ litre (5 pt)	3.3 g protein
chopped apple	25 g (1 oz)	60 g ($2\frac{1}{2}$ oz)	2.6 g fibre
ground ginger	6 g ($\frac{1}{4}$ oz)	15 g ($\frac{3}{4}$ oz)	
chopped chutney	1 dsp	$2\frac{1}{2}$ dsp	
desiccated coconut	25 g (1 oz)	60 g ($2\frac{1}{2}$ oz)	
salt			
cooked rice, white or wholegrain	10 g ($\frac{1}{2}$ oz)	25 g ($1\frac{1}{4}$ oz)	

1 Lightly brown the onion and garlic in the fat or oil.

2 Mix in the flour and curry powder, cook out for a few minutes, browning slightly.

3 Mix in the tomato purée. Cool slightly.

4 Gradually mix in the brown stock. Stir to the boil.

5 Add the remainder of the ingredients and season with salt.

6 Simmer for 30–45 minutes.

7 Pass firmly through a medium strainer or liquidise.

8 Return to a clean pan, reboil.

9 Correct the seasoning and consistency.
10 Place the rice in a warm soup tureen and pour in the soup.

21 – Okra or gumbo soup

	4 portions	10 portions
butter, oil or margarine	50 g (2 oz)	125 g (5 oz)
okra	200 g (8 oz)	500 g (1¼ lb)
leek, in brunoise	100 g (4 oz)	250 (10 oz)
chicken stock	750 ml (1½ pt)	2¼ litre (4½ pt)
lean ham	25 g (1 oz)	60 g (2½ oz)
cooked chicken	25 g (1 oz)	60 g (2½ oz)
salt and pepper		
tomato, peeled, deseeded and diced	50 g (2 oz)	125 g (5 oz)
cooked rice	25 g (1 oz)	60 g (2½ oz)

> Using butter
> I portion provides:
>
> 140 kcals/581 kJ
> 11.5 g fat
> (of which 7.1 g saturated)
> 4.5 g carbohydrate
> (of which 2.2 g sugars)
> 4.9 g protein
> 2.7 g fibre

1 Heat the fat or oil and sweat the sliced okra in a thick-bottomed pan, covered with a lid, until nearly cooked.
2 Add the leeks and cook until soft.
3 Add the stock, diced ham and chicken and simmer for 5 minutes.
4 Correct the seasoning, add the rice and tomato, bring to the boil and serve.

22 – Pumpkin soup

	4 portions	10 portions
chopped onion	100 g (4 oz)	250 g (10 oz)
pumpkin, peeled, seeded, chopped	800 g (2 lb)	2½ kg (5 lb)
butter or margarine	100 g (4 oz)	250 g (10 oz)
white stock	500 ml (1 pt)	1¼ litre (2½ pt)
flour	50 g (2 oz)	125 g (5 oz)
milk	500 ml (1 pt)	1¼ litre (2½ pt)
salt and pepper		
cream	125 ml (¼ pt)	300 ml (⅝ pt)
grated cheese	50 g (2 oz)	125 g (5 oz)
chopped parsley		

1 Sweat the onion and pumpkin in half of the butter for a few minutes.
2 Add the stock and simmer until cooked.
3 Make a white sauce with the remaining butter, flour and milk.
4 Add to the pumpkin, blend, purée and pass through a strainer.
5 Season, bring to the boil and finish with cream, cheese and parsley.

23 – Chive, potato and cucumber soup with cream

	4 portions	10 portions
onions ⎫	50 g (2 oz)	125 g (5 oz)
spring onions ⎬ chopped	50 g (2 oz)	125 g (5 oz)
celery ⎭	50 g (2 oz)	125 g (5 oz)
butter	50 g (2 oz)	125 g (5 oz)
chicken stock	375 ml ($\frac{3}{4}$ pt)	1 litre (2 pt)
potatoes, diced	400 g (1 lb)	1 kg (2 lb)
cucumber, diced	1	2–3
salt and pepper		
cream	125 ml ($\frac{1}{4}$ pt)	300 ml ($\frac{5}{8}$ pt)
chopped parsley		
chopped chives		

1 Sweat the onions and celery without colour in the butter.
2 Add the stock, potatoes and cucumber; season and simmer until soft.
3 Liquidise and cool. Correct the seasoning and consistency.
4 Finish with cream, parsley and chives.
5 Chill and serve.

Note This soup is usually served chilled but may be served hot.

I 24 – Chilled minty yoghurt and hazelnut soup

(DAVID REID)

	4 portions	10 portions
cucumber	1	$2\frac{1}{2}$
natural yoghurt	500 ml (1 pt)	$1\frac{1}{4}$ litre ($2\frac{1}{2}$ pt)
chopped toasted hazelnuts	50 g (2 oz)	125 g (5 oz)
chopped fresh mint	2 tbsp	5 tbsp
hazelnut oil	2 tbsp	5 tbsp
coarsely ground toasted cummin seeds	$\frac{1}{2}$ tsp	$1\frac{1}{4}$ tsp

1 portion provides:

187 kcals/748 kJ
13.7 g fat
(of which 1.8 g saturates)
9.0 g carbohydrate
(of which 8.7 g sugars)
7.5 g protein
1.1 g fibre

1 Place the cucumber and yoghurt in a blender and process until smooth.
2 Stir in the remaining ingredients and season.
3 Chill for 1 hour.
4 Garnish with mint sprigs.

25 – Chilled tomato and cucumber soup (Gazpacho)

This Spanish soup has many regional variations. It is served chilled and has a predominant flavour of cucumber, tomato and garlic.

	4 portions	10 portions	1 portion provides:
tomato juice	500 ml (1 pt)	1¼ litre (2½ pt)	91 kcals/382 kJ
tomatoes, skinned, deseeded and diced	100 g (4 oz)	250 g (10 oz)	6.71 g fat (of which 1 g is saturated)
cucumber, peeled and diced	100 g (4 oz)	250 g (10 oz)	6.2 g carbohydrate
green pepper, diced	50 g (2 oz)	125 g (5 oz)	1.83 g protein
onion chopped	50 g (2 oz)	125 g (5 oz)	1.56 g fibre
mayonnaise	1 tbsp	2–3 tbsp	
vinegar	1 tbsp	2–3 tbsp	
seasoning			
clove garlic	1	2–3	

1 Mix all the ingredients together.
2 Season and add crushed chopped garlic to taste.
3 Stand in a cool place for an hour.
4 Correct the consistency with iced water and serve chilled.

Note   Instead of serving with all the ingredients finely chopped, the soup can be liquidised and garnished with chopped tomato, cucumber and pepper. The soup may also be finished with chopped herbs.

A tray of garnishes may accompany the soup, e.g. chopped red and green pepper, chopped onion, tomato, cucumber and croûtons.

26 – Carrot and orange soup

	4 portions	10 portions	
			I portion provides:
carrots, sliced	400 g (1 lb)	1¼ kg (2½ lb)	138 kcals/579 kJ
white of leek	50 g (2 oz)	125 g (5 oz)	5.8 g fat
onion	50 g (2 oz)	125 g (5 oz)	(of which 3.6 g saturated)
butter or margarine	25 g (1 oz)	60 g (2½ oz)	19.1 g carbohydrate
flour	25 g (1 oz)	60 g (2½ oz)	(of which 13.4 g sugars)
tomato purée	1 tsp	2–3 tsp	3.5 g protein
white stock	1 litre (2 pt)	2½ litre (5 pt)	2.9 g fibre
oranges, zest and juice of	2	5	
bouquet garni			
salt and pepper			
natural yoghurt	125 ml (¼ pt)	300 ml (⅝ pt)	

1 Gently sweat the sliced vegetables in the butter or margarine without colour, until soft. Mix in the flour.
2 Cook over a gentle heat without colouring.
3 Mix in the tomato purée.
4 Gradually add the boiling stock. Stir well.
5 Prepare a fine julienne from the zest of the oranges, blanch and refresh.
6 Add the orange juice to the soup.
7 Add bouquet garni, salt and pepper.
8 Simmer gently for approximately 45 minutes.
9 Remove bouquet garni, liquidise and pass through a coarse strainer.
10 Return to a clean pan, reboil, correct the seasoning and consistency, finish with yoghurt. Garnish with the blanched julienne of orange zest.

Note Alternatively, the soup may be finished with cream or fromage frais.

27 – Cream of tomato and orange soup

Prepare a cream of tomato soup. Prior to straining, add thinly peeled strips of orange zest and simmer for a few minutes. The juice of one orange may be added and a blanched julienne of orange zest used for garnish to every 500 ml (1 pt) of soup. Serve hot.

28 – Fruit soups

Soups with a fruit base are usually served cold and may be offered for breakfast as well as lunch or dinner.

	4 portions	10 portions
raisins, seedless	50 g (2 oz)	125 g (5 oz)
currants	50 g (2 oz)	125 g (5 oz)
dried apples, diced	50 g (2 oz)	125 g (5 oz)
dried apricots, diced	50 g (2 oz)	125 g (5 oz)
prunes (stoned), diced	50 g (2 oz)	125 g (5 oz)
water	500 ml (1 pt)	1¼ litre (2½ pt)
orange, in segments	1	2–3
lemon, in segments	1	2–3
pineapple juice	500 ml (1 pt)	1¼ litre (2½ pt)

1 Soak the dried fruit overnight in the water or a mixture of water and wine.
2 Drain, cover the dried fruit with water and cook for 10 min.
3 Add the diced orange and lemon segments, free from pith, and the pineapple juice and simmer for a few minutes. Serve hot or cold.

Note   This soup may also be finished with 125 ml ($\frac{1}{4}$ pt) Madeira, port or dry sherry.

Many other fruit soups can be made using, for example, pineapple, apple, strawberries, raspberries, cherries, redcurrants, melon and peach. The fruits that require cooking, such as pineapple, apple and cherry, are prepared, cut up, cooked in sugar syrup and puréed. They are then mixed with white or red wine or garnished as follows:

Pineapple
Small dice of pineapple macerated in syrup and lemon juice.

Apple
Diced apple and sultanas cooked in sugar syrup with cinnamon or clove flavouring.

Cherry
This soup may require light thickening with diluted arrowroot or cornflour. Garnish with chopped stoned cooked cherries.

Fruits that do not require cooking must be fully ripe. They are puréed and mixed with a combination of sugar syrups and red or white wine.

I 29 – Roasted plum tomato and olive soup

(ANNA MILLER)

	4 portions	10 portions
plum tomatoes	400 g (1 lb)	1½ kg (3 lb)
cloves of garlic	1	2
small onions	1	2
sprigs of basil	2	4
tomato purée	2 tbsp	4 tbsp
balsamic vinegar	1 tsp	3 tsp
black and green olives	50 g (2 oz)	100 g (4 oz)
water	500 ml (1 pt)	1½ litre (3 pt)
salt and pepper		
sugar	10 g (½ oz)	25 g (1 oz)
dinner rolls	2	3
sun dried tomato paste	1 tbsp	3 tbsp
black olives	2	5
Parmesan	25 g (1 oz)	75 g (3 oz)
chopped parsley	25 g (1 oz)	50 g (2 oz)
olive oil	25 g (1 oz)	50 g (2 oz)

1 Roughly chop the plum tomatoes, onion, garlic and basil.
2 Place into a roasting tray with tomato purée and a few drops of olive oil. Roast at 204°C (400°F) for 10 minutes.
3 Remove from the oven and put into a saucepan. Add water.
4 Simmer for 20 minutes, occasionally stirring.
5 Liquidise for 2–3 minutes with olives. Pass through a conical sieve.
6 Check the consistency of the soup, add seasoning, a pinch of sugar and a few drops of balsamic vinegar.
7 Slice dinner rolls into rounds and lightly toast both sides.
8 Spread with sun dried tomato paste and Parmesan.
9 When the soup is required, bring to the boil. Put into soup cups and top with croûtons and a slice of black olive and chopped parsley.

30 – Mussel soup

	4 portions	10 portions
mussels	400 g (1 lb)	1¼ kg (2½ lb)
fish stock	1 litre (2 pt)	2½ litre (5 pt)
shallots or onions	50 g (2 oz)	125 g (5 oz)
celery	50 g (2 oz)	125 g (5 oz)
leek	50 g (2 oz)	125 g (5 oz)
parsley		
salt and pepper		
white wine	60 ml (⅛ pt)	150 ml (⅓ pt)
cream	125 ml (¼ pt)	300 ml (⅝ pt)
egg yolk	1	2–3

1 Scrape and thoroughly clean the mussels.
2 Place in a pan with the stock, chopped vegetables and herbs; season.
3 Cover with a lid and simmer for 5 minutes.
4 Extract the mussels from the shells and remove the beards.
5 Strain the liquid through a double muslin and bring to the boil, add the wine.
6 Correct the seasoning, finish with a liaison and garnish with the mussels and chopped parsley.

Note Variations for this soup include scallops in place of mussels, fennel and dill in place of parsley. A further variation is to prepare a potato soup using fish stock, garnish with mussels and finish with cream.

31 – Fish soup

	4 portions	10 portions
onions or shallots, chopped	50 g (2 oz)	125 g (5 oz)
clove garlic	1	2–3
butter, margarine or oil	50 g (2 oz)	125 g (5 oz)
monk fish or any white fish	400 g (1 lb)	1¼ kg (2½ lb)
potato	100 g (4 oz)	250 g (10 oz)
tomato	100 g (4 oz)	250 g (10 oz)
fish stock	1 litre (2 pt)	2½ litre (5 pt)
bouquet garni		
salt and pepper		
parsley		

1 Sweat the onion and garlic in the butter without colour.

2 Add the fish, free from skin and bone, cook for 2 to 3 minutes.
3 Add the remainder of the ingredients, season.
4 Simmer for 20 minutes.
5 Remove the bouquet garni, liquidise and reboil.
6 Correct the seasoning and consistency.
7 Finish with chopped parsley.

Note Variations to this soup include the addition of wine, cream or yoghurt or fromage frais, saffron, curry powder, tomato purée, rice, shrimps, or mushrooms.

32 – Lobster bisque

Bisque is the term applied to any thickened shellfish soups, e.g. crab, crayfish, prawn and shrimp.

	4 portions	10 portions
live lobster	400 g (1 lb)	1 kg (2½ lb)
butter	100 g (4 oz)	250 g (10 oz)
onion	50 g (2 oz)	125 g (5 oz)
carrot	50 g (2 oz)	125 g (5 oz)
brandy	60 ml ($\frac{1}{8}$ pt)	150 ml ($\frac{3}{8}$ pt)
flour	75 g (3 oz)	190 g (7½ oz)
tomato purée	50 g (2 oz)	125 g (5 oz)
white stock (beef or veal or chicken or a combination of any 2 or 3)	1¼ litre (2¼ pt)	3 litre (5½ pt)
white wine (dry)	120 ml ($\frac{1}{4}$ pt)	300 ml ($\frac{3}{4}$ pt)
bouquet garni		
salt, cayenne		
cream	120 ml ($\frac{1}{4}$ pt)	300 ml ($\frac{3}{4}$ pt)

> I portion provides:
>
> 438 kcals/1841 kJ
> 28.7 g fat
> (of which 17.2 g saturated)
> 18.8 g carbohydrate
> (of which 4.2 g sugars)
> 14.4 g protein
> 1.2 g fibre

1 Wash the live lobster.
2 Cut it in half lengthwise tail first, then the carapace.
3 Discard the sac from the carapace, clean the trail from the tail and wash all the pieces.
4 Crack the claws and the four claw joints.
5 Melt the butter in a thick-bottomed pan.
6 Add the lobster and the roughly cut onion and carrot.
7 Allow to cook steadily without colouring the butter for a few minutes stirring with a wooden spoon.

8 Add the brandy and allow it to ignite.
9 Remove from heat and mix in the flour and tomato purée.
10 Return to gentle heat and cook out the roux.
11 Cool slightly and gradually add the white stock and white wine.
12 Stir until smooth and until the bisque comes to the boil.
13 Add the bouquet garni and season lightly with salt.
14 Simmer for 15–20 minutes. Remove lobster pieces.
15 Remove lobster meat, crush the lobster shells, return them to the bisque and allow to continue simmering for further 15–20 minutes.
16 Cut lobster meat into large brunoise.
17 Remove bouquet garni and as much bulk from the bisque as possible.
18 Pass through a coarse and then fine strainer or liquidise, and then through a fine strainer again. Return the soup to a clean pan.
19 Reboil, correct seasoning with a little cayenne, and add the cream.
20 Add the brunoise of lobster meat and serve. At this stage 25 g (1 oz) butter may be stirred into the bisque as a final enriching finish.

In order to produce a less expensive soup, cooked lobster shell (not shell from the claws) may be crushed and used in place of a live lobster.

An alternative method of thickening is to omit the flour and, 10 minutes before the final cooked stage is reached, to thicken by stirring in 75 g (3 oz) rice flour diluted in a little cold water.

33 – Bortsch

This is an unclarified broth of Eastern European origin, mainly Russia and Poland.

	4 portions	10 portions
Stock		
duck (half-roasted)	1 × 2 kg (4 lb)	2 × 2 kg (4 lb)
boiling beef (blanched and refreshed)	200 g (½ lb)	500 g (1¼ lb)
beef stock	2 litre (4 pt)	5 litre (10 pt)
beetroot juice	*250 ml (½ pt)	600 ml (1¼ pt)
onion	50 g (2 oz)	125 g (5 oz)
carrots	50 g (2 oz)	125 g (5 oz)
celery	50 g (2 oz)	125 g (5 oz)
leek	50 g (2 oz)	125 g (5 oz)
bouquet garni		

Garnish

carrot	50g (2oz)	125g (5oz)
leek	50g (2oz)	125g (5oz)
cabbage	50g (2oz)	125g (5oz)
beetroot	50g (2oz)	125g (5g)
diced, cooked duck	50g (2oz)	125g (5oz)
diced, cooked beef	50g (2oz)	125g (5oz)

Accompaniments
*beetroot juice
sour cream
**small duck patties

1 Make a good brown stock, allow to simmer and reduce to half the amount.
2 Strain through a double muslin, skim well, correct the seasoning and add the garnish. (For the garnish, the vegetables are cooked in short, thick batons.)

Notes
* Grate raw peeled beetroot and squeeze firmly to obtain the juice.
** Duck patties can be made as small as possible from any type of paste, e.g. short or puff, and the filling should be a well-flavoured and seasoned duck mixture with, for example, sweated chopped onion and cabbage.

EGG DISHES

— *Introduction* —

HENS' EGGS

1 Eggshells should be clean, well shaped, strong and slightly rough.
2 When broken there should be a high proportion of thick white to thin white.
3 The yolk should be firm, round and of a good even colour. As eggs are kept, the thick white gradually changes into thin white and water passes from the whites to the yolks. The yolks lose their strength and shape and begin to flatten; water evaporates from the eggs and is replaced by air, and, as water is heavier than air, fresh eggs weigh more than stale ones.

FOOD VALUE

Eggs contain most nutrients and are low in calories (approximately 90 calories each). Egg protein is complete and easily digestible. They are a protective food and provide energy and material for growth and repair of the body.

STORAGE AND USE

1 Store in a cool place preferably under refrigeration 0–5°C (32–41°F) (eggshells are porous and should not be stored near strong-smelling foods, such as cheese, onion, fish and raw meat, because the odours will be absorbed).
2 Rotate the stocks – first in first out.
3 Wash your hands before and after handling eggs.
4 Do not use cracked eggs.

It is important to understand that food-poisoning *Salmonella* bacteria can be passed into eggs from hens. Department of Health advice to food manufacturers and caterers is that for all recipes using raw eggs which involve no cooking, pasteurised eggs (frozen, liquid or dried) should be used instead.

Turkeys' and guinea fowls' eggs may be used in place of hens' eggs. Goose or duck eggs should always be thoroughly cooked.

Quail eggs are popular and may be used in many ways for serving as a first course, as a light course or with salads and as a garnish to many other dishes.

1 – Poached eggs in potato nest with mushrooms and horseradish sauce

	4 portions	10 portions
eggs	4	10
duchess potato	200 g (8 oz)	500 g (1¼ lb)
finely chopped onion	100 g (4 oz)	250 g (10 oz)
butter or margarine	50 g (2 oz)	125 g (5 oz)
paprika	½ tsp	1¼ tsp
finely chopped mushrooms	100 g (4 oz)	250 g (10 oz)
horseradish sauce	250 ml (½ pt)	600 ml (1¼ pt)

1 Poach the eggs, keep in ice-cold water until required.
2 On a lightly greased and floured baking sheet, pipe a nest of duchess potato to hold each egg. Egg wash. Lightly brown in a moderate oven (180°C, 350°F).
3 Sweat the finely chopped onion in the butter without colour; add the paprika, sweat together for 2 minutes.
4 Add the mushrooms, cook out for a further 2–3 minutes.
5 Reheat the poached eggs in simmering salted water, drain and dry well on a clean cloth.
6 Place the potato nests on to a suitable plate, arrange a spoonful of the mushroom mixture on the bottom of each and carefully place an egg on the top. Coat with horseradish sauce (see below) and serve immediately.

– *Horseradish sauce*

	4 portions	10 portions
chicken velouté or natural yoghurt	125 ml (¼ pt)	300 ml (⅝ pt)
single cream	125 ml (¼ pt)	300 ml (⅝ pt)
freshly grated horseradish	1 tbsp	2½ tbsp
lemon juice		

1 Boil out the velouté, season with salt and pepper, add the cream.
2 Continue to cook until correct consistency and then strain. Add horseradish and a squeeze of lemon juice.

2 – Poached eggs with prawns, sherry and French mustard

	4 portions	10 portions
eggs	4	10
medium-sized tomatoes, peeled and sliced	4	10
prawns	100 g (4 oz)	250 g (10 oz)
butter or margarine	25 g (1 oz)	60 g (2½ oz)
sherry	2 tbsp	5 tbsp
Mornay sauce	250 ml (½ pt)	600 ml (1¼ pt)
French mustard	½ tsp	1¼ tsp
grated Parmesan cheese	50 g (2 oz)	125 g (5 oz)

1 Poach the eggs, reserve in a basin of cold water.
2 Divide the tomatoes into individual dishes, e.g. egg dishes, season lightly with salt and pepper. Place on a baking sheet in a moderate oven for approximately 5 minutes.
3 Warm the prawns in the butter and sherry.
4 Reheat the Mornay sauce and flavour with the French mustard.
5 Reheat the eggs, drain well. Place on top of the slices of cooked tomato.
6 Sprinkle the prawns over the eggs.
7 Coat with Mornay sauce and sprinkle with Parmesan cheese.
8 Glaze under the salamander. Serve immediately.

3 – Poached eggs with chicken and tomato and cream sauces

	4 portions	10 portions
eggs	4	10
short pastry	100 g (4 oz)	250 g (10 oz)
diced cooked chicken	50 g (2 oz)	125 g (5 oz)
tomatoes, peeled, deseeded and diced	50 g (2 oz)	125 g (5 oz)
butter or margarine	50 g (2 oz)	125 g (5 oz)
chicken velouté	125 ml (¼ pt)	300 ml (⅝ pt)
double cream	1 tbsp	2–3 tbsp
tomato sauce	125 ml (¼ pt)	300 ml (⅝ pt)
meat glaze		

1 Poach the eggs, retain in cold water.
2 Line tartlet moulds with short pastry, bake blind.

3 Reheat the diced chicken and tomatoes in the butter or margarine.
4 Place the chicken and tomato in the bottom of the tartlet cases.
5 Reheat the eggs in simmering salted water; drain well. Arrange the eggs on top of the chicken and tomato.
6 Boil the chicken velouté, add the cream and strain.
7 Mask each egg with the two sauces: tomato sauce on one half and suprême sauce on the other.
8 Separate the two sauces with a thin line of warm meat glaze and serve.

4 – Poached eggs on a muffin with hollandaise sauce (eggs Benedict)

	4 portions	10 portions
eggs	4	10
muffins	4	10
slices of tongue or ham	4	10
hollandaise sauce	250 ml ($\frac{1}{2}$ pt)	600 ml (1$\frac{1}{4}$ pt)

1 Poach the eggs, reserve in cold water.
2 Toast the muffins cut out with a round plain cutter, the size of the eggs.
3 Cut a slice of ham or tongue the same size; warm gently by brushing with a little butter and placing in a moderate oven.
4 Place the buttered muffin on a suitable plate, with the ham or tongue on top and the reheated, well-drained poached eggs on the ham or tongue.
5 Coat with hollandaise sauce and serve immediately.

5 – Eggs on the dish with sliced onion, bacon and potato

	4 portions	10 portions
shredded onion	50 g (2 oz)	125 g (5 oz)
oil	60 ml ($\frac{1}{8}$ pt)	150 ml ($\frac{1}{3}$ pt)
small potatoes	2	5
lardons of bacon	100 g (4 oz)	250 g (10 oz)
butter	50 g (2 oz)	125 g (5 oz)
eggs	4	10
salt and pepper		
cream	4 tbsp	10 tbsp
chopped parsley		

1 Sauté the onions in oil until they are lightly coloured.
2 Peel and slice the potatoes then separately fry them in oil until cooked and golden brown; drain.
3 Add the onions to the potatoes.
4 Blanch the lardons; quickly fry in the butter, do not drain.
5 Divide the potatoes, onions and lardons into individual egg dishes.
6 Break in the eggs, season with salt and pepper and mask with cream. Cook in a moderate oven until the eggs are set.
7 Sprinkle with chopped parsley and serve immediately.

6 – Eggs on the dish with chicken livers and mushrooms in Madeira sauce

	4 portions	10 portions
butter or margarine	75 g (3 oz)	180 g (7½ oz)
eggs	4	10
chicken livers	100 g (2 oz)	125 g (5 oz)
oil	1 tbsp	2–3 tbsp
salt and pepper		
sliced button mushrooms	50 g (2 oz)	125 g (5 oz)
demi-glace or jus-lié	125 ml (¼ pt)	300 ml (⅝ pt)
Madeira wine	2 tbsp	5 tbsp
parsley or chervil		

1 Divide two-thirds of the butter between egg dishes and allow to melt.
2 Break in the eggs, season with salt and pepper, place on a baking sheet. Cook in a moderate oven until set.
3 Clean the chicken livers, neatly slice.
4 Sauté the chicken livers in the oil, keeping them undercooked. Drain and season with salt and pepper.
5 Sauté the sliced mushrooms in the remaining butter or margarine.
6 Boil the demi-glace or jus-lié with the Madeira wine, strain and add the mushrooms.
7 Arrange a cordon of Madeira sauce and mushrooms around the eggs, garnish with chicken livers and a sprig of parsley or chervil and serve.

7 ~ Eggs on the dish with grilled lamb's kidney and Madeira sauce

	4 portions	10 portions
lamb's kidneys	2	5
salt and pepper		
oil	2 tbsp	5 tbsp
butter or margarine	50 g (2 oz)	125 g (5 oz)
eggs	4	10
demi-glace or jus-lié	125 ml ($\frac{1}{4}$ pt)	300 ml ($\frac{5}{8}$ pt)
Madeira wine	2 tbsp	5 tbsp

1 Remove the membrane from the kidneys, cut in half and remove centre core.
2 Place on a suitable tray. Season and brush with oil; grill under salamander, leaving them slightly under cooked.
3 Divide the butter between the egg dishes, melt, break in the eggs and season with salt and pepper.
4 Place on a baking sheet and cook in a moderate oven until set.
5 Boil the demi-glace or jus-lié, add the Madeira wine and strain.
6 Serve the eggs with a cordon of Madeira sauce, garnished with half a grilled kidney and a sprig of parsley or chervil.

8 ~ Soft-boiled eggs with mushroom duxelle and cheese sauce

	4 portions	10 portions
eggs	4	10
short pastry	100 g (4 oz)	250 g (10 oz)
Duxelle		
shallots	25 g (1 oz)	60 g (2$\frac{1}{2}$ oz)
mushrooms, chopped	100 g (4 oz)	250 g (10 oz)
butter or margarine	50 g (2 oz)	125 g (5 oz)
salt and pepper		
Mornay sauce	125 ml ($\frac{1}{2}$ pt)	600 ml (1$\frac{1}{4}$ pt)
grated Parmesan cheese	25 g (1 oz)	60 g (2$\frac{1}{2}$ oz)

1 Soft boil the eggs for 5–6 minutes then remove and place in a basin of cold water to cool. Shell. Retain in cold water.
2 Line individual tartlet moulds with short pastry and bake blind.
3 Prepare the mushroom duxelle and season.

4 Place tartlet cases in individual serving dishes and fill with the duxelle.
5 Reheat the eggs in simmering salted water, drain. Place the reheated eggs in the tartlet cases.
6 Mask with Mornay sauce, sprinkle with grated Parmesan cheese and gratinate. Serve immediately.

9 ~ Omelet with creamed smoked haddock and cheese (Arnold Bennett)

	4 portions	10 portions
butter or margarine	12 g ($\frac{1}{2}$ oz)	30 g ($1\frac{1}{4}$ oz)
cooked, flaked, smoked haddock	50 g (2 oz)	125 g (5 oz)
Mornay sauce	90 ml ($\frac{3}{16}$ pt)	225 ml ($\frac{1}{2}$ pt)
egg flat omelet	4 × 3	10 × 3
Parmesan cheese	10 g ($\frac{1}{2}$ oz)	25 g ($1\frac{1}{4}$ oz)

1 Melt the butter or margarine in a suitable pan, reheat the smoked haddock. Bind with a little of the Mornay sauce.
2 Prepare a flat omelet, place on to a plate.
3 Arrange the fish on top of the omelet, coat with the remainder of the sauce, sprinkle with Parmesan cheese and glaze under the salamander. Serve immediately.

10 ~ Omelet with mushrooms and chicken livers

	4 portions	10 portions
chicken livers	100 g (4 oz)	250 g (10 oz)
butter or margarine	50 g (2 oz)	125 g (5 oz)
sliced mushrooms	50 g (2 oz)	125 g (5 oz)
jus-lié	60 ml ($\frac{1}{8}$ pt)	150 ml ($\frac{1}{3}$ pt)
salt and pepper		
egg omelets	4 × 2	10 × 2
chopped tarragon		

1 Trim the livers, cut into quarters, sauté quickly in half the butter or margarine, keeping slightly under-cooked.
2 Sauté the mushrooms in the remaining butter or margarine.

144

3 Add the mushrooms to the chicken livers, bind with jus-lié and season with salt and pepper.
4 Make the omelets and fold.
5 Serve the omelets on individual plates. Cut an incision in the tops, fill with mushrooms and chicken livers, and sprinkle with chopped tarragon. Serve a little sauce around the omelets.

11 – Omelet with potatoes and gruyère cheese

	4 portions	10 portions
potatoes	100 g (4 oz)	250 g (10 oz)
oil	60 ml ($\frac{1}{8}$ pt)	150 ml ($\frac{1}{3}$ pt)
salt and pepper		
eggs	8	20
gruyère cheese	100 g (4 oz)	250 g (10 oz)
butter or margarine	100 g (4 oz)	250 g (10 oz)

1 Cut the potatoes into $\frac{1}{4}$ cm ($\frac{1}{8}$ in) dice, fry in the oil until lightly brown, drain and season with salt.
2 Beat the eggs well, season, add the potatoes.
3 Cut the cheese in $\frac{1}{4}$ cm ($\frac{1}{8}$ in) dice and add to the mixture.
4 Use the butter or margarine to make 4 or 10 flat omelets.
5 Serve on individual plates at once.

12 – Light fluffy omelet

For each omelet
2–3 egg yolks
salt and pepper
2–3 egg whites
25 g (1 oz) butter or margarine

1 Beat the yolks with salt and pepper.
2 Half beat the whites, fold the yolks into the whites.
3 Heat the butter or margarine in the omelet pan and pour in the mixture; cook, stirring with a fork, until nearly set.
4 Fold the omelet in half, finish cooking in the oven until set.
5 Serve on individual plates immediately.

13 – Eggs in cocotte with tomato and orange sauce

	4 portions	10 portions
tomato sauce	250 ml ($\frac{1}{2}$ pt)	600 ml (1$\frac{1}{4}$ pt)
orange	1	2–3
sugar	10 g ($\frac{1}{2}$ oz)	25 g (1$\frac{1}{4}$ oz)
vinegar	$\frac{1}{2}$ tbsp	1 tbsp
juice of lemon	$\frac{1}{2}$	1
Cointreau	1 tbsp	2–3 tbsp
butter or margarine	50 g (2 oz)	125 g (5 oz)
salt and pepper		
eggs	4	10

1 Boil the tomato sauce.
2 Segment the orange, retain the juice.
3 Boil the sugar and vinegar to a light caramel, add the orange and lemon juice. Boil out.
4 Add the tomato sauce, simmer for 2 minutes. Pass through a strainer.
5 Finish with the Cointreau.
6 Butter and season individual cocotte dishes. Place a half tablespoon of the sauce in each. Break in the eggs.
7 Place in a shallow tray containing 1 cm ($\frac{1}{2}$ in) water. Cook in a moderate oven until the eggs are lightly set.
8 Serve with a little of the sauce around each egg, garnished with a segment of orange.

T ## 14 – Tart of softly boiled quail's eggs on brioche with spinach and brunoise of smoked salmon

(DAVID ADLARD)

Quail's eggs (3 per person)
1 Plunge the quail's eggs into rapidly boiling water, cook for exactly 2 minutes. Plunge into iced water.
2 When they are cold, peel them carefully (if you leave them in the fridge in water overnight, it is easier to peel). They should be soft.
3 Put them in cold water and store in the fridge.

Spinach (200 g (8 oz) of uncooked for 4)
Blanch the spinach and refresh in cold water. Squeeze out as much water as possible.

146

Brioche
1 Before serving the dish, toast the brioche on both sides.
2 Cut out a circle 5 cm (2 in) across with a round cutter and keep warm.

Smoked salmon
Cut the salmon into small dice.

To finish the dish
1 Sauté the spinach in butter and season with salt, pepper and nutmeg.
2 Plunge the quail's eggs in very hot water for 30 seconds. Drain and season.
3 Boil up the sauce and add the smoked salmon.
4 Put the spinach on top of the brioche and 'nestle' the quail's eggs into the spinach.
5 Gently pour the sauce with smoked salmon on top of the quail's eggs.

For the sauce you need fish stock

	4 portions	10 portions
fish bones and heads	1 kg (2 lb)	2½ kg (5 lb)
sliced onions	50 g (2 oz)	125 g (5 oz)
chopped leek	50 g (2 oz)	125 g (5 oz)
bouquet garni		
water to cover and a little bit more		

1 Soak the bones in water for an hour to clean.
2 Put all the ingredients in a pan, boil, skim and simmer for 20 minutes.
3 Strain.

To make the sauce

	4 portions	10 portions
fish stock	2 litre (4 pt)	5 litre (10 pt)
dry white wine	250 ml (½ pt)	600 ml (1¼ pt)
Noilly Prat	30 ml (2 oz)	75 ml (¼ pt)
chopped shallots	2	5

1 Reduce the fish stock and wine by 75%.
2 Add the Noilly Prat and the shallots.
3 Reduce to demi-glaze and add ½ litre (1 pt) of double cream.
4 Boil up to consistency. Pass through a sieve.

FISH DISHES

Prepare and cook complex fish and shellfish dishes

1   Select the type, quantity and quality of fish and shellfish in accordance with recipe specifications.
2   Demonstrate that the nutritional value of fish and shellfish is adequately retained during the preparation and cooking procedures.
3   Recognise that fish and shellfish not for immediate consumption are stored in accordance with the recipe specification and the relevant legislation.

—— *Introduction* ——

More people are eating fish in preference to meat these days and customers should always be offered a reasonable choice. The dishes available should include simply prepared and cooked items. It is a mistake to include on the menu all rich and elaborate dishes as good fresh fish is often at its best when simply cooked, e.g. grilled sea bass with fennel.

The contemporary trend is for hot fish sauces to be lightly thickened, preferably without the use of a roux-based sauce. However, in large-scale cookery, when considerable quantities of fish sauces may be required, the use of fish velouté may be necessary.

The quality of fish stock must be of the highest level if good quality fish dishes are to be produced. Care must be taken at all times to use only fresh, clean, selected fish bones, then to sweat them in butter with onion, season lightly with herbs and where possible moisten with white wine. Never allow fish stock to cook for more than 20 minutes otherwise the flavour will be impaired.

Any fish or shellfish cooked by poaching can alternatively be cooked by steaming. Combination steam/convection ovens are commonly used in many kitchens and fish cooked in a controlled moist atmosphere at temperatures below 99°C (210°F) benefits as shrinkage is kept to the minimum, overcooking is easier to control and the texture of the fish is moist and succulent.

— *Fish* —

TYPES OR VARIETIES OF FISH

1 Oily fish. These are round in shape, e.g. herring, mackerel, salmon.
2 White fish:
    (a) Round, e.g. cod, whiting, hake.
    (b) Flat, e.g. plaice, sole, turbot.
3 Shellfish:
    (a) Crustacea, e.g. lobster, crabs.
    (b) Mollusca, e.g. oysters, mussels.

PURCHASING UNIT

Fresh fish is bought by the kilogram, by the number of fillets or whole fish of the weight that is required. For example, 30 kg (66 lb) of salmon could be ordered as 2 × 15 kg (33 lb), 3 × 10 kg (22 lb) or 6 × 5 kg (11 lb). Frozen fish can be purchased in 15 kg (33 lb) blocks.

SOURCE

Fish is plentiful in the UK, because we are surrounded by water, although overfishing and pollution are having a detrimental effect on the supplies of certain fish. Most catches are made off Iceland, Scotland, the North Sea, Irish Sea and the English Channel. Salmon are caught in certain English and Scottish rivers, and are also extensively farmed. Frozen fish is imported from Scandinavia, Canada and Japan; the last two countries export frozen salmon to Britain.

STORAGE

1 Fresh fish are stored in a fish-box containing ice, in a separate refrigerator or part of a refrigerator used only for fish.
2 The temperature must be maintained just above freezing-point.
3 Frozen fish must be stored in a deep-freeze cabinet or compartment.
4 Smoked fish should be kept in a refrigerator.

QUALITY POINTS FOR BUYING

When buying whole fish the following points should be looked for to ensure freshness.

1 Eyes: bright, full and not sunken; no slime or cloudiness.
2 Gills: bright red in colour; no bacterial slime.
3 Flesh: firm and resilient so that when pressed the impression goes quickly. The fish must not be limp.
4 Scales: these should lie flat, and be moist and plentiful.
5 Skin: this should be covered with a fresh sea slime, or be smooth and moist, with a good sheen and no abrasions.
6 Smell: this must be pleasant, with no smell of ammonia or sourness.

GENERAL BUYING POINTS

1 The flesh should be translucent.
2 It should be firm and not ragged or gaping.
3 The flesh should not retain an indentation when pressed with a finger.
4 There should be no smell of ammonia or sour odours.
5 There must be no bruising or blood clots.
6 There should not be areas of discoloration.
7 Fish should be purchased daily.
8 If possible, it ought to be purchased direct from the market or supplier.
9 The fish should be well iced so that it arrives in good condition.
10 The flesh of the fish should not be damaged.
11 Fish may be bought on the bone or filleted. (The approximate loss from boning and waste is 50 per cent for flat fish, 60 per cent for round fish.)
12 Fillets of plaice and sole can be purchased according to weight. They are graded from 45 g (1½ oz) to 180 g (6 oz) per fillet and go up in weight by 15 g (½ oz).
13 Medium-sized fish are usually better than large fish, which may be coarse; small fish often lack flavour.

FOOD VALUE

Fish is as useful a source of animal protein as meat. The oily fish, such as sardines, mackerel, herrings and salmon contain vitamins A and D in their flesh; in white fish, such as halibut and cod, these vitamins are present in the liver.

The bones of sardines, whitebait and tinned salmon, when eaten, provide the body with calcium and phosphorus.

Since all fish contains protein it is a good body-building food and oily fish is useful for energy and as a protective food because of its vitamins. Owing to its fat content oily fish is not so digestible as white fish.

BASIC FISH PREPARATION

Unless otherwise stated, as a guide, allow 100 g (4 oz) fish off the bone and 150 g (6 oz) on the bone for a portion.

Filleting of round fish

1 Remove the head and clean thoroughly.
2 Remove first fillet by cutting along the backbone from head to tail.
3 Keeping the knife close to the bone, remove the fillet.
4 Reverse the fish and remove the second fillet in the same way, this time cutting from tail to head.

Filleting of flat fish with the exception of Dover sole

1 Using a filleting knife make an incision from the head to tail down the line of the backbone.
2 Remove each fillet, holding the knife almost parallel to the work surface and keeping the knife close to the bone.

Skinning of flat fish with the exception of Dover sole

1 Hold the fillet firmly at the tail end.
2 Cut the flesh as close to the tail as possible, as far as the skin.
3 Keep the knife parallel to the work surface, grip the skin firmly and move the knife from side to side to remove the skin.

Preparation of whole Dover sole

1 Hold the tail firmly, then cut and scrap the skin until sufficient is lifted to be gripped.
2 Pull the skin away from the tail to the head.
3 Both black and white skins may be removed in this way.
4 Trim the tail and side fins with fish scissors, remove the eyes and clean and wash the fish thoroughly.

Boning a round fish through the back

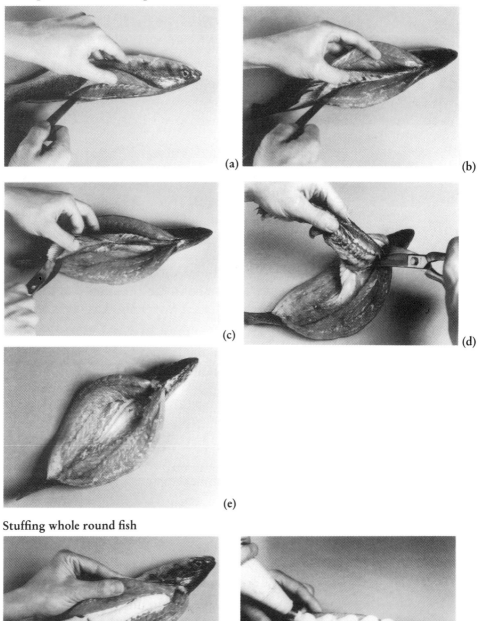

(a)

(b)

(c)

(d)

(e)

Stuffing whole round fish

(a)

(b)

Preparation of turbot

Allow approximately 300 g (12 oz) per portion on the bone.

1 Remove the head with a large chopping knife.
2 Cut off the side bones.
3 Commencing at the tail end, chop down the centre of the backbone, dividing the fish into two halves.
4 Divide each half into portions as required.

Note A $3\frac{1}{2}$ kg (7 lb) fish will yield approximately 10 portions.

METHODS OF COOKING FISH

Boiling

This method is suitable for whole fish, e.g. salmon, turbot, trout and certain cuts of fish, e.g. salmon, cod, turbot, halibut, brill, etc. In either case the fish should be completely immersed in the cooking liquid which can be water, water and milk, milk, fish stock (for white fish) or a court bouillon (water, vinegar, thyme, bay leaf, parsley stalks, onion, carrot, peppercorns) for oily fish.

Whole fish are covered with a cold liquid and brought to the boil, cut fish are usually placed in a simmering liquid.

Poaching

This is suitable for small whole fish, cuts or fillets. Barely cover the fish with fish stock, cover with a buttered paper, bring to the boil and cook in the oven without allowing the liquid to boil. The cooking liquor is usually used for the sauce which masks the fish.

Steaming

Any fish which can be poached or boiled may be cooked by steaming.

Grilling

This method is suitable for small whole fish, cuts and fillets. With the exception of fish cooked in butter and breadcrumbs, it is passed through seasoned flour, brushed with oil and grilled on both sides. When grilling fish under the salamander, grill bar marks may be made with a red-hot poker before cooking.

A gridiron holding fish for grilling

Shallow frying

Shallow fried fish, when termed meunière, is suitable for small whole fish, cuts and fillets. The fish is passed through seasoned flour, shallow fried on both sides, presentation side first, in clarified fat in a frying-pan. It is placed on a serving dish and masked with nut-brown butter, lemon juice, slice of lemon and chopped parsley.

Deep frying

This is suitable for small whole fish, cuts and fillets. The fish must be coated by one of the following:

1 flour
2 milk and flour
3 batter

The coating forms a surface to prevent penetration of the fat into the fish. Deep-fried fish is served with a quarter of lemon and/or a suitable sauce and fried parsley.

Baking

Many fish, whole (e.g. sea bass, mullet), portioned or filleted, may be baked. A savoury stuffing, e.g. with a duxelle, is often used, and the fish cooked on a bed of roots with sprigs of fresh herbs, e.g. fennel, parsley, in a buttered ovenproof dish with a lid. Whole fish can also be baked completely wrapped in sea salt or in pastry, e.g. puff, filo, brioche.

Roasting

Thick cuts of firm fish, e.g. salmon, turbot and monkfish, are suitable for roasting. The fish is usually portioned, lightly covered with oil and roasted in an oven in the usual way (do not over cook). Finely sliced vegetables and sprigs of herbs can be put in the roasting tray, and when the fish is cooked and removed the tray can be deglazed with a suitable wine to form the base of an accompanying sauce. Certain fish cuts, e.g. half a salmon steak, can have the skin left on both during cooking and for service. Alternatively, a crust of breadcrumbs mixed with chopped fresh herbs, or a duxelle-based mixture, or a light coating of creamed horseradish can be used.

CUTS OF FISH

Steaks	Thick slices of fish on or off the bone. Steaks of round fish, e.g. salmon and cod, may be called *darnes*. Steaks of flat fish, e.g. turbot and halibut, may be called *tronçons*
Fillets	Cuts of fish free from bone. A round fish yields two fillets, a flat fish four fillets.
Supremes	Prime cuts of fish without bone and skin, e.g. pieces cut from fillets of turbot, brill or salmon.
Goujons	Filleted fish cut into strips, approximately $8\,\text{cm} \times \frac{1}{2}\,\text{cm}$ ($3\,\text{in} \times \frac{1}{4}\,\text{in}$).
Paupiettes	Fillets of fish, e.g. sole, plaice and whiting, spread with a stuffing and rolled.
Plaited	Also known as *en tresse*, e.g. sole fillets cut into three even pieces lengthwise to within $1\,\text{cm}$ ($\frac{1}{2}\,\text{in}$) of the top, then neatly plaited.

Plaited (en tresse) fish can be prepared in two ways:

1 Fillets of fish, e.g. sole with the black-and-white skin removed, are cut into three even pieces lengthwise to within 1 cm ($\frac{1}{2}$ in) of the top. The fillets are then neatly plaited and may then be poached with a suitable sauce or egg and crumbed and deep fried.

2 Using two fish of different colours, e.g. salmon and brill, cut the filleted, skinned fish into strips 10 cm (4 in) long, 1 cm ($\frac{1}{2}$ in) wide. Use four strips of each colour per plait. Cover 10 cm (4 in) pieces of cardboard with foil, butter lightly and slide each plait on, poach gently and serve with a suitable sauce.

THE SMOKING OF FISH

Fish can be either cold smoked or hot smoked. In either case if the fish are not to be consumed immediately they are salted before smoking. This can be done either by soaking them in a brine solution (strong enough to keep a potato afloat) or rubbing in dry salt. This is to improve flavour and help the keeping quality.

Cold smoking

This takes place at a temperature of approximately 24°C (75°F) which smokes but does not cook the fish. Smoke boxes can be brought or improvised. Sawdust is used and different woods can impart different flavours. Herbs, e.g. thyme and rosemary, can also be incorporated. Fish can either be left whole or filleted. Smoked salmon is prepared by cold smoking usually over a fire of oak chips and peat. Kippers, haddock and young halibut are also cold smoked, as are bloaters which are lightly salted herring smoked without the gut being removed, which is what gives them the more pronounced gamey flavour.

Hot smoking

This takes place at approximately 82°C (180°F). Eel, trout, buckling, bloater (ungutted herring), sprats and mackerel are smoked and lightly cooked at one and the same time.

RECIPES

1 – Bouillabaisse

This is a thick, full-bodied fish stew – sometimes served as a soup – for which there are many variations. When made in the south of France, a selection of Mediterranean fish is used. If made in the north of France the following recipe could be typical.

	4 portions	10 portions
assorted prepared fish, e.g. red mullet, whiting, sole, gurnard, small conger eel, John Dory, crawfish tail	1½ kg (3 lb)	3¾ kg (7½ lb)
mussels (optional)	500 ml (1 pt)	1¼ kg (2½ pt)
chopped onion or white of leek	75 g (3 oz)	180 g (7½ oz)
crushed garlic	10 g (½ oz)	25 g (1¼ oz)
white wine	125 ml (¼ pt)	300 ml (⅝ pt)
water	500 ml (1 pt)	1¼ litre (2½ pt)
tomatoes, skinned, deseeded, diced *or*	100 g (4 oz)	250 g (10 oz)
tomato purée	25 g (1 oz)	60 g (2½ oz)
pinch of saffron		
bouquet garni (fennel, aniseed, parsley, celery)		
olive oil	125 ml (¼ pt)	300 ml (⅝ pt)
salt and pepper		
chopped parsley	5 g (¼ oz)	12 g (⅝ oz)
butter ⎤ beurre manié	25 g (1 oz)	60 g (2½ oz)
flour ⎦	10 g (½ oz)	25 g (1¼ oz)
French bread		

I portion provides:

689 kcals/2881 kJ
42.3 g fat
(of which 8.5 g saturated)
4.8 g carbohydrate
(of which 2.1 g sugars)
protein 67.6 g
0.5 g fibre

1 Clean, de-scale and wash the fish. Cut into 2 cm (1 in) pieces on the bone, the heads may be removed. Clean the mussels and leave in their shells.
2 Place the cut fish, with mussels and crawfish on top, in a clean pan.
3 Simmer the onion, garlic, wine, water, tomato, saffron and bouquet garni for 20 minutes.
4 Pour on to the fish, add the oil and parsley, bring to the boil and simmer for approximately 15 minutes.
5 Correct the seasoning and thicken with beurre manié.

6 The liquor may be served first as a soup, followed by the fish accompanied by French bread which has been toasted, left plain, or rubbed with garlic.

Note If using soft fish, e.g. whiting, add it 10 minutes after the other fish.

2 ~ Brioche bun filled with seafood perfumed with sauternes and orange

(DAVID PITCHFORD)

	4 portions	10 portions
fish stock	500 ml (1 pt)	1¼ litre (2½ pt)
double cream	250 ml (½ pt)	625 ml (1¼ pt)
fresh orange juice	125 ml (¼ pt)	300 ml (⅝ pt)
Sauternes	125 ml (¼ pt)	300 ml (⅝ pt)
tomatoes, skinned, deseeded and quartered	100 g (4 oz)	250 g (10 oz)
julienne of the green part of leek	50 g (2 oz)	125 g (5 oz)
brioche buns		
fresh scallops (with roes)	4	10
Dover sole fillets, cut into 8 (20) goujons	100 g (4 oz)	250 g (10 oz)
salmon, cut into 8 (20) slices	100 g (4 oz)	250 g (10 oz)
red mullet, cut into 8 (20) slices	100 g (4 oz)	250 g (10 oz)
clarified butter	50 g (2 oz)	125 g (5 oz)
chopped chives		

1 Reduce the fish stock, double cream, orange juice and Sauternes to the consistency of oil.
2 Cut the tomatoes into neat diamonds.
3 Lightly blanch the leek in boiling water and refresh.
4 Remove the top of each brioche and hollow out a little of the centre, retaining the lids. Keep warm.
5 Carefully toss the prepared fish in clarified butter and remove from the pan, discarding any excess butter.
6 Pass the Sauternes and orange reduction through a very fine chinois into the pan used for cooking the fish.

7 At service time add the fish to the reduction and gently reheat.
8 Place the warm brioche buns on hot plates.
9 Add the tomato diamonds, julienne of leek and chopped chives a few
   seconds before spooning the fish in and around the brioche buns.
10 Place the lids at an attractive angle and serve.

Notes This dish may be served as a first or fish course.

Any suitable combination of fish may be substituted for those given. In
a professional kitchen this dish may provide the means to use previously
prepared fish, e.g. lobster.

– Brioche paste

	10 small buns
yeast	12 g (½ oz)
milk	25 g (1 oz)
sieved strong flour	225 g (9 oz)
pinch of salt	
butter	125 g (5 oz)
sugar	12 g (½ oz)
beaten eggs	125 g (5 oz)

1 Dissolve the yeast in warm milk.
2 Make a leaven with 100 g (4 oz) of the flour, salt and dissolved yeast.
   Ferment for approximately 1½ hours in a warm place.
3 Cream the butter and sugar and add the beaten eggs.
4 Make the paste with the remaining flour and butter and egg mixture.
   Knead for 5 minutes.
5 Add the leaven to the paste and knead for a further 2 minutes. Cover
   and ferment for a further 20 minutes, beating on completion.
6 Use to one-third fill lightly greased brioche moulds and prove to the
   top of the moulds in a warm place.
7 Bake for 20 minutes in a hot oven (220°C, 435°F).

T 3 ~ Roast cod with artichoke mash

(MARTIN WEBB)

	4 portions	10 portions
portions of cod (scaled, skin on and bones out)	700 g (1¾ lb)	2¼ kg (4½ lb)
cream	1 dl (⅕ pt)	250 ml (½ pt)
freshly chopped parsley	1 tbsp	2–3 tbsp
salt		
ground black pepper		
olive oil	100 ml (⅕ pt)	250 ml (½ pt)
lemon oil	100 ml (⅕ pt)	250 ml (½ pt)
lemons	2	5
fresh watercress		

1 Once the cod has been filleted you need to de-scale, bone and cut the fillets into four portions cut across the fillet on angle. Make sure the skin and flesh are dry.

2 Peel the artichokes in a little lemon water (to stop the discolouring).

3 Drain off the water, place into a saucepan and cover with fresh water and salt to taste. Bring to the boil and treat as for mashed potatoes.

4 Once cooked, mash coarsely adding cream to obtain a moist, soft texture. Season with freshly ground black pepper and more salt if needed. Add the parsley and a little of the olive oil. Either keep warm or reheat.

5 To roast off the cod, have the oven on a high heat, using a thick cast steel frying pan which must be very hot before starting to cook the cod.

6 When the frying pan is very hot, add a little of the olive oil (only enough to coat the bottom of the pan). Season up the cod fillets with salt and ground black pepper and place skin side down. Leave on top of the flame for about 1–2 minutes before placing in the oven to roast. Do not turn over.

7 The fish should be cooked within 4–6 minutes. When ready remove from pan placing on to a hot plate *'skin side up'*. This should be dark and crispy. Place a kitchen spoon of the hot artichoke mash next to it, garnish with a wedge of lemon and a nice size bunch of picked watercress which has been previously washed.

8 Lastly, drizzle the roast cod with a little lemon oil and serve.

I 4 – Cod darnes on a bed of spätzle with a tomato butter sauce and smoked bacon

(PHILLIP ACCORSINI)

	4 portions	10 portions
Fish		
cod	400 g (1 lb)	1 kg (2.2 lb)
virgin olive oil	100 ml (4 fl oz)	250 ml (10 fl oz)
paprika	50 g (2 oz)	100 g (4 oz)
lemons	2	4
garlic	$\frac{1}{3}$ clove	1 clove
Spätzle		
milk	$62\frac{1}{2}$ ml ($2\frac{1}{2}$ fl oz)	$162\frac{1}{2}$ ml ($6\frac{1}{2}$ fl oz)
eggs	4	10
flour	$162\frac{1}{2}$ g ($6\frac{1}{2}$ oz)	400 g (1 lb)
salt		
pepper		
olive oil	50 ml (2 fl oz)	125 ml (5 fl oz)
Sauce		
plum tomatoes	200 g ($\frac{1}{2}$ lb)	600 g ($1\frac{1}{2}$ lb)
shallots	150 g (6 oz)	350 g (14 oz)
garlic	$\frac{1}{3}$ clove	1 clove
cream	100 ml (4 fl oz)	250 ml (10 fl oz)
white wine vinegar	50 ml (2 fl oz)	125 ml (5 fl oz)
peppercorns	3	9
fresh bay leaves	2	6
unsalted butter	150 g (6 oz)	350 g (14 oz)
smoked bacon (loin)	150 g (6 oz)	350 g (14 oz)
virgin olive oil	25 ml (1 fl oz)	50 ml (2 fl oz)
fresh basil	$\frac{1}{2}$ bunch	$1\frac{1}{2}$ bunches

1 Cut the cod into darnes and marinade in garlic, olive oil, paprika and lemon juice. Reserve to one side.

2 For the spätzle: sieve the flour, add the salt, pepper, milk and eggs. Mix to a smooth paste.

3 Place small pot of water on stove, season and put oil in water.

4 Push the dough mixture through a colander over the boiling water and cook for 2 minutes. (You should have irregular shapes. The water with oil stops the spätzle sticking.)

5 Remove from water and refresh in cold water and drain.

6 Sauté the spätzle in a small amount of olive oil and season. Cook until golden brown. Drain and serve.

7 For the sauce: blanch the plum tomatoes, skin them and remove seeds.

8 Cut tomatoes into rough squares and reserve.

9 Place vinegar in a saucepan with garlic, peppercorns and a bay leaf. Reduce by half.

10 Now add the cream and cool to blood temperature.

11 Cut cold butter into squares and whisk into cream. Reserve in a warm place.

12 Finely chop shallots, garlic and basil. Reserve.

13 Cut bacon into thin strips and sauté until crisp.

14 Season and seal the cod in a frying pan. Finish baking in the oven at 180–200°C (300–400°F) for 6–7 minutes.

15 Remove from oven, cover and reserve.

16 Sauté the shallots and garlic without colour then add tomatoes carefully.

17 Strain the butter sauce over the tomatoes and remove from heat. Add chopped basil and season. Reserve to one side in a warm place.

18 To serve: place the spätzle on your plate. Position the cod on top. Spoon the tomato butter sauce over the cod. Garnish with black olives and sprigs of fresh basil.

5 – Cod poached in white wine, tomato, garlic and parsley (Portuguese style)

	4 portions	10 portions
cod fillet or cod steaks	400 g (1 lb)	1¼ kg (2½ lb)
finely chopped shallot or small onion	1	2
olive oil	1 tbsp	2½ tbsp
tomatoes, skinned, deseeded and diced	300 g (12 oz)	1 kg (2 lb)
small garlic clove, crushed	1	2
chopped parsley		
white wine	125 ml (¼ pt)	300 ml (⅝ pt)
fish stock	125 ml (¼ pt)	300 ml (⅝ pt)
salt and pepper		
butter	50 g (2 oz)	125 g (5 oz)

Using 400 g cod fillet
Recipe provides:

238 kcals/992 kJ
14.3 fat
(of which 7.3 g saturated)
4 g carbohydrate
(of which 3.4 g sugars)
18.5 g protein
0.8 g fibre

1 Place the washed cod in a buttered ovenproof dish.

2 Cook the shallot in the oil without colour and add to the fish.

3 Add the tomatoes, garlic and parsley, and pour over the fish.
4 Add the wine, fish stock and season lightly with salt.
5 Cover with buttered paper and poach gently.
6 Remove the cod and drain.
7 Reduce the cooking liquor, mix in the butter, correct seasoning and add a pinch of fresh chopped parsley.
8 Pour over the cod and serve.

Note   This recipe can be used with any white fish, cooked on or off the bone. Always remove any bones or skin before coating with sauce. Filleted cod can be cooked in any of the other ways given for poached white fish.

6 – Fillet of halibut with a herb crust and lemon sauce

(Anna Miller)

	4 portions	10 portions
Fish		
halibut steaks	4 × 150 g (4 × 6 oz)	10 × 150 g (10 × 6 oz)
6 mm ($\frac{1}{2}$ in) thick		
breadcrumbs (dry)	100 g (4 oz)	200 g (8 oz)
sesame seeds	50 g (2 oz)	100 g (4 oz)
fresh mixed herbs	1 tbsp	3 tbsp
melted butter	50 g (2 oz)	225 g (5 oz)
sprigs of flat parsley for garnish		
Sauce		
shallots chopped	100 g (4 oz)	250 g (10 oz)
white wine	125 ml ($\frac{1}{4}$ pt)	250 ml ($\frac{1}{2}$ pt)
fish stock	250 ml ($\frac{1}{2}$ pt)	500 ml (1 pt)
dill stalks		
bay leaf, thyme		
cream (double)	250 ml ($\frac{1}{2}$ pt)	500 ml (1 pt)
unsalted butter (very cold)	200 g (8 oz)	400 g (1 lb)
lemon juice		

1 Put the breadcrumbs, sesame seeds, mixed herbs into a tray and mix together.
2 Season the halibut steaks with salt, pepper and paprika.
3 Put melted butter into a dish.
4 Coat the halibut in butter then in the sesame mix.

5 Put into a buttered tray suitable for grilling. Refrigerate.
6 For the sauce: put the shallots, a teaspoon of butter, dill stalks into a saucepan over a medium heat. Sweat off until lightly brown, add white wine. Allow to reduce for 5 minutes, add fish stock.
7 Simmer until you are left with about one-third of what you started with.
8 Add cream and allow to boil till the bubbles become large (2–3 minutes).
9 Cut the butter into cubes. Pull the saucepan slightly off the heat and gently whisk in the butter a little at a time. (Do not boil.)
10 Pass through a fine chinois, season with salt and pepper and fresh lemon juice. Keep the sauce warm to one side while you cook the fish.
11 Put the halibut under the grill and brown gently. Finish cooking in a moderate oven for 10–15 minutes or until firm.
12 To serve, place the fish on to the centre of the plates, put the sauce around it and garnish with a sprig of flat parsley.

Sole, plaice, turbot, halibut, hake, cod, fresh haddock, monkfish, whiting, or John Dory may be used for recipes 7 and 8.

7 – Fillets of fish on mushroom purée with cheese sauce (Cubat)

	4 portions	10 portions
button mushrooms	200 g (8 oz)	500 g (1¼ lb)
fish fillets	400–600 g (1–1½ lb)	1¼–1½ kg (2½–3 lb)
butter	50 g (2 oz)	125 g (5 oz)
Mornay sauce	250 ml (½ pt)	600 ml (1¼ pt)
slices of truffle	8	20

1 Roughly slice the mushrooms and cook in a little fish stock.
2 Poach the fish in butter and the mushroom cooking liquor.
3 Drain the fish well, reduce the cooking liquor and add it to the Mornay sauce.
4 Thoroughly dry the mushrooms and chop, place in serving dish.
5 Place the fish on top of the mushroom purée and add 2 slices of truffle on each portion.
6 Correct the seasoning and the consistency of the Mornay sauce.
7 Coat with the sauce, glaze and serve.

Note This is a simple classic dish with an excellent blend of flavours. Because truffles are so expensive it may not always be possible to use them. Using the basic flavours of cheese sauce and mushroom there is scope for variation, e.g. asparagus tips, prawns or shrimps, and turned mushrooms.

8 – Fillets of fish in a baked jacket potato with prawns and white wine and cheese sauce (Otéro)

	4 portions	10 portions
large baked jacket potatoes	2	5
fish fillets	400–600 g	1¼ kg
	(1–1½ lb)	(2½–3 lb)
shelled prawns	250 ml (½ pt)	600 ml (1¼ pt)
white wine sauce	125 ml (¼ pt)	300 ml (⅝ pt)
Mornay sauce	250 ml (½ pt)	600 ml (1¼ pt)
grated Parmesan cheese	50 g (2 oz)	125 g (5 oz)

> 1 portion provides:
>
> 538 kcals/2216 kJ
> 19 g fat
> (of which 9.3 g saturated)
> 42.1 g carbohydrate
> (of which 4.6 g sugars)
> 46.9 g protein
> 2.7 g fibre

1 Bake the potatoes, cut into halves, scoop out half of the flesh.
2 Cut the fish into suitable sized pieces, poach in fish stock and drain.
3 Strain off the cooking liquor, reduce and use in the Mornay sauce.
4 Mix the prawns with the white wine sauce and place in the base of the potatoes.
5 Add the fish, coat with Mornay sauce, sprinkle with grated cheese, gratinate and serve.

Note Using the basic principle of this dish, a number of variations can be made using different combinations of ingredients and sauces, e.g. a lobster, shrimp or white wine sauce in the bottom of the potato, then the fish, and finished with Mornay sauce.

9 – Grilled fish in butter and breadcrumbs (St Germain)

1 Clean and prepare the fish (usually filleted).
2 Pass through seasoned flour, melted butter or margarine and white breadcrumbs.
3 Neaten with a palette knife.
4 Place on a greased baking tray, brush with melted butter, margarine or oil.

5 Grill on both sides under salamander.

6 Serve with a sauceboat of béarnaise sauce (page 105).

Note As a variation, a little grated cheese or some chopped fresh herbs can be mixed in with the breadcrumbs.

10 – Grilled fish in butter and breadcrumbs with fried banana (caprice)

1 As for recipe 9, points 1–5.

2 Peel and halve a banana, pass through flour and shallow fry in butter.

3 Place half a banana on each portion of fish and serve a sauceboat of sauce Robert separately.

T 11 – Grilled Dover sole fillets with autumn salad and parsley pesto

(SHAUN HILL)

	4 portions	10 portions
fillets from 2 × 14 oz Dover soles	8	20
frisée lettuce	1	2½
sprigs corn salad – mâche, lamb's lettuce	4	10
plum tomatoes – skinned and deseeded	2	5
top-quality olive oil	2 tbsp	5 tbsp
lemon	1	2–3
Parsley pesto		
lemon, juice from	1	2–3
pine kernels	10 g (½ oz)	35 g (1½ oz)
fish stock – or water	50 ml (2 fl oz)	125 ml (¼ pt)
olive oil	50 ml (2 fl oz)	125 ml (¼ pt)
peeled shallot	1	2–3
peeled garlic clove	1	2–3
flat parsley	50 g (2 oz)	125 g (5 oz)
salt and pepper		

1 Make the dressing by blending in a liquidiser first the stock, pine kernels, garlic and shallot, then adding the olive oil, parsley, lemon juice and seasoning.

2 Wash and dry the lettuces. Arrange these round the outside of four plates. Cut the tomato into dice and sprinkle on top. Drizzle a little olive oil over the leaves.

3 Put a tablespoon of the parsley pesto dressing in the centre of each plate.

4 Grill the sole fillets. These cook quickly and depending on thickness will be cooked in 4–5 minutes. Squeeze lemon on the fish.

12 – Sole Colbert

1 Remove the black and white skins.
2 Remove the head and side fins. Clean well and wash.
3 Make an incision down the backbone on one side and proceed as though filleting, to within an inch of the sides.
4 Break the backbone in two or three places.
5 Curl the opened fillets back.
6 Pané, deep fry at 175°C and drain.
7 Carefully remove the backbone.
8 Serve as for fried fish with one or two slices of parsley butter at the last moment in the opened part of the fish.

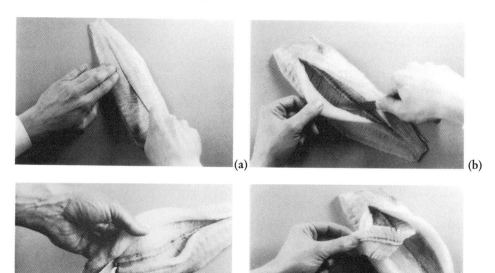

Preparation of sole for sole colbert

13 – Hake with shrimps, wild mushrooms and shrimp butter sauce

	4 portions	**10 portions**
hake slices on the bone or filleted	4 × 150 g (6 oz)	10 × 150 g (6 oz)
Court bouillon		
white wine	250 ml ($\frac{1}{2}$ pt)	300 ml ($\frac{5}{8}$ pt)
water	250 ml ($\frac{1}{2}$ pt)	300 ml ($\frac{5}{8}$ pt)
sliced onion	50 g (2 oz)	125 g (5 oz)
bouquet garni with fennel		
pinch of saffron soaked in boiling water		
salt and peppercorns		
butter	25 g (1 oz)	60 g (2$\frac{1}{2}$ oz)
oil	1 tbsp	2$\frac{1}{2}$ tbsp
small chopped garlic clove	1	2$\frac{1}{2}$
chopped shallot	1	2$\frac{1}{2}$
fresh ceps *or* } sliced	200 g (8 oz)	500 g (1$\frac{1}{4}$ lb)
dried ceps	25 g (1 oz)	60 g (2$\frac{1}{2}$ oz)
chopped parsley	5 g ($\frac{1}{4}$ oz)	12 g ($\frac{5}{8}$ oz)
chopped tarragon	5 g ($\frac{1}{4}$ oz)	12 g ($\frac{5}{8}$ oz)
grated cheese	50 g (2 oz)	125 g (5 oz)

> 1 portion provides:
>
> 555 kcals/2303 kJ
> 40.2 g fat
> (of which 21.4 g saturated)
> 1.8 g carbohydrate
> (of which 1.4 g sugars)
> 37 g protein
> 0.8 g fibre

1 To make the court bouillon, simmer all ingredients for 20 minutes and strain. Add the hake to the court bouillon and three-quarters cook.
2 Heat butter and the oil in a pan.
3 Add the garlic, shallot, ceps, parsley, tarragon and cook gently for 10 minutes; evaporate all moisture and season lightly.
4 Drain the fish, remove skin and bone.
5 Put the ceps in a shallow ovenproof dish. Lay the fish on top and sprinkle with grated cheese.
6 Bake in an oven at 220°C (425°F) until browned.
7 Serve a shrimp butter sauce separately (see below).

– Shrimp butter sauce

Reduction	
white wine	125 ml ($\frac{1}{4}$ pt)
wine vinegar	30 ml ($\frac{1}{16}$ pt)
crushed peppercorns	6

court bouillon	4 tbsp
egg yolks	2
butter, melted	100 g (4 oz)
salt and pepper	
picked shrimps	125 ml ($\frac{1}{4}$ pt)
chopped tarragon and parsley	

1 Make the reduction, add the court bouillon and reduce by a half, strain.
2 Add yolks and whisk over gentle heat to a sabayon.
3 Remove from the heat, slowly whisk in butter, correct seasoning, strain.
4 Add the shrimps, parsley and tarragon and serve.

14 – Poached hake with cockles and prawns

	4 portions	10 portions
finely chopped onion	100 g (4 oz)	250 g (10 oz)
oil	1 tbsp	$2\frac{1}{2}$ tbsp
fish stock	250 ml ($\frac{1}{2}$ pt)	600 ml ($1\frac{1}{4}$ pt)
chopped parsley	1 tbsp	$2\frac{1}{2}$ tbsp
hake steaks or fillets	4 × 150 g (6 oz)	10 × 150 g (6 oz)
shelled cockles	8–12	20–30
shelled prawns	8–12	20–30
salt and pepper		
hard boiled eggs, coarsely chopped	2	5
chopped parsley		

1 Lightly colour the onion in the oil, add fish stock and parsley and simmer for 10–15 minutes.
2 Place the fish in a shallow ovenproof dish, add cockles and prawns.
3 Pour on the fish stock and onion, season lightly.
4 Poach gently, remove any bones and skin from the fish.
5 If there is an excess of liquid, strain and reduce.
6 Serve coated with the unthickened cooking liquor, sprinkled with the egg and parsley.

15 – Stir-fried fish

Any firmly textured fish is suitable for stir frying, e.g. sole, turbot, brill and perch. The cleaned, filleted and skinned fish should be cut into pieces 2×4 cm ($1–1\frac{1}{2}$ in) which may then be used fresh or marinated for 15 minutes. Shrimp, prawn and squid are also used. Prawns should be shelled and de-veined by holding the tail firmly and making a small cut along the centre of the back. The black vein can be pulled out and thrown away. Squid should be cleaned and lightly scored in two directions. This is so that it can be quickly cooked in about 30 seconds and remain tender, delicate and juicy.

Stir-fry dishes originate mainly from Chinese cookery and are traditionally prepared in a wok. The whole essence of stir-fry cookery is that the food is only cooked to order and is cooked quickly over fierce heat. Because of this all ingredients to be used in the dish must be prepared and ready at hand before cooking begins.

EXAMPLES OF FISH	ADDITIONAL INGREDIENTS	MARINADE INGREDIENTS	SAUCE INGREDIENTS
shrimp	spring onion, shallots	oil, garlic	soy sauce
prawn	cucumber, courgette	ginger, wine	oyster sauce
lobster	mushrooms, chicken	salt, pepper	wine
scallops	ginger, wine	sugar	bean paste (yellow or black)

16 – Stir-fried brill, broccoli and mushrooms

	4 portions	10 portions
fillet of brill	400 g (1 lb)	$1\frac{1}{4}$ kg ($2\frac{1}{2}$ lb)
oil for frying (groundnut or corn)		
sliced, peeled ginger root	6	15
garlic cloves, peeled and sliced	1–2	3–4
shallots finely chopped	1–2	3–4
dry sherry	1 tbsp	3 tbsp
broccoli sprigs (blanched)	100 g (4 oz)	250 g (10 oz)
mushrooms (sliced)	100 g (4 oz)	250 g (10 oz)

173

Sauce

fish or chicken stock	60 ml ($\frac{1}{8}$ pt)	150 ml ($\frac{1}{3}$ pt)
oyster sauce	30 ml ($\frac{1}{16}$ pt)	75 ml ($\frac{1}{6}$ pt)
soy sauce	1 tsp	2–3 tsp
potato flour or cornflour	$\frac{1}{2}$ tsp	1$\frac{1}{2}$ tsp

If required to be marinated (15 minutes) the following could be used:

peeled root ginger, chopped and squeezed to extract juice (discard the pulp)	1 cm ($\frac{1}{2}$ in)	2 cm (1 in)
sherry or wine	1 tbsp	1 tbsp
egg white lightly beaten	1	2
salt, pepper, sugar		
cornflour	1 tsp	2 tsp

1 Heat the oil in a wok or thick frying pan.
2 Add the garlic, allow to sizzle, add the shallots and ginger.
3 Add the fish pieces, separate and cook for approximately 1 minute.
4 Add the mushrooms, broccoli sprigs, toss and cook for 30 seconds.
5 Add the wine.
6 Pour in the well mixed sauce, stir to the boil and serve.

Notes
- After (2), the garlic, shallots and ginger can be removed if required as the flavours will have been released into the oil.
- This recipe can be prepared with any other type of suitable fish.
- To lessen the risk of the fish breaking up, the fish pieces can be very quickly fried in deep hot oil for 30 seconds, then removed and added at a later stage.

17 – Shallow-fried fish with artichokes and potatoes (Murat)

	4 portions	10 portions
fish fillets	400–600 g (1–1$\frac{1}{2}$ lb)	1$\frac{1}{2}$ kg (2$\frac{1}{2}$–3 lb)
potatoes, peeled	300 g (12 oz)	750 g (2 lb)
artichoke bottoms, cooked in a blanc	2	5
butter	100 g (4 oz)	250 g (10 oz)
oil	60 ml ($\frac{1}{8}$ pt)	125 ml ($\frac{1}{4}$ pt)
juice of lemon	1	2
chopped parsley		

1 Cut the fish into goujons.
2 Cut the potatoes into short batons – $1\frac{1}{2} \times \frac{1}{2} \times \frac{1}{2}$ cm ($\frac{3}{4} \times \frac{1}{4} \times \frac{1}{4}$ in) – and shallow fry in butter and oil and drain in a colander.
3 Cut the artichokes into quarters or eighths, shallow fry and drain on top of the potatoes.
4 Flour the fish, shake off the surplus, and shallow fry quickly in oil and butter until golden grown. Place the fish on a serving dish.
5 Prepare 50 g (2 oz) noisette butter in a clean pan, add the potatoes, artichokes and seasoning, toss carefully to mix.
6 Sprinkle with lemon juice, mask over the fish, finish with chopped parsley to serve.

Note   If artichokes are unavailable, mushrooms (button or wild) can be used.

18 – Monkfish

Also known as angler fish, monkfish has firm, white flesh and is prepared by skinning, removing any dark patches, filleting and removing any gristle before cooking. It is suitable for adding to bouillabaisse and fish soups and can be prepared and cooked in a variety of ways, e.g. as for any of the cod or hake recipes.

19 – Fried monkfish scallops

1 Cut the thick part of the monkfish into slices 1–$1\frac{1}{2}$ cm ($\frac{1}{2}$–$\frac{3}{4}$ in) thick, flatten slightly.
2 Pass them through: (a) milk and flour, (b) a light batter, or (c) flour, egg and fresh breadcrumbs.
3 Deep fry, drain well and serve with quarters of lemon and a suitable sauce, e.g. tartare or tomato.

20 – Shallow-fried monkfish scallops

1 Prepare the monkfish as in stage 1 of previous recipe.
2 Pass them through a beaten egg mixed with a tablespoon of oil, salt and pepper and fine breadcrumbs.
3 Firm the coating with a palette knife, shake off surplus crumbs.
4 Shallow fry on both sides in butter and oil.
5 Serve with quarters of lemon and a suitable sauce.

T 21 – Fillet of monkfish in fresh lime sauce

(SOMERSET MOORE)

	4 portions	10 portions
trimmed monkfish fillets (1 per person)	1 kg (2 lb)	2½ kg (5 lb)
salt and pepper		
limes, juice of	3	7
lime, zest of	1	2½
finely chopped shallots	1 tbsp	2½ tbsp
double cream	250 ml (½ pt)	600 ml (1¼ pt)
unsalted butter	100 g (4 oz)	250 g (10 oz)
puff pastry fleurons	100 g (4 oz)	250 g (10 oz)
sprigs of dill or parsley		

1 Score the fillets, season and sauté until cooked through. Remove and keep warm.
2 Add lime juice and zest and shallots to pan, simmer until soft, not coloured. Reduce until 2 tablespoons remain (5 tablespoons for 10 portions).
3 Add cream, boil until thickened.
4 Remove from heat, whisk in cubes of cold butter.
5 Slice monkfish, coat plates with sauce and arrange monkfish in a circle.
6 Garnish with fleurons and dill or parsley to serve.

22 – Roast monkfish

	4 portions	10 portions
prepared monkfish	400–600 g (1–1½ lb)	1¼–1¾ kg (2½–3½ lb)
olive oil	30 ml (1⁄16 pt)	125 g (¼ pt)
large sprig of rosemary	1	2–3
garlic clove, crushed	1	2–3
lemon	1	2–3
butter, melted	50 g (2 oz)	125 g (5 oz)
salt and pepper		

1 Marinade the fish with the oil, rosemary, garlic, grated rind of the lemon, salt and pepper for 1 hour.

2 Place the fish and marinade in a roasting dish and cover with melted butter.
3 Roast in a hot oven 200°C (400°F) for approximately 15 minutes, squeeze over some lemon juice and serve.

Note Variation of additional flavourings can include, for example, mushrooms (button or wild), sliced shallots and chopped unsmoked bacon.

23 – Pot roasted monkfish

Proceed as above cooking the fish in a covered dish. A little dry white or red wine or vermouth can be added and tarragon or fennel used in place of rosemary.

24 – Eels

These must be bought live and kept alive until required because once killed they toughen and deteriorate quickly. A sharp blow to the head will kill them. To remove the skins, make an incision skin deep around the neck, ease the skin back and using a cloth with a firm grip tear off the skin in one move. Slit the bellies, gut them and remove the coagulated blood from the back bones. Cut off the fins and wash well in running water. They can then be cut into pieces 6 cm (3 in) or filleted according to dish requirements.

Eels can be prepared and cooked in a variety of ways: stewed, poached, braised, shallow or deep fried. They can also be made into pâtés, pies and terrines.

25 – Fried eels with spring onion and mustard sauce

	4 portions	10 portions
prepared eels cut in 8 cm (3 in) pieces	600 g (1½ lb)	2¼ kg (4½ lb)
onion, sliced	100 g (4 oz)	250 g (10 oz)
carrot, sliced	100 g (4 oz)	250 g (10 oz)
white wine	250 ml (½ pt)	600 ml (1¼ pt)
bouquet garni		
salt and pepper		

Sauce

hard-boiled egg yolks	3	8
Dijon mustard	1 tbsp	2½ tbsp
olive oil	125 ml (¼ pt)	300 ml (⅝ pt)
spring onions, chopped	4	10
flour, egg, breadcrumbs		

1 Simmer the eels, onions, carrots, wine, bouquet garni, seasoning until tender.
2 Remove the eels, drain and dry well.
3 Prepare the sauce by mashing the egg yolks and mixing in the mustard and oil, finally add the spring onions, salt and pepper.
4 Pané the eel pieces and deep fry at 195°C (350°F).
5 Serve accompanied with the sauce.

Note   This dish can also be prepared with boned-out eel pieces.

26 – Eels in white wine, onions and parsley

	4 portions	10 portions
prepared eels	600 g (1½ lb)	2¼ kg (4½ lb)
onion, chopped	200 g (½ lb)	500 g (1¼ lb)
butter	50 g (2 oz)	125 g (5 oz)
white wine	125 ml (¼ pt)	250 ml (⅝ pt)
bouquet garni		
slices of stale bread	4	10
butter	100 g (4 oz)	250 g (10 oz)
potatoes diced	200 g (½ lb)	500 g (1¼ lb)
oil or butter for frying		
chopped parsley		

1 Gently sweat the onions in butter without colour.
2 Add the pieces of eel.
3 Season lightly, add the wine and bouquet garni.
4 Cover with a lid, poach gently until tender, approximately 30–45 minutes.
5 Remove the eel, reduce the liquid by half and lightly thicken with kneaded butter if required.
6 Mix in the parsley and serve on bread croûtons, garnished with the diced potatoes.

27 – Fricassée of eels with fine herbs

	4 portions	10 portions
filleted eels cut into 8 cm (3 in) pieces	600 g (1½ lb)	2¼ kg (4½ lb)
butter	50 g (2 oz)	125 g (5 oz)
shallots, finely chopped	50 g (2 oz)	125 g (5 oz)
dry white or a light red wine	60 ml (⅛ pt)	150 ml (⅓ pt)
salt and pepper		
chopped tarragon, chives, chervil		

1 Gently fry the eel pieces in butter without colouring.
2 Add the shallots, cover with a lid and sweat gently until the shallots are tender. Pour off any surplus fat.
3 Add the wine, reduce slightly, correct the seasoning.
4 Serve sprinkled with herbs.

28 – Mousse, mousseline, quenelle

These are all made from the same basic mixture known as forcemeat. Salmon, sole, trout, brill, turbot, halibut, whiting, pike and lobster can all be used for fish forcemeat in the preparation of mousse of sole, mousselines of salmon, quenelles of turbot, all of which would be served with a suitable sauce, e.g. white wine, a butter sauce, lobster, shrimp, saffron and mushroom.

29 – Fish forcemeat or farce

	4 portions	10 portions
fish, free from skin and bone	300 g (12 oz)	1 kg (2 lb)
salt, white pepper		
egg whites	1–2	4–5
double cream, ice cold	250–500 ml (½–1 pt)	600 ml–1¼ litre (1¼–2½ pt)

1 Process the fish and seasoning to a fine purée.
2 Continue processing, slowly adding the egg white(s) until thoroughly absorbed.

3 Pass the mixture through a fine sieve and place into a shallow pan or bowl.
4 Leave on ice or in refrigerator until very cold.
5 Beating the mixture continuously, slowly incorporate the cream.

Notes When half the cream is incorporated, test the consistency and seasoning by cooking a teaspoonful in a small pan of simmering water. If the mixture is very firm, a little more cream may be added, then test the mixture again and continue until the mixture is of a mousse consistency.

As mousses are cooked in buttered moulds in a bain-marie in the oven and turned out for service, the mixture should not be made too soft otherwise they will break up.

Mousses are made in buttered moulds, usually one per portion but larger moulds for 2 to 4 can be made if required. It is sounder practice to use individual moulds because for large moulds the mousse needs to be of a firmer consistency to prevent them collapsing. They are cooked in a bain-marie in a moderate oven or in a low pressure steamer.

Mousselines are moulded using two tablespoons, dipping the spoons frequently into boiling water to prevent the mixture sticking. They are normally moulded into shallow buttered trays, covered with salted water or fish stock, covered with buttered greaseproof paper and gently poached in the oven or steamed.

Quenelles are made in various shapes and sizes as required:

1 moulded with dessert or teaspoons;
2 piped with a small plain tube.

They are cooked in the same way as mousselines. When making lobster mousse, use raw lobster meat and ideally some raw lobster roe which gives authentic colour to the mousse when cooked. For scallop mousse use cooked scallops and the roe. In order to achieve sufficient bulk it is sometimes necessary to add a little other fish, e.g. whiting, sole, pike. Shellfish mousselines are best cooked in shallow individual moulds because of the looser texture.

I 30 – Three fish terrine with butter sauce

(Mick Maguire)

	4 portions	10 portions
white fish (half whiting, half lemon sole) skinless and boned	500 g (1¼ lb)	1¼ kg (3 lb)
salmon fillet	50 g (2 oz)	125 g (5 oz)
lemon, squeezed	¼	1
chopped parsley	25 g (1 oz)	60 g (2½ oz)
pinch of cayenne pepper		
egg white	½	1½
whipping cream	315 ml (⅝ pt)	775 ml (1¾ pt)
dash of pastis		

Sauce		
dry white wine	60 ml (⅛ pt)	150 ml (⅜ pt)
shallots, chopped	25 g (1 oz)	50 g (2½ oz)
pinch of ground white pepper		
whipping cream	50 ml (2 fl oz)	110 g (5 fl oz)
unsalted butter, cut into 12 mm (½ in) dice	100 g (4 oz)	250 g (10 oz)

Garnish
picked watercress
star-shaped fleurons

> Without butter sauce,
> I portion provides:
>
> 416 kcals/1743 kJ
> 33.8 g fat
> (of which 19.9 g is saturated)
> 2.4 g carbohydrate
> (of which 2.4 g sugars)
> 25.8 g protein
> 0 g fibre

1 Cut the white fish into 12 mm (½ in) cubes, cut the salmon into thin 5 cm (2 in) wide strips and soak in the lemon juice for 10 minutes. Season, add salt, pepper and cayenne; sprinkle chopped parsley over.

2 In a food processor purée the white fish. Add the egg white and blend for 30 seconds. Place the purée in the fridge until chilled.

3 Return the purée to the blender and add the cream and pastis. Season and then test the consistency by cooking a little of the mixture in simmering water.

4 Line the base and sides of a lightly buttered terrine with the purée. Alternate layers of salmon and purée until full. Cover with oiled tinfoil.

5 Half-fill a roasting tin with hot (but not boiling) water and place the terrine in it. Make sure that the water is three-quarters of the way up the side. Place in a preheated oven (200°C, 390°F) for 50 minutes. Allow to rest 10 minutes before removal from the terrine.

6 For the sauce place the wine, pepper and shallots in a pan and reduce by half. Pass into a clean pan through a fine strainer, add the cream and boil for 30 seconds. Reduce the heat to its lowest setting and whisk in the butter.

7 Flood a warm plate with the sauce and lay the sliced terrine on top. Garnish with fleurons and watercress.

31 – Warm mousseline of pike with fresh water crayfish

	4 portions	10 portions
pike fillets (skinned and boned)	170 g (6 oz)	400 g (14 oz)
salt		
cayenne		
paprika		
large egg whites	2	5
double cream	300 ml (10 fl oz)	750 ml (25 fl oz)
live freshwater crayfish	285 g (10 oz)	740 g (1 lb 10 oz)
carrot	1	2
onion	1	2
shallots	4	10
bunch fresh tarragon	$\frac{1}{2}$	1
bay leaf	$\frac{1}{2}$	1
celery stalks	1	3
leeks	1	2
tomatoes (plum if available)	2	5
glass dry white wine	$\frac{1}{2}$	3
butter (unsalted)	45 g (1$\frac{1}{2}$ oz)	140 g (5 oz)
sherry vinegar	1 tbsp	3 tbsp

1 Purée fish with egg white and season with salt and cayenne, pass through fine sieve. Place in mixing bowl on a bed of crushed ice.

2 Incorporate two-thirds of the cream. Poach a little quenelle and check for seasoning and consistency. Refrigerate.

3 Plunge crayfish into boiling salted water for 4 minutes. Keep the water for the sauce and 4 or 10 for garnish.

4 Peel and remove meat from crayfish, chop shells, sprinkle with paprika and roast in a hot oven with finely chopped carrot, onion, shallot, tarragon, bay leaf, celery, leek, tomato and cayenne. Then add wine and enough of the cooking liquor from the crayfish to barely

cover. Bring to the boil, stir with plastic spoon – transfer to another pan and simmer for 2 hours.

5 Pass and reduce by two-thirds, add remaining cream, reduce, add nob of cold butter and season as necessary. Pass through fine sieve.

6 Spoon mousse mixture around bottom and sides of a buttered dariole mould. Fill the centre with crayfish meat and cover with more mousse. Smooth off cover with buttered foil. Cook in a bain-marie at 177°C (350°F) for 20 minutes or until mixture rises.

7 Turn out on a plate. Mark with sauce and garnish with whole peeled crayfish (tail peeled), tomato concasse and snipped chives.

32 – Paupiettes

These are fillets of suitable fish, e.g. sole, whiting, lightly flattened with a moistened meat bat or large knife to prevent shrinkage during cooking, coated with fish forcemeat (page 179) and rolled. They can be kept in a shape by: (1) tying with fine string, (2) placing in dariole moulds, or (3) placing them close together in the cooking pan.

Paupiettes are gently poached in fish stock and/or white wine in a well buttered pan and may be prepared and served as for any of the poached fish recipes.

Variations in the flavour of and/or additions to the forcemeat can give variety to a dish of paupiettes, e.g. paupiettes of sole stuffed with a lobster forcemeat and a lobster sauce, paupiettes of whiting stuffed with a forcemeat containing dice of wild mushrooms and a white wine sauce.

33 – Red mullet

Sometimes known as the woodcock of the sea because, like the game bird, it has no gall bladder, red mullet can be cooked undrawn which enhances the flavour of the flesh. The gills are removed and the vent end must, however, be checked to ensure that it is clean. Red mullet is considered to be an essential constituent of bouillabaisse.

I 34 – Grilled red mullet on saffron creamed potato with roasted garlic and cherry tomato

(JAMES GRIMES)

	4 portions	10 portions
red mullets, scaled	4 × 175–200 g (7–8 oz)	10 × 175–200 g (7–8 oz)
large baking potato	4–5	10
saffron		
double cream	125 ml ($\frac{1}{4}$ pt)	300 ml ($\frac{3}{4}$ pt)
garlic cloves (whole)	16	40
cherry tomatoes	16	40
lemon juice and zest		
clarified butter	15 g ($\frac{1}{2}$ oz)	40 g ($1\frac{1}{2}$ oz)
salt and pepper		

I portion provides:

483 kcals/2023 kJ
19.5 g fat
(of which 11.6 g saturated)
44.7 g carbohydrate
(of which 4.1 g sugars)
35.1 g protein
5.4 g fibre

1 Infuse saffron into cream and leave aside.
2 Put potatoes in the oven to bake.
3 With a sharp knife, separate the flesh of the fish from tail to head along the bone. Do not separate the head from the fillet. Turn the fish over and repeat the process. Snap the bone away leaving the head attached to two fillets.
4 Pin-bone the fillets and remove the gills, then wash, drain well and place on a greased tray and leave in the refrigerator.
5 Blanch and roast the garlic. Cross and peel the tomatoes
6 When the potatoes are cooked, scoop out the flesh and pass through a sieve with the saffron cream. Season and mix until smooth. Keep hot.
7 Grill the fish with the lemon, a little butter and seasoning. When fish is half cooked, put the tomatoes on the tray and complete the cooking.
8 Put the saffron creamed potato into a piping bag and pipe a plait on each plate of roughly the same size as the fish.
9 Place the grilled fish on top and arrange alternate garlic cloves and tomato alongside the potato about 2.5 cm (1 in) from edge of plate. Serve immediately.

35 – Grilled red mullet with anchovy butter

1 Allow 1 × 200–300 g (8–12 oz) mullet per portion, clean and cut as in previous recipe.
2 Marinade in oil, lemon juice, salt and pepper for 20 minutes, then grill.

3 Cut bread croûtons the shape of the fish, fry in butter and spread with anchovy butter.
4 Place a mullet on each croûton, garnish with fried parsley, straw potatoes and accompany with tomato sauce finished with 25–50 g (1–2 oz) anchovy butter.

36 – Red mullet in a paper bag (en papillotte)

1 Grill or fry the prepared red mullets.
2 Place 1–2 tablespoons thick Italian sauce (below) on a large, oiled heart-shaped piece of greaseproof paper, or aluminium foil, allowing one for each fish.
3 Place the mullets on top of the sauce, surround with cooked tomato concassé and sliced cooked mushrooms.
4 Cover with a little more Italian sauce and sprinkle with brown breadcrumbs and melted butter.
5 Carefully fold and tightly pleat the paper so that the fish is completely enclosed.
6 Place on a tray in a hot oven (220°C, 425°F) until the bag balloons up and lightly browns, then serve immediately in the bag.

Notes There are many other variations of fillings and sauces that can be added to red mullet when cooking 'en papillotte'.

Sometimes only small mullet are available, in which case serve 2–3 per portion according to weight.

– Italian sauce

	4 portions	10 portions
margarine, oil or butter	25 g (1 oz)	60 g (2½ oz)
chopped shallots	10 g (½ oz)	25 g (1¼ oz)
chopped mushrooms	50 g (2 oz)	125 g (5 oz)
demi-glace or jus-lié	250 ml (½ pt)	600 ml (1¼ pt)
chopped lean ham	25 g (1 oz)	60 g (2½ oz)
tomatoes, skinned, deseeded and diced	100 g (4 oz)	250 g (10 oz)
chopped parsley, chervil and tarragon		

1 Melt the fat or oil in a small sauteuse.

2 Add the shallots and gently cook for 2–3 minutes.
3 Add the mushrooms and gently cook for 2–3 minutes.
4 Add the demi-glace or jus-lié, ham and tomatoes.
5 Simmer for 5–10 minutes. Correct the seasoning.
6 Add the chopped herbs.

T 37 – Red mullet with artichokes and olive oil

(CHRIS SUTER)

	4 portions	10 portions
red mullet	600 g (1½ lb)	2 kg (4 lb)
onion cut in brunoise	1	2–3
carrot cut in brunoise	1	2–3
olive oil	2 tbsp	5 tbsp
artichokes bottoms (finely sliced)	3	7
bouquet garni	1	2
cloves garlic	2	5
Sauce		
olive oil	375 ml (¾ pt)	1 litre (2 pt)
lemon, juice of	1	2–3
red pepper	1 small	2–3 small
green pepper, peeled and diced	1	2–3
tomato peeled, seeded and diced	1	2–3
chopped parsley	1 tsp	2–3 tsp
chopped chervil	1 tsp	2–3 tsp
tarragon, finely chopped	1 sprig	2–3 sprigs
salt		
freshly ground pepper		

1 Clean scale and fillet fish, set aside.
2 Sweat the onion, carrot in olive oil.
3 Add the artichoke, bouquet garni and garlic, cook until just tender.
4 To make sauce, whisk the oil with the lemon juice. Add the pepper, tomato, chopped herbs and seasoning to taste.
5 Cook the mullet skin side down.
6 To serve, divide the artichoke mixture between plates, arrange fish on top and pour sauce over.
7 Garnish with chervil and pasta and serve.

38 – Russian fish pie (Coulibiac)

This dish can be made using brioche or puff paste.

	4 portions	10 portions
brioche or puff paste	200 g (8 oz)	500 g (1¼ lb)
coarse semolina or rice, cooked in good stock as for pilaff	100 g (4 oz)	250 g (10 oz)
salmon, cut in small thick slices and very lightly fried in butter	400 g (1 lb)	1¼ kg (2½ lb)
finely chopped onion	50 g (2 oz)	125 g (5 oz)
chopped mushrooms	100 g (4 oz)	250 g (10 oz)
chopped parsley	1 tbsp	2½ tbsp
hard-boiled egg, chopped	1	2½
fresh vesiga (50 g/2 oz if dried), cooked and roughly chopped		
melted butter	200 g (8 oz)	500 g (1¼ lb)

1 Roll out the paste thinly into a rectangle approximately 30 × 18 cm (12 × 7 in).
2 Place the ingredients in layers one on top of the other along the centre, alternating the layers, starting and finishing with the semolina or rice.
3 Egg wash the edges of the paste and fold over to enclose the filling completely.
4 Seal the ends and turn over on to a lightly greased baking sheet so that the sealed edges are underneath.
5 Allow to prove in a warm place for approximately 30 minutes.
6 Brush all over with melted butter and cut two small holes neatly in the top to allow steam to escape.
7 Bake at 190°C (375°F) for approximately 40 minutes.
8 When removed from the oven, pour some melted butter into the two holes.
9 To serve, cut into thick slices and offer a butter-type sauce, e.g. Hollandaise, separately.

Notes
1 If using puff pastry, egg wash the completed dish before baking instead of brushing with butter.

2 Individual coulibiacs can be made using a 20 cm (8 in) pastry cutter.
3 Vesiga is the spinal cord of the sturgeon obtained commercially in the shape of white, semi-transparent dry gelatinous ribbon. It must be soaked in cold water for 4–5 hours when it will swell to 4–5 times the size and the weight will increase 6-fold. It is then gently simmered in white stock for $3\frac{1}{2}$–$4\frac{1}{2}$ hours. If it is not possible to obtain vesiga, a layer of fish forcemeat may be substituted.
4 Coulibiac has been for many years a popular dish in high-class restaurants around the world. If the ingredients in this recipe are not available or are too expensive then other fish may be used to replace salmon, e.g. haddock. If vesiga is unobtainable then use more of all the other ingredients. With imagination many variations of this dish can be conceived.

39 – Fillet of salmon en croûte with dill and yoghurt sauce

	4 portions	10 portions
puff pastry	140 g (6 oz)	350 g (14 oz)
salmon fillet	300 g (12 oz)	750 g (1 lb 14 oz)
nori seaweed	1–2 sheets	4 sheets
wild rice	25 g (1 oz)	60 g ($2\frac{1}{2}$ oz)
long-grain rice	48 g (2 oz)	120 g (5 oz)
shi-take and oyster mushrooms	34 g ($1\frac{1}{2}$ oz)	85 g ($3\frac{1}{2}$ oz)
finely chopped shallots	20 g ($\frac{3}{4}$ oz)	50 g (2 oz)
sieved or grated hard boiled egg	48 g (2 oz)	120 g (5 oz)
parsley	10 g ($\frac{1}{3}$ oz)	25 g (1 oz)
finely chopped ginger	10 g ($\frac{1}{3}$ oz)	25 g (1 oz)
finely chopped lemon grass	8 g ($\frac{1}{4}$ oz)	20 g ($\frac{3}{4}$ oz)
lime juice	$\frac{1}{2}$	1
salt, mill pepper		
eggwash		

1 Cook and refresh the rice.
2 Sweat the shallot in a little butter and oil. Add ginger, lemon grass, chopped mushrooms and seasoning.
3 Cook gently for 8 minutes.
4 Combine the mushroom mixture with the rice, egg, parsley and lime juice. Correct the seasoning.
5 Roll out the pastry to a 50 × 25 cm (20 × 10 in) rectangle.

6 Using a lattice pastry cutter, roll over the centre of the pastry along the whole length.
7 Gently pull the pastry to show the lattice effect.
8 Place the dampened seaweed over the lattice design.
9 Place the rice mixture along the centre of the pastry, no longer or wider than the fillet of salmon.
10 Place the seasoned fillet of salmon on the rice mixture.
11 Eggwash the edges of the pastry and wrap, sealing well.
12 Gently turn over to show the top and place on a baking sheet.
13 Eggwash and leave to rest for 20 minutes in a cool place.
14 Eggwash again and bake at 425°C (797°F) for 10 minutes and 175°C (347°F) for a further 20 minutes.
15 Rest for 5 minutes before slicing.
16 Serve with a dill and yoghurt sauce.

⁓ Dill and yoghurt sauce

		4 portions	10 portions
leek	} white mirepoix	25 g (1 oz)	50 g (2 oz)
celery		25 g (1 oz)	50 g (2 oz)
onion		25 g (1 oz)	50 g (2 oz)
white peppercorns		4	10
lemon juice		$\frac{1}{4}$	$\frac{1}{2}$
bay leaf		$\frac{1}{2}$	1
coriander seeds		3	8
dill and tarragon stalks		8 g ($\frac{1}{4}$ oz)	20 g (1 oz)
fish velouté		250 ml ($\frac{1}{2}$ pt)	$\frac{1}{2}$ litre (1 pt)
Noilly Prat		50 ml ($\frac{1}{8}$ pt)	125 ml ($\frac{1}{4}$ pt)
double cream		30 ml ($\frac{1}{16}$ pt)	60 ml ($\frac{1}{8}$ pt)
natural yoghurt		125 ml ($\frac{1}{4}$ pt)	250 ml ($\frac{1}{2}$ pt)
fresh dill (chopped)		10 g ($\frac{1}{3}$ oz)	25 g (1 oz)
salt, pepper			

1 Sweat the mirepoix without colour in 25 g (1 oz) of butter.
2 Add the wine and reduce by half.
3 Add the fish velouté and bring to the boil.
4 Add the cream and finally the yoghurt.
5 Simmer gently for 15 minutes.
6 Adjust the seasoning and pass through a fine chinois.
7 Add the chopped dill and serve.

The following three recipes illustrate the use of salmon over different seasons of the year.

T 40 – Millander of Tay salmon with button onions and red wine gravy

(ALAN HILL)

	4 portions	10 portions
cubed Scottish salmon	4 × 160 g (5 oz)	10 × 160 g (5 oz)
salt and freshly ground pepper		
button onions (blanched)	60 g (2 oz)	125 g (5 oz)
button mushrooms	60 g (2 oz)	125 g (5 oz)
garlic clove	1	2–3
Chambertin red wine	20 cl ($\frac{1}{2}$ pt)	600 ml ($1\frac{1}{4}$ pt)
batons of Ayrshire bacon (blanched)	60 g (2 oz)	200 g (5 oz)
few thyme leaves		
butter	100 g (4 oz)	250 g (10 oz)
double cream	10 cl ($\frac{1}{4}$ pt)	300 ml ($\frac{5}{8}$ pt)
heart-shaped croûtons	4	10
chopped parsley		

1 Place a touch of butter into a saucepan and cook the button onions and mushrooms until golden brown, remove, dry and keep warm.
2 Remove any excess fat, add the garlic clove and pour in the red wine.
3 Reduce by half and allow to cool slightly.
4 In a teflon pan cook the cubed salmon to taste, remove and keep warm.
5 Return the mushrooms and onions to the reduced red wine and add the blanched bacon.
6 Slowly add the firm butter to the pan and gently fold together to form a silky sauce.
7 Add the thyme leaves and the double cream then check the seasoning of the sauce.
8 Place the salmon upon the serving bowl and nap the sauce over the top.
9 Garnish with the heart shaped croûtons and chopped parsley.
10 Serve warm and immediately.

41 – Barbecue skree of Tay salmon with heather honey and seasonal greens

(ALAN HILL)

	4 portions	10 portions
fillets of Tay salmon	4×160 g (5 oz)	10×160 g (5 oz)
salt and freshly ground pepper		
dark sugar	15 g ($\frac{1}{2}$ oz)	$37\frac{1}{2}$ g ($1\frac{1}{4}$ oz)
heather honey	25 g (1 oz)	60 g ($2\frac{1}{2}$ oz)
Lea & Perrins	5 cl ($\frac{1}{8}$ pt)	75 ml ($\frac{1}{4}$ pt)
lemon zest and juice	$\frac{1}{2}$	1
lime zest and juice	$\frac{1}{2}$	1
grapefruit zest and juice	$\frac{1}{2}$	1
summer salad leaves	400 g (1 lb)	$1\frac{1}{4}$ kg ($2\frac{1}{2}$ lb)
hazelnut oil	10 cl ($\frac{1}{4}$ pt)	20 cl ($\frac{1}{2}$ pt)
lemons	2	5
picked herbs for garnish		

1 Place the sauce, honey and citrus juices into a bowl and thoroughly mix together.
2 Add the dark sugar and then place the salmon in a marinating tray.
3 Season with salt and freshly ground pepper then pour the marinade over the top. Leave overnight to marinate.
4 Remove from the marinade and barbecue to taste, remove and keep warm.
5 Place the washed salad leaves into a bowl and season with salt and freshly ground pepper.
6 Add the salad leaves and dressing, fold together and place in a serving bowl.
7 Place the barbecued salmon upon the serving plate and garnish with a half a lemon and some freshly picked herbs.
8 Serve immediately.

T 42 ~ Stir-fry of salmon with glazed chestnuts and Brussels sprouts

(ALAN HILL)

	4 portions	10 portions
fillets of salmon	4 × 160 g (5 oz)	10 × 160 g (5 oz)
salt and freshly ground pepper		
bean shoots	60 g (2 oz)	125 g (5 oz)
bamboo shoots	60 g (2 oz)	125 g (5 oz)
carrots ⎫	30 g (1 oz)	60 g (2½ oz)
celery ⎬ cut in slivers	30 g (1 oz)	60 g (2½ oz)
courgettes ⎭	30 g (1 oz)	60 g (2½ oz)
sliced waterchestnuts	30 g (1 oz)	60 g (2½ oz)
five spice powder	pinch	pinch
fresh ginger root	15 g (½ oz)	25 g (1 oz)
whole glazed chestnuts	12	30
button Brussels sprouts	12	30
sesame seed oil	10 cl (¼ pt)	30 cl (⅝ pt)
soy sauce	1 tbsp	2½ tbsp
chopped chives	30 g (1 oz)	60 g (2½ oz)
toasted sesame seeds		

1 Season and pan fry the salmon in a touch of hot sesame seed oil, remove, dry and keep warm.
2 In a wok quickly stir-fry the vegetables and water chestnuts, season with a touch of ginger and five spice powder.
3 Reheat the glazed chestnuts and Brussels sprouts, season with salt and freshly ground pepper.
4 On the serving plate place a plastic or stainless steel ring.
5 Pour in a touch of soy sauce and sesame seed oil on to the vegetables then place in the ring.
6 Place the button Brussels sprouts and chestnuts around the ring.
7 Nap with a cordon of the remaining sauce then remove the ring.
8 Place the salmon on top and sprinkle with the toasted sesame seeds and chopped chives.
9 Serve hot and immediately.

I 43 – Salmon with Thai spices

(SEAN O'BRIAN)

	4 portions	10 portions
salmon fillet	500 g (1.1 lb)	1 kg (2.2 lb)
white peppercorns	level tsp	12 g ($\frac{1}{2}$ oz)
coarse sea salt	25 g (1 oz)	50 g (2 oz)
sugar	25 g (1 oz)	50 g (2 oz)
coriander leaf	50 g (2 oz)	75 g (3 oz)
juice and zest of lime	1	2
lime leaves	3	6
lemon grass stalk	$\frac{1}{2}$	1
galangel or ginger	level tsp	25 g (1 oz)
fish sauce (Thai)	1 tbsp	1$\frac{1}{2}$ tbsp

1 Carefully remove small bones along length of salmon fillet with tweezers, wash carefully and pat dry with paper.
2 Mix the peppercorns, coriander seeds, sea salt, sugar, two-thirds of the coriander leaf (roughly chopped), juice and zest of limes, finely chopped lime leaves and lemon grass, galangel or ginger and fish sauce.
3 Take a sheet of foil twice the size of the salmon and line with cling film. Divide the salt/spice mix in two and spread over the salmon fillets. Place one fillet on top of the other, marinating surfaces together. Place on cling film and seal tightly.
4 Leave to marinade in the fridge for 6–8 hours, turn the fillets over and marinate for a further 6–8 hours, repeat the process for 24–36 hours.
5 After 24 hours check taste and consistency of the salmon. Do not leave it to marinate too long as the salmon will go dry.
6 When salmon has reached desired stage, scrape off marinade ingredients, keeping juice to baste. Sprinkle remaining one-third of roughly chopped coriander over salmon and reseal in cling film ready for carving.
7 To serve: dress some rocket leaves with olive oil and preferably rice wine vinegar and lightly season.
8 Place the dressed leaves on the middle of plates, cover thinly with carved slices of salmon.
9 Serve separately a sauce of crème fraîche with chopped coriander, chillies and lime juice to taste.

I 44 – Salmon wrapped in garlic leaves with a chive sauce

(PHILLIP ACCORSINI)

	4 portions	10 portions
salmon fillet	500 g (1¼ lb)	1¼ kg (3 lb 2 oz)
garlic leaves	1 bunch	2 bunches
fish stock	500 ml (1 pt)	1 litre (2 pt)
cream	150 ml (¼ pt)	300 ml (½ pt)
chives	1 bunch	2 bunches
shallots	150 g (6 oz)	300 g (12 oz)
olive oil	150 ml (5 fl oz)	300 ml (10 fl oz)
garlic	¼ clove	½ clove
sea salt		
white peppercorns		
white wine vinegar		

1 Remove the little bones of the salmon by using tweezers.
2 Cut fillet into suprêmes.
3 Rub each fillet with olive oil, salt and pepper.
4 Remove the spine from the garlic leaves, and then wrap around salmon suprême (reserve garlic flowers for garnish).
5 Steam the salmon for 10 minutes or until just pink (too much cooking will dry the fish out, leaving it flavourless).

Sauce
1 Finely chop shallots and garlic, reserve to one side.
2 Finely chop chives.
3 Sauté shallots and garlic without colour in a light amount of olive oil.
4 Add fish stock which has been passed. Bring to a simmer and reduce by half.
5 Add double cream.
6 Add chives, salt and pepper to taste and a drop of white wine vinegar. (The vinegar counterbalances the fatty taste of the cream and brings forward the other flavours.)
7 To serve: pour sauce on to a warmed plate. Place salmon fillet on top and garnish with the garlic flowers.

45 – Salmon in red wine sauce

	4 portions	10 portions
slices of salmon on the bone	4 × 150–200 g (6–8 oz)	10 × 150–200 g (6–8 oz)
carrot, sliced	100 g (4 oz)	250 g (10 oz)
onion, sliced	100 g (4 oz)	250 g (10 oz)
sprig of thyme, bay leaf, parsley stalks		
red wine	125 ml ($\frac{1}{4}$ pt)	312 ml ($\frac{3}{4}$ pt)
fish stock	60 ml ($\frac{1}{8}$ pt)	150 ml ($\frac{1}{3}$ pt)
onion, sliced	50 g (2 oz)	125 g (5 oz)
carrot, sliced	50 g (2 oz)	125 g (5 oz)
thyme, parsley stalks		
butter	50 g (2 oz)	125 g (5 oz)
salmon head and bones	1 kg (2 lb)	2$\frac{1}{2}$ kg (5 lb)
Genevoise sauce		
red wine	125 ml ($\frac{1}{4}$ pt)	312 ml ($\frac{3}{4}$ pt)
fish stock	60 ml ($\frac{1}{8}$ pt)	150 ml ($\frac{1}{3}$ pt)
butter	100 g (4 oz)	250 g (10 oz)
salt and pepper		

1 To braise the salmon: place the fish on the vegetables and herbs. Add wine and fish stock to come two-thirds of the way up.
2 Cover and braise gently for 10 minutes.
3 Remove lid, baste frequently and continue cooking until centre bones are easily removed from the salmon.
4 Remove all skin and bones, keep warm, strain off cooking liquor.
5 Make genevoise sauce by lightly browning onion, carrot and herbs in 50 g (2 oz) butter.
6 Add the salmon head, cook for 15 minutes.
7 Add wine, stock and fish cooking liquid, simmer for 10 minutes.
8 Strain, reduce to a light glaze, incorporate butter and correct seasoning.
9 Dress salmon, mask lightly with sauce, garnish with fish quenelles (page 179), turned mushrooms, fried soft roes, cooked crayfish and slices of truffle.
10 Serve remainder of sauce separately.

Note The salmon may also be braised in one whole piece.

T 46 – Envelope of salmon and turbot

(DAVID DORRICOTT)

	4 portions	10 portions
diced avocado	100 g (4 oz)	250 g (10 oz)
diced tomato	100 g (4 oz)	250 g (10 oz)
chopped tarragon	5 g ($\frac{1}{4}$ oz)	12 g ($\frac{5}{8}$ oz)
fresh white breadcrumbs	10 g ($\frac{1}{2}$ oz)	25 g (1 oz)
walnut oil	2 tsp	5 tsp
salt and pepper		
turbot } batted out	4 × 75 g (3 oz)	10 × 75 g (3 oz)
salmon }	4 × 75 g (3 oz)	10 × 75 g (3 oz)
fish cream sauce	250 ml ($\frac{1}{2}$ pt)	600 ml (1$\frac{1}{4}$ pt)

1 Mix 85 g (3$\frac{1}{2}$ oz) avocado, 85 g (3$\frac{1}{2}$ oz) tomato, half the tarragon, all the breadcrumbs and walnut oil and season (200 g, 8$\frac{3}{4}$ oz for 10 portions).
2 Place in a dome shape in the centre of the turbot.
3 Cover with salmon and gently seal around the edges.
4 Sauté quickly in a hot non-stick pan.
5 Finish cooking under the salamander.
6 Heat the fish cream sauce.
7 Add the remaining tarragon, avocado and tomato, and correct the seasoning.
8 Place fish on a plate, coat with sauce and garnish with a sprig of tarragon.

Note This dish is served as a first course.

– Fish cream sauce

	4 portions	10 portions
butter	5 g ($\frac{1}{4}$ oz)	12 g ($\frac{5}{8}$ oz)
shallot, sliced	1 medium	2–3 medium
fish stock	375 ml ($\frac{3}{4}$ pt)	1 litre (2 pt)
bay leaf	$\frac{1}{2}$	1$\frac{1}{2}$
peppercorns	7–8	20
white wine	125 ml ($\frac{1}{4}$ pt)	300 ml ($\frac{5}{8}$ pt)
Noilly Prat vermouth	60 ml ($\frac{1}{8}$ pt)	150 ml ($\frac{1}{3}$ pt)
double cream	250 ml ($\frac{1}{2}$ pt)	600 ml (1$\frac{1}{4}$ pt)
salt and pepper		

1 Melt butter and add shallot, sauté without colour for 1 minute.
2 Add fish stock, bay leaf, peppercorns and reduce by three-quarters.
3 Add white wine and Noilly Prat, reduce by two-thirds.
4 Add double cream, simmer and reduce until of a sauce consistency.
5 Pass through a fine strainer, correct seasoning and use as above.

47 – Fresh sardines with tomato sauce

	4 portions	10 portions
large fresh sardines	400–600 g (1–1½ lb)	1¼–1½ kg (2½–3¾ lb)
oil for frying		
finely sliced onion	150 g (6 oz)	375 g (15 oz)
dry white wine	60 ml (⅛ pt)	150 ml (⅓ pt)
tomatoes, skinned, deseeded, diced	400 g (1 lb)	1¼ kg (2½ lb)
salt and pepper		
chopped parsley		

1 Scale, gut, wash and dry the sardines.
2 Shallow fry rapidly in oil on both sides, remove from pan.
3 In the same oil gently cook the onions without colour.
4 Add wine, reduce by two-thirds, add tomatoes, season, reduce by half.
5 Pour the sauce into an ovenproof dish, place sardines on top.
6 Cook for 5–7 minutes in oven at 220°C (425°F) and serve, sprinkled with parsley.

48 – Deep-fried sardines with an egg, butter, tarragon and caper sauce

1 Remove heads and tails from sardines, gut and wash.
2 Flour, egg, crumb and deep fry.
3 Serve with a béarnaise sauce (see page 105) containing a few capers.

49 – Baked stuffed sardines

1 Slit the stomach openings of the sardines and gut.
2 From the same opening carefully cut along each side of the backbones and remove by cutting through the end with fish scissors.
3 Scale, wash, dry and season the fish.

4 A variety of stuffings can be used, e.g.
   (a) cooked chopped spinach with cooked chopped onion, garlic, nutmeg, salt, pepper;
   (b) fish forcemeat;
   (c) thick duxelle.
5 Place the stuffed sardines in a greased ovenproof dish.
6 Sprinkle with breadcrumbs and oil.
7 Bake in hot oven (200°C, 400°F) for approximately 10 minutes and serve.

Notes   Herring, mackerel, sea-bass and trout can also be prepared and cooked in this way, and there is considerable scope for flair and imagination in the different stuffings and methods of cooking the fish.

Fresh sardines are also popular when plainly grilled and served with quarters of lemon.

I 50 – Seafood file gumbo

(PAUL BURTON)

	4 portions	10 portions
Stock		
lightly crushed garlic	2	5
allspice berries, lightly crushed	3	8
lightly crushed green peppercorns	$\frac{1}{2}$ tsp	$1\frac{1}{4}$ tsp
sliced onion	$\frac{1}{2}$	1
lemon (sliced)	$\frac{1}{2}$	$1\frac{1}{2}$
chopped celery stalk with leaves	1	2
water	600 ml (1 pt)	$1\frac{1}{2}$ litre (3 pt)
garnish with sprigs of fresh dill	4	10
redfish (flaked)	180 g (6 oz)	450 g (1 lb)
shelled cooked prawns	360 g (13 oz)	800 g (2 lb)
white crabmeat	140 g (5 oz)	350 g (12 oz)
vegetable oil	50 ml ($1\frac{1}{2}$ fl oz)	125 ml (4 fl oz)
flour	30 g (1 oz)	75 g (3 oz)
chopped onion	120 g (4 oz)	300 g (10 oz)
diced green pepper	60 g (2 oz)	150 g (5 oz)
diced red pepper	60 g (2 oz)	150 g (5 oz)

diced celery	30 g (1 oz)	75 g (3 oz)
crushed cloves garlic	3–4	8–10
large bay leaf	$\frac{1}{2}$	1
chopped fresh thyme	1 tsp	2 tsp
chopped fresh parsley	1 tsp	2 tsp
cayenne pepper	$\frac{1}{4}$ tsp	$\frac{1}{2}$ tsp
file powder*	1 tsp	2 tsp
freshly cooked long grain and wild rice	300 g (10 oz)	750 g (25 oz)

1 Place all the stock ingredients in a large saucepan, bring to boil and simmer for 1 hour. Strain.
2 Heat oil in a large heavy saucepan, stir in the flour and cook out stirring constantly until the roux is a sandy texture and colour.
3 Remove from heat, add onion, pepper and garlic.
4 Return to heat and cook to soften.
5 Gradually stir in stock, add herbs and seasonings.
6 Bring to the boil, lower the heat and simmer for 1 hour.
7 Add the prawns, simmer for 5 minutes.
8 Add redfish and simmer for a further 3 minutes.
9 Add crabmeat and simmer for a further 2 minutes.
10 Remove from the heat, stir in the file powder.
11 Ladle into plates or bowls over the freshly cooked rice. Serve.

* File powder is an American spice.

Note Always add the file powder just prior to serving. Adding too early causes a 'bitter' taste to be developed.

51 – Grilled sea bass with fennel

	4 portions	10 portions
sea bass or two fish double the weight	4 × 300–400 g (12 oz–1 lb)	10 × 300–400 g (12 oz–1 lb)
salt and pepper		
fennel sprigs	50 g (2 oz)	125 g (5 oz)
oil for grilling		

1 Scale, trim, gut and wash the fish.
2 Cut 3–4 incisions on either side and season.
3 Pack as much sprig fennel into the stomach cavity as possible.

4 Brush with oil and grill.

5 Serve sprinkled with chopped fennel and quarters of lemon.

Note 2–3 tablespoons of an anise liquor, e.g. Pernod, may be flamed and poured over the fish.

52 – Baked stuffed sea bass

	4 portions	10 portions
finely chopped shallot	50 g (2 oz)	125 g (5 oz)
butter	150 g (6 oz)	375 g (15 oz)
chopped mushrooms	150 g (6 oz)	375 g (15 oz)
salt and pepper		
tomato, skinned, deseeded, diced	100 g (4 oz)	250 g (10 oz)
pinch of chopped marjoram		
beaten egg	1	2–3
few drops of lemon juice		
fresh breadcrumbs		
sea bass	1 kg (2 lb)	2½ kg (5 lb)
white wine	60 ml ($\frac{1}{8}$ pt)	150 ml ($\frac{1}{3}$ pt)

1 Cook the shallots in the butter without colour.

2 Add mushrooms, season and cook until dry.

3 Add tomato, marjoram, remove from heat, mix in the egg and lemon juice.

4 Bring to suitable consistency by adding breadcrumbs.

5 Clean, wash and stuff the fish. Place in buttered ovenproof dish and season.

6 Pour on the wine, sprinkle with breadcrumbs and remainder of butter in small thin pieces.

7 Bake at 200°C (400°F), basting frequently until cooked and lightly browned, approximately 30–40 minutes and serve.

T 53 ‑ Ceviche of sea bass or red mullet

(STEPHEN BULL)

	4 portions	10 portions
lemon, juice of	1	$2\frac{1}{2}$
limes	2	5
crushed coriander seeds	1 heaped tsp	$2\frac{1}{2}$ heaped tsp
castor sugar	40 g ($1\frac{1}{2}$ oz)	100 g (4 oz)
sea bass or red mullet fillets (leave skin on some)	300 g (12 oz)	1 kg (2 lb)
chives, finely chopped		
diced tomato flesh, skinned and seeded	50 g (2 oz)	125 g (5 oz)
small shallots, finely chopped	2	5

1 Mix juices, coriander and sugar to dissolve sugar. Salt lightly.
2 Slice fish very thinly (flatten with heavy knife if necessary).
3 Lay in wide shallow dish and pour marinade over. Leave for 3 hours.
4 Serve on individual plates, sprinkled with chives, tomato and shallots.

Note Ceviche is a word of Spanish/Peruvian origin, meaning 'fish marinaded in lime and lemon juice'.

This dish is served as a first course.

T 54 ‑ Steamed sea bass with angel-hair pasta, bean sprouts and mango

(STANLEY BERWICK)

	4 portions	10 portions
Stock		
cleaned and chopped carrot	200 g (8 oz)	500 g ($1\frac{1}{4}$ lb)
white of leek	50 g (8 oz)	125 g (5 oz)
onions	50 g (2 oz)	125 g (5 oz)
unsalted butter	100 g (4 oz)	250 g (10 oz)
dry white wine	125 ml (5 fl oz)	300 ml ($\frac{5}{8}$ pt)
fish stock	500 ml (1 pt)	$1\frac{1}{4}$ litre ($2\frac{1}{2}$ pt)
white chicken stock	125 ml (5 fl oz)	300 ml ($\frac{5}{8}$ pt)

1 Place vegetables in a heavy saucepan with the butter and cook on a low heat until tender.
2 Add the wine and cook until nearly dry.

3 Add the fish and chicken stock and cook out until half the quantity has evaporated.
4 Pass through a sieve into a clean pan and continue cooking until only 250 ml ($\frac{1}{2}$pt) remains (625 ml, 1$\frac{1}{4}$pt for 10 portions).

Fish

sea bass fillets with scales and bones removed and cut into diamonds	2 × 150 g (6 oz)	10 × 150 g (6 oz)
salt and pepper		
taglioni or vermicelli pasta	100 g (4 oz)	250 g (10 oz)
enriched fish stock	250 ml ($\frac{1}{2}$pt)	600 ml (1$\frac{1}{4}$pt)
bean sprouts	100 g (4 oz)	250 g (10 oz)
firm mango, diced	100 g (4 oz)	250 g (10 oz)
unsalted butter	50 g (2 oz)	125 g (5 oz)

1 Place the sea bass, skin side up, in a container for steaming (or poach if necessary) and season.
2 Cook the pasta and set to one side, lightly seasoned and buttered.
3 Rapidly boil the stock while the fish is cooking.
4 When reduced by half, add the bean sprouts and mango and beat in the butter.
5 Remove from the heat and correct seasoning.
6 Place the hot pasta in the centre of pre-heated plates and arrange the sea bass diamonds, skin side up, around this.
7 Spoon the sauce between each piece of sea bass and serve.

55 – Baked sea bass or bream in a salt crust

	4 portions	10 portions
fish	1–1$\frac{1}{2}$kg (2–3 lb)	2–3 kg (5–7 lb)
sea salt	1$\frac{1}{2}$kg (3 lb)	3 kg (7 lb)

1 Do not scale or degut the fish, the scales are covered with a salty deposit which strengthens the fish flavour and also makes it easier to remove the skin when cooked.
2 Gut the fish and remove the fins.
3 Spread 1 lb salt evenly in the bottom of a cast iron dish, lay the fish on and spread the remainder of the salt around and over, completely covering it.
4 Bake in a hot oven 220°C (425°F) for 25 minutes approximately; the salt should have set hard and may have cracks.

5 The fish can be presented to the customer, after which the salt layer can be removed.

6 Remove the fish, peel off the skin (with the scales) and serve accompanied by lemon quarters and/or a suitable sauce.

Note This method can be used with many other whole fish of suitable sizes, e.g. red or grey mullet, mackerel.

56 – Grilled sea bass or bream with fennel

	4 portions	10 portions
fish	1–2	3–5
sprigs of fresh fennel		
oil for basting		
lemon for accompaniment		

1 Place the lightly seasoned fish on to preheated oiled grill bars.
2 Brush with oil.
3 Sprinkle generously with fennel
4 Turn the fish half way through cooking.
5 Serve accompanied with quarters of lemon.

57 – Skate

Only the wings of the smaller common and thornback skate are used; they are usually purchased skinned and cleaned.

58 – Fried skate

	4 portions	10 portions
skate	1 kg (2 lb)	2½ kg (5 lb)
Marinade		
lemons, juice of	2	5
oil	125 ml ($\frac{1}{4}$ pt)	300 ml ($\frac{5}{8}$ pt)
thyme, bayleaf, salt,		
pepper, parsley stalks		

1 Cut skate into small slices and marinade for 2–3 hours.
2 Dip the skate pieces in a light batter and deep fry in hot fat.
3 Serve garnished with fried or sprig parsley and quarters of lemon.

I 59 – Skate wing cooked inside a paper parcel on a compote of mung beans and rhubarb

(GARY WITCHALLS)

	4 portions	10 portions
fresh skate wings	4 × 200 g (8 oz)	10 × 200 g (8 oz)
mung beans (soaked overnight)	200 g (8 oz)	500 g (1¼ lb)
large sprigs fresh coriander	8	20
rhubarb, 1 cm (½ in) dice	150 g (6 oz)	400 g (1 lb)
clove smoked garlic	1	3
shallots	2	5
vegetable oil	2 tbsp	5 tbsp
fish stock	500 ml (1 pt)	1.25 litre (2 pt)
egg white	1	3
seasoning		
circles greaseproof paper	4 × 36 cm (14 in)	10 × 36 cm (14 in)

> I portion provides:
>
> 271 kcals
> 6.9 g fat
> (of which 0.3 g saturated)
> 19.4 g carbohydrate
> (of which I g sugars)
> 33.9 g protein
> I1.9 g fibre

1 Gently sauté the finely diced shallots and garlic in the vegetable oil for 2–3 minutes.
2 Add rhubarb and mung beans and cook for a further 2 minutes.
3 Add three-quarters of fish stock, seasoning and gently simmer for approximately 20 minutes until all stock has been absorbed.
4 Lightly oil the greaseproof circles and brush edges with egg white.
5 Divide rhubarb compote evenly between the parcels and then place on top the lightly seasoned skate wing and a sprig of coriander.
6 Spoon over the remaining stock, seal the parcels and bake in a moderate oven for approximately 15–20 minutes.
7 Break open the parcels and garnish with fresh sprigs of coriander.

60 – Skate with mustard and lemon on spinach

	4 portions	10 portions
skate	4 × 150–200 g (6–8 oz)	10 × 150–200 g (6–8 oz)
spinach, cooked	1 kg (1½ lb)	2½ kg (4 lb)
butter	200 g (8 oz)	500 g (1¼ lb)
lemon, juice of	1	2
French mustard (according to taste)	2–3	5–6

1 Poach or steam the fish, drain well.
2 Reheat spinach in half the butter, add a rub of nutmeg and season.
3 Boil the lemon juice and an equal amount of water and reduce.
4 Remove from heat, incorporate the remaining butter, then the mustard and correct seasoning.
5 Place the spinach on serving dish, add the skate.
6 Coat with sauce and serve.

Note The skate flesh may be removed from the bones if desired.

61 – Squid

Squid should be cooked very quickly or braised for an hour or so. Only fresh squid is suitable for stir-frying, shallow frying or grilling.

Preparation (see page 206)
1 Pull the head away from the body together with the innards.
2 Cut off the tentacles just below the head, remove the small round cartilage at the base of the tentacles.
3 Discard the head, innards and pieces of cartilage.
4 Taking care not to break the ink bag remove the long transparent blade of cartilage (the backbone).
5 Scrape or peel off the reddish membrane which covers the pouch, rub with salt and wash under cold water.

62 – Baby squid with parsley

	4 portions	10 portions
prepared baby squid	600 g (1½ lb)	2¾ kg (5½ lb)
olive oil	60 ml (⅛ pt)	150 ml (⅓ pt)
garlic cloves, crushed	1–2	3–4
sprigs, finely chopped parsley	3–4	4–6
lemon, juice of	½	1

1 Heat the oil, add the garlic until it begins to brown and then discard it.
2 Add the well dried squid, season lightly with salt and pepper.
3 Cook over a fierce heat for 8–10 minutes.
4 Sprinkle with lemon juice and parsley and serve.

Cleaning and preparation of squid

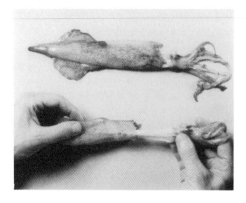

Pull off head – the interior organs will come out with it

Pull out plastic-like 'quill' from the body sac and rinse out the sac

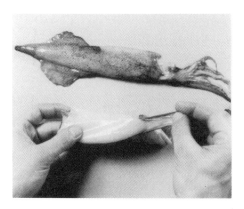

Pull off the skin

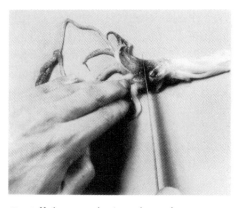

Cut off the tentacles just above the eye. Discard the head, organs and 'beak' which is in the centre of the tentacle

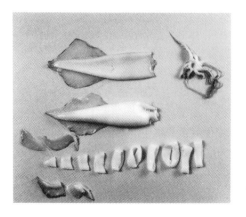

From top to bottom: cleaned whole body sac and tentacles; stuffed squid fastened with a pick; a squid sliced into rings

63 – Squid with white wine, garlic and chilli

	4 portions	10 portions
squid	600 g (1½ lb)	2¾ kg (5½ lb)
olive oil	60 ml (⅛ pt)	150 ml (⅓ pt)
garlic cloves, crushed	2	3–4
sprigs chopped parsley	3–4	4–6
small piece of hot chilli pepper, finely chopped		
dry white wine	60 ml (⅛) pt	150 ml (⅓ pt)
stock	60 ml (⅛ pt)	150 ml (⅓ pt)

1 Gently fry the garlic in the oil until golden brown, discard the garlic.
2 Add the well dried squid, chilli, a little salt and cook over fierce heat for 8–10 minutes.
3 Add the wine and reduce by half.
4 Add the stock, simmer gently until tender.
5 Add parsley, correct seasoning and serve.

64 – Stuffed squid

The pocket of the cleaned squid is suitable for stuffing and a variety of ingredients and flavourings can be used, for example:

1 anchovy, garlic, chilli, parsley;
2 rice, onions, spinach, dill;
3 oil, garlic, parsley, white wine, white breadcrumbs.

After stuffing, the openings must be secured with string and the squid can then either be baked or braised.

65 – Fish soufflés

	4 portions
raw fish, free from skin and bone	300 g (10 oz)
butter	50 g (2 oz)
thick béchamel	250 ml (½ pt)
eggs, separated	3
salt and cayenne pepper	

Haddock, sole, salmon, turbot, lobster, crab, etc. can all be used for soufflés.

1 Cook the fish in the butter and process to a purée.
2 Mix with the béchamel, pass through a fine sieve and season well.
3 Warm the mixture and beat in the yolks.
4 Carefully fold in the stiffly beaten whites.
5 Place into individual buttered and floured soufflé moulds.
6 Bake at 220°C (425°F) for approximately 14 minutes; serve immediately.

Notes   If individual moulds are used, less cooking time is required. A suitable sauce may be offered, e.g. white wine, mushroom, shrimp, saffron, lobster.

The use of an extra beaten egg white will increase the lightness of the soufflé.

Lobster soufflés can be cooked and served in the cleaned half shells of the lobsters.

T 66 – Fish and shellfish soufflé

(René Pauvert)

	4 portions	10 portions
Fish mousseline preparation		
scallop (white only)	50 g (2 oz)	125 g (5 oz)
sole fillet	50 g (2 oz)	125 g (5 oz)
unsalted soft butter	5 g ($\frac{1}{4}$ oz)	12$\frac{1}{2}$ g ($\frac{1}{2}$ oz)
egg white	1	2$\frac{1}{2}$
single cream	80 g (3 oz)	200 g (7$\frac{1}{2}$ oz)
salt and cayenne to taste		
Soufflé		
egg whites	7	17$\frac{1}{2}$
salt and cayenne to taste		

1 Lightly salt the flesh of the fish (sole and scallop) and place to rest for 10 minutes in the fridge until really cold.
2 Purée the flesh with the egg whites and the soft butter and cayenne.
3 Pass the flesh through a fine sieve and place into a stainless-steel bowl over ice.

4 Carefully incorporate the cream little by little.

5 Season to taste and keep cool.

6 Take individual soufflé moulds, grease them with soft unsalted butter and coat with fresh breadcrumbs.

7 Whisk the egg whites with a touch of salt, until stiff.

8 Add a small amount of egg white into the mousseline, incorporate well, then fold in gently the rest of the egg. Season to taste.

9 Pour the mixture into the moulds up to the rim.

10 Cook for about 14 minutes at 200°C (392°F)

You could serve this soufflé with a sauce Americaine with small dice of poached scallop. Or you could incorporate in the middle of the soufflé the same sauce Americaine reduced to a glaze with dice of sole fillet and scallop and tarragon.

67 – Soufflés of sole or chicken turbot

These soufflés may be prepared by boning the whole fish and stuffing with a forcemeat, they are then poached, garnished and served whole with a suitable sauce.

Sole

1 Allow 1×300 g (12 oz) sole per person.

2 Remove black and white skins and the head.

3 Trim the edges of the fish lightly with scissors.

4 With a filleting knife cut along the backbone and loosen the fillets on both sides, stopping about $1\frac{1}{2}$ cm ($\frac{3}{4}$ in) from the edge and leaving the same space at the head and tail end of the backbone.

5 Make a pocket in the sole by carefully cutting through the backbone and removing it.

6 Wash and dry the fish, season lightly.

7 Fill the pockets of the sole with fish forcemeat, page 179.

8 Draw the edges of the fish together leaving a gap of about 4 cm ($1\frac{1}{2}$ in) in the middle and 1 cm ($\frac{1}{2}$ in) at each end.

9 Smooth with a palette knife dipped in boiling water and wiped dry before use.

10 Place the fish into well buttered ovenproof dishes, covered with well buttered greaseproof paper.

11 Poach gently in fish stock and white wine for approximately 15 minutes. The filling will expand during cooking.

12 When cooked, carefully remove the fish, strain off cooking liquid and reduce and make into the required fish sauce.

13 Dress the soles, garnish as required, coat with sauce and serve.

Notes There is considerable scope for variation in this dish. The forcemeat can be a contrasting fish, e.g. crab, scallop, lobster, and can also contain diced or flaked fish or shrimps, prawns, mushrooms or truffles. Any of the many variations of fish sauce may be used and the garnish may be simple, e.g. a prawn, or more lavish, e.g. mussel, oyster, turned mushrooms.

Chicken turbot

1 Allow $1 \times 1\frac{1}{2}$–2 kg (3–4 lb) chicken turbot for 4 portions.

2 Gut the turbot and clean the head, removing the gills and eyes.

3 Cut down backbone on black skin side and raise the fillets as in stage 4 for sole.

4 Proceed as for sole for preparation and cooking, allowing more cooking time.

5 Remove the black skin carefully, without damaging the flesh of the fish, before serving.

Note All the notes for sole apply equally to chicken turbot.

68 – Tuna

Because tuna fish can be very large slices they are usually cut without bone 1–2 cm ($\frac{1}{2}$–1 in) thick. Slices on the bone from smaller fish (darnes) are sometimes named rouelles. Large pieces of fish are also braised.

69 – Braised tuna

	4 portions	10 portions
piece of tuna	1×600 g ($1\frac{1}{2}$ lb)	3×600 g ($1\frac{1}{2}$ lb)
onion, thickly sliced	100 g ($\frac{1}{4}$ lb)	250 g (10 oz)
carrot, thickly sliced	100 g ($\frac{1}{4}$ lb)	250 g (10 oz)
bouquet garni		
olive oil	60 ml ($\frac{1}{8}$ pt)	150 ml ($\frac{1}{3}$ pt)
white wine	125 ml ($\frac{1}{4}$ pt)	300 ml ($\frac{5}{8}$ pt)
white stock		

1 Well oil a small braising pan.
2 Add the onion and carrot.
3 Place the tuna on top, cover with a lid and sweat in the oven for
   15–20 minutes.
4 Add white wine and sufficient stock to barely cover the fish.
5 Season *very* lightly with salt and pepper, add bouquet garni.
6 Return to the oven, cover and cook gently for approximately
   45 minutes.
7 Remove the fish when cooked and reduce the cooking liquid.
8 Correct seasoning, strain and skim.
9 To serve moisten the fish with a little stock and serve the remainder
   separately.

70 – Braised tuna Italian style

	4 portions	10 portions
piece of tuna	$1 \times 600\,g$ ($1\frac{1}{2}$lb)	$3 \times 600\,g$ ($1\frac{1}{2}$lb)
Marinade		
lemon, juice of	1	2–3
olive oil	60 ml ($\frac{1}{8}$pt)	150 ml ($\frac{1}{3}$pt)
onion, sliced	100 g ($\frac{1}{4}$lb)	250 g (10 oz)
carrot, sliced	100 g ($\frac{1}{4}$lb)	250 g (10 oz)
bay leaf	$\frac{1}{2}$	1
thyme, salt and pepper		
shallots, chopped	100 g ($\frac{1}{4}$lb)	250 g (10 oz)
mushrooms, chopped	200 g ($\frac{1}{2}$lb)	250 g (10 oz)
white wine	125 ml ($\frac{1}{4}$lb)	300 ml ($\frac{5}{8}$pt)
fish stock	125 ml ($\frac{1}{4}$pt)	300 ml ($\frac{5}{8}$pt)

1 Marinade the pieces of fish for 1 hour.
2 Remove, dry well and colour in hot oil.
3 Place in braising pan, add shallots and mushrooms.
4 Cover with a lid, cook gently in oven for 15–20 minutes.
5 Add white wine and fish stock, cover, return to oven.
6 Braise gently for approximately 45 minutes until cooked.
7 Carefully remove the fish, correct the seasoning of the liquid (which
   may be lightly thickened with beurre manié, if required) and serve.

Notes
- Other ingredients that may be used when braising tuna include: tomatoes, garlic, basil, vinegar.
- Slices of tuna can also be shallow fried or cooked meunière with or without the meunière variations.

71 – Grilled tuna

	4 portions	10 portions
pieces of tuna	4 × 150 g (6 oz)	10 × 150 g (6 oz)
Marinade		
small onion, thinly sliced	1	$2\frac{1}{2}$
bay leaf	$\frac{1}{2}$	1
sprig of thyme		
parsley stalks		
juice of a lemon		
olive oil	125 ml ($\frac{1}{4}$ pt)	300 ml ($\frac{5}{8}$ pt)

1 Season the fish.
2 Marinade for an hour using half the oil.
3 Drain well, dry, oil and grill gently on both sides.
4 Serve with quarters of lemon and/or a suitable sauce, e.g. tartare.

72 – Shallow-fried whiting

1 Allow 1 × 250–300 g (10–12 oz) fish per person.
2 Cut on either side of the backbones and remove.
3 Flour, egg and crumb the fish, leaving the fillets joined but flat and unseparated.
4 Shallow fry on both sides in oil and butter.
5 Serve with parsley butter.

73 – Whiting colbert

Prepare as in previous recipe, deep fry and add 2–3 slices of parsley butter just before serving.

74 – Whiting poached in white wine with shrimps, mussels and mushrooms

1 Cut fish on either side of the backbones and remove.
2 Poach fish in white wine, mushroom cooking liquor and fish stock.
3 Strain off cooking liquor and make into a white wine sauce, strain.
4 Garnish fish with shrimps, mussels and mushrooms.
5 Add a little chopped parsley to the sauce, coat the fish and serve.

—— *Shellfish* ——

FOOD VALUE

Shellfish is a good body-building food. As the flesh is coarse and therefore indigestible a little vinegar may be used in cooking to soften the fibres.

QUALITY, PURCHASING POINTS AND STORAGE

SHELLFISH	SEASON	PURCHASING UNIT
cockles	all year, best in summer	weight
common crab	all year, best April to December	number and weight
spider crab	all year	number and weight
swimming crab	all year	number and weight
king crab, red crab	check with supplier	imported frozen, shelled, prepared
soft-shelled crab	check with supplier	number and weight
crawfish	April to October	number and weight
cuttlefish	all year	number and weight
Dublin Bay prawn	all year	number and weight
freshwater crayfish	mainly imported, some farmed in UK, wild have short season	number, weight and by case
lobster	April to November	number and weight
mussels	September to March	weight
oysters	May to August	by the dozen
prawn and shrimp	all year	number and weight
scallop	best December to March	number and weight
sea urchin	all year	number and by case

1 With the exception of shrimps and prawns all shellfish, if possible, should be purchased alive, so as to ensure freshness.
2 They should be stored in a cold room.
3 Shellfish are kept in boxes and covered with damp sacks.
4 Shellfish should be cooked as soon as possible after purchasing.

Shrimps and prawns are usually bought cooked and may be obtained in their shell or peeled. They should be freshly boiled, of an even size and not too small. Frozen shrimps and prawns are obtainable in packs ready for use.

TYPES OR VARIETIES OF SHELLFISH

Cockles

These are enclosed in pretty cream-coloured shells of 2–3 cm (1–1½ in). Cockles are soaked in salt water to purge and then steamed. They may be used in soups, salads and fish dishes, or served as a dish by themselves.

Shrimps

Shrimps are used for garnishes, decorating fish dishes, cocktails, sauces, salads, hors-d'oeuvre, potted shrimps, omelets and savouries.

Prawns

Prawns are larger than shrimps; they may be used for garnishing and decorating fish dishes, for cocktails, canapés, salad, hors-d'oeuvre and for hot dishes, such as curried prawns.

Scampi, Dublin Bay prawn

Scampi are found in the Mediterranean. The Dublin Bay prawn, which is the same family, is caught around the Scottish coast. These shellfish resemble small lobster about 20 cm (8 in) long and only the tail flesh is used.

Crayfish

Crayfish are a type of small freshwater lobster used for garnishing cold buffet dishes and for recipes using lobster. They are dark brown or grey, turning pink when cooked. Average size is 8 cm (3 in).

Lobster

Quality and purchasing points

1 Live lobsters are bluish black in colour and when cooked they turn bright red.
2 They should be alive when bought in order to ensure freshness.
3 Lobsters should have both claws attached.
4 They ought to be fairly heavy in proportion to their size.
5 Price varies considerably with size. For example, small $\frac{1}{2}$kg (1 lb) lobsters are more expensive per kilogram than large lobsters.
6 Lobster prices fluctuate considerably during the season.
7 Hen lobsters are distinguished from the cock lobsters by a broader tail.
8 There is usually more flesh on the hen, but it is considered inferior to that of the cock.
9 The coral of the hen lobster is necessary to give the required colour for certain soups, sauces and lobster dishes. For these, 1 kg (2 lb) hen lobster should be ordered.
10 When required for cold individual portions, cock lobsters of $\frac{1}{4}$–$\frac{1}{2}$kg ($\frac{1}{2}$–1 lb) are used to give two portions.

Use Lobsters are served cold in cocktails, hors-d'oeuvre, salads, sandwiches and on buffets. When hot they are used for soup, grilled and served in numerous dishes with various sauces. They are also used as a garnish to fish dishes.

Crawfish

Crawfish are like large lobsters without claws, but with long antennae. They are brick red in colour when cooked. Owing to their size and appearance they are used mostly on cold buffets but they can be served hot. The best size is $1\frac{1}{2}$–2 kg (3–4 lb).

Crab

Quality and purchasing points

1 Crab should be alive when bought to ensure freshness and both claws should be attached to the body.
2 The claws should be large and fairly heavy.
3 The hen crab has a broader tail, which is pink. The tail of the cock is narrow and whiter.

4 There is usually more flesh on the hen crab, but it is considered to be of inferior quality to that of the cock.

Use Crabs are used for hors-d'oeuvre, cocktails, salads, dressed crab, sandwiches and bouchées. Soft-shelled crabs are eaten in their entirety. They are considered to have an excellent flavour and may be deep or shallow fried or grilled.

Oysters

Whitstable and Colchester are the chief English centres for oysters where they occur naturally and are also farmed. Since the majority of oysters are eaten raw it is essential that they are thoroughly cleansed before the hotels and restaurants receive them.

Quality and purchasing points

1 Oysters must be alive; this is indicated by the firmly closed shells.
2 They are graded in sizes and the price varies accordingly.
3 Oysters should smell fresh.
4 They should be purchased daily.
5 English oysters are in season from September to April (when there is an R in the month).
6 During the summer months oysters are imported from France, Holland and Portugal.

Storage

Oysters are stored in barrels or boxes, covered with damp sacks and kept in a cold room to keep them moist and alive. The shells should be tightly closed; if they are open, tap them sharply, and if they do not shut at once, discard them.

Use The popular way of eating oysters is in the raw state. They may also be served in soups, hot cocktail savouries, fish garnishes, as a fish dish, in meat puddings and savouries.

Mussels

Mussels are extensively cultivated on wooden hurdles in the sea, producing tender, delicately flavoured, plump fish. British mussels are considered good; French mussels are smaller; Dutch and Belgian mussels are plumper. All vary in quality from season to season.

Buying and quality points

1 The shells must be tightly closed.
2 The mussels should be large.
3 There should not be an excessive number of barnacles attached.
4 Mussels should smell fresh.

Storage   Mussels are kept in boxes, covered with a damp sack and stored in a cold room.

Use   They may be served hot or cold or as a garnish.

Scallops

Great scallops are up to 15 cm (6 in) in size; Bay scallops up to 8 cm (3 in); Queen scallops are small-cockle-sized, and are also known as 'Queenies'. Scallops may be steamed, poached, fried or grilled.

Buying and quality points

1 Scallops are found on the sea-bed, and are therefore dirty, so it is advisable to purchase them ready cleaned.
2 If scallops are not bought cleaned, the shells should be tightly closed.
3 The orange part, roe, should be bright in colour and moist.
4 If they have to be kept, they should be stored in an ice-box or refrigerator.

Use   Scallops are usually poached or fried.

RECIPES

75 – Lobster Mornay

	4 portions	10 portions
cooked lobsters (400 g/1 lb)	2	5
butter	25 g (1 oz)	60 g (2½ oz)
salt, cayenne		
Mornay sauce	250 ml (½ pt)	625 ml (1¼ pt)
grated cheese (Parmesan)		

1 Remove lobsters' claws and legs.
2 Cut lobsters carefully in half lengthwise.
3 Remove all meat. Discard the sac and trail.

4 Wash shell and drain on a baking sheet upside down.
5 Cut the lobster meat into escalopes.
6 Heat the butter in a thick-bottomed pan, add the lobster and season.
7 Turn two or three times; overcooking will toughen the meat.
8 Meanwhile, finish the Mornay sauce.
9 Place a little sauce in the bottom of each shell.
10 Add the lobster, press down to make a flat surface.
11 Mask completely with sauce, sprinkle with grated cheese, and brown under the salamander and serve garnished with pickled parsley.

76 – Lobster Thermidor

	4 portions	10 portions
cooked lobsters	2	5
butter	25 g (1 oz)	60 g ($2\frac{1}{2}$ oz)
finely chopped shallot	12 g ($\frac{1}{2}$ oz)	30 g ($1\frac{1}{4}$ oz)
dry white wine	60 ml ($\frac{1}{8}$ pt)	150 ml ($\frac{1}{3}$ pt)
diluted English mustard	$\frac{1}{2}$ tsp	1 tsp
chopped parsley		
Mornay sauce	$\frac{1}{4}$ litre ($\frac{1}{2}$ pt)	$\frac{5}{8}$ litre ($1\frac{1}{4}$ pt)
grated Parmesan cheese	25 g (1 oz)	60 g ($2\frac{1}{2}$ oz)

1 Remove lobsters' claws and legs
2 Cut lobsters carefully in halves lengthwise. Remove the meat.
3 Discard the sac and remove the trail from the tail.
4 Wash the halves of shell and drain on a baking sheet.
5 Cut the lobster meat into thick escalopes.
6 Melt the butter in a sauteuse, add the chopped shallot and cook until tender without colour.
7 Add the white wine to the shallot and allow to reduce to a quarter of its original volume.
8 Mix in the mustard and chopped parsley.
9 Add the lobster slices, season lightly with salt, mix carefully and allow to heat slowly for 2–3 minutes. If this part of the process is overdone the lobster will become tough and chewy.
10 Meanwhile spoon a little of the warm Mornay sauce into the bottom of each lobster half shell.
11 Neatly add the warmed lobster pieces and the juice in which they were re-heated. If there should be an excess of liquid it should be reduced and incorporated into the Mornay sauce.

12 Coat the half lobsters with the remaining Mornay sauce, sprinkle with Parmesan cheese and place under a salamander until a golden brown, and serve garnished with picked parsley.

77 – Lobster American style

	4 portions	10 portions
live hen lobster	1 kg (2 lb)	2½ kg (5 lb)
butter	100 g (4 oz)	250 g (10 oz)
oil	60 ml (⅛ pt)	150 ml (⅓ pt)
finely chopped shallot	50 g (2 oz)	125 g (5 oz)
chopped clove of garlic	1	2–3
brandy	60 ml (⅛ pt)	150 ml (⅓ pt)
dry white wine	125 ml (¼ pt)	300 ml (⅝ pt)
fish stock	250 ml (½ pt)	600 ml (1¼ pt)
tomatoes, skinned, deseeded, diced	200 g (8 oz)	500 g (1¼ lb)
tomato purée	25 g (1 oz)	50 g (2½ oz)
coarsely chopped parsley		
salt, cayenne pepper		

1 Wash the lobster.
2 Remove the legs and claws. Crack the claws.
3 Cut the lobster in halves crosswise between the tail and carapace.
4 Cut the carapace in two lengthwise.
5 Discard the sac but retain the coral and place in a basin.
6 Cut the tail across in thick slices through the shell.
7 Remove the trail. Wash the lobster pieces.
8 Heat 50 g (2 oz) of the butter with the oil, in a sauté-pan.
9 Add the pieces of lobster, season with salt and fry off rapidly until a red colour on all sides. Pour off all the butter.
10 Add the shallot and garlic, cover the pan with a lid and allow to sweat for a few seconds.
11 Add the brandy and allow it to ignite.
12 Add the white wine, fish stock, tomatoes, tomato purée and a little of the chopped parsley. Allow to simmer for 20 minutes.
13 Remove the lobster, pick the meat from the shells and place in a covered serving dish and keep warm.
14 Reduce the cooking liquor by a half.
15 Pound lobster coral, mix in the other 50 g (2 oz) butter until smooth.
16 Add this lobster butter to the sauce, mix in well until the sauce

thickens then remove it from the heat.

17 Add a little cayenne and correct the seasoning.

18 Pass the sauce through a coarse strainer, mix in a little fresh coarsely chopped parsley and pour over the lobster.

19 Decorate with the head and tail of the lobster and serve.

20 Serve accompanied with a pilaff of rice.

78 ~ Grilled lobster

	4 portions	10 portions
live lobster	2 × 400 g (1 lb)	5 × 400 g (1 lb)

Method A

1 Cut the lobster in halves lengthwise.

2 Remove the sac in the head and clean the tail.

3 Brush with butter and grill over a moderate heat for 15–20 minutes.

Method B

1 Plunge the lobster into a boiling court bouillon and cook for 10 minutes.

2 Remove from the liquid, split in half, remove sac and clean the tails.

3 Grill for 5–10 minutes over a moderate heat.

Serve with a suitable sauce, e.g. melted or herb butter.

Note   Method A can sometimes leave the lobster flesh a little tough and chewy.

79 ~ Lobster Newburg

	4 portions	10 portions
cooked lobster meat cut into thickish pieces	400 g (1 lb)	1¼ kg (2½ lb)
butter	50 g (2 oz)	125 g (5 oz)
Madeira	60 ml (⅛ pt)	150 ml (⅓ pt)
cream } liaison	120 ml (¼ pt)	300 ml (⅝ pt)
egg yolks }	2	5

1 Gently reheat the lobster pieces in the butter.

2 Add Madeira and allow to gently almost completely reduce.
3 With the pan over gentle heat, pour in the liaison and allow to thicken by gentle continuous shaking, do not allow to boil, correct seasoning using a touch of cayenne if required.
4 Serve with pilaff rice separate.

Note   A lobster butter made from the crushed soft lobster shells will improve the colour of the sauce.

1 Sweat the crushed lobster shells in 1–2 oz butter over a fierce heat, stirring well.
2 Moisten with stock or water, boil for 10 minutes, strain.
3 Clarify the butter by simmering to evaporate the liquid.

T **80 – Langoustine provençale**

(RORY KENNEDY)

	4 portions	10 portions
large fresh langoustine	20	50
small bunches mixed salad leaves	4	10
French dressing	2 tbsp	5 tbsp
large cooked artichoke (diced)	2	2–3
large head of fennel (cooked and diced)	1	2–3
bunch fresh chives (chopped)	1	3
cloves of garlic (crushed)	2	5
langoustine oil	300 ml ($\frac{3}{5}$ pt)	600 ml ($1\frac{1}{4}$ pt)
olive oil	60 ml (2 fl oz)	125 ml ($\frac{1}{4}$ pt)
lemon	$\frac{1}{2}$	1
butter	25 g (1 oz)	60 g ($2\frac{1}{2}$ oz)
salt and pepper		
pinch saffron		

1 Remove flesh from langoustine tails, retaining one nice head per portion for garnish.
2 Remove any trail from the centre of the tails, lay them on a dry cloth and refrigerate.
3 In a small pan add the diced artichoke, fennel and crushed garlic. Cover with langoustine oil and heat gently (matignon).

4 When the above is warm check for seasoning. Add a few drops of lemon juice and the chopped chives, reserving a few for garnish. Keep warm.
5 In the large frying pan sauté the langoustine tails with the olive oil and butter. When the tails are almost cooked add a pinch of saffron. When cooked remove from the pan on to a dry cloth to remove excess oil.
6 Place a bouquet of salad leaves on each plate, seasoned and mixed with a little vinaigrette, then decorate with a cleaned langoustine head.
7 Surround each salad with a good 3 dessertspoons of matignon (artichoke mixture). Place 5 langoustine tails attractively around each salad.
8 Finish with some freshly chopped chives.

81 – Crab

Crab meat can be used in a variety of recipes:

First courses – on halves of mango or papaya coated with a mayonnaise or natural yoghurt based sauce lightly flavoured with tomato ketchup, lemon juice, Worcester sauce, etc.

Crab tartlets or barquettes – made with short puff or filo pastry cooked blind and filled with a crab mixture, for example:

	4 portions	10 portions
shallot, finely chopped, cooked in oil or butter	100 g (4 oz)	250 g (10 oz)
raw mushroom, finely chopped	200 g (8 oz)	500 g (1¼ lb)
white wine	30 ml ($\frac{1}{16}$ pt)	125 ml ($\frac{1}{4}$ pt)
crab meat	200 g (8 oz)	500 g (1¼ lb)
salt and cayenne pepper		

Sprinkle with fresh white breadcrumbs and melted butter and lightly brown.

Soup, au gratin, Mornay, devilled, curried, soufflé, pancakes, etc., are obvious other ways of preparing and serving crab.

However, crabs are at their best during the summer – simple crab salads will always be popular.

82 – Crab rissoles with a light mustard and vermouth sauce

(EUGENE CARTWRIGHT)

	4 portions	10 portions
baking potatoes	2 large	5 large
tabasco sauce	$\frac{1}{2}$ tsp	$1\frac{1}{4}$ tsp
egg yolks	5	13
lump crabmeat	600 g ($1\frac{1}{2}$ lb)	$1\frac{1}{2}$ kg ($3\frac{3}{4}$ lb)
fresh white breadcrumbs	150 g (6 oz)	375 g (1 lb)
finely chopped red and green peppers	75 g (3 oz)	187 g ($7\frac{1}{2}$ oz)
salt	$\frac{1}{2}$ tsp	$1\frac{1}{4}$ tsp
fresh ground pepper	$\frac{1}{2}$ tsp	$1\frac{1}{4}$ tsp
olive oil	60 ml (4 tbsp)	150 ml (10 tbsp)
Mustard sauce		
dry white wine	225 ml (9 fl oz)	562 ml (23 fl oz)
dry mustard	1–$1\frac{1}{2}$ tsp	$2\frac{1}{2}$–4 tsp
butter	25 g (1 oz)	60 g ($2\frac{1}{2}$ oz)
chopped shallots	60 ml (4 tbsp)	150 ml (10 tbsp)
fish stock	200 ml (8 fl oz)	500 ml (20 fl oz)
dry vermouth	125 ml (5 fl oz)	312 ml (13 fl oz)
double cream	225 g (9 oz)	562 g (1 lb 6 oz)

> Without sauce,
> 1 large rissole provides:
>
> 478 kcals/2002 kJ
> 20.2 g fat
> (of which 3.7 g saturated)
> 40.4 g carbohydrate
> (of which 1.7 g sugars)
> 36.3 g protein
> 3.7 g fibre

1 Bake the potatoes until soft, about 45 minutes. Skin and mash with a fork and leave to cool completely. Blend the tabasco and egg yolks, combine with crab, one-third of the breadcrumbs, the red and green peppers, salt and ground pepper. Mix lightly and form into cakes 2.5 cm (1 in) thick, 7.5 cm (3 in) in diameter.

2 To prepare the sauce, blend together 2 tablespoons of the white wine with 1 teaspoon of the mustard and set aside. Melt the butter in a small pan over a moderately low heat, add the shallots and stir for about 2 minutes until softened. Add the remaining white wine, fish stock and dry vermouth. Boil to reduce to 8 fl oz (about 15 minutes). Add the cream, boil again to reduce to 8 fl oz or the desired consistency. Add the mustard mixture. Stir in additional dry mustard as desired (first dissolving in water), season and pass through a fine strainer.

3 Dredge the cakes in the remaining breadcrumbs. Heat the olive oil in a wide frying pan over low heat. Fry the cakes for 6 minutes on each side. Raise the heat to moderate. Fry for 1 minute longer on each side

until golden brown. Heat the sauce, pour into a warmed sauce boat. Serve the rissoles on a silver dish lined with dish paper.

83 – Crawfish

Both the body and the flesh of the crawfish are similar to the lobster, the main difference being that the crawfish does not have main claws. All the flesh is contained in the tail.

Crawfish are boiled in the same way as lobsters and the meat can be used for any of the lobster recipes. Because of its spectacular image the crawfish cooked, dressed and presented whole is a popular addition to cold buffets.

84 – Dublin Bay prawns

Langoustines also known as scampi, freshwater crayfish, ecrevisses and prawns are used in a wide variety of dishes, hot and cold, and also as garnishes for many other dishes. Where possible they are best bought live and cooked in a court bouillon for 5–10 minutes.

If they have to be kept then this should be in a cool, moist place covered with damp sacking or seaweed.

Cleaning
The intestines can be removed either before or after cooking by grasping the middle tail fin, twisting once each way right and left then giving a sharp pull away from the tail.

Salads
After removing the fish from the shells they can be mixed with one or two of a variety of ingredients, e.g.:

1 Sliced cooked artichoke hearts.
2 Finely sliced raw button mushrooms.
3 Sliced roast or smoked duck or chicken, salmon (fresh or smoked).
4 Chopped parsley, chive, chervil, tarragon, basil lamb's lettuce, spinach or any other salad leaves a suitable gentle salad dressing.

Dublin Bay prawns, crayfish and prawns can also be prepared as for any lobster recipe hot or cold.

85 – Dublin Bay prawns or crayfish with pasta

	4 portions	10 portions
pasta, e.g. noodles, tagliatelle	400 g (1 lb)	1¼ kg (2½ lb)
cooked, cleaned fish tails	400 g (1 lb)	1¼ kg (2½ lb)
butter	50 g (2 oz)	125 g (5 oz)
chopped onion	50 g (2 oz)	125 g (5 oz)
garlic clove crushed (optional)	1	2–3
fish stock	250 ml (½ pt)	600 ml (1¼ pt)
chopped tomatoes	100 g (4 oz)	250 g (10 oz)
or tomato purée	1 tsp	2½ tsp
white wine	30 ml (1/16 pt)	75 ml (3/16 pt)
single cream (optional)	30 ml (1/16 pt)	75 ml (3/16 pt)
salt and pepper		

1 Sweat the crushed fish shells, onions and garlic in the butter.
2 Add the tomatoes, white wine and stock, simmer for 20 minutes.
3 Pass through a fine strainer, reboil, reduce if necessary.
4 Correct the seasoning, add the cream and fish tails, reheat.
5 Cook and drain pasta, mix in the sauce and serve.

Note　This recipe can be adapted and used for any other shellfish.

86 – Cockles

Cockles live in sand, therefore it is essential to wash them well under running cold water and then leave them in cold salted water changed frequently until no traces of sand remain.

Cockles are cooked:

1 In unsalted water until the shells open.
2 On a preheated griddle.
3 As for any of the mussel recipes.

They can be used for soup, sauces, salads and as garnishes for fish dishes.

87 – Clams

To ensure freshness, the shells of clams should be tightly shut. They can be steamed or poached like mussels and certain types are eaten raw.

Clams should be soaked in salt water for a few hours so that the sand in which they exist can be ejected.

Clams can be prepared and served raw (certain types only) or cooked with lemon juice; au gratin (fresh breadcrumbs, chopped garlic, parsley, melted butter); in pasta, stir fry and fish dishes as garnishes or/and a component of a sea food mixture; and as a soup, clam chowder.

88 – Mussels

When mussels are fresh the shells should be tightly closed. If the shells are open there is the possibility of danger from food poisoning therefore the mussels should be discarded.

Preparation for cooking
1 Scrape the shells to remove any barnacles, etc.
2 Wash well and drain in a colander.

To cook
1 Take a thick-bottomed pan with a tight-fitting lid.
2 For 1 litre (2 pt) mussels, place in the pan 25 g (1 oz) chopped shallot or onion.
3 Add the mussels, cover with a lid and cook on a fierce heat for 4–5 minutes until the shells open completely.

Preparation for use
1 Remove mussels from shells, checking carefully for sand, weed, etc.
2 Retain the liquid.

89 – Mussels in white wine sauce

	4 portions	10 portions
fine chopped shallot	50 g (2 oz)	125 g (5 oz)
chopped parsley		
dry white wine	60 ml ($\frac{1}{8}$ pt)	150 ml ($\frac{1}{3}$ pt)
mussels	2 litre (4 pt)	5 litre (10 pt)
fish stock if necessary		
beurre manié (butter/flour)	25 g (1 oz)	60 g ($2\frac{1}{2}$ oz)
salt, pepper		

1 portion provides:

133 kcals/559 kJ
3.0 g fat
(of which 0.5 g saturated)
0.7 g carbohydrate
(of which 0.7 g sugars)
26.1 g protein
0.2 g fibre

1 Take a thick-bottomed pan.
2 Add chopped shallot, parsley, wine and the well-cleaned and washed mussels.
3 Cover with a tight-fitting lid.
4 Cook over fierce heat till shells open, approximately 4–5 minutes.
5 Drain off all cooking liquor into a basin, allow to stand in order to allow any sand to sink to the bottom.
6 Carefully check the mussels for sand, etc. If in doubt, discard.
7 Place mussels in an earthenware casserole, cover with a lid and keep warm.
8 Carefully pour the cooking liquor into a small sauteuse.
9 If necessary make up to $\frac{1}{4}$ litre ($\frac{1}{2}$pt) with fish stock.
10 Bring to the boil, whisk in the beurre manié.
11 Correct the seasoning, add a little chopped parsley.
12 Pour over the mussels and serve.

90 – Mussels with a butter and lemon sauce

	4 portions	10 portions
large live mussels	2 litre (4 pt)	5 litre (10 pt)
sliced onion	100 g (4 oz)	250 g (10 oz)
parsley stalks		
finely chopped onion	50 g (2 oz)	125 g (5 oz)
butter	75 g (3 oz)	180 g (7$\frac{1}{2}$oz)
lemon, juice of	$\frac{1}{4}$	$\frac{3}{4}$
salt and pepper		

1 Scrape and thoroughly wash the mussels.
2 Place in a pan with sliced onion, parsley stalks and a little water.
3 Cover with tight-fitting lid and cook rapidly until mussel shells open.
4 Drain off all cooking liquid, allow it to settle, then strain carefully – being careful of any sand or grit.
5 Cook the chopped onion without colour in a little butter.
6 Reduce the mussel cooking liquid and make into a lightly thickened fish sauce; incorporate the butter and lemon juice, and correct seasoning.
7 Remove mussels from shells, mix with the sauce, replace them and the sauce into the larger shells, glaze and serve.

Note Mussels may be mixed with a fish sauce plus other ingredients if required, e.g. mushrooms, and served in a puff pastry case of any desired shape. They may also be served in the centre of a ring of pilaff rice which has been set in a savarin mould to give a neat presentation. In these ways they are suitable for serving either as a first, fish or main course.

91 – Fried mussels

1 Select large mussels and cook them as for recipe 88, remove from shells.
2 Marinate for 20 minutes in lemon juice, olive or vegetable oil and chopped parsley.
3 Dip in a thin frying batter and deep fry in hot fat.
4 Drain well and serve with quarters of lemon or a tartare type sauce.

92 – Oysters

Oysters are most popular when freshly opened and eaten raw, together with their own natural juice which should be carefully retained in the deep shell.

The shells should be tightly shut to indicate freshness. The oysters should be carefully opened with a special oyster knife so as to avoid scratching the inside shell, then turned and arranged neatly in the deep shell and served on a bed of crushed ice on a plate. They should not be washed unless gritty and the natural juices should always be left in the deep shell.

Accompaniments – brown bread and butter and lemon. It is usual to serve six oysters as a portion.

Oysters can also be cooked in a variety of ways. In all the following recipes they may be initially gently poached for a short time (10–15 seconds) in their own juice and the beards removed (over-cooking will toughen them).

Examples
(a) Warm the shells, add a little cheese sauce, place two oysters in each shell, coat with sauce, grated cheese, glaze and serve.
(b) As previous recipe, dressing the oysters on a bed of leaf spinach.

(c) Place two oysters in each shell, coat with white wine sauce, glaze and serve.

(d) As previous recipe, using champagne in place of white wine.

(e) Place one oyster on each shell, add a few drops of lemon, barely cover with breadcrumbs lightly fried in butter and gratinate under the salamander or in a very hot oven.

(f) Pass the well-dried oysters through a light batter, or flour, egg and crumb, deep fry and serve with quarters of lemon or lime.

Note Oysters can also be mixed with any of the poached fish sauces together with other ingredients if required, e.g. a few lightly poached bean sprouts, button or wild mushrooms and served in a bouchée, vol-au-vent, or any other shape of puff paste case – square, rectangular or diamond. They may then be served as a first course, fish course or main course, as required.

93 – Scallops

Scallops can be served as a first, fish or main course.

1 Always use live scallops if possible, in order to ensure freshness, and open them at the last possible moment.
2 Slide the blade of a knife under the flat lid of the shell and cut through the muscle by which it is attached.
3 Carefully scoop out the scallop with a spoon, separate the coral, discard the frilly outer membranes and wash well.

Note Alternatively, place the shells on top of the stove in the oven for a few seconds; the shells will then open and the scallops can be cut away with a small knife.

94 – Scallop mousseline

Some fish can be made into mousselines without using egg white in the preparation, e.g. scallops as in the following recipe:

scallops	6 large
sole or pike flesh	100 g (4 oz)
salt, pepper	
cream (very cold)	250 ml ($\frac{1}{2}$ pt)

1 Trim, wash and thoroughly dry the scallops.
2 Finely mince or process with the sole or pike.

3 Season lightly, place in the refrigerator or in a bowl of ice to cool thoroughly.
4 Gradually beat in the cream.
5 Pass the mixture through a fine sieve.
6 Poach a teaspoon of the mixture to test the seasoning and consistency.
7 Spoon into small buttered moulds.
8 Poach in a bain-marie or steam for approximately 10–15 minutes.
9 Allow to rest for 3–4 minutes before carefully turning out.
10 Serve with a suitable sauce, e.g. white wine, vermouth, tarragon, fennel or mousseline.

Note
1 Alternatively, five scallops can be used in the preparation with the remaining one cut into dice and put into the mixture before moulding.
2 Mousselines made without egg white will have a lighter consistency and must be handled carefully when cooked.

T 95 ~ Seared scallops with wild mushroom duxelle with a sauce of leeks and thyme

(CHRIS SUTER)

	4 portions	10 portions
large scallops	24	60
leeks *or* baby leeks	400 g (1 lb)	1¼ kg (2½ lb)
small bunch of thyme		
vegetable stock	500 ml (1 pt)	1¼ litre (2½ pt)
cream	150–250 ml (¼–½ pt)	500 ml (1 pt)
butter	200 g (8 oz)	500 g (1¼ lb)
salt and pepper		
Duxelle		
flat mushrooms	200 g (½ lb)	500 g (1¼ lb)
wild mushrooms	400 g (1 lb)	1¼ kg (2½ lb)
zest of orange	1	2–3
cloves of garlic (finely diced)	2	5
shallots (finely diced)	6	15
chopped parsley		
thyme		
a little bay leaf		
salt and pepper		
a little port		

1 Wash off all the mushrooms carefully to remove any grit.
2 Select the best of the wild mushrooms for garnishing the dish (approximately half).
3 The remaining half of the wild mushrooms and the flat mushrooms can be roughly chopped.
4 Fry the shallots and garlic, add the mushrooms, thyme and bay leaf.
5 Continue to fry and add the orange zest and the port.
6 Allow to cook out for 10–15 minutes until quite dry.
7 Stir in a little chopped parsley and check the seasoning.
8 Turn into the food processor, then strain through a fine strainer to allow any excess moisture to drain away.
9 Meanwhile prepare the scallops and cut the leeks into diamonds.
10 Bring the vegetable stock to the boil, add the cream and thyme and allow to infuse.
11 Add the butter to enrich and the diamonds of leeks, check the seasoning.
12 Season the scallops and sear quickly on the stove top or in a red hot skillet.
13 Warm the duxelle.
14 Pan fry the remaining wild mushrooms.
15 Check the seasoning and add a little chopped parsley.
16 Form the duxelle into 4 or 10 large quenelles.
17 Place one in the middle of each plate, dress with the leek sauce and the thyme.
18 Arrange the wild mushroom garnish and the seared scallops and serve.

96 – Scallops with cider

4 portions

finely chopped shallot	10 g ($\frac{1}{2}$ oz)
butter	25 g (1 oz)
scallops, prepared, cleaned and halved	12–16
dry cider	500 ml (1 pt)
salt and pepper	
double cream	250 ml ($\frac{1}{2}$ pt)
chopped parsley	

1 Cook shallot in the butter without colour.

2 Add scallops and cider, season, and poach for 2 minutes.
3 Remove scallops, keep warm.
4 Reduce liquid to 60 ml ($\frac{1}{8}$pt) and strain (×2$\frac{1}{2}$ for 10 portions).
5 Add cream, reboil, correct seasoning and consistency.
6 Add well-drained scallops, chopped parsley and serve.

Note   30 ml ($\frac{1}{16}$pt) calvados can be added to the sauce if desired (×2$\frac{1}{2}$ for 10 portions).

T 97 – Seafood risotto, scallop tempura and crispy ginger

(A. WORRALL-THOMPSON)

	4 portions	10 portions
shallot, finely chopped	1	2–3
ginger, peeled and finely chopped	2$\frac{1}{2}$cm (1 in)	2–3 cm (2$\frac{1}{2}$in)
garlic, finely chopped	1 clove	2–3 cloves
olive oil	3 tbsp	7 tbsp
dry white wine	125 ml ($\frac{1}{4}$pt)	300 ml ($\frac{5}{8}$pt)
mussels, cleaned	400 g (1 lb)	1$\frac{1}{4}$kg (2$\frac{1}{2}$lb)
littleneck clams, cleaned	8	20
fish stock	1$\frac{1}{2}$ litre (3 pt)	3$\frac{1}{2}$ litre (7 pt)
squid, cleaned, cut into small pieces	200 g (8 oz)	500 g (1$\frac{1}{4}$lb)
plum tomatoes, peeled, seeded and diced	3	7
coriander, chopped	2 tbsp	5 tbsp
flat parsley, chopped	2 tbsp	5 tbsp
basil, finely chopped	2 tbsp	5 tbsp
onion, finely chopped	1 cup	2$\frac{1}{2}$ cups
garlic, finely chopped	2 cloves	5 cloves
hot chilli, finely chopped	1	2$\frac{1}{2}$
unsalted butter	4 tbsp	10 tbsp
extra virgin olive oil	2 tbsp	5 tbsp
arborio rice	2 cups	2–3 cups
saffron, soaked in warm water	1 pinch	2 pinches
unsalted butter	50 g (2 oz)	125 g (5 oz)
salt and freshly ground black pepper		

1 Sweat the shallot, ginger and one clove garlic in half the olive oil until

soft but not brown.

2 Add the white wine, bring to the boil and add mussels and clams. Cover and cook until the shellfish have opened.
3 Remove shellfish and set aside.
4 Remove the flesh from shells and chop.
5 Add fish stock to the shellfish juices and bring to the boil. Simmer for 20 minutes and strain.
6 Sweat the remaining garlic in the remaining olive oil and add squid.
7 Cook fast for 2 minutes, add tomatoes, coriander, basil and parsley. Set aside.
8 Sweat the onion, garlic and chilli in the olive oil and butter until soft but brown.
9 Add rice and cook for 1 minute. Add simmering broth 125 ml ($\frac{1}{4}$ pt) at a time stirring frequently. Wait until each addition is almost completely absorbed. Stir frequently to prevent sticking.
10 Add saffron halfway through the cooking process.
11 After approximately 22 minutes when rice is tender, add squid mix, clams and mussels, and butter.
12 Stir vigorously to combine; serve immediately with scallop tempura and crispy ginger.

~ Scallop tempura

	4 portions	10 portions
scallops	4	10
nori seaweed		
flour	200 g (8 oz)	500 g (1$\frac{1}{4}$ lb)
beer	500 ml (1 pt)	1$\frac{1}{4}$ litre (2$\frac{1}{2}$ pt)
fresh yeast	70 g (3 oz)	175 g (7 oz)
pinch salt		

1 Wrap the scallops in nori seaweed, first removing coral (use coral in the risotto).
2 Make batter by combining remaining ingredients.
3 Allow to rest in a warm place for at least 1 hour.
4 Dip scallops in batter and deep fry.

~ Crispy ginger

1 Cut ginger as long and as thin as possible; julienne.
2 Cook separately in very hot clean oil.

MEAT DISHES

Prepare and cook complex meat, offal, game and poultry dishes

1   Select the type, quantity and quality of meat, offal, game and poultry in accordance with recipe specifications.

2   Demonstrate that the nutritional value of meat, offal, game and poultry is adequately retained during the preparation and cooking procedures.

3   Recognise that meat, offal, game and poultry not for immediate consumption are stored in accordance with the recipe specification and the relevant legislation.

—— *Introduction* ——

To cook meat properly it is necessary to know and understand the structure of meat. Lean flesh is composed of muscles, which are numerous bundles of fibres held together by connective tissue. The size of these fibres is extremely small, especially in tender cuts or cuts from young animals, and only the coarsest fibres may be distinguished by the naked eye. The size of the fibres varies in length, depth and thickness and this variation will affect the grain and the texture of the meat.

The quantity of connective tissue binding the fibres together will have much to do with the tenderness and eating quality. There are two kinds of connective tissue, the yellow (*elastin*) and the white (*collagen*). The thick yellow strip that runs along the neck and back of animals is an example of elastin. Elastin is found in the muscles, especially in older animals or those muscles receiving considerable exercise. Elastin will not cook, and it must be broken up mechanically by pounding or mincing. The white connective tissue (collagen) can be cooked, as it decomposes in moist heat to form gelatine. The amount of connective tissue in meat is determined by the age and breed of the animal, and the care and feed given to it.

The quantity of fat and its condition are important factors in determining eating quality. Fat is found on the exterior and interior of the carcass and in the flesh itself. Fat deposited between muscles or between the bundles of fibres is called marbling. If marbling is present, the meat is likely to be tender, of better flavour and moist. Much of the flavour of meat is given by fats found in lean or fatty tissues of the meat. Animals absorb flavour from the food they are given, therefore the type of feed is important in the final eating quality of the meat.

Extractives in meats are also responsible for flavour. Muscles that receive a good deal of exercise have a higher proportion of flavour extractives than those receiving less exercise. Shin, shank, neck and other parts receiving exercise will give richer stock and gravies, and meat with more flavour than the tender cuts.

Tenderness, flavour and moistness are increased if beef is hung after slaughter or pre-tenderised. Pork and veal are hung for 3–7 days according to the temperature. Meat is generally hung at a temperature of 1°C (34°F).

Meat, having a high protein content, is valuable for growth and repair of the body and as a source of energy.

STORAGE

1 Fresh meat must be hung to allow it to become tender.
2 Ideal storage temperature for fresh meat is −1°C (30°F) at a relative humidity of 90 per cent. Safe storage times, under hygienic conditions, at these temperatures are:
    beef up to 3 weeks
    veal up to 1–3 weeks
    lamb up to 10–15 days
    pork up to 7–14 days.
3 Meat should be suspended on hooks.

CLARIFICATION OF FAT

All fat trimmings can be chopped or minced and placed in a pan with a little water, then allowed to cook until there is no movement, and the fat is golden in colour. When cool, pass through a clean cloth, then use as required.

—— *Lamb and mutton* ——

As a guide when ordering, allow approximately 100 g (4 oz) meat off the bone per portion, and 150 g (6 oz) on the bone per portion.

It must be clearly understood that the weights given can only be approximate. They must vary according to the quality of the meat and also for the purpose for which the meat is being butchered. For example, a chef will often cut differently from a shop butcher, i.e. a chef frequently needs to consider the presentation of the particular joint whilst the butcher is more often concerned with economical cutting. We have given simple orders of dissection for each carcass. In general, bones need to be removed only when preparing joints, so as to facilitate carving. The bones are used for stock and the excess fat can be rendered down for second-class dripping.

BUTCHERY

Joints, uses and weights

| | | APPROX. WEIGHT | |
| | | LAMB | MUTTON |
JOINT	USES	KG (LB)	KG (LB)
Whole carcass		16 (32)	25 (50)
1 Shoulder (two)	roasting, stewing	3 (6)	$4\frac{1}{2}$ (9)
2 Leg (two)	roasting (mutton boiled)	$3\frac{1}{2}$ (7)	$5\frac{1}{2}$ (11)
3 Breast (two)	roasting, stewing	$1\frac{1}{2}$ (3)	$2\frac{1}{2}$ (5)
4 Middle neck	stewing	2 (4)	3 (6)
5 Scrag end	stewing, broth	$\frac{1}{2}$ (1)	1 (2)
6 Best-end (two)	roasting, grilling, frying	2 (4)	3 (6)
7 Saddle	roasting, grilling, frying	$3\frac{1}{2}$ (7)	$5\frac{1}{2}$ (11)
Kidneys	grilling, sauté		
Heart	braising		
Liver	frying		
Sweetbreads	braising, frying		
Tongue	braising, boiling		

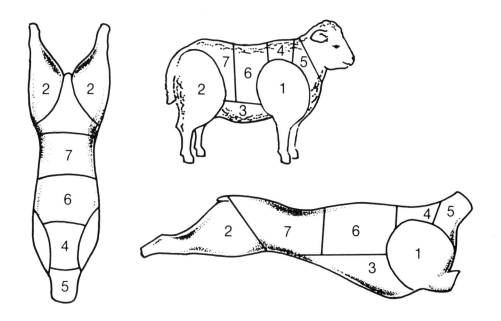

Quality of lamb and mutton

(Lamb is under 1 year old)

1 A good quality animal should be compact and evenly fleshed.
2 The lean flesh should be firm, of a pleasing dull red colour and of a fine texture or grain.
3 There should be an even distribution of surface fat which should be hard, brittle and flaky in structure and a clear white colour.
4 In a young animal the bones should be pink and porous, so that, when cut, a degree of blood is shown in their structure. As age progresses the bones become hard, dense, white and inclined to splinter when chopped.

Order of dissection of a carcass

1 Remove the shoulders.
2 Remove the breasts.
3 Remove the middle neck and scrag.
4 Remove the legs.
5 Divide the saddle from the best-end.

PREPARATION OF THE JOINTS AND CUTS

Shoulder

Boning   Remove the blade bone and upper arm bone, tie with string. The shoulder may be stuffed before tying.

Cutting for stews   Bone out, cut into even 25–50 g (1–2 oz) pieces.

Roasting   Remove the pelvic or aitchbone. Trim the knuckle cleaning 3 cm (1½ in) bone. Trim off excess fat and tie with string if necessary.

Breasts

Remove excess fat and skin.

Roasting   Bone, stuff and roll, tie with string.

Stewing   Cut into even 25–50 g (1–2 oz) pieces.

Middle neck

Stewing   Remove excess fat, excess bone and the gristle. Cut into even 50 g (2 oz) pieces. This joint, when correctly butchered, can give good uncovered second-class cutlets.

Scrag-end

Stewing   This can be chopped down the centre, the excess bone, fat and gristle removed and cut into even 50 g (2 oz) pieces, or boned out and cut into pieces.

Saddle

A full saddle includes the chumps and the tail. For large banquets it is sometimes found better to remove the chumps and use short saddles. Saddles may also be boned and stuffed.

saddle	roasting, pot roasting
loin	roasting
fillet	grilling, frying
loin chop	grilling, frying, stewing
chump chop	grilling, frying, stewing
kidney	grilling, sauté

Preparation of saddle of lamb

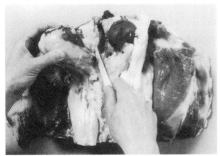

Removing kidneys

Removing sinew

Knife point indicates fillet

Trim off flaps

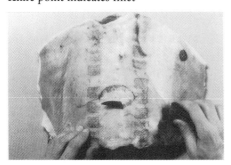

Trim excess fat

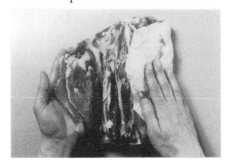

Fold over flaps

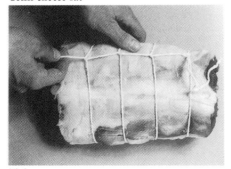

Tying

The saddle may be divided as follows:

Remove skin, starting from head to tail and from breast to back, split down the centre of the backbone to produce two loins. Each loin can be roasted whole, boned and stuffed, or cut into loin and chump chops.

Saddle for roasting
1 Skin and remove the kidney.
2 Trim the excess fat and sinew.
3 Cut off the flaps leaving about 15 cm (6 in) each side so as to meet in the middle under the saddle.
4 Remove the aitch or pelvic bone.
5 Score neatly and tie with string.
6 For presentation the tail may be left on, protected with paper and tied back.
7 The saddle can also be completely boned, stuffed and tied.

Loin for roasting
Skin, remove excess fat and sinew, remove pelvic bone, tie with string.

Loin boned and stuffed
Remove the skin, excess fat and sinew. Bone out, replace the fillet and tie with string. When stuffed, bone out, season, stuff and tie.

Chops
Loin chops
Skin the loin, remove the excess fat and sinew, then cut into chops approximately 100–150 g (4–6 oz) in weight. A first-class loin chop should have a piece of kidney skewered in the centre.

Double loin chop
Also known as a Barnsley chop. These are cut approximately 2 cm (1 in) across a saddle on the bone. When trimmed they are secured with a skewer and may include a piece of kidney in the centre of each chop.

Chump chops
These are cut from the chump end of the loin. Cut into approximately 150 g (6 oz) chops, trim where necessary.

Noisette
This is a cut from a boned-out loin. Cut slantwise into approximately 2 cm (1 in) thick slices, bat out slightly, trim cutlet shape.

Rosette
This is a cut from a boned out loin approximately 2 cm (1 in) thick. It is shaped round and tied with string.

Best-end

Best-end preparation
1 Remove the skin from head to tail and from breast to back.
2 Remove the sinew and the tip of the blade bone.
3 Complete the preparation of the rib bones as indicated in the diagram.
4 Clean the sinew from between the rib bones and trim the bones.
5 Score the fat neatly to approximately 2 mm ($\frac{1}{12}$ in) deep as shown.

The overall length of the rib bones to be trimmed to two and a half times the length of the nut of meat.

Roasting – prepare as above.

Cutlets – prepare as for roasting, excluding the scoring and divide evenly between the bones, or the cutlets can be cut from the best-end and prepared separately. A double cutlet consists of two bones; therefore a six bone best-end yields six single or three double cutlets.

PREPARATION OF LAMB OFFAL

Kidney

Grilling   Skin and split three-quarters the way through lengthwise, cut out gristle and skewer.

Sauté   Skin and remove the gristle. Cut slantways into 6–8 pieces.

Hearts

Braising   Remove the tubes and excess fat.

Liver

Remove skin, gristle and tubes and cut into thin slices on the slant.

Sweetbreads

Soak in salted water for 2–3 hours to remove any traces of blood. Wash well, blanch and trim.

Tongue

Remove bone and gristle from the throat end and soak in cold water for 24 hours. If pickled soak for 4 hours.

RECIPES

1 – Best-end or rack of lamb with herbs and garlic

	4 portions	10 portions
best-end of lamb prepared for roasting	1 × 8 or 2 × 4 bone	3 × 8 or 5 × 4 bone
Marinade		
oil	30 ml ($\frac{1}{16}$ pt)	125 ml ($\frac{1}{4}$ pt)
chopped cloves of garlic (optional)	4	10
chopped thyme	5 g ($\frac{1}{4}$ oz)	12 g ($\frac{5}{8}$ oz)
chopped rosemary	5 g ($\frac{1}{4}$ oz)	12 g ($\frac{5}{8}$ oz)
chopped savory	5 g ($1\frac{1}{4}$ oz)	12 g ($\frac{5}{8}$ oz)
salt and pepper		

1 Place meat in marinade for 30 minutes, turning frequently.
2 Roast, keeping meat slightly pink, and serve with a herb butter.

Notes   If dried herbs are used, halve the quantities. Other combinations of fresh herbs and spices may also be used. A well-browned boulangère potato makes a good accompaniment for this dish. Instead of marinading the meat, a coating of fresh breadcrumbs and rosemary (a herb particularly compatible with lamb) can be firmly pressed into the fat side of the meat half-way through cooking. Here again a range of herbs may be used as a variation, e.g. parsley, tarragon, basil.

If 3 cutlets are being served per portion, then 3 bone racks of lamb can be prepared, cooked and served uncut.

2 – Crumbed lamb cutlets with asparagus

	4 portions	10 portions
lamb cutlets (flattened)	8	20
butter	50 g (2 oz)	125 g (5 oz)
oil		
slices of truffle (optional)	8	20
asparagus tips	16–24	40–60

1 Flour, egg and crumb the cutlets, then shallow fry them in butter and oil on both sides.
2 Dress neatly, place slice of truffle on each.
3 Garnish with asparagus tips and serve.

Note   If truffles are unobtainable, slices of cooked button mushroom may be used.

3 – Crumbed lamb cutlets with artichokes, onions and mushrooms

	4 portions	10 portions
lamb cutlets	8	20
butter	50 g (2 oz)	125 g (5 oz)
oil		
cooked artichoke bottoms	4	10
chopped mushrooms	200 g (8 oz)	500 g (1¼ lb)
chopped onion	50 g (2 oz)	125 g (5 oz)

1 Prepare the cutlets as above, then shallow fry in butter and oil on both sides.
2 Dress neatly, garnish with artichoke bottoms reheated in butter and filled with mushroom and onion purée.

4 – Noisettes of lamb in a cream herb sauce

	4 portions	10 portions
noisettes	8 × 50 g (2 oz)	20 × 50 g (2 oz)
butter	100 g (4 oz)	250 g (10 oz)
dry white vermouth	60 ml ($\frac{1}{8}$ pt)	150 ml ($\frac{1}{3}$ pt)
white chicken, lamb or veal stock	250 ml ($\frac{1}{2}$ pt)	600 ml (1$\frac{1}{4}$ pt)
double cream	250 g ($\frac{1}{2}$ oz)	600 ml (1$\frac{1}{4}$ pt)
chopped fresh herbs, e.g. tarragon, basil, parsley	10 g ($\frac{1}{2}$ oz)	25 g (1$\frac{1}{4}$ oz)
salt and pepper		

> 1 portion provides:
>
> 606 kcals/2502 kJ
> 55 g fat
> (of which 34.2 g saturated)
> 2.5 g carbohydrates
> (of which 2.5 g sugars)
> 21.5 g protein
> 0 g fibre

1 Sauté noisettes in a little of the butter, keeping them pink. Remove from pan and keep warm.
2 Pour off excess fat, add vermouth and reduce by three-quarters.
3 Add stock, reduce by half, then add cream.
4 Reduce to a light consistency. Strain, add herbs, and incorporate remainder of butter.
5 Correct seasoning and consistency, coat noisettes and serve.

Note Two or three noisettes may be offered according to size and the prices charged.

White wine, sherry or port may be used in place of vermouth. One or a mixture of the herbs may be used. Cultivated or wild mushrooms may be added.

5 – Noisettes of lamb in cider, calvados and cream

	4 portions	10 portions
noisettes	8 × 50 g (2 oz)	20 × 50 g (2 oz)
butter	50 g (2 oz)	125 g (5 oz)
white lamb, veal or chicken stock	250 ml ($\frac{1}{2}$ pt)	600 ml (1$\frac{1}{4}$ pt)
dry cider	125 ml ($\frac{1}{4}$ pt)	300 ml ($\frac{5}{8}$ pt)
calvados	30 ml ($\frac{1}{16}$ pt)	125 ml ($\frac{1}{4}$ pt)
double cream	250 ml ($\frac{1}{2}$ pt)	600 ml (1$\frac{1}{4}$ pt)
salt and pepper		

1 Sauté noisettes in a little butter, keep warm.

2 Pour off excess fat, add stock and reduce by two-thirds.

3 Add cider, calvados and cream and reduce to a light consistency.

4 Strain, correct seasoning and consistency, pour over noisettes and serve.

Note This dish may be garnished with apples, e.g. cut in rings and fried, caramelised, baked in quarters etc.

T 6 – Lambs' kidneys with juniper and wild mushrooms

(PAUL GAYLER)

	4 portions	10 portions
English lambs' kidneys	12	30
chopped shallots	25 g (1 oz)	60 g (2½ oz)
crushed juniper berries	12	30
gin marinaded with the berries for one day	60 ml (⅛ pt)	150 ml (⅓ pt)
English white wine	125 ml (¼ pt)	300 ml (⅝ pt)
strong lamb stock	½ litre (1 pt)	1¼ litre (2½ pt)
selected wild mushrooms	50 g (2 oz)	125 g (5 oz)
large potatoes	2	5

1 Remove fat and thin film of tissue covering the kidneys.

2 Season well and sauté in a hot pan, keeping them pink. Remove and keep warm.

3 Add the shallots and some crushed juniper berries to the pan, flambé with a little gin, pour in the white wine and reduce well. Add the lamb stock and reduce by half. Pass and finish with butter.

4 Prepare the mushrooms and sauté in hot oil, adding butter to maintain their earthy flavour, then keep warm.

5 Finely shred the potatoes into matchsticks on a mandolin, dry in a clean cloth, season and cook in butter as a fine potato cake.

6 To serve, place the potato cake in the centre of a serving dish, slice the kidneys and arrange attractively in a circle on the potato. Garnish the kidney with the wild mushrooms, cordon the dish with the sauce and serve immediately.

▣ 7 – Sliced fillet of lamb with fresh herbs

(NICK GILL)

	4 portions	10 portions
double loin of young English lamb	$\frac{1}{2}$	1
olive oil, salt and pepper		
tarragon, chervil, mint, thyme and parsley		
watercress and spinach		
strong lamb stock	400 ml (1 pt)	1 litre (2 pt)
shallots, finely chopped	2	5
glass dry vermouth	$\frac{1}{2}$	1
double cream	220 ml ($\frac{1}{2}$ pt)	500 ml (1 pt)
turnips and carrots	400 g (1 lb)	1 kg (2 lb)
potatoes (Dutch binje)	400 g (1 lb)	1 kg (2 lb)
young mange-tout	80 g (3 oz)	200 g (8 oz)
fresh asparagus tips	8	20

1 Prepare the lamb a day in advance. Strip it of all bone, fat, and sinew, producing long fillets.
2 Marinate the fillets overnight in olive oil, seasoning and finely chopped herbs. Reserve the bones.
3 To prepare the herb sauce: blanch bunches of fresh tarragon, chervil, mint, thyme, parsley (reserving a few leaves), watercress and spinach, by plunging into rapidly boiling water, then almost immediately into cold water. Drain, purée, put into a clean bowl and refrigerate.
4 Reduce the lamb stock, with the lightly roasted and finely chopped lamb bones, to a syrupy residue. Remove the bones.
5 In a clean saucepan, sweat the shallots with the vermouth and the lamb glaze until almost evaporated.
6 Add the cream and simmer gently for 5–10 minutes until slightly thickened. Sieve and keep warm.
7 To prepare the vegetable garnish: using a small Parisienne cutter, cut balls out of the turnips, carrot, and potatoes. Top and tail the mange-tout and bundle the asparagus. Cook carrot and turnip glacé, fry the potato, blanch the asparagus and mange-tout.
8 Heat a little olive oil in a heavy pan, add the drained and seasoned fillets of lamb, and cook over a fairly fierce heat, turning occasionally, until the lamb is well sealed and nicely pink inside. Remove from the pan and keep warm.

9 Add the herb purée to the stock and cream until a deep green colour and good flavour is obtained.

10 Sieve and adjust seasoning and consistency to taste.

11 To serve: coat large hot plates with the sauce. Slice the lamb into thin medallions and lay these around the plate. Decorate with the vegetables and herb leaves.

8 – Roast stuffed saddle of lamb

1 Select a short saddle, i.e. the chump-ends removed, and allow 150–200 g (6–8 oz) per portion.

2 Carefully remove the skin, starting from a breast flap at the head end.

3 Remove kidneys, excess fat and sinew.

4 Placing saddle fat down, carefully cut away the two fillets to expose the bones and bone-out.

5 Season the joint and insert a neat roll of stuffing in the space left by the bones, replace the fillets.

6 Thin out the breast flaps with a meat bat and trim so that they meet, forming a complete layer of fat around the saddle.

7 Turn the saddle over, lightly score the fat to form a pattern and tie securely with string at 2 cm (1 in) intervals.

The saddle may be roasted and served with roast gravy and redcurrant jelly or pot-roasted, in which case it may be garnished in a variety of ways, for example:

Quarters of artichoke bottoms, cocotte potatoes, tomatoes, French beans.

Tartlets garnished with Brussels sprouts and finished Mornay, potato croquettes.

Tartlets or artichoke bottoms filled with purée of peas, small château potatoes.

Artichoke bottoms filled with carrots and turnips. French beans, peas, asparagus tips, cauliflower coated with hollandaise sauce, new potatoes.

With thought and imagination other garnishes making use of a wide variety of vegetables can be offered.

The stuffing can be varied in many ways, for example:

• Basic stuffing or forcemeat for lamb joints.

- Duxelle base thickened with fresh breadcrumbs and bound with egg.
- Diced lamb kidneys quickly sautéed in a little butter can be added.
- Diced or quartered cultivated or wild mushrooms can be added.
- Thicken forcemeat can be used as a base.

I 9 – Lambs' liver flavoured with lavender and sage, served with avocado and sherry sauce

(PHILLIP ACCORSINI)

	4 portions	10 portions
lambs' liver	400 g (1 lb)	1 kg (2.2 lb)
milk	250 ml ($\frac{1}{2}$ pt)	625 ml (1$\frac{1}{4}$ pt)
garlic cloves	2	4
sage (chopped) bunch	1	2
lavender bunch	1	2
honey	50 g (2 oz)	125 g (5 oz)
sesame oil	25 ml (1 fl oz)	50 ml (2 fl oz)
avocado	1	1
unsalted butter	50 g (2 oz)	125 g (5 oz)
Sauce		
veal stock	250 ml ($\frac{1}{2}$ pt)	625 ml (1$\frac{1}{4}$ pt)
sherry	50 ml (2 fl oz)	125 ml (5 fl oz)
baby onions	200 g (8 oz)	500 g (1$\frac{1}{4}$ lb)
garlic clove	1	1
sesame oil	25 ml (1 fl oz)	50 ml (2 fl oz)

1 Remove skin and arteries from the liver and place on one side.
2 Mix milk, honey and half chopped sage, with the lavender and uncrushed garlic clove.
3 Place the liver in the milk mixture and leave for 24 hours.
4 Peel the baby onions, blanch them, then refresh.
5 Sauté the crushed garlic in sesame oil with the baby onions. Add the sherry and reduce by half.
6 Add the veal stock and reduce this by two-thirds. Take off heat and cool slightly.
7 Whisk in the unsalted butter and season.
8 Peel the avocado, stone it and cut into chunks. Reserve.
9 Heat sesame oil, remove liver from marinade and drain. Season liver with salt, pepper, sage and any remaining lavender

10 Sauté liver lightly until pink.
11 Sauté the avocado in the butter until soft, season with salt.
12 To serve: pour the sauce on to the plate, place the liver on top. Garnish with the avocado and the onions from the sauce. If you have any remaining sage or lavender use this also.

— *Beef* —

BUTCHERY

Side of beef, approximate weight 180 kg (360 lb).

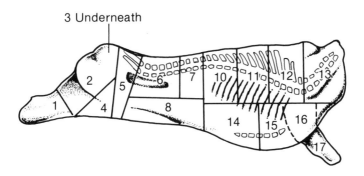

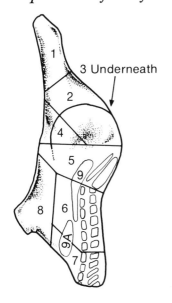

Hindquarter of beef

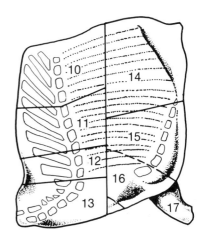

Forequarter of beef

Hindquarter: joints, uses and weights

JOINT	USES	APPROX. WEIGHT (KILO)	(LB)
1 Shin	Consommé, beef tea, stewing	7	14
2 Topside	Braising, stewing, second-class roasting	10	20
3 Silverside	Pickled in brine then boiled	14	28
4 Thick flank	Braising and stewing	12	24
5 Rump	Grilling and frying as steaks, braised in the piece	10	20
6 Sirloin	Roasting, grilling and frying in steaks	9	18
7 Wing ribs	Roasting, grilling and frying in steaks	5	10
8 Thin flank	Stewing, boiling, sausages	10	20
9 Fillet	Roasting, grilling and frying in steaks	3	6
Fat and kidney		10	20
	Total weight	90	180

Quality of beef

1 The lean meat should be bright red, with small flecks of white fat (marbled).
2 The fat should be firm, brittle in texture, creamy white in colour and odourless.

Older animals and dairy breeds have fat which is usually a deeper yellow colour.

Order of dissection

A whole side is divided between the wing ribs and the fore ribs.

Dissection of the hindquarter

1 Remove the rump suet and kidney.
2 Remove the thin flank.
3 Divide the loin and rump from the leg (topside, silverside, thick flank and shin).
4 Remove the fillet.
5 Divide rump from the sirloin.

6 Remove the wing ribs.
7 Remove the shin.
8 Bone-out the aitchbone.
9 Divide the leg into the three remaining joints (silverside, topside and thick flank).

Dissection of the forequarter
1 Remove the shank.
2 Divide in half down the centre.
3 Take off the fore ribs.
4 Divide into joints.

― Brine

cold water	$2\frac{1}{2}$ litres (4 qt)
saltpetre	15 g ($\frac{3}{4}$ oz)
salt	$\frac{1}{2}$–1 kg (1–2 lb)
bayleaf	1
juniper berries	6
brown sugar	50 g (2 oz)
peppercorns	6

Boil the ingredients together for 10 minutes, skimming frequently. Strain into a china, wooden or earthenware container. When the brine is cold, add the meat. Immerse the meat for up to 10 days under refrigeration.

PREPARATION OF THE JOINTS AND CUTS

Hindquarter

Shin
Bone-out, remove excess sinew. Cut or chop as required.

Topside
Roasting – remove excess fat, cut into joints and tie with string.
Braising – as for roasting.
Stewing – cut into dice or steaks as required.

Silverside
Remove the thigh bone. This joint is usually kept whole and pickled in brine prior to boning.

Thick flank
As for topside.

Rump
Bone-out. Cut off the first outside slice for pies and puddings. Cut into 1½cm (¾in) slices for steaks. The point steak, considered the tenderest, is cut from the pointed end of the slice.

Sirloin
Roasting
Method I: whole on the bone
Saw through the chine bone, lift back the covering fat in one piece for approximately 10cm (4in). Trim off the sinew and replace the covering fat. String if necessary. Ensure that the fillet has been removed.

Method II: boned-out strip loin
The fillet is removed and the sirloin boned-out and the sinew is removed as before. Remove the excess fat and sinew from the boned side. This joint may be roasted open, or rolled and tied with string.

Grilling and frying
Prepare as for Method II above and cut into steaks as required.

Minute steaks
Cut into 1cm (½in) slices, flatten with a cutlet bat dipped in water, making as thin as possible, then trim.

Sirloin steaks
Cut into 1cm (½in) slices and trim. Approx. weight 150g (6oz).

Double sirloin steaks
Cut into 2cm (1in) thick slices and trim. Approx. weight 250–300g (10–12oz).

Porterhouse and T-bone steak
Porterhouse steaks are cut including the bone from the rib end of the sirloin.

T-bone steaks are cut from the rump end of the sirloin, including the bone and fillet.

Fillet

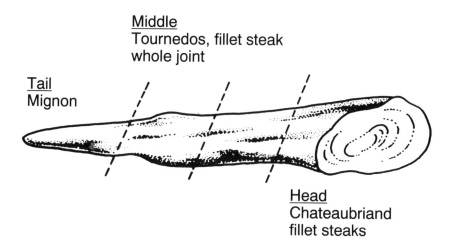

Middle
Tournedos, fillet steak
whole joint

Tail
Mignon

Head
Chateaubriand
fillet steaks

As a fillet of beef can vary from $2\frac{1}{2}$–$4\frac{1}{2}$ kg (5–9 lb) it follows that there must be considerable variation in the number of steaks obtained from it. A typical breakdown of a 3 kg (6 lb) fillet would be as above.

Chateaubriand
Double fillet steak 3–10 cm ($1\frac{1}{2}$–4 in) thick 2–4 portions. Average weight 300 g–1 kilo ($\frac{3}{4}$–2 lb). Cut from the head of the fillet, trim off all nerve and leave a little fat on the steak.

Fillet steaks
Approximately 4 steaks of 100–150 g (4–6 oz) each $1\frac{1}{2}$–2 cm ($\frac{3}{4}$–1 in) thick. These are cut as shown in the diagram and trimmed as for chateaubriand.

Tournedos
Approximately 6–8 at 100 g (4 oz) each, 2–4 cm (1–$1\frac{1}{2}$ in) thick. Continue cutting down the fillet. Remove all the nerve and all the fat and tie each tournedos with string.

Tail of fillet
Approximately $\frac{1}{2}$ kg (1 lb). Remove all fat and sinew and slice or mince as required.

Whole fillet

Preparation for roasting and pot roasting. Remove the head and tail of the fillet leaving an even centre piece from which all nerve and fat is removed. This may be larded by inserting pieces of fat bacon cut into long strips, with a larding needle.

Larding a fillet of beef – method 1

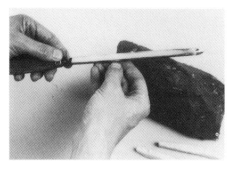

Larding a fillet of beef – method 2

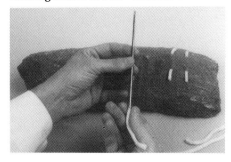
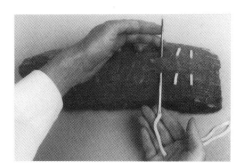

Wing rib

This joint usually consists of the last three rib bones which, because of their curved shape, act as a natural trivet and because of its prime quality make it a first-class roasting joint, for hot or cold, particularly when it is to be carved in front of the customer.

To prepare, cut seven-eighths of the way through the spine or chine bone, remove the nerve, saw through the rib bones on the underside 5–10 cm (2–4 in) from the end. Tie firmly with string. When the joint is cooked the chine bone is removed to facilitate carving.

Thin flank

Trim off excessive fat and cut or roll as required.

Forequarter

Fore ribs and middle ribs – prepare as for wing ribs.

chuck ribs
sticking piece
brisket } bone-out, remove excess fat and sinew,
plate   use as required.
leg of mutton cut
shank

PREPARATION OF BEEF OFFAL

Tongue	Remove bone and gristle from the throat end.
Hearts	Remove arterial tubes and excess fat.
Liver	Skin, remove the gristle and cut in thin slices on the slant.
Kidney	Skin, remove the gristle and cut as required.
Sweetbreads	Soak in salted water for 2–3 hours to remove any traces of blood. Wash well, trim, blanch and refresh.
Tripe	Wash well and soak in cold water, then cut into even pieces.
Tail	Cut between the natural joints, trim off excess fat. The large pieces may be split in two.

OFFAL	USES
Tongue	Pickled in brine, boiling, braising
Heart	Braising
Liver	Braising, frying
Kidney	Stewing, soup
Sweetbread	Braising, frying
Tripe	Boiling, braising
Tail	Braising, soup
Suet	Suet paste and stuffing or rendered down for first-class dripping
Bones	Beef stocks
Marrow	Savouries and sauces

RECIPES

10 – Fillet of beef

Fillet of beef served as a joint may be roasted or pot-roasted. The joint can be larded with strips of pork fat in order to give an added flavour and succulence to the meat whilst cooking. There are numerous ways of garnishing the fillet, such as:

Artichoke bottoms filled with broad beans (whole or in purée), sprigs of cauliflower coated with sauce hollandaise, parsley potatoes.

Small tartlet cases filled with peas à la française or purée of peas and macaire potatoes.

Bouquets of buttered asparagus tips, Lorette potatoes.

A well-flavoured roast gravy or a lightly thickened sauce made from the cooking juices should accompany this dish.

Attractive garnishes can also be made from the wide range of local and international vegetables available.

Do not over-elaborate when garnishing dishes, keep items to a minimum – simple, attractive and complementary to the meat.

11 – Tournedos

Tournedos and sirloin steaks (also known as entrecôte steaks) may be cooked and served, in many ways according to the classical repertoire with classical sauces, e.g. bordelaise, marchand de vins; but with thought and ingenuity numerous appetising variations can be evolved.

1 Always trim steaks well, so that no sinew, gristle or excess fat remains on the meat.
2 Flavour is enhanced if steaks are cooked in butter, but margarine or oil can be used.
3 If chopped onion, shallots or mushrooms are added, cook them in the same fat in the same pan after removing the steaks.
4 Drain off all fat.
5 Always utilise cooking juices by deglazing the pan with stock, wine (red or white), a fortified wine (vermouth, port, sherry, Madeira) or a spirit such as brandy, and use in making the accompanying sauce.

6 The sauce can be made in many ways, e.g.
   (a) adding a thin demi-glaze (plain or tomato flavoured), thickened gravy or a good, rich veal, beef or chicken stock.
   (b) adding cream, yoghurt or a thin veal or chicken velouté:

Either sauce may have a little butter incorporated to enrich and enhance the shine and presentation, e.g.:

– Red wine sauce

	4–6 portions
finely chopped onion	100 g (4 oz)
red wine	250 ml ($\frac{1}{2}$ pt)
beef or veal stock	250 g ($\frac{1}{2}$ pt)
crushed cloves garlic (optional)	2
sprig of thyme	1
butter	150 g (6 oz)
French mustard	2 tsp
salt and pepper	

1 After the steaks are cooked, drain off almost all the fat from the pan.
2 Add chopped onion and cook until soft.
3 Add wine, stock, garlic and thyme. Reduce by three-quarters and strain into a clean pan.
4 Incorporate the butter and mustard, season and pour over steaks.

– Shallot sauce

	4–6 portions
finely chopped shallots	100 g (4 oz)
dry white wine	250 ml ($\frac{1}{2}$ pt)
beef or veal stock	250 ml ($\frac{1}{2}$ pt)
butter	150 g (6 oz)
salt and pepper	
chopped parsley	5 g ($\frac{1}{4}$ oz)

1 After the steaks are cooked, drain off almost all the fat from the pan.
2 Add shallots and cook until soft. Add wine and stock, reduce by three-quarters and strain.
3 Incorporate butter, season, add parsley and pour over the steaks.

12 – Fillet of beef Wellington

	4 portions	10 portions
even-shaped beef fillet	400 g (1 lb)	1 kg (2 lb)
Duxelle		
chopped mushrooms	160 g (5 oz)	400 g (1 lb)
chopped shallot or onion	20 g (¾ oz)	50 g (2 oz)
oil	50 ml (⅛ pt)	125 ml (¼ pt)
chopped parsley	2 g (⅛ oz)	5 g (¼ oz)
salt and pepper		
puff or brioche pastry	400 g (1 lb)	1 kg (2 lb)
egg wash		

> 1 portion provides:
>
> 616 kcals/2573 kJ
> 40.8 g fat
> (of which 3.7 g saturated)
> 37.6 g carbohydrates
> (of which 1.7 g sugars)
> 26.8 g protein
> 0.5 g fibre

1 Trim off all sinew from the fillet, season and fry rapidly on all sides in very hot oil. Remove, drain and thoroughly cool.
2 Prepare the duxelle, keeping it fairly dry, and allow to cool.
3 Roll out the pastry 3 mm (⅛ in) thick and with a large knife neatly cut a rectangle sufficiently wide to envelope the meat and long enough to seal the ends.
4 A layer of thin pancakes may now be added to keep the pastry crisp.
5 Place half the duxelle in the centre, add the meat and cover with the other half.
6 Egg wash the edges of the paste and fold to make a neat roll, overlapping slightly, and neaten the ends to seal in the meat completely.
7 Place on to a greased baking sheet, egg wash generously.
8 Lightly score the surface into portion sizes to lessen the risk of the pastry breaking up when cut for service. If the joint is to be presented whole, further decoration can be added from the pastry trimmings at this stage.
9 Allow to rest in refrigerator for 1–2 hours.
10 Egg wash again and bake at 220°C (425°F) approximately 30 minutes; the meat should be pink in the centre.
11 Serve whole or cut into portions, as required, accompanied by a suitable sauce, e.g. Madeira.

Notes Variations can include additions to the duxelle, e.g. pâté, sliced or quartered button mushrooms, chopped ham or chicken, or purée of raw chicken or veal. Beef Wellington can also be prepared in single or double portions.

13 – Fillet of beef en croûte Richelieu

The prepared fillet is larded, the duxelle omitted and it is wrapped in pastry and cooked in the same way as beef Wellington, garnished with stuffed tomatoes and mushrooms, braised lettuce and château potatoes.

Other classical garnishes can also be used, such as:

Artichoke bottoms filled with carrot, turnips, dice of French beans and peas, sprigs of cauliflower coated with hollandaise sauce and château potatoes.

Morels tossed in butter, dice of bacon, and Parmentier potatoes.

Quarters of artichoke bottoms tossed in butter, cocotte potatoes, and slices of truffle.

Alternatively, garnishes can be prepared from selected seasoned vegetables according to one's own choice and an appropriate name given to the dish.

14 – Peppered steak in cream sauce

	4 portions	10 portions
steaks (fillet, rump or sirloin)	4×100–$150\,g$ (4–6 oz)	10×100–$150\,g$ (4–6 oz)
crushed peppercorns	50 g (2 oz)	125 g (5 oz)
butter	50 g (2 oz)	125 g (5 oz)
brandy	30 ml ($\frac{1}{16}$ pt)	125 ml ($\frac{1}{4}$ pt)
double cream	125 ml ($\frac{1}{4}$ pt)	300 ml ($\frac{5}{8}$ pt)
French mustard (optional)	1–2 tsp	5 tsp

1 Lightly salt the steaks and press them firmly into the peppercorns on each side, ensuring that the peppercorns stick. Leave for 30–45 minutes.
2 Shallow fry steaks on both sides in hot butter to just below required degree of cooking, remove and keep warm.
3 Pour off surplus fat, deglaze pan with brandy, add cream and boil to required consistency. Mix in mustard, correct seasoning.
4 Pour over steaks and serve.

Notes   Variations include:

(a) A thin demi-glace in place of cream, with the sauce finished by mixing in 50–75 g (2–3 oz) butter.
(b) 25–50 g (1–2 oz) finely chopped shallots placed in the pan and cooked for 20 seconds before adding the steaks.

I 15 – Fajitas

(Paul Burton)

	4 portions	10 portions
rump steak, cut into strips	450 g (1 lb)	1⅛ kg (2½ lb)
lime juice (fresh is best)	80 ml (⅕ pt)	200 ml (⅖ pt)
unsaturated margarine	35 g (1½ oz)	87 g (3½ oz)
onion, cut into strips	180 g (6½ oz)	450 g (1 lb)
mixed green and red peppers, seeded and cut into strips	180 g (6½ oz)	450 g (1 lb)
meat magic*	1½ tbsp	3½ tbsp
seasoning to taste		
flour or corn tortillas	8 × 6 in	20 × 6 in

1 Marinate the steak in lime juice, meat magic and seasoning for 15 minutes.
2 In a fry pan, melt the margarine, sauté vegetables and remove.
3 Drain the meat (reserve marinade), sauté rapidly, add vegetables, marinade mixture and cook for a further minute.
4 Serve with warmed tortillas, sour cream, guacamole and salsa.

*Commercial flavouring product.

Note   Try chicken as an alternative to steak, or a mixture of both. Traditionally, fajitas are eaten as envelopes of tortillas filled with sour cream, guacamole, salsa and the meat mixture.

16 – Tripe with dry cider in the Normandy style

Traditionally this dish is made using equal quantities of each of the four types of tripe – paunch, honeycomb, manyplies and reed – and an ox trotter.

	4 portions	10 portions
tripes cut into squares, well washed and blanched	800 g (1½ lb)	2 kg (4 lb)
ox trotter boned and cut into pieces	½	1
carrots peeled and thickly sliced	160 g (6½ oz)	400 g (1 lb)
onions peeled and thickly sliced	160 g (6½ oz)	400 g (1 lb)
bouquet garni		
cloves ⎱ tied in muslin	1	2
garlic cloves ⎰	2	4
dry cider	200 ml (¾ pt)	500 ml (1 pt)
beef fat or pork rind	80 g (3 oz)	200 g (½ lb)
salt, mill pepper		

1 Place tripe, onions, carrots, bouquet garni, cloves and cider in a braising pan.
2 Season lightly with salt and mill pepper.
3 Add the chopped bones from the ox trotter.
4 Cover with thick slices of beef fat or pork rind.
5 Add the pan and seal with a rim of flour and water paste.
6 Cook in a slow preheated oven for 12 hours.
7 Break the seal, remove lid, cloves, bones and all fat.
8 Correct seasoning and serve.

Note This recipe is for fresh uncooked tripe. If the tripe has been blanched and pre-cooked then the cooking time needs to be considerably reduced to 2–2½ hours.

17 – Oxtail braised in white wine with chestnuts

	4 portions	10 portions
oxtail	1 kg (2 lb)	2½ kg (5 lb)
butter	50 g (2 oz)	125 g (5 oz)
bottles dry white wine	1	2
lean bacon	200 g (8 oz)	500 g (1¼ lb)
peeled chestnuts	12	30
button onions or shallots	24	60
bouquet garni		
salt and pepper		

1 Cut the oxtail into pieces, remove excess fat.
2 Lightly fry on both sides in the butter without colouring.
3 Place the oxtail into a braising pan.
4 Add the wine, bring to the boil, add the bouquet garni and a little salt, cover with a lid and allow to cook gently in an oven until almost tender.
5 Cut the bacon into cubes, blanch and refresh.
6 Cook the onions gently in butter and a little wine without colouring.
7 Add the bacon, onions and chestnuts to the oxtail and complete cooking.
8 Pick out the oxtail and garnish, skim the cooking liquor well and reduce if necessary.
9 Correct seasoning, pass through a fine strainer, add the oxtail and garnish and serve.

18 – Oxtail braised in red wine

	4 portions	10 portions
oxtail	1 kg (2 lb)	2½ kg (5 lb)
oil	30 ml ($\frac{1}{16}$ pt)	90 ml ($\frac{3}{16}$ pt)
bottles red wine	1	2
pork rind	100 g (4 oz)	250 g (10 oz)
bouquet garni	1	2
peeled shallots	8	20
unpeeled crushed garlic cloves	4	10
peeled carrots cut in thick rounds	300 g (12 oz)	1 kg (2 lb)
mushrooms	200 g (8 oz)	500 g (1¼ lb)
celeriac	300 g (12 oz)	1 kg (2 lb)
salt, mill pepper		

1 Cut the oxtail into pieces, remove excess fat.
2 Heat the oil in a pan and briskly fry the oxtail to a golden brown on both sides.
3 Place the pork rind in a braising pan, add the oxtail, garlic, bouquet garni, whole shallots, carrots and wine; season lightly with salt; cover with a lid and cook in an oven until almost tender.
4 Add the mushrooms and celeriac cut into neat pieces and continue cooking until tender.
5 Lift out the oxtail and garnish into a clean pan.

6 Discard the pork rind and bouquet garni.
7 Reduce the cooking liquor if necessary, skim well, correct seasoning and strain on to the oxtail.

Note Alternatively, half a bottle of wine can be used with the balance of liquid being made up from a good white veal stock.

—— *Veal* ——

BUTCHERY

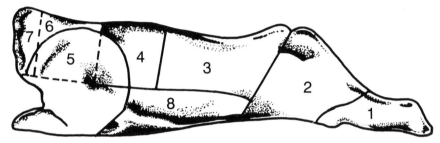

Joints, uses and weights

JOINT	USES	APPROX. WEIGHT	
		(KILO)	(LB)
1 Knuckle	Osso buco, sauté, stock	2	4
2 Leg	Roasting, braising, escalopes, sauté	5	10
3 Loin	Roasting, frying, grilling	$3\frac{1}{2}$	7
4 Best-end	Roasting, frying, grilling	3	6
5 Shoulder	Braising, stewing	5	10
6 Neck-end	Stewing, sauté	$2\frac{1}{2}$	5
7 Scrag	Stewing stock	$1\frac{1}{2}$	3
8 Breast	Stewing, roasting	$2\frac{1}{2}$	5
Kidneys	Stewing (pies and puddings), sauté	–	–
Liver	Frying	–	–
Sweetbreads	Braising, frying	–	–
Head	Boiling, soup	4	8
Brains	Boiling, frying	–	–
Bones	Used for stock	–	–

Joints of the leg

Average weight of English or Dutch milk fed – 18 kg (36 lb).

CUTS	WEIGHT	PROPORTION OF LEG	USES
Cushion or nut	2.75 kg (5½ lb)	15%	Escalopes, roasting, braising, sauté
Under cushion or under nut	3 kg (6 lb)	17%	Escalopes, roasting, braising, sauté
Thick flank	2.5 kg (5 lb)	14%	Escalopes, roasting, braising, sauté
Knuckle (whole)	2.5 kg (5 lb)	14%	Osso buco, sauté
Bones (thigh and aitch)	2.5 kg (5 lb)	14%	Stock, jus-lié
Usable trimmings	2 kg (4 lb)	11%	Pies, stewing, Pojarski
Skin and fat	2.75 kg (5½ lb)	15%	

Corresponding joints in beef

Cushion = topside
Under cushion = silverside
Thick flank = thick flank

Dissection of leg of veal

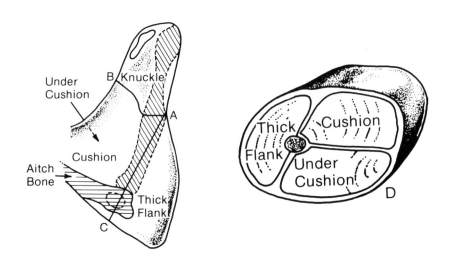

1 Remove knuckle by dividing knee joint (A) and cut through the meat away from the cushion-line A–B.

2 Remove aitch bone (C) at thick end of leg separating it at the ball and socket joint.
3 Remove all outside skin and fat thus exposing the natural seams. It will now be seen that the thigh bone divides the meat into $\frac{2}{3}$ and $\frac{1}{3}$ (thick flank).
4 Stand the leg on the thick flank with point D uppermost. Divide the cushion from the under-cushion, following the natural seam, using the hand and the point of a knife. Having reached the thigh bone, remove it completely.
5 Allowing the boned leg to fall open the 3 joints can easily be seen joined only by membrane. Separate and trim the cushion removing the loose flap of meat.
6 Trim the undercushion removing the layer of thick gristle. Separate into 3 small joints through the natural seams. It will be seen that one of these will correspond with the round in silverside of beef.
7 Trim the thick flank by laying it on its round side and making a cut along the length about 1 in deep. A seam is reached and the two trimmings can be removed.

The anticipated yield of escalopes from this size leg would be 220 ounces, i.e. 55×4 oz or 73×3 oz.

Quality of veal

1 Veal is available all the year round, but is best from May to September.
2 The flesh should be pale pink in colour.
3 The flesh should be firm in structure, not soft or flabby.
4 Cut surfaces should be slightly moist, not dry.
5 Bones, in young animals, should be pinkish white, porous and with a degree of blood in their structure.
6 The fat should be firm and pinkish white.
7 The kidney should be hard and well covered with fat.

Order of dissection

1 Remove the shoulders.
2 Remove the breast.
3 Take off the leg.
4 Divide the loin and best-end from the scrag and neck-end.
5 Divide the loin from the best-end.

PREPARATION OF THE JOINTS AND CUTS

Shin

Stewing (on the bone) – osso buco   Cut and saw into 2–4 cm (1–1½ in) thick slices through the knuckle.

Sauté   Bone-out and trim and cut into even 25 g (1 oz) pieces.

Leg

Braising or roasting whole   Remove the aitch bone, clean and trim 4 cm (1½ in) off the knuckle bone. Trim off excess sinew.

Braising or roasting the noix, sous-noix or quasi   Remove the sinew and if there is insufficient fat on the joint then bard thinly and secure with string.

Escalopes   Remove all sinew and cut into large 50–75 g (2–3 oz) slices against the grain and bat out thinly.

Sauté   Remove all sinew and cut into 25 g (1 oz) pieces.

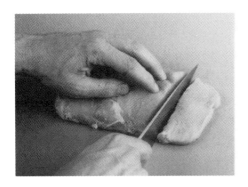 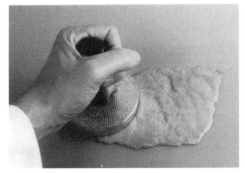

Preparation of veal escalope

Loin and Best-end

Roasting   Bone-out and trim the flap, roll out and secure with string. This joint may be stuffed before rolling.

Frying   Trim and cut into cutlets.

Boning a loin of veal

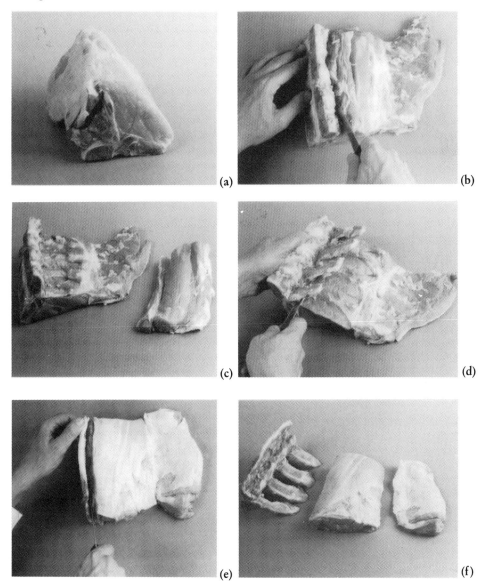

(a)

(b)

(c)

(d)

(e)

(f)

Shoulder

Braising Boned-out as for lamb and usually stuffed (page 240).

Stewing Bone-out, remove all sinew and cut into 25 g (1 oz) pieces.

Neck-end and Scrag

Stewing and sauté Bone-out and remove all sinew and cut into approx. 25 g (1 oz) pieces.

Breast

Stewing As for neck-end.

Roasting Bone-out, season, stuff and roll up then tie with string.

Kidneys

Remove the fat and skin and cut down the middle lengthwise. Remove sinew and cut into thin slices or neat dice.

Liver

Skin if possible, remove gristle and cut into thin slices on the slant.

Sweetbreads

Soak in salted water for 2–3 hours to remove any trace of blood. Wash well, blanch and trim.

Head

1 Bone-out by making a deep incision down the middle of the head to the nostrils.
2 Follow the bone carefully and remove all the flesh in one piece.
3 Lastly remove the tongue.
4 Wash the flesh well and keep covered in acidulated water.
5 Wash off, blanch and refresh.
6 Cut into 2–5 cm (1–2 in) squares.
7 Cut off the ears and trim the inside of the cheek.

Brains

Using a chopper or saw, remove the top of the skull, making certain that the opening is large enough to remove the brain undamaged. Soak the brains in running cold water, then remove the membrane, or skin and wash well to remove all blood. Keep in cold salted water till required.

RECIPES

19 – Veal sauté with mushrooms

	4 portions	10 portions
stewing veal	500 g (1¼ lb)	1½ kg (3 lb)
seasoned flour	25 g (1 oz)	60 g (2½ oz)
butter	25 g (1 oz)	60 g (2½ oz)
oil	1 tbsp	2–3 tbsp
chopped onion	100 g (4 oz)	250 g (10 oz)
crushed clove of garlic	1	2–3
tomato purée	1 tbsp	2–3 tbsp
white wine	125 ml (¼ pt)	300 ml (⅝ pt)
brown stock	500 ml (1 pt)	1¼ litre (2½ pt)
bouquet garni		
salt and pepper		
button mushrooms	200 g (8 oz)	500 g (1¼ lb)

1 Trim meat, cut into even pieces, pass through seasoned flour.
2 Quickly brown on all sides in hot butter and oil, drain off excess fat.
3 Add onion and garlic and cook for a few minutes.
4 Mix in tomato purée, add white wine and reduce by half.
5 Add stock and bouquet garni, cover with lid and simmer gently until almost cooked.
6 Pick meat into a clean pan, discard bouquet garni, correct the seasoning and strain on to the meat. If there is too much sauce, allow to reduce before straining.
7 Bring to boil, add whole or quartered button mushrooms, cover with lid and simmer until tender, then serve.

Notes The mushrooms can be cultivated or wild. If button mushrooms are used, they may be sliced and added for the last 1–2 minutes of cooking.

This recipe will produce a very thin sauce. If a thicker sauce is required use half brown stock and half demi-glace.

20 – Veal sauté with white wine, button onions, mushrooms and tomatoes (Marengo)

	4 portions	10 portions
prepared stewing veal	500 g (1¼ lb)	1½ kg (3 lb)
seasoned flour	25 g (1 oz)	60 g (2½ oz)
butter	25 g (1 oz)	60 g (2½ oz)
oil	1 tbsp	2–3 tbsp
chopped onion	100 g (4 oz)	250 g (10 oz)
crushed clove garlic	1	2–3
white wine	125 ml (¼ pt)	300 ml (⅝ pt)
brown stock	500 ml (1 pt)	1¼ litre (2½ pt)
tomatoes, skinned, deseeded and diced	1 kg (2 lb)	2½ kg (5 lb)
bouquet garni		
button onions	16	40
button mushrooms	16	40
salt and pepper		
heart-shaped bread croûtons fried in butter	8	20
chopped parsley		

> 1 portion provides:
>
> 524 kcals/2195 kJ
> 25.4 g fat
> (of which 10.8 g saturated)
> 36.3 g carbohydrate
> (of which 12.1 g sugars)
> 35 g protein
> 4.2 g fibre

1 Proceed as for previous recipe, stages 1–6, adding the tomatoes with the stock.
2 Add button onions, simmer 15 minutes, add button mushrooms and cook until tender.
3 Serve with tips of croûtons dipped in sauce and chopped parsley.

21 – Veal escalope with tomatoes, cheese and white wine

	4 portions	10 portions
escalopes, according to size, slightly batted	4, 8 or 12	10, 20 or 30
seasoned flour	25 g (1 oz)	60 g (2½ oz)
tomatoes, skinned, deseeded and diced	100 g (4 oz)	250 g (10 oz)
butter	50 g (2 oz)	125 g (5 oz)
white wine	125 ml (¼ pt)	300 ml (⅝ pt)
thin slices mozzarella cheese	4	10
chopped parsley		

1 Pass the escalopes through the flour.
2 Cook the tomatoes in a little butter for 5 minutes, season.
3 Cook the veal to a golden brown on both sides in butter, remove from pan.
4 Pour off any fat, deglaze with white wine, reduce by half, strain and season.
5 Lay a slice of cheese on each escalope, place under salamander until cheese has melted, add the tomatoes on the cheese and heat through.
6 Dress the escalopes on a serving dish, pour the reduced wine around the edge of the dish, sprinkle with chopped parsley and serve.

Note Variations can include the addition of sliced mushrooms, double cream, rosemary, tarragon, basil or chives.

22 – Veal chops with mushrooms, onions and potatoes

	4 portions	10 portions
veal chops	4	10
butter	50 g (2 oz)	125 g (5 oz)
small button mushrooms	16	40
small button onions	16	40
small potatoes	16	40
salt and pepper		
dry white wine	60 ml ($\frac{1}{8}$ pt)	150 g ($\frac{1}{3}$ pt)

1 Brown chops on both sides in butter and place in an earthenware dish.
2 Quickly brown mushrooms, onions and potatoes, and add to chops.
3 Season lightly, cover and cook in oven at 180°–190°C (350°–375°F) for approximately $\frac{1}{2}$–1 hour.
4 Remove the chops and garnish; dress on a serving dish.
5 Deglaze the pan with the wine, strain over chops and serve.

23 – Veal chops with cream and mustard sauce

	4 portions	10 portions
veal chops	4	10
butter or oil	50 g (2 oz)	125 g (10 oz)
dry white wine	125 ml ($\frac{1}{4}$ pt}	300 ml ($\frac{5}{8}$ pt)
veal stock	125 ml ($\frac{1}{4}$ pt)	300 ml ($\frac{5}{8}$ pt)

273

bouquet garni
salt and pepper
double cream   60 ml ($\frac{1}{8}$ pt)   150 ml ($\frac{1}{3}$ pt)
French mustard, to taste
chopped parsley

1 Shallow fry the chops on both sides in hot butter, pour off the fat.
2 Add white wine, stock, bouquet garni and season lightly; cover and
  simmer gently until cooked.
3 Remove chops and bouquet garni, reduce liquid by two-thirds, then
  add cream, the juice from the chops and bring to boil.
4 Strain the sauce, mix in the mustard and parsley, correct seasoning,
  pour over chops and serve.

24 – Veal chop or escalope in a paper bag (en papillotte)

	4 portions	10 portions
veal chops (well trimmed)	4 × 150 g (6 oz)	10 × 10 g (6 oz)
butter	50 g (2 oz)	125 g (5 oz)
butter or oil	25 g (1 oz)	60 g (2$\frac{1}{2}$ oz)
shallots chopped	25 g (1 oz)	60 g (2$\frac{1}{2}$ oz)
mushrooms chopped	100 g (4 oz)	250 g (10 oz)
white wine	30 ml ($\frac{1}{16}$ pt)	75 ml ($\frac{3}{16}$ pt)
lean ham chopped	50 g (2 oz)	125 g (5 oz)
tomato concassé	100 g (4 oz)	250 g (10 oz)
demi-glace or jus-lié	250 ml ($\frac{1}{2}$ pt)	600 ml (1$\frac{1}{4}$ pt)
chopped parsley		
greaseproof paper, oil, or aluminium foil		

1 Fry or grill the chops on both sides.
2 Sweat the shallots in the butter, add mushrooms, cook for
  2–3 minutes.
3 Add white wine and allow to reduce.
4 Add ham, tomato, sauce and reduce to a thickish consistency.
5 Correct seasoning, add a little chopped parsley.
6 Cut greaseproof paper or aluminium foil into large heart shapes, big
  enough to hold one chop each. Oil the paper liberally.
7 Place a spoonful of the sauce to one side of the centre.
8 Place a chop on top and cover with more sauce.

9 Fold and pleat the paper or foil tightly.
10 Place on an oiled tray in a hot oven 220°C (425°F) until the bag
   expands and lightly browns. Serve immediately.

Note Instead of chopped ham in the sauce, the chops can be
sandwiched between two slices of ham in the bag.

Preparation of foods en papilotte

Cut out heart-shaped piece of parchment on
greaseproof paper. This is done by folding a
piece of parchment in half and cutting a heart
from the folded side. Oil or butter on both
sides

Place the veal or other item/s on one side of
the heart

Fold over, make a crimp

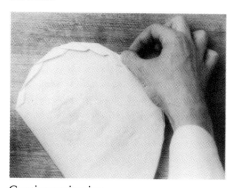

Continue crimping

Fold over at the bottom to hold in place

25 – Veal kidneys with mustard and cream sauce

	4 portions	10 portions
skinned and trimmed kidneys, cut in walnut-sized pieces	400 g (1 lb)	1¼ kg (2½ lb)
butter	100 g (4 oz)	250 g (10 oz)
double cream	250 ml (½ pt)	600 ml (1¼ pt)
lemon, grated zest of	1	2–3
French mustard, according to taste	1–2 tbsp	3–5 tbsp
salt and pepper		

1 Sauté the kidneys in a little hot butter for 3–4 min, drain in a colander.
2 Boil the cream, lemon zest, mustard, salt and pepper for 2–3 min.
3 Strain into a clean pan and incorporate remaining butter. Add kidneys, do *not* reboil, correct seasoning and serve.

Notes Variations can include: brandy, chopped shallots, a chopped herb, e.g. tarragon, chervil or chives, and cultivated or wild mushrooms, either singly or in combination.

26 – Veal kidneys with ceps

	4 portions	10 portions
oil	2 tbsp	5 tbsp
fresh ceps *or*	200 g (8 oz)	500 g (1¼ lb)
dried ceps (soaked and dried)	50 g (2 oz)	125 g (5 oz)
finely chopped shallots	50 g (2 oz)	125 g (5 oz)
salt and pepper		
few drops of lemon juice		
chopped parsley	1 tbsp	2–3 tbsp
tomatoes, skinned, deseeded and diced	200 g (8 oz)	500 g (1¼ lb)
butter	25 g (1 oz)	60 g (2½ oz)
lardons of streaky bacon	100 g (4 oz)	250 g (10 oz)
skinned and trimmed kidneys, cut in walnut-sized pieces	400 g (1 lb)	1¼ kg (2½ lb)

1 Heat the oil and cook the ceps for 4–5 minutes until brown.

2 Reduce heat, continue cooking until tender, and add shallots and season.
3 Add lemon juice and chopped parsley.
4 Cook the tomatoes in a little oil until soft, then add to ceps.
5 Heat the butter and a little oil and brown the lardons.
6 Drain and mix lardons with ceps and tomato.
7 Quickly sauté the kidneys in butter for 4–5 minutes until brown but slightly pink in the centre, season lightly and drain.
8 Place the cep mixture on a serving dish with the kidneys on top and serve.

27 – Fricassée of kidneys and sweetbreads with flageolets and broad beans

	4 portions	10 portions
heart-shaped sweetbreads	200 g (8 oz)	500 g (1¼ lb)
butter	25 g (1 oz)	60 g (2½ oz)
oil	1 tbsp	2–3 tbsp
veal kidneys, skinned, trimmed, 1 cm (½ in) dice	200 g (8 oz)	500 g (1¼ lb)
white wine	60 ml (⅛ pt)	150 ml (⅓ pt)
finely chopped shallot	25 g (1 oz)	60 g (2½ oz)
double cream	125 ml (¼ pt)	300 ml (⅝ pt)
salt and pepper		
chopped parsley, tarragon or chervil		
cooked flageolet beans	50 g (2 oz)	125 g (5 oz)
cooked broad beans	50 g (2 oz)	125 g (5 oz)

> 1 portion provides:
>
> 353 kcals/1464 kJ
> 28.7 g fat
> (of which 15.2 g saturated)
> 4 g carbohydrate
> (of which 1.4 g sugars)
> 17.6 g protein
> 1.5 g fibre

1 Blanch sweetbread for 5 minutes, drain, refresh, skin, remove any fat or gristle, and cut into walnut-sized pieces.
2 Heat butter and oil in a frying pan, add sweetbreads and cook for 2–3 minutes, then add kidneys and cook for 4–5 minutes to a golden brown, drain and keep warm.
3 Add white wine and shallot to the pan, strain and reduce by half, add cream and simmer 3–4 minutes.
4 Correct seasoning, add sweetbreads, kidneys, flageolets and broad beans. Mix carefully, correct seasoning and serve sprinkled with chopped herbs.

[T] 28 – Gratin of veal medallions and sweetbreads with herbs

(MARK DODSON)

	4 portions	10 portions
trimmed loin of veal	800 g (2 lb)	2½ kg (5 lb)
veal sweetbreads	75 g (3 oz)	7½ g (18 oz)
veal stock	400 ml (¾ pt)	1 litre (2 pt)
double cream	350 ml (⅝ pt)	1 litre (2 pt)
white wine	100 ml (¼ pt)	300 ml (⅝ pt)
egg white	1	2–3
shallots	50 g (2 oz)	125 g (5 oz)
butter	40 g (2 oz)	125 g (5 oz)
carrots	50 g (2 oz)	125 g (5 oz)
fresh herbs (parsley, tarragon, thyme)	20 g (1 oz)	50 g (2 oz)
brioche crumbs	45 g (2 oz)	125 g (5 oz)
clarified butter		
salt and pepper		

1 From the loin of veal, cut four or ten slices 4 cm (1½ in) thick, place each one between two sheets of cling film and bat them slightly, trim them to an even shape, each medaillon should weigh approximately 140 g (6 oz). Keep all the trimming and remaining loin, for the mousse and the sauce.
2 Dice up 170 g (7 oz) of veal (×2½ for 10 portions), reserve from the loin, and place it into the robot coupe, work it well, until smooth.
3 Place this into a bowl set on ice and leave it to become cold.
4 Blanch the veal sweetbreads in salted water and leave them to stand.
5 Beat the egg white into the mousse and then gradually add the double cream beating well. Season with salt. (To test the seasoning of the mousse, a teaspoonful can be poached in a little water.)
6 Remove any membrane from the sweetbread and separate it into its natural pieces, add these to the mousse.
7 Dice up all the remaining veal and cook off in a pan with the shallots, carrots, stalks from the herbs and half the butter; when all of this is a nice golden colour add the white wine and leave to reduce.
8 When most of the wine has evaporated, add the veal stock. Leave the sauce to cook slowly and skim from time to time.
9 After 20–25 minutes, when the sauce has reduced by about one-third, pass it through a fine strainer, or preferably through a muslin cloth.

10 In a pan, seal the medallions well on all sides, and then leave them to cool.
11 Finely chop the herbs, mixing half with the brioche crumbs, keep the remainder for finishing the sauce.
12 When the medallions are cool, spread the mousse on to the top of each one, so it is slightly raised in the centre.
13 Place the medallions on to a baking sheet and into the preheated oven, 220°C (475°F), for 8 minutes (ideally the mousse should be cooked through and the veal still pink).
14 Brush each medallion with the clarified butter and then sprinkle the brioche crumbs and herbs evenly over the top of each one.
15 Finish the sauce by stirring in the rest of the butter and the chopped herbs and seasoning.
16 Gratinate the veal under the salamander until golden brown. Lift the medallion off the baking sheet, on to a cloth and then directly on to the serving dish or plates, pour the sauce around. Serve immediately.

29 – Grenadines of veal

Grenadines are smaller, thicker escalopes, approximately 4 cm (1½ in) thick, larded with thin strips of fresh pork fat. They are usually pot-roasted or braised and can be cooked and garnished in a variety of ways, for example:

Stuffed mushrooms and quarters of artichoke bottoms.

Carrots, turnips, French beans, peas and cauliflower coated with hollandaise sauce.

Green peas, carrots and duchess potatoes.

The above are examples of the many classical garnishes but there are other ways of garnishing, such as:

- A type of pasta, e.g. noodles or spaghetti, either with butter or butter and cheese, or with a sauce.
- One or two carefully selected vegetables.
- A variety of vegetables.

The sauce made from the cooking liquor of the grenadines can also be varied in many ways, with imagination and careful thought.

30 – Calves' liver with raspberry vinegar

	4 portions	10 portions
calves' liver, sliced	400 g (1 lb)	1¼ kg (2½ lb)
butter	100 g (4 oz)	250 g (10 oz)
finely chopped shallots	50 g (2 oz)	125 g (5 oz)
raspberry vinegar	60 ml ($\frac{1}{8}$ pt)	150 ml ($\frac{1}{3}$ pt)
veal stock	90 ml ($\frac{3}{16}$ pt)	300 ml ($\frac{5}{8}$ pt)
salt, mill pepper		

1 Shallow fry the liver on both sides in half the butter and remove from the pan.
2 Cook the shallots in the same pan.
3 Add raspberry vinegar and stock, reduce slightly and strain.
4 Mix in the remaining butter, correct seasoning and pour over the liver.

Note   This recipe can also be prepared using any other fruit vinegar.

31 – Veal sweetbreads with white wine, tomato and mushrooms

	4 portions	10 portions
heart-shaped sweetbreads	500 g (1¼ lb)	1½ kg (3 lb)
seasoned flour	25 g (1 oz)	60 g (2½ oz)
chopped shallot	25 g (1 oz)	60 g (2½ oz)
sliced mushrooms	100 g (4 oz)	250 g (10 oz)
brandy	30 ml ($\frac{1}{16}$ pt)	75 ml ($\frac{3}{16}$ pt)
white wine	60 ml ($\frac{1}{8}$ pt)	150 ml ($\frac{1}{3}$ pt)
tomato, skinned, deseeded and diced	100 g (4 oz)	250 g (10 oz)
lemon, juice of	1	2–3
double cream	60 ml ($\frac{1}{8}$ pt)	125 ml ($\frac{1}{3}$ pt)
chopped parsley, chervil, tarragon		

1 Soak, blanch and refresh the sweetbreads, remove skin, fat and gristle.
2 Dry the sweetbreads well, pass through seasoned flour, and cook gently in butter on both sides until golden brown.
3 Add shallots, cover with a lid and cook for 2–3 minutes, then add mushrooms, cover with a lid and cook 4–5 minutes.
4 Add brandy and flame, add white wine, tomatoes, lemon juice and season lightly.

5 Simmer gently until cooked.

6 Add cream, reboil, correct seasoning, and serve sprinkled with herbs.

Note This is a dish that lends itself to many variations, e.g.

- lemon juice may be omitted or reduced in quantity;
- red wine can be used in place of white;
- tomatoes can be omitted and the quantity of mushrooms increased;
- wild mushrooms can be used in place of cultivated;
- jus-lié can be used in place of cream.

—— *Pork* ——

BUTCHERY

Cuts, uses and weights

ENGLISH	USES	APPROX. WEIGHT (KILO)	(LB)
1 Leg	Roasting and boiling	5	10
2 Loin	Roasting, frying, grilling	6	12
3 Spare rib	Roasting, pies	$1\frac{1}{2}$	3
4 Belly	Pickling, boiling	2	4
	Stuffed, rolled and roasted		
5 Shoulder	Roasting, sausages, pies	3	6
6 Head (whole)	Brawn	4	8
7 Trotters	Grilling, boiling		
Kidneys	Sauté, grilling		
Liver	Frying, pâté		

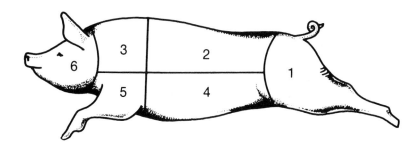

When 5–6 weeks old a piglet is known as a sucking or suckling pig. The weight is then between 5–10 kg (10–20 lb).

Signs of quality

1 Lean flesh should be pale pink, firm and of a fine texture.
2 The fat should be white, firm, smooth and not excessive.
3 Bones should be small, fine and pinkish.
4 The skin or rind should be smooth.

Order of Dissection

1 Remove the head.
2 Remove the trotters.
3 Remove the leg.
4 Remove shoulder.
5 Remove spare ribs.
6 Divide loin from the belly.

PREPARATION OF THE JOINTS AND CUTS

Belly

Remove all the small rib bones, season with salt, pepper and chopped sage, roll and secure with string. This joint may be stuffed.

Shoulder

Roasting
The shoulder is usually boned-out, excess fat and sinew removed, seasoned, scored and rolled with string. It may be stuffed and can also be divided into two smaller joints.

Sausages and pies
Skin, bone-out, remove the excess fat and sinew and cut into even pieces or mince.

Head

Brawn
1 Bone-out as for calf's head (page 270) and keep in acidulated water till required.
2 Split down the centre and remove the brain and tongue.

Trotters

Boil in water for a few minutes, scrape with the back of a knife to remove the hairs, wash off in cold water and split in half.

Kidneys

Remove the fat and skin, cut down the middle lengthwise. Remove the sinew and cut into slices or neat dice.

Liver

Skin if possible, remove the gristle and cut into thin slices on the slant.

Leg

Roasting
Remove the pelvic or aitch bone, trim and score the rind neatly. That is to say with a sharp-pointed knife, make a series of 3 mm ($\frac{1}{8}$ in) deep incisions approx. 2 cm (1 in) apart all over the skin of the joint. Trim and clean the knuckle bone.

Boiling
It is usual to pickle the joint either by rubbing dry salt and saltpetre into the meat or by soaking in a brine solution (page 253). Then remove the pelvic bone, trim and secure with string if necessary.

Loin

Roasting (on the bone)
Saw down the chine bone in order to facilitate carving; trim excess fat and sinew and score the rind in the direction that the joint will be carved. Season and secure with string.

Roasting (boned-out)
Remove the filet mignon and bone-out carefully. Trim off excess fat and sinew, score the rind and neaten the flap, season, replace the filet mignon, roll up and secure with string.

This joint is sometimes stuffed (recipe 32, page 284).

Grilling or frying chops
Remove the skin, excess fat and sinew, then cut and saw or chop through the loin in approx. 1 cm ($\frac{1}{2}$ in) slices, remove excess bone and trim neatly.

Spare rib

Roasting
Remove excess fat, bone and sinew and trim neatly.

Pies
Remove excess fat and sinew, bone-out and cut as required.

RECIPES

32 – Roast stuffed suckling pig

10–20 portions
Suckling pig is young milk-fed pig, 8–10 weeks old, weighing 3–5 kg
(6–10 lb), which takes approximately 2–2½ hours to roast. If the stuffing
is cooked separately allow about half an hour less.

A golden-brown, crisp skin is essential, therefore the cooking must
always be timed so that the pig does not have to stand for too long
before serving. Brush the skin with oil frequently during cooking to
ensure its crispness.

– *Basic stuffing*

finely chopped onion, cooked without colour in pork fat or butter	1 kg (2 lb)
fresh bread cubes, soaked in milk and squeezed dry, or fresh breadcrumbs	400 g (1 lb)
butter	100 g (4 oz)
freshly chopped sage	50 g (2 oz)
or dried sage	25 g (1 oz)
parsley	50 g (2 oz)
grated nutmeg	
salt and pepper	
eggs	2

Thoroughly mix all the ingredients.

Variations can include the addition of any of the following: 200 g (8 oz)
chopped chestnuts; 200 g (8 oz) chopped dessert apple or stoned cherries
or cranberries; 100 g (4 oz) chopped mushrooms; 100 g (4 oz) chopped

bacon, ham or pork sausage meat; juice of 2 crushed cloves of garlic; rosemary or basil in place of sage, or a combination of all three; 60 ml ($\frac{1}{8}$ pt) brandy.

1 Stuff the pig loosely with the stuffing mixture and sew up the opening securely with string.
2 Truss the forelegs and hindlegs so that the pig lies flat on its belly during cooking.
3 Place a block of wood in its mouth to keep it open, and cover the ears and tail with foil to prevent burning.
4 Score the pig's back to allow fat to escape.
5 Brush with oil or melted butter and roast at 200°C (400°F), basting frequently. Allow 25 minutes for every $\frac{1}{2}$ kg (1 lb).
6 A few minutes before the pig is cooked, remove foil from ears and tail.
7 When cooked, transfer the pig to a wooden board, deglaze the pan and make roast gravy. Apple sauce should also be served.
8 Place a red apple in the mouth, cherries or cranberries in the eye sockets and serve.

33 – Fillet of pork in pastry

This can be prepared, cooked and served in the same way as Beef fillet en croûte or Wellington, recipe 12, page 260.

As pork fillets are smaller, two or three can be pressed together, with stuffing in between, before covering with pastry.

Alternatively, the lean meat from a loin completely trimmed of all fat and sinew can be used.

A variety of sauces may be offered but a slightly piquant sauce is particularly suitable, e.g. Robert, charcutière.

34 – Pork escalopes with prunes

Escalopes can be taken from prime cuts of pork, e.g. fillet, loin, best-end and leg, cut into 75–100 g (3–4 oz) slices, free from fat and sinew and batted. They may then be cooked plain, with prunes as here, or egg and crumbed and served in a wide variety of ways with different sauces, garnishes or accompaniments.

285

	4 portions	10 portions
prunes	12–16	30–40
white wine	250 ml ($\frac{1}{2}$pt)	600 ml (1$\frac{1}{4}$pt)
piece of cinnamon stick or pinch of ground cinnamon		
seasoned flour	25 g (1 oz)	60 g (2$\frac{1}{2}$oz)
pork escalopes (if small allow 2–3 per portion)	4	10
butter	50 g (2 oz)	125 g (5 oz)
double cream	75 ml ($\frac{1}{6}$pt)	150 g ($\frac{1}{3}$pt)
redcurrant jelly	1 tbsp	2–3 tbsp
salt and pepper		

1 Soak prunes overnight in wine.
2 Remove and discard stones from prunes and simmer with the liquid and cinnamon until soft.
3 Flour the escalopes, shallow fry in butter on both sides until cooked through.
4 Remove from pan and keep warm.
5 Drain off prunes (reserving liquid) and add to the escalopes.
6 Add prune liquid to the pan in which escalopes were cooked and reduce by half.
7 Incorporate cream and redcurrant jelly, bring to boil and correct seasoning. If sauce is too sweet, add a few drops of lemon juice.
8 Strain sauce over pork and serve.

Note   Well-trimmed pork chops can also be cooked in this way.

35 – Pork escalopes with apples, cream and calvados

	4 portions	10 portions
seasoned flour	25 g (1 oz)	60 g (2$\frac{1}{2}$oz)
escalopes (if small allow 2–3 per portion)	4	10
butter	50 g (2 oz)	125 g (5 oz)
sliced onion	100 g (4 oz)	250 g (10 oz)
cooking apples, peeled and sliced	200 g (8 oz)	500 g (1$\frac{1}{4}$lb)
calvados	60 ml ($\frac{1}{8}$pt)	150 ml ($\frac{1}{3}$pt)
stock	125 ml ($\frac{1}{4}$pt)	300 ml ($\frac{5}{8}$pt)
double cream	75 ml ($\frac{1}{6}$pt)	150 g ($\frac{1}{3}$pt)
salt and pepper		

> 1 portion provides:
>
> 432 kcals/1798 kJ
> 26.3 g fat
> (of which 15.2 g saturated)
> 14.2 g carbohydrate
> (of which 8.8 g sugars)
> 32 g protein
> 1.2 g fibre

1 Flour escalopes and shallow fry in butter on both sides until cooked through. Remove from pan, keep warm.
2 Gently cook the onions in the same pan, add the apples, cover with a lid and cook gently until apples are soft.
3 Drain off the fat, add the calvados and flame.
4 Add the stock, simmer 5 minutes, liquidise, or pass firmly through a strainer, and return to a clean pan.
5 Add the cream, bring to boil, correct seasoning and consistency, pour over the escalopes and serve.

Note Well-trimmed pork chops can also be cooked this way. Caramelised apple slices can be served with this dish and are prepared as follows:

butter	50 g (2 oz)	125 g (5 oz)
medium-sized cooking apples, cored, unpeeled, cut in thick slices	2	5
sugar	25 g (1 oz)	60 g (2½ oz)

1 Heat the butter in a thick-bottomed pan.
2 Dip one side of the apple slices in the sugar. Place sugar side down in the hot butter.
3 Cook over high heat until caramelised.
4 Sprinkle with the rest of the sugar, turn the slices over and brown on the other side.

36 – Sauté of pork with leeks

	4 portions	10 portions
boned shoulder of pork	500 g (1¼ lb)	1½ kg (3 lb)
seasoned flour	25 g (1 oz)	60 g (2½ oz)
oil	1–2 tbsp	3–4 tbsp
sliced leeks	400 g (1 lb)	1¼ kg (2½ lb)
stock	250 ml (½ pt)	600 ml (1¼ pt)
bouquet garni, including a little sage		
cloves garlic (optional)	1–2	3–4
salt and pepper		

1 Trim meat, cut into even pieces and pass through seasoned flour.
2 Thoroughly brown on all sides in hot oil.

3 Transfer to an ovenproof dish, mix in the leeks, cover with a lid and cook for 3–4 minutes.
4 Mix in the stock, add bouquet garni and garlic, bring to boil and simmer until tender.
5 Remove bouquet garni and garlic, check consistency and seasoning and serve.

I 37 – Bacon, avocado and walnuts in a filo parcel with fresh basil sauce

(Lloyd Stoll)

	4 portions	10 portions
Parcels		
rashers of bacon, diced	4	10
avocado diced	100 g (4 oz)	250 g (10 oz)
walnuts roughly chopped	50 g (2 oz)	125 g (5 oz)
white wine	4 tsp	10 tsp
filo pastry cut thickly into 12.5 × 20 cm sheets	4	10
Sauce		
butter	50 g (2 oz)	125 g (5 oz)
onion finely diced	25 g (1 oz)	$62\frac{1}{2}$ g ($2\frac{1}{2}$ oz)
flour	50 g (2 oz)	125 g (5 oz)
vegetable stock	1 litre (2 pt)	$2\frac{1}{2}$ litre (5 pt)
fresh basil	25 g (1 oz)	$62\frac{1}{2}$ g ($2\frac{1}{2}$ oz)
cream	125 ml ($\frac{1}{4}$ pt)	312 ml ($\frac{5}{8}$ pt)
English mustard	$\frac{1}{2}$ tsp	$1\frac{1}{2}$ tsp

1 Heat a frying pan with no oil, fry off bacon and avocado for 1 min, then add walnuts and remove from heat, allow to cool. Lay out filo pastry and put the mixture in the centre of each one.
2 Gather the 4 corners and pinch tightly to seal pastry then open out the top of the parcel to give it a frill.
3 Bake in the oven for 15–20 minutes at 170–180°C (350°F).
4 To make the sauce, melt butter in a pan, add onion and chopped basil. Fry for 2 min and then add the flour and cook for a further 2 minutes until the roux comes away from the side of the pan.
5 Over a low heat gradually add the hot vegetable stock until the sauce is smooth. Add the mustard and cook for 20 minutes on a low heat.

6 To finish add the cream and season to taste.

7 Serve parcels on a pool of sauce and garnish with fresh basil.

I **38 ~ Roasted pork fillet on a thyme flavoured drop scone with sautéed turned pears and a Madeira sauce**

(PHILLIP ACCORSINI)

	4 portions	10 portions
pork fillet	400 g (1 lb)	1 kg (2½ lb)
thyme, bunch of	1	1
garlic clove	⅓	⅔
sesame oil	50 ml (2 fl oz)	75 ml (3 fl oz)
Sauce		
pears	3	6
butter	25 g (1 oz)	50 g (2 oz)
shallots	150 g (6 oz)	300 g (12 oz)
garlic powder, pinch	1	2
Madeira wine	50 ml (2 fl oz)	100 ml (4 fl oz)
veal stock	500 ml (¾ pt)	1 litre (1¾ pt)
sesame oil	12½ ml (½ fl oz)	25 ml (1 fl oz)
butter	50 g (2 oz)	100 g (4 oz)
sea salt		
black pepper		

1 Trim the pork free of sinew and cut to 100 g (4 oz) portions.

2 Season the pork with finely chopped thyme, garlic and salt and pepper.

3 Heat a frying pan and season; the pork on all sides.

4 Roast in a moderate oven for 6–7 minutes.

5 Cut the pears into 4 lengthways then again in half.

6 Turn these into barrel shapes.

7 Lightly sauté the pears in butter until tender.

8 To make the sauce: finely chop shallots and garlic.

9 Sauté shallots and garlic without colour in sesame oil. Add Madeira wine and reduce this by half. (This removes the roughness of the alcohol and leaves the Madeira flavour).

10 Add the veal stock making sure it has been passed. Reduce by three-quarters. Season and cool slightly.

11 Mount the sauce with unsalted butter and correct seasoning (this will thicken and give a glossy sheen to the sauce).

12 Pour sauce on to plate and place a drop scone in the centre. Set the pork fillet on the scone and garnish with scattered turned pears and fresh thyme sprigs.

– Drop scone

	1	2
thyme, bunch of	1	2
flour	200 g (8 oz)	400 g (1 lb)
baking powder	5 g ($\frac{1}{4}$ oz)	10 g ($\frac{1}{2}$ oz)
eggs	1$\frac{1}{2}$	3
milk	100 ml ($\frac{1}{5}$ pt)	200 ml ($\frac{2}{5}$ pt)
shallots	200 g (8 oz)	400 g (1 lb)
butter	13 g ($\frac{1}{2}$ oz)	26 g (1 oz)
sesame oil	50 ml (2 fl oz)	100 ml (4 fl oz)

1 Sift the flour into a mixing bowl and add the salt, pepper and baking powder.
2 Finely chop garlic, shallots and thyme.
3 Sauté the shallots, garlic and thyme in sesame oil without colour. Remove from heat to cool and reserve.
4 Melt butter to a liquid, remove from heat and cool.
5 Add the shallots and thyme to the flour.
6 Mix in the milk, eggs and melted butter. Beat thoroughly and rest for 10 minutes in a cool place.
7 Warm a frying pan to medium heat. Using a spoon, drop the required amount of mixture into the pan (without oil as the butter should stop it sticking). Cook until bubbles form and golden brown then turn over and cook the other side. Serve once cooked.

39 – Braised ham with Madeira sauce

	4 portions	10 portions
piece of ham	600 g (20 oz)	1$\frac{1}{2}$ kg (3 lb)
Madeira	50 ml ($\frac{1}{8}$ pt)	125 ml ($\frac{1}{4}$ pt)
demi-glace or jus-lié	200 ml ($\frac{1}{2}$ pt)	500 ml (1 pt)
brown sugar	40 g (1$\frac{1}{2}$ oz)	100 g (4 oz)
cloves	5	12

1 Boil the ham for 1 hour.
2 Remove the rind and surplus fat.
3 Stud with cloves and place in a braising pan.

4 Add the Madeira, cover with a lid and cook in an oven for 1 hour basting frequently.
5 Remove the ham and place on a dish.
6 Remove the cloves and sprinkle the surface with sugar.
7 Return to the oven until the surface caramelises.
8 Meanwhile add the sauce to the cooking liquid.
9 Reboil, skim off all the fat, correct seasoning and strain.
10 Carve ham into slices and coat with sauce.

Note Suggested serving accompaniments, e.g.: purée of spinach; purée of dried yellow or green peas; buttered noodles.

40 – Mousselines of ham

	4 portions	10 portions
raw lean ham	400 g (1 lb)	1¼ kg (2½ lb)
egg white	1	2–3
paprika	5 g (¼ oz)	12 g (⅝ oz)
double cream (very cold)	125 ml (¼ pt)	300 ml (⅝ pt)
white stock	½ litre (1 pt)	1¼ litre (2½ pt)

1 Finely mince the ham and place in a basin.
2 Thoroughly beat in the egg white, add paprika and pass mixture through a fine sieve.
3 Place in refrigerator until thoroughly cold.
4 Gradually add the cream, beating well, correct seasoning.
5 Using 2 tbsp and a pan of hot water mould the mousselines by taking a spoonful of mixture, dipping the second spoon into hot water and spooning out the mixture from the first spoon to give a neat shape.
6 Place the mousselines on to a buttered deep tray.
7 Gently pour on the stock, cover with a buttered paper, bring almost to the boil and poach in a moderate oven for approx. 15 minutes.

Note Mousselines can be served with a variety of sauces and garnishes, e.g. on a bed of leaf spinach coated with Mornay sauce, sprinkled with Parmesan cheese and gratinated.

POULTRY AND GAME

Prepare and cook complex meat, offal, game and poultry dishes

1   Select the type, quantity and quality of meat, offal, game and poultry in accordance with recipe specifications.
2   Demonstrate that the nutritional value of meat, offal, game and poultry is adequately retained during the preparation and cooking procedures.
3   Recognise that meat, offal, game and poultry not for immediate consumption are stored in accordance with the recipe specification and the relevant legislation.

—— *Poultry* ——

The term 'poultry' in its general sense applies to all domestic fowl bred for food, fowls, turkeys, duck, geese and pigeons.

HANDLING AND PREPARING POULTRY

Nutritional value

Poultry is a good source of energy giving protein.

Signs of quality

1 Plump breast.
2 Pliable breast bone.
3 Flesh firm.
4 Skin white, unbroken, and with a faint tint.

Old birds have coarse scales and large spurs on the legs and long hairs on the skin.

Cleaning

1 Pick out any pens or down, using a small knife.
2 Singe in order to remove any hairs, take care not to scorch the skin.
3 Split the neck skin by gripping firmly and make a lengthwise incision on the underside, cut off the neck as close to the body as possible.

4 Cut off the head.
5 Remove the crop and loosen intestines and lungs with forefinger.
6 Cut out vent and wipe clean.
7 Loosen intestines with forefinger.
8 Draw out the innards being careful not to break the gall bladder.
9 Wipe vent end if necessary.
10 Split and clean the gizzard.
11 Cut off the gall bladder from the liver and discard.
12 Keep the neck and heart for stock.

Trussing for roasting

1 Clean the legs by dipping in boiling water for a few seconds then remove the scales with a cloth.
2 Cut off the outside claws leaving the centre ones, trim these to half their length.
3 To facilitate carving remove the wish-bone.
4 Place the bird on its back.
5 Hold the legs back firmly.
6 Insert the trussing needle through the bird, midway between the leg joints.
7 Turn on to its side.
8 Pierce the winglet, the skin of the neck, the skin of the carcass and the other winglet.

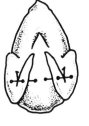

9 Tie ends of string securely.
10 Secure the legs by inserting the needle through the carcass and over the legs, take care not to pierce the breast.

Trussing for boiling and entrées

1 Proceed as for roasting.
2 Cut the leg sinew just below the joint.
3 Either:
 (a) bend back the legs so that they lie parallel to the breast and secure when trussing, or
 (b) insert the legs through incisions made in the skin at the rear end of the bird and secure when trussing.

CUTS OF CHICKEN

Leg { 4 drumstick
      3 thigh

1 Wing
2 Breast
5 Winglet
6 Carcass

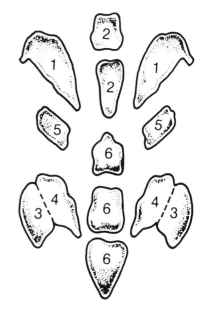

Preparation for grilling

1 Remove the wish-bone.
2 Cut off the claws at the first joint.
3 Place bird on its back.
4 Insert a large knife through the neck-end and out of the vent.
5 Cut through the backbone.
6 Open out.
7 Remove back and rib bones.

Preparation for ballottines

Ballottine – this is a boned stuffed leg of bird.

1 Using a small sharp knife remove the thigh bone.
2 Scrape the flesh off the bone of the drumstick towards the claw joint.
3 Sever the drumstick bone leaving approximately 2–3 cm ($\frac{3}{4}$–1 in) at the claw joint end.
4 Fill the cavities in both the drumstick and thigh with a savoury stuffing.
5 Neaten the shape and secure with string using a trussing needle.

Cutting of cooked chicken (roasted or boiled)

1 Remove the legs and cut in two (drumstick and thigh).
2 Remove the wings.
3 Separate breast from the carcass and divide in two.
4 Serve a drumstick with a wing and the thigh with the breast.

Preparation for ballottines

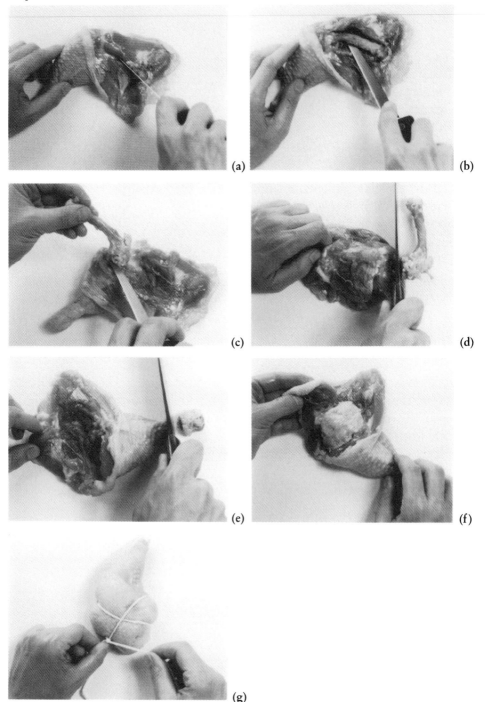

(a)

(b)

(c)

(d)

(e)

(f)

(g)

RECIPES

1 – Chicken mousse, mousselines and quenelles

These chicken dishes are smooth and light in texture and easy to digest. They are made from a mixture known as chicken forcemeat or farce.

Mousses are cooked in buttered moulds in a bain-marie in a moderate oven, then turned out of the mould for service. Therefore the basic mixture must be fairly firm so that the mousse does not break up. They can be cooked in individual or 2- or 4-portion moulds.

Mousselines are moulded using two tablespoons which are dipped into hot water to prevent the mixture sticking to the spoons. The mousselines are then placed into a buttered shallow dish and carefully covered with chicken stock. They are then covered with a buttered paper and cooked gently in the oven. Usually two mousselines are served to a portion.

Quenelles are shaped with two spoons as for mousselines but the sizes can be varied by using different sized spoons, according to requirement, e.g. using teaspoons if the quenelles are required for vol-au-vent. The mixture can also be piped into pea-sized shapes and used to garnish soups.

Note   Mousse, mousseline and quenelles may also be made from other foods, e.g. ham, hare, partridge, pheasant, quail. They can be prepared in different sizes according to the dish requirement and can be used as a light first course, e.g. mousselines of quail, fresh herb sauce, as a main course, e.g. mousselines of ham with spinach and cheese sauce, or as a garnish to other dishes. See mousseline of duck page 324.

2 – Chicken forcemeat or farce

	4 portions
prepared chicken (without skin or bone)	400 g (1 lb)
salt and pepper	
nutmeg	
whites of egg	3
double cream, very cold	375–500 ml ($\frac{3}{4}$–1 pt)

1   Remove all the sinew from the flesh of the chicken.

2 Lightly season and process to a purée.
3 Gradually add the egg whites, mixing thoroughly, and then pass through a sieve.
4 Place mixture in a bowl on ice until very cold.
5 Whilst on ice gradually combine the cream, mixing thoroughly. Test a little of the mixture by gently cooking in simmering water. If the mixture is too light add a little more white of egg, if too stiff, add a little more cream. Check seasoning.

3 – Mousseline of chicken using a panada

A panada is sometimes used as a cost-saving factor and to extend the flavouring ingredient. There are three basic panadas:

1 Equal quantities of white breadcrumbs and milk soaked and squeezed dry.
2 A basic choux pastry mixture without the addition of eggs.
3 A frangipan panada.

– Frangipan panada

	4 portions	10 portions
butter or margarine	50 g (2 oz)	125 g (5 oz)
flour	100 g (4 oz)	250 g (10 oz)
egg yolks	4	10
milk	250 ml ($\frac{1}{2}$ pt)	625 ml ($1\frac{1}{4}$ pt)

1 Cream the butter, flour and yolks together well; boil the milk and add to the mixture, then return to the saucepan and bring back to the boil.
2 Allow to cool.

Allow all panadas to cool before adding to the basic mixture.

– Chicken forcemeat using a panada

	4 portions	10 portions
raw chicken flesh	400 g (1 lb)	1 kg ($2\frac{1}{2}$ lb)
egg whites	3	$7\frac{1}{2}$
panada	150–200 g (6–8 oz)	375–500 g (15–20 oz)
double cream	500 ml (1 pt)	$1\frac{1}{4}$ litre ($2\frac{1}{2}$ pt)
seasoning, mace, nutmeg		

1 Remove all sinew, bones and skin from the chicken.
2 Purée in a food processor.
3 Beat in egg whites and panada.
4 Pass through a fine sieve then place into a basin over a bowl of ice.
5 Add the cream slowly, beating well between each addition.
6 Season with salt, pepper, mace and nutmeg. Use as required.

4 – Chicken soufflé

	4 portions	10 portions
raw chicken, without skin or sinew	250 g (10 oz)	600 g (1½ lb)
butter	50 g (2 oz)	125 g (5 oz)
thick velouté	250 ml (½ pt)	600 ml (1¼ pt)
salt and pepper		
eggs, separated	3	8

1 Finely dice the chicken and cook in the butter.
2 Add to the velouté and purée in a food processor.
3 Pass through a fine sieve and season.
4 Beat the yolks into the warm mixture.
5 Fold in the stiffly beaten whites carefully.
6 Place into individual buttered moulds or one mould.
7 Bake at 220°–230°C (425°–450°F) for approximately 15 minutes and serve.
8 Serve a suitable sauce separately, for example mushroom or suprême sauce.

Note For a lighter soufflé use 3 egg yolks and 4 egg whites.

⊤ 5 – Chicken soufflé with creamed mushrooms

(René Pauvert)

	4 portions	10 portions
chicken breast	100 g (4 oz)	250 g (10 oz)
soft unsalted butter	5 g ($\frac{1}{4}$ oz)	12$\frac{1}{2}$ g ($\frac{1}{2}$ oz)
single cream	80 g (3 oz)	200 g (7$\frac{1}{2}$ oz)
salt and cayenne to taste		
egg whites	7	18

1 Lightly season the chicken, purée with the butter and place in refrigerator for 10–15 minutes until cold.
2 Pass the mixture through a fine sieve and place in a stainless-steel bowl on ice.
3 Carefully incorporate the cream little by little.
4 Check seasoning and keep it cool.
5 Lightly butter individual soufflé moulds and coat with fresh white breadcrumbs.
6 Whisk the egg whites with a pinch of salt until stiff.
7 Add a small amount of egg white to the mousseline, incorporate well, then gently fold in the remainder, season to taste.
8 Pour half the mixture into the moulds, add a spoonful of the ragoût, then the remainder of the mixture.
9 Bake at 200°C (392°F) for about 14 minutes.
10 Serve with a morille cream sauce.

– Ragout of mushrooms with cream

diced raw chicken breast or thigh	25 g (1 oz)	60 g (2$\frac{1}{2}$ oz)
mushrooms quartered	25 g (1 oz)	60 g (2$\frac{1}{2}$ oz)
shallots finely chopped	5 g ($\frac{1}{4}$ oz)	12 g ($\frac{1}{2}$ oz)
white wine	2 tbsp	5 tbsp
brown chicken stock	10 cl ($\frac{1}{8}$ pt)	25 cl ($\frac{1}{3}$ pt)
double cream	5 cl ($\frac{1}{16}$ pt)	12 cl ($\frac{1}{4}$ pt)
butter	5 g ($\frac{1}{4}$ oz)	12 g ($\frac{1}{2}$ oz)
salt and cayenne to taste		

1 Sauté the chicken in butter. Add the mushrooms, finely chopped shallots, deglaze with white wine, reduce, add the chicken stock, reduce and then add the cream.
2 Adjust to a sauce consistency, season to taste and let it cool.

6 – Roast stuffed spring chicken

	4 portions	10 portions
Stuffing		
bacon	100 g (¼lb)	250 g (¾lb)
butter or oil	50 g (2 oz)	125 g (5 oz)
bay leaf	½	1
small sprig of thyme		
onion (chopped)	25 g (1 oz)	60 g (2½oz)
chicken livers, raw (optional)	200 g (½lb)	500 g (1¼lb)
spring chickens	4 single or	10 single or
	2 double	5 double
brown stock	¼ litre (½pt)	¾ litre (1¼pt)
butter	100 g (4 oz)	250 g (10 oz)
white or wholemeal	25 g (1 oz)	60 g (2½oz)
breadcrumbs		
lemon, juice of	½	1
chopped parsley		

1 Prepare the stuffing by cutting the bacon in small pieces.
2 Fry off quickly in a frying pan with the butter or oil, herbs and chopped onion for a few seconds.
3 Add the trimmed chicken livers.
4 Season with salt and pepper. Fry quickly until brown.
5 Pass all the mixture through a fine sieve.
6 Clean, prepare, season and truss the spring chicken as for entrée.
7 Fill the chicks with the prepared stuffing.
8 Roast or pot-roast the chicks.
9 Remove the lid half way through to obtain a golden brown colour.
10 When cooked, remove the string and place the chicks on a flat serving dish and keep warm.
11 Remove the fat from the cooking dish, deglaze with brown stock and lightly thicken with a little diluted arrowroot. Pass through a fine chinois and serve separately.
12 Cook the butter in a frying pan to a beurre noisette.
13 Mix in the breadcrumbs and the lemon juice and pour over the chicks. Sprinkle with chopped parsley and serve.

7 – Chicken in casserole or cocotte

A casserole is made of earthenware, a cocotte of porcelain.

	4 portions
1 chicken	1¼–1½ kg (2½–3 lb)
onion	50 g (2 oz)
carrot	50 g (2 oz)
celery	50 g (2 oz)
bouquet garni	
butter, margarine or oil	50 g (2 oz)
jus-lié	¼ litre (½ pt)
chopped parsley	

> Using hard margarine
> I portion provides:
>
> 530 kcals/2224 kJ
> 41.5 g fat
> (of which 16.7 g saturated)
> 2.0 g carbohydrate
> (of which 1.5 g sugars)
> 37.0 g protein
> 0.9 g fibre

1 Prepare the chicken and truss for entrée (page 296).
2 Slice the onion, carrot and celery, place in the bottom of the casserole or cocotte with the bouquet garni.
3 Season the chicken and place on the bed of roots.
4 Spread the butter on the bird.
5 Cover with a lid and place in a hot oven (230–250°C, 446–482°F).
6 Baste occasionally, allow approximately ¾–1 hour.
7 When cooked remove the chicken and the string.
8 Pour off the fat from the casserole, remove the bouquet garni.
9 Deglaze the casserole or cocotte with the demi-glace or jus-lié.
10 Pour the sauce into a sauteuse, boil, skim and correct the seasoning and consistency.
11 Clean the casserole, and place the bird in the casserole.
12 Pass the sauce through a fine strainer on to the bird.
13 Sprinkle with chopped parsley and serve.

Chicken casserole is usually served garnished, for example:

• Cocotte potatoes, glazed button onions, lardons
• Dice of mushrooms and croûtons
• Parmentier potatoes, white wine in the sauce
• Paysanne of vegetables

8 – Chicken sauté

Chickens 1¼–1½ kg (2½–3 lb) in weight are suitable to cut into 8 pieces for 4 portions. The pieces can be prepared on the bone or skinned and bone out. Boning out slightly increases shrinkage, the portions look smaller and preparation time is increased, but it facilitates ease of eating.

Chicken is prepared in this manner for fricasseé, blanquette and chicken pies; the winglets, giblets and carcass are used for chicken stock. There are many garnishes for chicken sauté and a few examples follow. Further variety can be introduced by using herbs, e.g. tarragon, basil, rosemary etc., wines, e.g. dry white, dry sherry, vermouth, and different garnishes, e.g. wild mushrooms and ceps.

9 – Cutting for sauté, fricassée, pies, etc.

1 Remove the feet at the first joint.
2 Remove the legs from the carcass.
3 Cut each leg in two at the joint.
4 Remove the wish-bone. Remove winglets and trim.
5 Remove the wings carefully, leaving two equal portions on the breast.
6 Remove the breast and cut in two.
7 Trim the carcass and cut into three pieces.

10 – Chicken sauté with mushrooms and curry-flavoured sauce

	4 portions	10 portions
chicken cut for sauté	1	$2\frac{1}{2}$
butter	50 g (2 oz)	125 g (5 oz)
finely chopped onions	150 g (6 oz)	375 g (15 oz)
curry powder	1 dsp	$2\frac{1}{2}$ dsp
button mushrooms	100 g (4 oz)	250 g (10 oz)
cream	125 ml ($\frac{1}{4}$ pt)	300 g ($\frac{5}{8}$ pt)

1 Allow seasoned chicken to cook for a few minutes in butter without colour.
2 Add the onion, curry powder and cayenne and cover with a lid to finish cooking in the oven.
3 Cook the mushrooms in butter without colour and place with the chicken on the serving dish and keep warm.
4 Add the cream to the pan, cook for several minutes and pass through a sieve.
5 Finish with 25 g (1 oz) of the butter and pour over the chicken.

The following recipes are examples of the different ways of using chicken cut for sauté:

1 Shallow fried and coloured brown with jus-lié
2 Cooked without colour and a sauce
3 Crumbed and fried (e.g. Maryland, page 311)

11 – Chicken sauté in whisky-flavoured cream sauce

	4 portions	10 portions
butter or margarine	50 g (2 oz)	125 g (5 oz)
chicken cut for sauté	1¼–1½ kg (2½–3 lb)	3–3¾ kg (6¼–7½ lb)
finely chopped onion	50 g (2 oz)	125 g (5 oz)
carrots ⎫	50 g (2 oz)	125 g (5 oz)
celery ⎬ cut in brunoise	50 g (2 oz)	125 g (5 oz)
leek ⎭	50 g (2 oz)	125 g (5 oz)
whisky or port wine	60 ml (⅛ pt)	150 ml (⅓ pt)
chicken velouté	250 ml (½ pt)	600 ml (1¼ pt)
single cream or non-dairy unsweetened creamer	125 ml (¼ pt)	300 ml (⅝ pt)
lemon juice	2–3 drops	5–7 drops
seasoning, chopped parsley		

1 Heat the butter or margarine in a sauté pan.
2 Season the chicken and place in the pan: legs, then breasts and wings.
3 Set quickly on both sides without colour, remove from the sauté pan. Add to the pan in which the chicken has been cooked the finely chopped onion and the brunoise of vegetables, sweat without colour.
4 Deglaze with whisky or port wine, add chicken velouté and bring to the boil.
5 Replace the chicken into the pan with the velouté and vegetables, cover with a lid and gently simmer until cooked.
6 Finish with lemon juice and single cream or non-dairy creamer.
7 Arrange the pieces of chicken neatly in a suitable dish and coat with sauce. Sprinkle with chopped parsley and serve.

12 – Chicken sauté with ceps

Proceed as for chicken sauté. Before swilling the pan add 50 g (2 oz) chopped shallots and 200 g (8 oz) ceps and cook for a few minutes, add the jus-lié and finish with chopped parsley (increase proportions $2\frac{1}{2}$ times for 10 portions).

13 – Chicken sauté with button onions and potatoes (champeaux)

Proceed as for chicken sauté. Deglaze the pan with white wine and jus-lié, strain and finish with butter. Garnish with 100 g (4 oz) button onions cooked in butter and 100 g (4 oz) cocotte potatoes (increase proportions $2\frac{1}{2}$ times for 10 portions).

14 – Breast and wing of chicken (suprême)

The word suprême is traditionally used to describe half of the white meat of a whole chicken. In contemporary menu practice the word wing or breast is often used in place of suprême.

Therefore there are two suprêmes to a chicken. Each has a fillet which is lifted off, the sinew is removed, an incision is made along the thick side of the suprême and the fillet inserted, then the suprême is lightly batted.

Suprêmes can be poached or shallow fried in butter, oil or margarine. When shallow fried they can be garnished as for sauté of chicken. For certain dishes the breasts can be stuffed (see page 314), floured or crumbed before shallow frying.

15 – Preparation for suprêmes

Suprême – this is the wing and half the breast of a chicken with the trimmed wing bone attached, i.e. the white meat of one chicken yields two suprêmes.

1 Use chicken weighing $1\frac{1}{4}$–$1\frac{1}{2}$ kg ($2\frac{1}{2}$–3 lb).
2 Cut off both legs from the chicken.
3 Remove the skin from the breasts.
4 Remove the wishbone.
5 Scrape the wing bone bare adjoining the breasts.
6 Cut off the winglets near the joints leaving $1\frac{1}{2}$–2 cm ($\frac{1}{2}$–$\frac{3}{4}$ in) of bare bone attached to the breasts.
7 Cut the breasts close to the breastbone and follow the bone down to the wing joint.

8 Cut through the joint.
9 Lay the chicken on its side and pull the suprêmes off assisting with the knife.
10 Lift the fillets from the suprêmes and remove the sinew from each.
11 Make an incision lengthways, along the thick side of the suprêmes, open and place the fillets inside.
12 Close, lightly flatten with a bat moistened with water and trim if necessary.

16 – Poached chicken breast with mushrooms

	4 portions	10 portions
suprêmes of chicken	4	10
button mushrooms	100 g (4 oz)	250 g (10 oz)
lemon, juice of	1	$2\frac{1}{2}$
suprême sauce	500 ml (1 pt)	$1\frac{1}{4}$ litre ($2\frac{1}{2}$ pt)

1 Gently poach the chicken breasts in mushroom cooking liquor, produced by cooking the mushrooms in water containing lemon juice.
2 Place the suprêmes on the dish with the mushrooms and keep warm.
3 Reduce cooking liquor and add to the suprême sauce.
4 Correct the seasoning and consistency and strain over the chicken and mushrooms.

17 – Poached chicken breast with cheese sauce and asparagus

Poach the breast of chicken in chicken stock and add the reduced cooking liquor to the cheese sauce. Mask the suprême with the finished sauce, glaze and garnish with asparagus.

18 – Poached chicken wing in chicken cream sauce and mushrooms

Poach the breast of chicken and add the reduced cooking liquor to the chicken cream sauce (suprême sauce). Mask the chicken with the sauce, which contains 50 g (2 oz) julienne of mushrooms cooked in a little butter.

I 19 ~ **Breast of chicken filled with clove, ham, spinach and sundried tomato served with a light reduction Madeira sauce and roasted shallots**

(CARLOS DIAZ)

- Filled chicken breast

	4 portions	10 portions
chicken breasts	4	10
slices of honey and clove roast ham	4	10
sundried tomatoes	75 g (3 oz)	187 g (7½ oz)
leaf spinach	100 g (4 oz)	250 g (10 oz)
ground white pepper		
salt		
honey	2 tbsp	5 tbsp
olive oil	1 tbsp	3 tbsp
soft butter	2 tbsp	5 tbsp

1 Remove breast fillets and open with a sharp knife with an envelope cut from the centre.
2 Gently bat out and season lightly. Blanch and refresh spinach, lay on a clean towel to dry.
3 Cover each breast with a thin layer of blanched spinach, followed by a thin layer of sundried tomatoes topped with ham and a further layer of spinach.
4 Roll carefully and evenly like a swiss roll, gently seam edges by batting out thinly.
5 Brown with butter and honey. Roast in oven at 180–200°C (356–392°F) for 12–15 minutes. Rest for 3 minutes keeping warm. Slice evenly and surround with Madeira sauce and roasted shallots.

~ Roasted shallots

	4 portions	10 portions
shallots, whole	24	60
virgin olive oil	1 tbsp	3 tbsp
butter	25 g (1 oz)	62½ g (2½ oz)
freshly ground black pepper		
coarse sea salt	½ tsp	1 tsp

Place shallots in suitable pan, add olive oil and melted butter, season, roast in hot oven

⁓ Madeira sauce

	4 portions	10 portions
Madeira	50 ml (2 fl oz)	125 ml (5 fl oz)
brown chicken stock	300 ml ($\frac{1}{2}$ pt)	750 ml (1$\frac{1}{2}$ pt)
unsalted butter	25 g (1 oz)	62 g (2$\frac{1}{2}$ oz)
seasoning		

1 Reduce the chicken stock to a glaze, add Madeira.
2 Remove from heat and shake in butter in small pieces.
3 Adjust seasoning to taste, use as above.

20 ⁓ Fried chicken breast with mushrooms and chicken sauce

Shallow fry the chicken in butter to a golden colour on both sides, garnish with mushrooms cooked in butter and coat with suprême sauce.

21 ⁓ Fried chicken wing with asparagus and nut brown butter

Shallow fry the chicken, garnish with asparagus tips and finish with nut brown butter.

22 ⁓ Fried chicken breast with artichokes

Shallow fry the chicken, garnish with sliced cooked artichoke bottoms and finish with nut brown butter and chopped parsley. Jus-lié is served separately.

23 ⁓ Fried suprême of chicken with vegetables

Shallow fry the chicken, garnish with batons of vegetables and finish with nut brown butter.

24 – Crumbed breasts or wings of chicken

Prepare the chicken by passing through seasoned flour, egg and crumbs. Shallow fry to a golden colour on both sides.

25 – Fried crumbed chicken wing with cucumber and nut brown butter

Shallow fry the chicken, garnish with turned pieces of cucumber cooked in butter and finish with nut brown butter.

Some examples of garnishes and sauces suitable for use with these dishes include the following:

Vegetables	Sauces
stir-fry vegetables	wine sauces
chicory	asparagus
courgettes	broccoli
sugar peas (mange-tout)	leek
peppers	watercress
spinach	

26 – Suprême of chicken Maryland

	4 portions	10 portions
chicken suprêmes	4	10
breadcrumbs	100 g (4 oz)	250 g (10 oz)
eggs	2	5
tomatoes	4	10
rashers streaky bacon	4	10
bananas	2	5
sweetcorn	100 g (4 oz)	250 g (10 oz)

1 The suprêmes, after being egg and crumbed, may be deep or shallow fried to a golden colour ensuring that they are cooked through.
2 Garnish with grilled tomatoes, grilled bacon, fried halved bananas and fried sweetcorn fritters. (Not all establishments serve tomato, however it does add colour to the presentation.)

Sweetcorn fritters
The sweetcorn is bound in a thick white sauce, or a little flour and egg, and shallow fried on both sides. Alternatively, the mixture can be made into croquettes, flour, egg and crumbed and deep fried.

Note Hot horseradish sauce is served separately. The horseradish sauce is made from cream sauce with freshly grated horseradish.

The banana may also be crumbed or passed through batter and deep fried.

27 – Chicken Kiev

	4 portions	10 portions
suprêmes of chicken	4	10
butter	100 g (4 oz)	250 g (10 oz)
seasoned flour	25 g (1 oz)	60 g (2½ oz)
eggs	2	5
breadcrumbs	100 g (4 oz)	250 g (10 oz)

1 Make an incision along the thick sides of the suprêmes.
2 Insert 25 g (1 oz) cold butter into each. Season.
3 Pass through seasoned flour, eggwash and crumbs, ensuring complete coverage. Eggwash and crumb twice if necessary.
4 Deep fry, drain and serve.

Note To vary the flavour, garlic, parsley, tarragon or chive butter can be used.

The chicken could be stuffed, for example, with duxelle, chopped yellow, green and red peppers (pimentos), or lemon or thyme stuffing, in which case it would not be named Kiev and so leaves room for personal interpretation and names to suit.

28 – Chicken escalopes

These can be prepared in a number of ways:

1 75–100 g (3–4 oz) slices of chicken breast thinly beaten out using a little water, then left plain or flour, egg and crumbed.
2 Boned and skinned chicken thighs treated as above.

3 Minced raw breast and/or leg of chicken bound with a little egg white, shaped, flattened and either left plain or egg and crumbed.

Chicken escalopes can then be cooked and served in a wide variety of ways using different garnishes and sauces. Any recipe using a cut of chicken can be adapted to use chicken escalopes, but often the simpler recipes are most effective, e.g. egg and crumbed chicken escalope with asparagus tips.

29 – Chicken fricassée in cream and wine sauce

	4 portions	10 portions
chicken cut for sauté	$1\frac{1}{4}$–$1\frac{1}{2}$ kg ($2\frac{1}{2}$–3 lb)	3–$3\frac{3}{4}$ kg (6–$7\frac{1}{2}$ lb)
butter	75 g (3 oz)	180 g ($7\frac{1}{2}$ oz)
leeks	100 g (4 oz)	250 g (10 oz)
celery	100 g (4 oz)	250 g (10 oz)
onions	100 g (4 oz)	250 g (10 oz)
white wine	250 ml ($\frac{1}{2}$ pt)	600 ml ($1\frac{1}{4}$ pt)
double cream	250 ml ($\frac{1}{2}$ pt)	600 ml ($1\frac{1}{4}$ pt)

leeks, celery, onions: cut into $\frac{1}{4}$ cm ($\frac{1}{8}$ in) dice

1 Gently cook the seasoned chicken in 50 g (2 oz) butter without colour in a sauté pan.
2 Add the diced vegetables, cover with a lid and cook until tender on top of the stove or in the oven.
3 Remove the chicken and keep warm.
4 Deglaze the pan with wine.
5 Add the cream, simmer for 2 minutes, whisk in the remaining butter and correct the seasoning. (Alternatively, use half chicken velouté and half double cream.)
6 Pour over the chicken to serve.

Note   Various garnishes can be used which would be added to the sauce before being poured over the chicken, for example:

• julienne of leek, cooked in butter
• diced pimento cooked in butter
• turned blanched cucumber
• peeled white grapes without pips

Yoghurt may be used in place of cream.

Deep-fried fine julienne of root vegetables can be sprinkled over this dish just before serving.

313

30 – Stuffed crumbed fried breast of chicken

	4 portions	10 portions
suprêmes of chicken	4	10
salt and pepper		
stuffing	100 g (4 oz)	250 g (10 oz)
seasoned flour ⎫	1	3
egg ⎬ if crumbed		
breadcrumbs ⎭	25 g (1 oz)	60 g (2½ oz)
oil	50 g (2 oz)	125 g (5 oz)
butter	50 g (2 oz)	125 g (5 oz)

1 Make an incision along the thick side of the suprêmes and season.
2 Add the stuffing and enclose.
3 Flour or, if to be breadcrumbed, pass through flour, eggwash and breadcrumbs.
4 Shallow fry gently to a golden colour on both sides.
5 Ensure that the chicken is thoroughly cooked, if necessary by finishing in the oven.
6 Finish with nut brown butter or serve with parsley or garlic butter.

Note Suggested stuffings include: duxelle; pimentoes or leeks, chopped and cooked in butter; ham; and liver paté. Always add the stuffing cold unless the suprêmes are to be cooked immediately.

31 – Stuffed legs of chicken (ballottines) with vegetable garnish

		4 portions	10 portions
legs of chicken		4	10
stuffing			
salt and pepper			
butter		50 g (2 oz)	125 g (5 oz)
carrots ⎫	cut half in	100 g (4 oz)	250 g (10 oz)
onion ⎪	paysanne,	100 g (4 oz)	250 g (10 oz)
celery ⎬	remainder in	100 g (4 oz)	250 g (10 oz)
leeks ⎭	mirepoix	100 g (4 oz)	250 g (10 oz)
jus-lié or brown chicken and veal stock		375 ml (¾ pt)	1¼ litre (2½ pt)

1 Bone out the chicken legs: first, remove the thigh bone.
2 Scrape the flesh off the bone of the drumstick towards the claw joint.

3 Sever the drumstick bone, leaving 2–3 cm ($\frac{3}{4}$–1 in) at the end.

4 Fill legs with a savoury stuffing, neaten the shape and secure with string using a trussing needle. Season with salt and pepper.

5 Pot-roast in butter with mirepoix in a covered pan or sauté until cooked.

6 Ensure that the stuffing is cooked through, approximately 20–30 minutes.

7 Remove the ballottines and keep warm in a clean pan.

8 Deglaze the pan with wine, if desired, add the jus-lié or stock and simmer for several mins.

9 Strain, correct the seasoning and consistency.

10 Add to the sauce the paysanne of vegetables which have been sweated together in a little butter.

11 Pour the sauce on to the chicken, simmer gently for a few minutes and serve.

– Stuffing for ballottines

	4 portions	10 portions
chopped onion (cooked)	25 g (1 oz)	60 g (2$\frac{1}{2}$ oz)
breadcrumbs	50 g (2 oz)	125 g (5 oz)
butter or margarine	50 g (2 oz)	125 g (5 oz)
salt and pepper		
or use		
minced chicken and veal, in place of the breadcrumbs, seasoned and bound with an egg	100 g (4 oz)	250 g (10 oz)

Mix all the ingredients together, adding the required herb or flavouring e.g. thyme, parsley, rosemary etc. If desired, chopped crushed garlic, chopped chicken livers and chopped mushrooms could also be used.

Note Wines such as Madeira, Marsala or white port could also be added to the sauce.

I 32 – Chicken sausages with lemon balm

(GRAHAM MELLISH)

	4 portions	10 portions
chicken breast	3 × 150–200 g (6–8 oz)	6 × 150 g–200 g (6–8 oz)
double cream	375 ml ($\frac{3}{4}$ pt)	875 ml (1$\frac{3}{4}$ pt)
fresh lemon balm	$\frac{1}{2}$ bunch	1 bunch
dry sherry	2 tsp	6 tsp
sausage skins		
salt and pepper		

1 Remove all fat, skin and bone from chicken.
2 Mince finely and blend chicken with cream, seasoning, lemon balm and sherry.
3 Remove from blender, chill in fridge for 30 minutes.
4 When cold add more cream if necessary.
5 Pipe into sausage skins.
6 Poach for 10–15 minutes.
7 Grill for colour and serve with a watercress sauce.

33 – Turkey

Turkeys can vary in weight from 3$\frac{1}{2}$–20 kg (7–40 lb).

They are cleaned and trussed in the same way as chicken. The wish-bone should always be removed before trussing. The sinews should be drawn out of the legs. Allow 200 g ($\frac{1}{2}$ lb) per portion raw weight.

Note When cooking a large turkey the legs may be removed, boned, rolled, tied and roasted separately from the remainder of the bird. This will reduce the cooking time and enable the legs and breast to cook more evenly.

Stuffings may be rolled in foil, steamed or baked and thickly sliced. If a firmer stuffing is required, mix in one or two raw eggs before cooking.

34 – Stuffed leg of turkey

Ensure that the sinews are withdrawn from the turkey leg, remove the leg from the turkey and bone out, season and stuff, then tie with string. Roast, braise or pot roast, remove the string and allow to stand before carving in thick slices.

Suitable stuffings include chestnut, walnut, peanuts or mixed nuts in pork sausage meat or those stuffings suggested for chicken or duck ballottines.

Sauces such as jus-lié containing cranberries, blackcurrants or redcurrants may be served.

35 – Breast and wing of turkey

Suprêmes of 100–150 g (4–6 oz) can be cut from the boned-out breast and wing of turkey and used in a similar manner to chicken (see pages 307–308).

36 – Turkey escalopes

4 oz slices cut from boned out turkey breast can be beaten out using a little water then flour, egg and crumbed. They may then be shallow fried on both sides and served with a variety of sauces and garnishes. The escalopes can also be left in a thicker cut, stuffed and then egg and crumbed. For simpler dishes they can be lightly coated in seasoned flour and gently cooked in butter, margarine or oil on both sides with the minimum of colour.

Examples of recipes which can be adapted using turkey include:

Veal escalopes with tomatoes, cheese and white wine, page 272.
Veal kidneys with mustard and cream sauce, page 276.
Pork escalopes with prunes, page 285.
Pork escalopes with apples, cream and calvados, page 286.
Chicken recipes.

37 – Roast Turkey

Chestnut stuffing

chestnuts	200 g (½ lb)
sausage meat	600 g (1½ lb)
chopped onion	50 g (2 oz)

Parsley and thyme stuffing

chopped onion	50 g (2 oz)
oil, butter or margarine	100 g (4 oz)
salt, pepper	
white or wholemeal breadcrumbs	100 g (4 oz)
pinch powdered thyme	
pinch chopped parsley	
chopped turkey liver (raw) (optional)	

turkey	5 kg (10 lb)
fat bacon	100 g (4 oz)
brown stock	375 ml (¾ pt)
bread sauce	

No accompaniments
1 portion (200 g raw with skin, bone):

200 kcals/836 kJ
11.75 g fat
(of which 4.0 g saturated)
0.0 g carbohydrate
(of which 0.0 g sugars)
29.0 g protein
0.0 g fibre

With stuffing, roast gravy, bread sauce
1 portion (200 g raw, with skin, bone):

380 kcals/1589 kJ
24.0 g fat
(of which 8.4 g saturated)
8.6 g carbohydrate
(of which 1.6 g sugars)
34.0 g protein
0.9 g fibre

1 Slit the chestnuts on both sides using a small knife.
2 Boil chestnuts in water for 5–10 minutes.
3 Drain and remove outer and inner skins whilst warm.
4 Cook the chestnuts in a little stock for 5 minutes approximately.
5 When cold, dice and mix into the sausage meat and onion.
6 For the parsley and thyme stuffing, cook the onion in oil, butter or margarine without colour.
7 Remove from the heat, add the seasoning, crumbs and herbs.
8 Mix in the raw chopped liver (optional).
9 Truss the bird firmly (removing wish-bone first).
10 Season with salt and pepper.
11 Cover the breast with fat bacon.
12 Place the bird in a roasting tray on its side and coat with 200 g (4 oz) dripping or oil.
13 Roast in a moderate oven (200–300°C, 392–446°F).
14 Allow to cook on both legs and complete the cooking with the breast upright for the last 30 minutes.
15 Baste frequently and allow 15–20 minutes per lb.
16 Bake the two stuffings separately in greased trays until well cooked.

17 When cooked prepare the gravy from the sediment and the brown stock. Correct the seasoning and remove the fat.
18 Remove the string and serve with stuffings, roast gravy, bread sauce and/or hot cranberry sauce.
19 The turkey may be garnished with chipolata sausages and bacon rolls.

38 – Duck

1 The feet and bills should be bright yellow.
2 The upper bill should break easily.
3 The web feet must be easy to tear.

Duck and duckling are prepared and trussed in the same way as chicken.

Use Ducks and geese may be roasted or braised.

39 – Roast duck or duckling

	4 portions	10 portions
duck	1 × 2 kg (4 lb)	3 × 2 kg (4 lb)
oil		
salt		
brown stock	¼ litre (½ pt)	600 ml (1¼ pt)
watercress	1 bunch	2 bunches
apple sauce	125 ml (¼ pt)	300 ml (⅝ pt)

With apple sauce, watercress
I portion provides:

734 kcals/3083 kJ
60.5 g fat
(of which 16.9 g saturated)
8.2 g carbohydrate
(of which 7.8 g sugars)
40.0 g protein
1.4 g fibre

1 Lightly season the duck inside and out with salt.
2 Truss and brush lightly with oil.
3 Place on its side in a roasting tin, with a few drops of water.
4 Place in hot oven for approximately 20–25 minutes.
5 Turn on to the other side.
6 Cook for a further 20–25 minutes approximately. Baste frequently.
7 To test if cooked, pierce with a fork between the drumstick and thigh and hold over a plate. The juice issuing from the duck should not show any signs of blood.
8 Prepare roast gravy with the stock and the sediment in the roasting tray. Correct the seasoning, remove surface fat.
9 Serve garnished with picked watercress.

10 Accompany with a sauceboat of hot apple sauce and a sauceboat of gravy and game chips. Also serve sauceboat of sage and onion stuffing as prepared in the following recipe for roast stuffed duck.

40 – Roast stuffed duck

	4 portions	10 portions
Stuffing		
chopped onion	100 g (4 oz)	250 g (10 oz)
duck dripping or butter	100 g (4 oz)	250 g (10 oz)
powdered sage	$\frac{1}{2}$ tsp	1 tsp
chopped parsley		
salt, pepper		
white or wholemeal breadcrumbs		
chopped duck liver (optional)	50 g (2 oz)	125 g (5 oz)

1 Gently cook the onion in the dripping without colour.
2 Add the herbs and seasoning. Mix in the crumbs and liver. Stuff the neck end and cook remaining stuffing separately. Cook and serve as for roast duck.

41 – Braised duck with celery

	4 portions	10 portions
butter or oil	50 g (2 oz)	125 g (5 oz)
bacon trimmings	50 g (2 oz)	125 g (5 oz)
carrots	50 g (2 oz)	125 g (5 oz)
onions	50 g (2 oz)	125 g (5 oz)
celery	200 g (8 oz)	600 g (1¼ lb)
duck	2 kg (4 lb)	3 × 2 kg (4 lb)
brown stock	375 ml ($\frac{3}{4}$ pt)	1 litre (2 pt)
demi-glace	375 ml ($\frac{3}{4}$ pt)	1 litre (2 pt)
bouquet garni		
pieces of braised celery	4	10

(carrots, onions, celery bracketed as mirepoix)

1 Place the butter in a braising pan and lightly fry the mirepoix.
2 Add the seasoned, trussed duck and brown on all sides.
3 Drain off the fat, add the stock and demi-glace so as to three-parts cover the duck, add the bouquet garni and bring to the boil.

4 Cover with a lid and cook in a moderate oven (200°C, 400°F approximately.) and allow to simmer until cooked, approximately $1\frac{1}{2}$ hours.
5 Put the duck aside to keep warm, remove the string.
6 Degrease the sauce, strain and correct the seasoning and consistency.
7 Cut the duck into portions, mask with the sauce, garnish with braised celery and serve.

Notes
(a) In place of demi-glace or jus-lié, brown stock may be used and the stock thickened slightly with cornflour or arrowroot.
(b) 1 or 2 heads of celery, according to size, would be required for braising for the garnish.
(c) In place of celery, braised duck could be served with, for example, chicory, salsify, fennel, leeks or spring vegetables.

42 – Duckling with gooseberries

	4 portions	10 portions
duckling	1 × 2 kg (4 lb)	3 × 2 kg (4 lb)
butter	50 g (2 oz)	125 g (5 oz)
carrots ⎫	50 g (2 oz)	125 g (5 oz)
onions ⎪	50 g (2 oz)	125 g (5 oz)
celery ⎬ mirepoix	25 g (1 oz)	60 g (2½ oz)
bay leaf ⎪		
thyme ⎭		
brown stock	250 ml (½ pt)	600 ml (1¼ pt)
arrowroot (optional)	10 g (½ oz)	25 g (1¼ oz)
gooseberries, topped and tailed	200 g (8 oz)	500 g (1¼ lb)

Based on 100 g cooked meat
1 portion provides:

309 kcals/1287 kJ
20.2 g fat
(of which 9.5 g saturated)
5.9 g carbohydrate
(of which 3.2 g sugars)
26.2 g protein
1.8 g fibre

1 Clean, truss and season the duckling for pot-roasting.
2 Place the duck in a buttered pan with mirepoix and coat with butter. Cover pan with tight-fitting lid.
3 Cook in the oven at 200°C (400°F) for 1 hour, basting occasionally.
4 Remove the lid, continue cooking for a further half hour until tender and baste frequently.
5 Remove the duck and keep warm.
6 Drain all fat from pan, deglaze with the brown stock and thicken with arrowroot (if required).

7 Add the gooseberries to the sauce and simmer gently for a few minutes, until just cooked.
8 Carve the duck, coat with sauce and serve.

Notes
(a) If gooseberries are very tart, a little sugar or honey can be added to the sauce.
(b) In place of gooseberries, blackcurrants or peaches, cut into quarters, could be used.
(c) For service the duck can be cut into pieces retaining the bone or by removing the legs, boning out and cutting into slices, and by removing the breast from the bone and carving into slices.

43 – Duckling with orange sauce (bigarade)

4 portions

duckling	2 kg (4 lb)
butter	50 g (2 oz)
carrots	50 g (2 oz)
onions	50 g (2 oz)
celery mirepoix	25 g (1 oz)
bay leaf	1
small sprig thyme	1
brown stock	250 ml (½ pt)
arrowroot	10 g (½ oz)
oranges	2
lemon	1
vinegar	2 tbsp
sugar	25 g (1 oz)

Using butter
1 portion provides:

744 kcals/3125 kJ
60.1 g fat
(of which 17.1 g saturated)
11.8 g carbohydrate
(of which 9.3 g sugars)
39.9 g protein
0.1 g fibre

1 Clean and truss the duck. Use some butter to grease a deep pan. Add the mirepoix.
2 Season the duck. Place the duck on the mirepoix.
3 Coat the duck with the remaining butter.
4 Cover the pan with a tight fitting lid.
5 Place the pan in oven (200–230°C, Reg. 6–8).
6 Baste occasionally, cook for approximately 1 hour.
7 Remove the lid and continue cooking the duck basting frequently until tender (approximately a further ½ hour).
8 Remove the duck, cut out the string and keep the duck in a warm

place. Drain off all the fat from the pan.

9 Deglaze with the stock, bring to the boil and allow to simmer for a few minutes.

10 Thicken by adding the arrowroot diluted in a little cold water.

11 Reboil, correct seasoning, degrease and pass through a fine chinois.

12 Thinly remove the zest from one orange and the lemon and cut into fine julienne.

13 Blanch the julienne of zest for 3–4 minutes, refresh.

14 Place the vinegar and sugar in a small sauteuse and cook to a light caramel stage.

15 Add the juice of the oranges and the lemon.

16 Add the sauce and bring to the boil.

17 Correct seasoning and pass through a fine chinois.

18 Add the julienne to the sauce, keep warm.

19 Remove the legs from the duck, bone out and cut in thin slices.

20 Carve the duck breasts into thin slices and neatly dress.

21 Coat with the sauce and serve.

Note An alternative method of service is to cut the duck into eight pieces which may then be either left on the bone or the bones removed.

44 – Stuffed leg of duck

Proceed as for stuffed chicken legs, page 314.

The stuffing recommended for chicken can be used for duck as well but consider also sage and onion, and sauces such as orange, and port wine.

45 – Breast of duck

Remove the breast of duck in a similar manner to suprême of chicken (page 307). Grill, sauté or roast in a hot oven and cook as required, either slightly underdone or cooked through.

Serve whole or sliced and garnish as required.

Note The fat and skin may be removed from the breast: discard the fat and tie the skin back on to the breast to protect it during the cooking.

46 – Breast of duck with pineapple

	4 portions	10 portions
duck suprêmes	4	10
oil or butter	100 g (4 oz)	250 g (10 oz)
pineapple	4 slices	10 slices
jus-lié or brown stock	250 ml ($\frac{1}{2}$pt)	600 ml ($1\frac{1}{4}$pt)

1 Shallow fry the duck in butter or oil.
2 Carefully fry the pineapple to colour. If canned pineapple is used, shallow fry quickly; if fresh pineapple is used, cook until tender.
3 Quarter the pineapple and neatly arrange three-quarters on the duck; cut remaining quarter into dice and add to the jus-lié.
4 Deglaze the pan with the jus-lié, strain and pour over the duck to serve.

Note   Variations to this garnish may be kiwi fruit, mango, and banana, and a liquor such as curaçao or rum may be added to the sauce.

47 – Mousseline of duck

	4 portions	10 portions
breast of duck	150 g (6 oz)	375 g (15 oz)
chopped garlic, shallots, juniper berries, peppercorns and thyme		
port	$\frac{1}{2}$ tbsp	$1\frac{1}{2}$ tbsp
brandy	$\frac{1}{2}$ tbsp	$1\frac{1}{2}$ tbsp
large beaten egg	$\frac{1}{2}$	$1\frac{1}{2}$
salt and pepper	$\frac{1}{2}$ tsp	$1\frac{1}{2}$ tsp
reduced duck and juniper-flavoured veal stock	2 tbsp	5 tbsp
double cream	125 ml ($\frac{1}{2}$pt)	300 ml ($\frac{5}{8}$pt)
whipping cream	125 ml ($\frac{1}{2}$pt)	300 ml ($\frac{5}{8}$pt)

1 Slice raw breast and marinate together with chopped garlic, shallots, juniper berries, peppercorns, thyme, port and brandy for 12 hours.
2 Remove duck from marinade and dry thoroughly on kitchen paper.
3 Chop finely in a food processor and add the egg, salt and pepper, the

brandy and port from the marinade, and the reduction and mix well.

4 Whilst the machine is in motion slowly add all the cream until well amalgamated. Correct seasoning.

5 Place into equal-sized well greased moulds, cover with tin foil and cook in a bain-marie at 160°C (325°F) until firm for approximately 25 minutes.

6 Serve with a rich juniper berry sauce.

Notes This is served as a first course.

(a) The reduction must be of a very intense flavour and consistency in order to balance the lack of flavour in the cream, without impairing the texture of the mousseline. Therefore the quality of the reduction is of paramount importance to achieve the best result.

(b) All ingredients, barring the reduction, which must be kept warm to prevent setting, must be kept very cold to compensate, as the cream is vulnerable to curdling when warm.

(c) A ragoût of diced mushrooms with a little reduction, cooled until set, can be placed into the centre of each mousseline prior to cooking. Be sure this is well enclosed all round.

I 48 – Breast of maigret duck with peaches and redcurrants

(ANNA MILLER)

	4 portions	10 portions
maigret ducks	2 × 2½ kg (5 lb)	5 × 2½ kg (5 lb)
peaches	2	5
redcurrants (punnets)	1	2
peach brandy	2 tbsp	4 tbsp
shallots chopped	50 g (2 oz)	250 g (10 oz)
veal stock	250 ml (½ pt)	750 ml (1½ pt)
thyme		
bay leaf		
red wine		
icing sugar		

1 Take the legs off ducks and reserve.
2 Remove breasts and trim well.
3 Keep any trimmings for sauce.
4 Using a couple of the legs and shallots, fry off in a saucepan with a

little oil till brown, add red wine and half the brandy.

5 Allow to reduce, add veal stock, thyme and bay leaf. Simmer.
6 Wash peaches and slice into segments allowing 3 per person.
7 Put any peach trimmings into sauce.
8 Season duck breasts and fry in a little hot oil.
9 Place skin side down first, allow to colour, remove from pan.
10 Put into a hot oven at 204°C (400°F) for 8 minutes until just firm.
11 Pass sauce through a fine chinois. Season and add rest of brandy.
12 Put peaches and redcurrants on a tray, dust with icing sugar and warm under grill.
13 To serve slice duck breasts lengthways into 5 slices.
14 Arrange plate with peaches and redcurrants.
15 Pour over sauce till just covering the plate.

I **49 ~ Roast galantine of duck with hot Cumberland sauce**

(IAN PERKINS)

	4 portions	10 portions
duck	1 × 1 kg (2 lb)	1 × 2½ kg (5 lb)
chicken breasts	2 × 50 g (2 oz)	2 × 125 g (5 oz)
egg whites	1	2
double cream	100 ml (⅕ pt)	250 ml (½ pt)
pistachio nuts, peeled and shelled	20 g (¾ oz)	50 g (2 oz)
chives, chopped	¼ bunch	½ bunch
mushrooms	40 g (1½ oz)	100 g (4 oz)
onions, chopped	40 g (1½ oz)	100 g (4 oz)
reduced duck stock	500 ml (1 pt)	1¼ litre (2½ pt)
port	50 ml (2 fl oz)	125 ml (5 fl oz)
shallots, chopped	40 g (1¼ oz)	100 g (4 oz)
redcurrant jelly	40 g (1¼ oz)	100 g (4 oz)
oranges, zest from	¾	2
oranges, juice of	1½	4
oranges for garnish, cut into segments	¾	2
chives for garnish, chopped	¼ bunch	½ bunch

1 Bone duck by removing carcass without breaking skin. Remove leg bones leaving knuckle to seal end, trim wing. Open out duck with skin side down, season and place in fridge.

2 Make the mousse by blending the chicken breasts and egg white, place under ice, beat in the double cream slowly, pass through a sieve, season and place in the fridge.

3 Chop $\frac{1}{2}$ bunch of chives, chop duck livers (saved from giblets).

4 Sweat down mushrooms and onions. When cool, add to the mousse with the chives, duck livers and pistachio nuts.

5 Place mousse in the centre of the duck to replace carcass, ensuring leg cavity is also filled.

6 Sew carcass together using trussing needle and string. (Alternatively hold together with cocktail sticks.)

7 Wrap tightly in tin foil to reform shape. Bake in oven for 1 hour.

8 Remove foil and finish cooking for approximately $\frac{1}{2}$ hour basting with juices and allowing to colour.

9 Sweat shallots and orange zest, add port, recurrant jelly and orange juice.

10 Reduce, add duck stock and reduce to required consistency. Check seasoning and flavour.

11 Allow duck to rest for 10 minutes, carve or serve whole and carve as required.

12 Lay duck on sauce and garnish with orange segments and chopped chives.

50 – Goose

Goose, average weight 5–6 kg (10–12 lb)
Gosling, average weight $2\frac{1}{2}$–$3\frac{1}{2}$ kg (5–7 lb)

The preparation for cleaning and trussing is the same as for chicken.

Roast goose is traditionally served with sage and onion stuffing and apple sauce. Other stuffings include peeled apple quarters and stoned prunes, and peeled apple quarters and peeled chestnuts.

For roasting goose proceed as for roast duck (page 319) using a moderate oven 200–230°C (392–446°F), allowing 15–20 minutes per lb.

51 – Guinea fowl

Guinea fowl can be used in a similar manner to chicken. The flesh is of a dry nature and has little fat, therefore when roasted or pot roasted it is usual to bard the guinea fowl and not to over-cook it.

52 – Guinea fowl breast with bacon and mushrooms

	4 portions	10 portions
suprêmes of guinea fowl	4	10
oil or butter	100 g (4 oz)	250 g (10 oz)
lardons of bacon, blanched	100 g (4 oz)	250 g (10 oz)
button mushrooms	200 g (8 oz)	500 g (1¼ lb)
potatoes (diced and shallow fried)	100 g (4 oz)	250 g (10 oz)

1 Season and sauté the suprêmes in oil or butter on both sides for 3–4 minutes.
2 Remove and keep warm.
3 Fry the lardons for a few minutes, add the quartered mushrooms and cook quickly for a minute or two. Add the cooked potatoes.
4 Add the garnish to the suprêmes and finish with nut brown butter.

Note   In place of button mushrooms, wild mushrooms can be used and jus-lié or reduced stock containing chopped cooked mushrooms can be served separately.

53 – Sauté of guinea fowl with tomatoes and herbs

	4 portions	10 portions
guinea fowl, cut for sauté	1 × 1¼–1½ kg (2½–3 lb)	3 × 1¼–1½ kg (2½–3 lb)
butter	50 g (2 oz)	125 g (5 oz)
chopped onion or shallots	100 g (4 oz)	250 g (10 oz)
Madeira	60 ml (⅛ pt)	150 ml (⅓ pt)
jus-lié or brown stock	250 ml (½ pt)	600 ml (1¼ pt)
tomatoes, skinned, deseeded, diced	200 g (8 oz)	500 g (1¼ lb)
salt and pepper		
chopped tarragon, chervil and parsley		

1 Shallow fry the seasoned pieces of guinea fowl in the butter to a golden colour.
2 Cover with a lid and cook on the stove or in the oven until tender.
3 Remove the guinea fowl and keep warm.
4 Add the shallots or onions and cook for 2 minutes.
5 Drain off the fat, add the wine, jus-lié and tomatoes.

6 Bring to the boil and simmer for 3–4 minutes.

7 Correct the seasoning, add the herbs and pour over the guinea fowl to serve.

T 54 ~ Guinea fowl with yellow pepper sauce

(TERRY FARR)

	4 portions	10 portions
cleaned guinea fowl	2 × 1¼ kg (2½ lb)	5 × 1¼ kg (2½ lb)
salt and pepper		
veal or chicken forcemeat	100 g (4 oz)	250 g (10 oz)
pink peppercorns	1 tsp	2½ tsp
unsalted butter	25 g (1 oz)	60 g (2½ oz)
chopped shallots	75 g (3 oz)	180 g (7½ oz)
yellow pepper	200 g (8 oz)	500 g (1¼ lb)
dry white wine	125 ml (¼ pt)	300 ml (⅝ pt)
thin chicken velouté or béchamel	125 ml (¼ pt)	300 ml (⅝ pt)
double cream	125 ml (¼ pt)	300 ml (⅝ pt)
julienne of red, green and yellow pepper	100 g (4 oz)	250 g (10 oz)

1 Remove suprêmes and legs from carcasses.
2 Remove bones from legs and tap out lightly with cutlet bat.
3 Season insides of legs, and spread with forcemeat combined with peppercorns. Roll up legs and tie lightly.
4 Melt the butter in a thick-bottomed pan, add the seasoned suprêmes and legs, cover with a lid.
5 Cook gently for 8–10 minutes, remove suprêmes and cook legs for a further 5–6 minutes. Keep the joints in a covered dish in a warm place.
6 Add the shallots to the juices in the pan and cook without colour.
7 Add the diced yellow pepper and cook gently for about 5 minutes.
8 Add white wine and reduce by half.
9 Add velouté and cream and cook gently for 5 minutes.
10 Liquidise the sauce (or rub through a sieve), strain through fine chinois, adjust seasoning and consistency.
11 Arrange the suprêmes on one side of the warmed plates, and the leg, cut into 5 slices, on the other.
12 Surround the joints with the sauce and garnish the centre with the julienne of mixed peppers.

—— *Game* ——

Game is the name given to certain wild birds and animals which are eaten; there are two kinds of game:

(a) feathered;
(b) furred.

HANDLING AND PREPARING GAME

Food value

As it is less fatty than poultry or meat, game is easily digested, with the exception of water fowl, owing to their oily flesh. Game is useful for building and repairing body tissues and for energy.

Storage

1 Hanging is essential for all game. It drains the flesh of blood and begins the process of disintegration which is vital to make the flesh soft and edible, and also to develop flavour.
2 The hanging time is determined by the type, condition and age of the game and the storage temperature.
3 Old birds need to hang for a longer time than young birds.
4 Game birds are not plucked or drawn before hanging.
5 Venison and hare are hung with the skin on.
6 Game must be hung in a well-ventilated, dry, cold storeroom; this need not be refrigerated.
7 Game birds should be hung by the neck with the feet down.

Quality points for buying

Venison
Joints of venison should be well fleshed and a dark brownish-red colour.

Hares and rabbits
The ears of hares and rabbits should tear easily. With old hares the lip is more pronounced than in young animals. The rabbit is distinguished from the hare by shorter ears, feet and body.

Birds
1 The beak should break easily.
2 The breast plumage ought to be soft.

3 The breast should be plump.
4 Quill feathers should be pointed, not rounded.
5 The legs should be smooth.

FEATHERED GAME

Grouse, pheasant, partridge are the most popular game birds. Woodcock, snipe, wild duck, plover are used but much less so. All these birds are protected by game laws and can only be shot in season. Quail is a game bird but large numbers of quail are reared and are available all year round.

The term includes all edible birds which live in freedom, but only the following are generally used in catering today:

pheasant
partridge
woodcock
snipe
wild duck
teal
grouse

The flavour of most game birds is improved by their being hung for a few days in a moderate draught before being plucked. Hanging is to some degree essential for all game. It drains the flesh of blood and begins a process of disintegration which is essential to make the flesh tender and develop flavour – this is due to the action of enzymes. Game birds should be hung with the feet down. Care should be taken with the water-birds: wild duck, teal, etc., not to allow them to get too high, because the oiliness of their flesh will quickly turn them rancid.

When game birds are roasted they should always be served on a croûte of fried bread, garnished with thick round pieces of toasted French bread spread with game farce (see overleaf), game chips and picked watercress.

As game birds are deficient in fat, a thin slice of fat bacon (bard) should be tied over the breast during cooking to prevent it from drying; this is also placed on the breast when serving. Roast gravy, bread sauce and browned breadcrumbs (toasted or fried) are served separately.

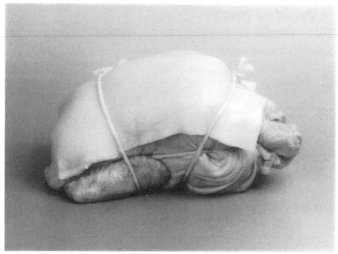

Barding of a bird

55 – Game farce

	4 portions	10 portions
butter or margarine	50 g (2 oz)	125 g (5 oz)
game livers	100 g (4 oz)	250 g (10 oz)
chopped onion	25 g (1 oz)	60 g (2½ oz)
sprig of thyme		
bay leaf	1	2–3
salt, pepper		

1 Heat half the butter in a frying-pan.
2 Quickly toss the seasoned livers, onion and herbs, browning well but keeping underdone. Pass through a sieve or mincer.
3 Mix in the remaining butter. Correct the seasoning.

56 – Pheasant

Young birds have a flexible beak, pliable breast bone, grey legs and underdeveloped spurs or none at all. The last large feather in the wing is pointed.

- They may be roasted or braised or pot roasted.
- Season – 1 October to 1 February.
- They should be well hung.

332

57 – Partridge

Young birds indicated as for pheasant, the legs should also be smooth.

- May be roasted, braised, etc.
- Season – 1 September to 1 February.
- Three to five days' hanging is ample time.

58 – Woodcock

A good quality bird should have soft supple feet, clean mouth and throat, fat and firm breast. It has a distinctive flavour which is accentuated by the entrails being left in during cooking. The vent must be carefully checked for cleanliness.

- Usually roasted.
- Season – October to November.
- Hang for 3–4 days.

59 – Snipe

Snipe resemble woodcock but are smaller. Points of quality are the same as for woodcock. The flavour of the flesh can be accentuated in the same way as the woodcock.

- May be roasted and are sometimes cooked in steak pudding or pies.
- Season – October to November.
- Hang for 3–4 days.

Snipe and woodcock are prepared with the head left on and the beak is used for trussing. The head is prepared by removing the skin and eyes.

60 – Wild duck

The most common is the mallard, which is the ancestor of the domestic duck. The beak and webbed feet should be soft and pliable.

- They may be roasted, slightly underdone or braised.
- Season – August to February.

It is particularly important that water-birds be eaten only in season; out of season the flesh becomes coarse and acquires a fishy flavour.

61 – Teal

This is a smaller species of wild duck. Select as for wild duck.

- May be roasted or braised.
- Season – October to January.

62 – Grouse

This is one of the most popular game birds.

Young birds have soft downy plumes on the breast and under the wings. They also have pointed wings and a rounded, soft spur knob, the spur becomes hard and scaly in older birds.

- Usually served roasted, left slightly underdone.
- Grouse is equally popular hot or cold.
- Season – 12 August to 10 December.

63 – Salmis of game

This is usually prepared from partridge or pheasant.

	4 portions	10 portions
cooked pheasant	1	$2\frac{1}{2}$
or cooked partridges	2	5
butter or margarine	25 g (1 oz)	60 g ($2\frac{1}{2}$ oz)
onion	50 g (2 oz)	125 g (5 oz)
carrot	50 g (2 oz)	125 g (5 oz)
celery	25 g (1 oz)	60 g ($2\frac{1}{2}$ oz)
red wine	4 tbsp	10 tbsp
bouquet garni		
mushrooms, quartered or turned	100 g (4 oz)	250 g (10 oz)
demi-glace	$\frac{1}{2}$ litre (1 pt)	$1\frac{1}{4}$ litre ($2\frac{1}{2}$ pt)

> Using hard margarine
> 1 portion provides:
>
> 310 kcals/1300 kJ
> 15.2 g fat
> (of which 5.6 g saturated)
> 2.4 g carbohydrate
> (of which 1.5 g sugars)
> 38.1 g protein
> 1.3 g fibre

1 Cut the bird into portions. Chop the carcass.
2 Melt the butter in a thick-bottomed pan.
3 Add the carcass, sliced onion, carrot, celery and colour slightly.
4 Pour off the fat. Deglaze with the wine.

5 Add the bouquet garni and mushroom trimmings and demi-glace. Simmer for 1 hour. Correct the seasoning.
6 Pass the sauce through a fine strainer on to the bird and heat through in a sauté pan, together with the cooked mushrooms.

Serve garnished with heart-shaped croûtons spread with game farce.

T 64 – Roast partridge with elderberries and a ginger bread sauce

(CLIVE HOWE)

	4 portions	10 portions
young partridge	4	10
slices of pancetta	8	20
elderberry sauce	250 ml ($\frac{1}{2}$pt)	600 ml (1$\frac{1}{4}$pt)
ginger bread crumbs	50 g (2 oz)	125 g (5 oz)
milk	200 ml ($\frac{1}{2}$pt)	500 ml (1 pt)
small onion (studded with a clove and bay leaf)	1	2–3
double cream	50 ml ($\frac{1}{8}$pt)	125 g (5 oz)
seasoning		
butter	15 g ($\frac{1}{2}$oz)	35 g (1$\frac{1}{2}$oz)

1 Season the partridge and place over the breast two slices of pancetta.
2 Roast in a hot oven for 15 minutes.
3 Remove and keep warm.
4 Place the milk into a saucepan with the studded onion and simmer for 20 minutes.
5 Strain, whisk in the ginger bread crumbs and the double cream and bring to the boil.
6 Whisk in the butter and correct the seasoning.
7 Heat the elderberry sauce and whisk in a little butter.
8 Remove the pancetta from the partridge.
9 Take off the legs and remove the breast.
10 Place a pool of the ginger bread sauce in the middle of four or ten large plates.
11 Place the two breasts of each partridge on the ginger bread sauce.
12 Place the two legs of each partridge at the top of the plate.
13 Place on top the two slices of pancetta.
14 Pour around the elderberry sauce.

Note Pancetta is Italian smoked bacon.

65 – Partridge with apple, cream and calvados

	4 portions	10 portions
young partridges, trussed and barded	4	10
butter	200 g (8 oz)	500 g (1¼ lb)
large dessert apples, peeled and cored	4	10
calvados	1 dsp	2½ dsp
double cream	125 ml (¼ pt)	300 ml (⅝ pt)

1 Season the partridges, rub all over with butter and place in an ovenproof dish. Brown in a hot oven 220°C (425°F) and remove from the dish.
2 Cut apples in thick slices and half-cook them by shallow frying in butter on both sides.
3 Place apples in the ovenproof dish, add calvados and place the partridges on top (removing the bards and trussing strings).
4 Pour over the cream, leave uncovered and return to the oven at 190°C (375°F) for approximately 20 minutes. Ensure the dish is clean and serve.

Note Variations can include: pears in place of apples; alternatives to calvados, e.g. white wine, vermouth or cider; cultivated or wild mushrooms; peeled and pipped grapes.

66 – Braised partridge with cabbage

Older or red-legged partridges are suitable for this dish.

	4 portions	10 portions
old partridges	2	5
lard, butter, margarine or oil	100 g (4 oz)	250 g (10 oz)
cabbage	400 g (1 lb)	1¼ kg (2½ lb)
belly of pork or bacon (in the piece)	100 g (4 oz)	250 g (10 oz)
carrot, peeled and grooved	1	2–3
studded onion	1	2–3
bouquet garni		
white stock	1 litre (2 pt)	2½ litre (5 pt)
frankfurter sausages or pork chipolatas	8	20

Based on 100 g cooked meat and oil
1 portion provides:

750 kcals/3137 kJ
57.6 g fat
(of which 14 g saturated)
11.5 g carbohydrate
(of which 6.2 g sugars)
47.8 g protein
3.3 g fibre

1 Season the partridges, rub with fat, brown quickly in a hot oven and remove.
2 Trim the cabbage, remove the core, separate the leaves and wash thoroughly.
3 Blanch the cabbage leaves and the belly of pork for 5 minutes. Refresh and drain well to remove all water. Remove the rind from the pork.
4 Place half the cabbage in a deep ovenproof dish; add the pork rind, the partridges, carrot, onion, bouquet garni, the remaining fat, and stock, and season lightly.
5 Add the remaining cabbage and bring to the boil, cover with greased greaseproof paper, a lid and braise slowly until tender, approximately $1\frac{1}{2}$–2 hours.
6 Add the sausages half-way through the cooking time by placing them under the cabbage.
7 Remove bouquet garni and the onion and serve everything else, the pork and carrot being sliced.

67 – Pheasant in casserole

	4 portions	10 portions
carrot ⎱	100 g (4 oz)	250 g (10 oz)
onion ⎬ sliced	100 g (4 oz)	250 g (10 oz)
celery ⎰	50 g (2 oz)	125 g (5 oz)
small sprig of thyme		
pheasant, cleaned, trussed and barded	$1 \times 1\frac{1}{2}$–2 kg (3–4 lb)	$3 \times 1\frac{1}{2}$–2 kg (3–4 lb)
salt and pepper		
butter	50 g (2 oz)	125 g (5 oz)
brandy	1 tbsp	3 tbsp
game stock	125 ml ($\frac{1}{4}$ pt)	300 ml ($\frac{5}{8}$ pt)

1 Place vegetables and thyme in casserole.
2 Add the seasoned and buttered pheasant.
3 Cover with a lid and place in oven at 200°C (400°F), basting occasionally until cooked.
4 Remove pheasant, pour off fat and deglaze casserole with brandy and gravy.
5 Bring to the boil (in a saucepan if necessary), correct the seasoning, skim off any fat, strain and serve.

Note This is a basic recipe which can be garnished in a variety of ways, for example:

(a) button onions, olive-shaped potatoes and lardons of bacon;
(b) button or wild mushrooms;
(c) braised celery or fennel.

68 – Pheasant with cream

1 Three-quarters cook the pheasant.
2 Add 125 ml ($\frac{1}{4}$ pt) double cream and a few drops of lemon juice and continue cooking without a lid, basting frequently until tender.
3 Remove pheasant, strain off the liquid, degrease, correct seasoning and consistency and serve.

Notes This is also a basic recipe to which other garnishes may be added, such as:

• wild or button mushrooms;
• a little meat glaze to alter the colour and flavour of the sauce;
• peeled and pipped grapes;
• quennelles of game, etc.

Pheasant can also be cooked with apples, as on page 336.

Old pheasants should only be braised, e.g. as in Partridge with cabbage, page 336.

Pheasant may be cut up raw and cooked as a sauté with a variety of sauces and garnishes.

Pheasant can also be prepared as suprêmes, left plain or stuffed, e.g. with a mousseline-type mixture, and shallow fried, e.g. Stuffed breasts of pheasant with a cream, brandy and mushroom sauce. Pheasant may be stuffed in a variety of ways, e.g. Pheasant stuffed with mushrooms and chestnuts.

T 69 ~ Stuffed breast of pheasant Aviona

(KEITH PODMORE)

	4 portions	10 portions
hen pheasants	2	5
cold water	750 ml (1½ pt)	2 litre (4 pt)
onion	50 g (2 oz)	125 g (5 oz)
carrot	50 g (2 oz)	125 g (5 oz)
stick celery	1	2½
leek	50 g (2 oz)	125 g (5 oz)
bouquet garni		
salt and pepper		
each of parsley, chervil, chives and tarragon, chopped	10 g (½ oz)	25 g (1¼ oz)
carrot ⎫	40 g (1½ oz)	100 g (4 oz)
white of leek ⎬ in julienne	40 g (1½ oz)	100 g (4 oz)
celery ⎭	40 g (1½ oz)	100 g (4 oz)
dry white wine	60 ml (2½ fl oz)	150 ml (⅓ pt)
butter	75 g (3 oz)	180 g (7½ oz)
mange-tout ⎫ in julienne	40 g (1½ oz)	100 g (4 oz)
beetroot ⎭	40 g (1½ oz)	100 g (4 oz)

1 Remove the legs and suprêmes from the pheasants and bone the thighs. Make pockets in the suprêmes.
2 Prepare stock from the carcass, bones and drumsticks, using the water and vegetables and bouquet garni.
3 Finely mince the thigh meat, incorporating the herbs and season. Use to fill the suprêmes.
4 Prepare a fine julienne of the carrot, celery and leek, keeping each separate.
5 Butter and season a suitable pan and sprinkle with the julienne of vegetables.
6 Lay on the suprêmes, sprinkle with the white wine and season.
7 Heat the pan on top of the stove, cover and cook in the oven till ready.
8 Strain the pheasant stock and reduce till lightly syrupy. Strain in the cooking liquor from the pheasant and further reduce if needed.
9 Finish with butter and season.

10 Dress the suprêmes on plates, sprinkling the cooked julienne garnish over.

11 Blanch the mange-tout and beetroot separately.

12 Pour the sauce over the pheasant, sprinkle with the mange-tout and beetroot and serve.

70 – Pheasant stuffed with mushrooms and chestnuts

	4 portions	10 portions	
young pheasant	1	3	Based on 75 g cooked pheasant per portion. I portion provides:
finely minced pork (half lean, half fat)	150 g (6 oz)	375 g (15 oz)	
finely chopped shallots	2	3	494 kcals/2078 kJ
or small onion	1	2	30.1 g fat
oil			(of which 8.8 g saturated)
finely chopped mushroom	150 g (6 oz)	375 g (15 oz)	21.4 g carbohydrate (of which 6.4 g sugars)
chopped parsley	1 tsp	3 tsp	33.5 g protein
salt, pepper			2.6 g fibre
peeled chestnuts cooked in stock	200 g (8 oz)	500 g (1¼ lb)	
brandy	1–2 tbsp	3–5 tbsp	
chopped pheasant liver			

1 Truss and bard the pheasant.

2 Use the remaining ingredients to make a stuffing.

3 Stuff the pheasant and either roast or pot-roast it.

4 Prepare a gravy from the pan juices after the pheasant is cooked, strain and serve.

71 – Quails

Only plump birds with firm white fat should be selected. When prepared, the entrails are drawn but the heart and liver are retained inside the birds. They may be roasted, spit-roasted, cooked 'en casserole' or poached in a rich well-flavoured chicken or veal stock (or a combination of both).

Quails may also be boned-out from the back, stuffed with a forcemeat made as follows, then cooked by any of the above mentioned methods.

	4 portions	10 portions
Forcemeat		
finely minced pork (half lean, half fat)	200 g (8 oz)	500 g (1¼ lb)
quail and chicken livers	400 g (1 lb)	900 g (2¼ lb)
chopped shallot or onion	50 g (2 oz)	125 g (5 oz)
chopped mushroom	25 g (1 oz)	60 g (2½ oz)
pinch of thyme, half bay leaf		
salt, pepper, mixed spice		

1 Gently fry the pork to extract the fat.
2 Increase the heat, add the livers and the remainder of the ingredients.
3 Fry quickly to brown the livers but keep them pink.
4 Allow to cool and pass through a sieve or mince finely.

72 – Quails with cherries

	4 portions	10 portions
carrot ⎤	100 g (4 oz)	250 g (10 oz)
onion ⎬ sliced	100 g (4 oz)	250 g (10 oz)
celery ⎦	50 g (2 oz)	125 g (5 oz)
small sprig of thyme		
quails, cleaned and trussed (stuffing optional)	4	10
butter	50 g (2 oz)	125 g (5 oz)
brandy	1 tbsp	2–3 tbsp
port wine	2 tbsp	5 tbsp
veal or chicken stock	125 ml (¼ pt)	300 ml (⅝ pt)
orange, juice of	¼	½
lemon juice	3–4 drops	8–10 drops
morello or black cherries, stoned and poached in stock syrup	36–40	80–100

Based on 75 g cooked meat per bird
1 portion provides:

327 kcals/1363 kJ
15.9 g fat
(of which 8.2 g saturated)
13.9 g carbohydrate
(of which 13.2 g sugars)
28.7 g protein
1.8 g fibre

1 Place vegetables and thyme in casserole.
2 Add seasoned and buttered quails and cover with a lid.
3 Place in a hot oven (230°C, 450°F), basting frequently until cooked.
4 Remove quails, pour off fat, deglaze with brandy, port and stock.
5 Add orange and lemon juice, correct seasoning, strain and allow to simmer.
6 When reduced to the required quantity, add the cherries, pour over the quails and serve.

73 ~ Quails with grapes

Prepare as in previous recipe, stuffing quails if required, substituting white wine for port and peeled and pipped grapes for cherries.

74 ~ Quails in aspic

The quails are boned, stuffed and gently poached. When cold they are lightly coated with a well-flavoured aspic in which the cooking liquid from the quails has been incorporated.

75 ~ Pigeon

As pigeons do not have gall-bladders it is not necessary to remove the livers when they are drawn and cleaned.

Tender young pigeons less than 12 months old can be roasted, pot-roasted or split open and grilled and served, for example, with a Robert, charcutière or devilled sauce.

Young pigeons can be cut in halves, flattened slightly, seasoned, shallow fried in butter and cooked and finished as for sautés of chicken, e.g. chasseur, bordelaise.

Pigeons may be cooked in casserole, as recipe 67, page 337 or as a salmis. Older pigeons should only be braised.

FURRED GAME

76 ~ Hare

Young hare $2\frac{1}{2}$–3 kg (5–6 lb) in weight should be used. To test a young hare it should be possible to take the ear between the fingers and tear it quite easily, also the hare lip which is clearly marked in old animals, should only be faintly defined.

A hare should be hung for about a week before cleaning it out.

77 – Jugged hare

	4 portions	10 portions
young hare	1	$2\frac{1}{2}$
oil	50 g (2 oz)	125 g (5 oz)
flour, white or wholemeal	25 g (1 oz)	60 g ($2\frac{1}{2}$ oz)
tomato purée	50 g (2 oz)	125 g (5 oz)
brown stock	$\frac{1}{2}$ litre (1 pt)	$1\frac{1}{4}$ litre ($2\frac{1}{2}$ pt)
clove garlic	1	2–3
red wine	$\frac{1}{4}$ litre ($\frac{1}{2}$ pt)	600 ml ($1\frac{1}{4}$ pt)
Garnish		
button onions	100 g (4 oz)	250 g (10 oz)
button mushrooms	100 g (4 oz)	250 g (10 oz)
streaky bacon	100 g (4 oz)	250 g (10 oz)
stale bread	100 g (4 oz)	250 g (10 oz)
chopped parsley		

Using sunflower oil
1 portion provides:

744 kcals/3125 kJ
39.2 g fat
(of which 11.9 g saturated)
20.5 g carbohydrate
(of which 3.7 g sugars)
68.3 g protein
2.3 g fibre

1 Skin hare carefully.
2 Make an incision along the belly. Clean out the intestines.
3 Clean out the forequarter end carefully collecting all the blood into a basin.
4 Cut as follows: each leg into two pieces, each foreleg into two pieces, the forequarter into two, the saddle into three or four pieces.
5 Soak in a marinade, as for venison, for 5–6 hours, but omit the vinegar.
6 Drain well in a colander.
7 Quickly fry the pieces of hare until brown on all sides.
8 Place into a thick-bottomed pan, mix in the flour, cook out, browning slightly.
9 Mix in the tomato purée. Gradually add the stock.
10 Add all the juice and vegetables and herbs from the marinade.
11 Bring to the boil, skim, add the garlic and the wine.
12 Cover with a lid and allow to simmer till tender.
13 Pick out the hare into a clean pan.
14 Reboil the sauce, correct the seasoning and thicken by gradually pouring in the blood (after which it must not be reboiled).
15 Check that the temperature is above 73°C and hold for 2 minutes.
16 Pass through a fine strainer on to the hare.
17 Meanwhile prepare the garnish by cooking the button onions glacé, cooking the mushrooms whole, turned or in quarters in a little stock and cutting the bacon into lardons, strips $2 \times \frac{1}{2} \times \frac{1}{2}$ cm ($1 \times \frac{1}{4} \times \frac{1}{4}$ in), and

lightly browning them in a little fat in a frying-pan. Cut the bread into heart-shaped croûtons and fry to a golden brown.

18 Mix the garnish with the civet, serve in an entrée dish, dip the point of the croûtons into the sauce, then into the chopped parsley and place on the edge of the dish.

Redcurrant jelly may be spread on the heart-shaped croûtons.

78 – Saddle of hare

This joint is cut from the back of the hare, usually in a similar way to a short saddle of lamb, that is, a pair of uncut loins. All skin and sinew must be removed, the joint trimmed and, if desired, the joint may be larded with pork fat.

It is not essential to marinade the saddle if obtained from a young hare, but if in doubt as to its tenderness, or if it is required to be kept for a few days, then the joint should be marinaded in the following:

– Raw marinade for furred game

		4 portions	10 portions
carrot		200 g (8 oz)	400 g (1 lb)
onion	finely sliced	200 g (8 oz)	400 g (1 lb)
celery		100 g (4 oz)	200 g (8 oz)
cloves garlic		2	4
parsley stalks		25 g (1 oz)	50 g (2 oz)
sprig of thyme			
bay leaf		$\frac{1}{2}$	1
cloves		2	4
peppercorns		12	24
red wine		500 ml (1 pt)	1 litre (2 pt)
wine vinegar		125 ml ($\frac{1}{4}$ pt)	250 ml ($\frac{1}{2}$ pt)
oil		125 ml ($\frac{1}{4}$ pt)	250 ml ($\frac{1}{2}$ pt)

1 Season the joints with salt and pepper.
2 Place the joints in a suitable container, e.g. stainless steel or china.
3 Cover with the marinade, keep in the refrigerator and turn the joint over frequently.

79 – Saddle of hare, German style

One saddle yields 1–2 portions according to size.

1 Remove the saddle from the marinade and dry thoroughly.
2 Place the saddle on a bed of vegetables from the marinade and roast in the oven at 220°C (425°F).
3 When the saddle is three-quarters cooked, remove the vegetables.
4 Add 125 ml (¼pt) cream and, basting frequently with the cream, complete the cooking, keeping the meat pink.
5 Remove the saddle, add a few drops of lemon juice to the sauce, correct seasoning and consistency, pass through a fine strainer and serve with the saddle.

Examples of variations include:

- Poivrade sauce mixed with redcurrant jelly and cream.
- As for German style, the sauce well flavoured with onion.
- By the addition of more lemon or wine vinegar.
- Garnished with glazed cherries.

There are many other variations that can be made, for example, after the saddle is removed from the roasting tray, the tray can be deglazed with brandy, whisky or gin. Sliced mushrooms (cultivated or wild) can be added to the sauce.

Suitable accompaniments include: braised chestnuts, or chestnut purée, or Brussels sprouts with chestnuts; purée of celeriac, or celeriac or parsnips, or celeriac and onion; buttered noodles, etc.

80 – Venison

Venison is the meat of the red deer, fallow deer and roebuck. Of these three, the meat of the roebuck is considered to have the best and most delicate eating quality. The prime cuts are the legs, loins and best ends. The shoulder of young animals can be boned, rolled and roasted but if in any doubt as to its tenderness, it should be cut up and used for stewed or braised dishes.

After slaughter, carcasses should be well hung in a cool place for several days and when cut into joints are usually marinaded before being cooked (see page 344 for marinade).

81 – Roast leg or haunch of venison

1 Prepare and trim leg, removing pelvic or aitch bone.
2 After marinading (see recipe 78) for 24 hours, remove, dry well and roast, basting frequently. The cooking time will vary according to the weight of the joint which is generally kept slightly pink in the centre. As a guide allow approximately 15–20 minutes per 400 g (1 lb).
3 Deglaze the roasting pan and incorporate the juices in the accompanying sauce, which is traditionally peppery and spicy.

Roast haunch of venison is popular served hot or cold.

82 – Venison cutlets, chops and steaks

1 Venison cutlets, cut from the best-end, and chops, cut from the loin, are usually well trimmed and cooked by shallow frying, provided that the meat is tender. If in doubt they should be braised.
2 After they are cooked they should be removed from the pan, the fat poured off and the pan deglazed with stock, red wine, brandy, Madeira, or sherry, which is then added to the accompanying sauce.
3 A spicy peppery sauce is usually offered, which can be varied by the addition of any one or more extra ingredients, e.g. cream, yoghurt, redcurrant jelly, choice of cooked beetroot, sliced button or wild mushrooms, cooked pieces of chestnut, etc.
4 Accompaniments can include, for example, a purée of green, brown or yellow lentils, a purée of any other dried bean, purée of braised chestnuts, braised red cabbage, or purée of a root vegetable, e.g. celeriac, turnip, swede, carrot, parsnip or any combination of these.
5 Venison steaks or escalopes are cut from the boned-out nuts of meat from the loins, well trimmed and slightly thinned with a meat bat.
6 The escalopes can be quickly shallow fried and finished as for cutlets and chops, with a variety of accompanying sauces and garnishes.

83 – Wild boar

For good quality, buy animals obtained from suppliers using as near as possible 100% pure breeding stock wild boars that are free to roam and forage for food rather than those that have been penned and fed.

Animals between 12–18 months old, weight 60–75 kg (140–150 lb) on the hoof, are best slaughtered late summer when the fat content is lower. The meat should be hung for 7–10 days before being used.

Young boar up to the age of 6 months are sufficiently tender for cooking in noisettes and cutlets and joints for roasting. The prime cuts of older animals, leg, loin, best end, can be marinaded and braised. Boar's head is prepared by boning the head and stuffing it with a forcemeat in which strips of ox tongue, foie gras and truffles and pistachio nuts can be added. The head is securely tied in a cloth and gently simmered. When cooled it is completed coated with a brown game aspic jelly and imitation eyes and tusks are inserted. Boar's head is a traditional Christmas cold buffet dish served with a spicy sauce, e.g. Cumberland.

T 84 ‒ Marinade for wild boar

(Marc Sanders)

	4 portions	10 portions
red wine	$\frac{1}{2}$ litre (1 pt)	$1\frac{1}{4}$ litre ($2\frac{1}{2}$ pt)
red wine vinegar	3 tbsp	$7\frac{1}{2}$ tbsp
bay leaf	1	$2\frac{1}{2}$
onion, sliced	$\frac{1}{2}$	$1\frac{1}{4}$
gin	1 measure	$2\frac{1}{2}$ measures
crushed juniper berries	1 tbsp	$2\frac{1}{2}$ tbsp

T 85 ‒ Ragôut of wild boar with wild rice

(Marc Sanders)

	4 portions	10 portions
diced wild boar	400 g (1 lb)	$1\frac{1}{4}$ kg ($2\frac{1}{2}$ lb)
walnut oil		
matignon	400 g (1 lb)	$1\frac{1}{4}$ kg ($2\frac{1}{2}$ lb)
flour (for roux)	100 g (4 oz)	250 g (10 oz)
tomato purée	50 g (2 oz)	125 g (5 oz)
wild boar brown stock	1 litre (2 pt)	$2\frac{1}{2}$ litre (5 pt)
marinade	$\frac{1}{2}$ litre (1 pt)	$1\frac{1}{4}$ litre ($2\frac{1}{2}$ pt)
smoked bacon strips	100 g (4 oz)	250 g (10 oz)
button onions	100 g (4 oz)	250 g (10 oz)
wild mushrooms	300 g (12 oz)	1 kg (2 lb)
heart-shaped fried bread croûtons	4	10
seasoning		

1 Place diced wild boar in marinade for 24 hours (see previous recipe).
2 Remove wild boar from marinade and drain.
3 Seal the meat in butter and walnut oil and sweat off.
4 Add matignon to pan with a little butter and cook the roux out.
5 Add stock and sieved marinade and cook for 1 hour.
6 Add meat and cook for a further 1 hour.
7 Add bacon, button onions, and mushrooms and simmer for 15–20 minutes.
8 Add measure of brandy and remove from heat.
9 Correct seasoning.
10 Serve with wild rice, chopped chives and heart-shaped fried bread croûtons.

T 86 ~ Wild boar medallions with morels and lentils

(MARC SANDERS)

	4 portions	10 portions
lentils	100 g (4 oz)	250 g (10 oz)
ham stock	$\frac{1}{2}$ litre (1 pt)	1$\frac{1}{4}$ litre (2$\frac{1}{2}$ pt)
onion	1	2–3
rashers smoked bacon	3	7–8
butter	10 g ($\frac{1}{2}$ oz)	25 g (1$\frac{1}{4}$ oz)
walnut oil		
medallions wild boar	8 × 50–75 g (2–3 oz)	20 × 50–75 g (2–3 oz)
chopped shallots	2	5
washed morels	100 g (4 oz)	250 g (10 oz)
brandy	30 ml ($\frac{1}{16}$ pt)	75 ml ($\frac{3}{8}$ pt)
marinade	2 tbsp	5 tbsp
brown wild boar stock	$\frac{1}{4}$ litre ($\frac{1}{2}$ pt)	600 ml (1$\frac{1}{4}$ pt)
chopped chives		
seasoning		

1 Place the wild boar medallions in the marinade and leave overnight. Soak the lentils overnight.
2 When thoroughly soaked, drain the lentils and add to the ham stock, 1 chopped onion and 3 slices chopped smoked bacon and bake in the oven for approximately 45 minutes.
3 Sauté the medallions of wild boar in the walnut oil and butter, remove from the pan and place on the cooked lentils and keep hot.

4 Add a little butter to the pan and add the chopped shallots, morels, measure of brandy, stock and marinade and reduce to a sauce consistency, pour over the medallions and finish with chopped chives.

87 – Rabbits

Are available wild or farm reared.

Preparation
1 Carefully remove the fur.
2 Cut an incision along the belly.
3 Remove the intestines.
4 Clean out the forequarter and removing all traces of blood.

Depending on the required use and size of rabbit can be cut:

1 Legs, forelegs, forequarter (well trimmed) into two pieces each, saddle into two or three pieces.
2 Saddles can be removed and left whole for roasting, braising or pot roasting.
3 The two nuts of meat can be removed from the saddle, half cut through lengthwise and carefully beaten out using a little cold water to form escalopes.

Rabbit can be used in a wide variety of dishes, e.g. pâtés, terrines, pies, salads, roast, braised, pot roasted, white and brown stews, curries.

T 88 – Trio of roast farmed rabbit with braised cabbage and thyme sauce

(Robert Mabey)

	4 portions	10 portions
Savoy cabbage	$1 \times \frac{3}{4}$–1 kg (1½–2 lb)	$2\frac{1}{2} \times \frac{3}{4}$–1 kg (1½–2 lb)
butter	150 g (6 oz)	375 g (15 oz)
salt, mill pepper		
dry white wine	100 ml (4 fl oz)	250 ml (10 fl oz)
whole farmed rabbits	2×1–1½ kg (2–3 lb)	5×1–1½ kg (2–3 lb)
whole cloves of garlic	2	5
sprigs of fresh thyme	3	7
veal and rabbit stock	500 ml (1 pt)	1¼ litre (2½ pt)

1 Discard the outside leaves of the cabbage, cut into four quarters, discard the stalk and finely slice the cabbage.

2 Heat 50 g (2 oz) of butter in a casserole dish, add the cabbage and season (125 g, 5 oz) for 10 portions. Gently sweat the cabbage until soft, then cover with butter papers and cook in the oven at 190°C (375°F) for 1 hour (turning every 15 minutes).

3 When the cabbage is cooked, add half a glass of white wine and keep warm.

4 Remove the legs from the rabbits at the ball joint. Then cut the saddle from the ribs, remove the sinews and flap from the saddles and set aside for the sauce. Keep the kidneys in the fat to be served later. Cut the first seven ribs from the rabbit and prepare as for a miniature version of rack of lamb. Chop the rest of the carcass for making stock.

5 Heat 50 g (2 oz) butter (125 g, 5 oz for 10 portions) in a large sauteuse, add the seasoned pieces of rabbit and trimmings and fry to obtain colour; the kidneys and racks will need about 2 minutes on each side.

6 Add the unpeeled cloves of garlic and thyme (reserving some picked leaves for the garnish). Cover with butter papers and roast in a hot oven.

7 Remove the saddle after 10 minutes and the legs after 20 minutes. Allow to relax in a warm place on a wire rack.

8 Drain off the fat, add the rest of the wine, reduce by half, add the stock, simmer and remove any scum.

9 Pass the stock and reduce by half (or to the consistency of single cream). Peel the cloves of garlic and keep warm.

10 Place the cabbage in a circle in the middle of the warmed dish.

11 Remove the bones from the rabbit thighs, cut into 4 slices (10 slices for 10 portions) and place in the centre of the dish.

12 Cut the loins and the fillets from the saddles and slice lengthways, fanning the pieces around the leg.

13 Cut the kidneys in 2 and arrange with the cloves of garlic around the dish.

14 Finish the sauce with 50 g (2 oz) butter (125 g, 5 oz for 10 portions), check the seasoning, pour the sauce over the meat and serve immediately.

For quenelles and mousselines, see page 299.

ETHNIC FOOD

—— *Introduction* ——

As the multi-ethnic society and the popularity of overseas dishes continue to grow, it becomes increasingly important to have a basic working knowlege of ethnic cookery.

Many countries, such as China, Japan and India, and areas like the Middle East, have long-established culinary traditions with a wide range of dishes dating back for two to three thousand years. Now, because of customer demands and changes in society, all students of cookery need to have at least a basic but sound understanding of ethnic dishes. The following recipes are examples of such dishes, however these will vary according to different regions.

—— *Caribbean* ——

1 – Piononos   Deep filled plantain rings with spiced minced-beef filling

	4 portions	10 portions
large ripe plantains	2	5
butter or margarine	50 g (2 oz)	125 g (5 oz)
vegetable oil	2 tsp	5 tsp
vegetable oil mixed with 1 (2½) tsp annatto	2 tbsp	5 tbsp
lean minced topside of beef	400 g (1 lb)	1¼ kg (2½ lb)
finely chopped onion	50 g (2 oz)	125 g (5 oz)
finely chopped green pepper	50 g (2 oz)	125 g (5 oz)
finely chopped red chilli	1	2–3
garlic clove crushed and chopped	1	2–3
plain flour	25 g (1 oz)	60 g (2½ oz)
ham chopped	100 g (4 oz)	250 g (10 oz)
tomato concassé	100 g (4 oz)	250 g (10 oz)
brown stock or water	125 ml (¼ pt)	300 ml (⅝ pt)
chopped olives	6	15
chopped capers	25 g (1 oz)	60 g (2½ oz)
malt vinegar	1 tbsp	2–3 tbsp
eggs	4	10
seasoning		

1 Peel the plantains and cut each one lengthways into thick strips, approximately 6 mm ($\frac{1}{4}$ in)
2 In a suitable pan fry the plantains both sides until golden brown, drain well.
3 Heat the vegetable oil and annatto in a suitable pan, quickly fry the minced beef.
4 Add the onions, peppers, chillies and garlic and cook for 5 minutes stirring frequently.
5 Add the flour, stir well and cook for a further 5 minutes.
6 Stir in the ham, tomatoes and seasoning.
7 Moisten with a little water or brown stock.
8 Continue to cook until the mixture resembles a paste like consistency.
9 Add chopped olives and capers, vinegar and correct seasoning.
10 To make the piononos, shape each strip of plaintain into a ring about 7.5 cm (3 in) in diameter, overlap by 8 mm ($\frac{1}{2}$ in). Secure with a cocktail stick.
11 Fill each with the beef mixture. *Do not overfill.*
12 Dip each piononos into seasoned flour, brush off excess flour. Dip into beaten egg.
13 Carefully deep fry in a suitable pan at 180°C (350°F) for approximately 3 minutes.
14 Serve immediately with red beans and rice.

Red beans and rice
The easiest way to serve this dish is to prepare a braised rice and garnish with cooked red beans.

2 – Salt fish and akee

	4 portions	10 portions
salt cod	400 g (1 lb)	1$\frac{1}{4}$ kg (2$\frac{1}{2}$ lb)
salt pork	100 g (4 oz)	250 g (10 oz)
chopped onion	100 g (4 oz)	250 g (10 oz)
red chilli chopped	1	2–3
tin akee	400 g (1 lb)	1$\frac{1}{4}$ kg (2$\frac{1}{2}$ lb)
mill pepper		
thyme		
tomato to garnish		

1 Soak the cod for 12 hours, change water 3–4 times.
2 Drain the cod, rise under cold water.
3 Poach it in boiling water or fish stock for approximately 10–15 minutes.
4 Remove it from the cooking liquor and flake it free from the skin and bone.
5 Deep fry the diced pork in a frying pan until crisp and brown and all the fat is rendered. Discard the pork.
6 Add the onions and chillies to the pork fat, cook for approximately 5 minutes.
7 Add the flaked cod, akee, thyme, mill pepper, cook for 2 minutes.
8 Serve in a suitable dish garnished with tomato.

Note Akee is a Caribbean fruit which may be purchased in cans.

3 – Blaff Poached marinated fish in lime and herb broth

	4 portions	10 portions
water	1 litre (2 pt)	2½ litre (5 pt)
limes, juice of	4	10
salt	2 tsp	5 tsp
filleted cod, halibut or turbot	4 × 150 g (6 oz)	10 × 150 g (6 oz)
finely chopped onions	50 g (2 oz)	125 g (5 oz)
garlic cloves crushed and chopped	2	5
red chillies finely chopped	2	5
bay rum berries or leaves or ½ tsp of allspice	2	5
chopped parsley		
fresh thyme		

1 Mix together the water, lime juice and salt in a suitable bowl.
2 Place the fish and allow to marinade for 1 hour.
3 Remove from marinade.
4 In a suitable pan, place approximately 1 litre (2 pt) of water (2½ litres, 5 pt for 10 portions).
5 Add the onions, garlic, chillies, bay rum berries or leaves or the allspice parsley and thyme.
6 Bring to the boil, simmer for approximately 10 minutes.
7 Add the fish carefully, bring back to the boil, then reduce the heat. Poach until the fish is cooked.

8 Serve the fish in the cooking liquor, garnished with wedges of fresh lime.

Notes Bay rum is native to the West Indies.

The dark berries are known as malagueta pepper, and are used in a similar way to allspice.

4 – Baked christophenes with onion and cheese filling

	4 portions	10 portions
large christophenes, approx. 300 g (12 oz) each	2	5
butter or margarine	75 g (3 oz)	180 g (7½ oz)
onions, finely chopped	150 g (6 oz)	375 g (15 oz)
Parmesan cheese, finely grated	25 g (1 oz)	60 g (2½ oz)
seasoning		

1 Wash and cut the chistophenes in half lengthways.
2 Place in boiling salted water and gently simmer until slightly under cooked (*al dente*).
3 Refresh and drain.
4 Remove the seeds.
5 Cut into boat-like shells, approximately 6 mm (¼ in) thick.
6 Chop the scooped out pulp coarsely.
7 In half the butter, sweat the onions without colour.
8 Add the pulp, cheese and seasoning.
9 Stir until the mixture is thick and most of the liquid has been evaporated.
10 Fill the christophene shells with the mixture.
11 Place in a suitable dish, brush with butter, sprinkle with a little more cheese.
12 Place in oven at 180°C (350°F) to reheat and brown. Serve immediately.

Note The christophenes may also be coated with a cheese sauce and glazed.

—— *India* ——

5 – Beef Do-piazza   A medium spiced dish from the Punjab

	4 portions	10 portions
topside or chuck steak cubed	400 g (1 lb)	1 kg (2½ lb)
vegetable ghee or oil	60 ml (⅛ pt)	125 ml (¼ pt)
finely chopped onion	100 g (4 oz)	250 g (10 oz)
finely chopped fresh ginger	12 g (½ oz)	30 g (1¼ oz)
clove crushed and chopped garlic	1	3
medium curry powder	3 tsp	7½ tsp
natural yoghurt	125 ml (¼ pt)	300 ml (⅝ pt)
lemon, juice of	½	1
large onion cut into rings	1	2
salt to taste		
julienne of lemon rind		

1 Fry the beef in the oil until brown.
2 Add the onions and continue to fry until brown. Drain off any excess oil.
3 Add the ginger, garlic and curry powder, and fry for a further 5 minutes.
4 Remove from heat, and add the yoghurt and lemon juice.
5 Simmer for 1–1½ hours, adding small amounts of water or stock during the cooking to prevent sticking.
6 Fry the onion rings in oil until golden brown. Keep some for garnish and add the remainder to the beef.
7 Season with salt.
8 Serve garnished with onion rings and the julienne of lemon rind.

6 – Beef Madras   A hot curry from the south of India

	4 portions	10 portions
cubed topside or chuck steak	400 g (1 lb)	1 kg (2½ lb)
finely chopped onion	100 g (4 oz)	250 g (10 oz)
clove garlic, crushed	2	5
vegetable ghee or oil	60 ml (⅛ pt)	125 ml (¼ pt)

hot Madras curry paste	3 tsp	$7\frac{1}{2}$ tsp
brown beef stock	500 ml (1 pt)	$1\frac{1}{4}$ litre ($2\frac{1}{2}$ pt)
tomato purée	50 g (2 oz)	125 g (5 oz)
chopped mango chutney	50 g (2 oz)	125 g (5 oz)
lemon, juice of	$\frac{1}{2}$	$1\frac{1}{2}$
season to taste		
coriander leaves for garnish		

1 Fry the beef in the oil until sealed and brown. Add the onion and garlic and continue to fry for a further 5 minutes.
2 Add the curry paste and mix well. Cook for a further 2 minutes.
3 Add the remaining ingredients, cover with brown stock and bring to the boil. Simmer until tender ($1–1\frac{1}{2}$ hours).
4 Correct the seasoning and consistency.
5 Garnish with coriander leaves.
6 Serve with pilaff rice.

7 – Kashmira lamb   A medium spiced dish from north India

	4 portions	10 portions
diced 2.5 cm (1 in) shoulder loin or leg of lamb	400 g (1 lb)	1 kg ($2\frac{1}{2}$ lb)
tikka paste	100 g (4 oz)	250 g (10 oz)
natural yoghurt	125 ml ($\frac{1}{4}$ pt)	312 ml ($\frac{5}{8}$ pt)
ghee or oil	62 ml ($\frac{1}{8}$ pt)	155 ml ($\frac{3}{8}$ pt)
cumin seeds	1 tsp	$2\frac{1}{2}$ tsp
cardamon pods	4	10
cloves	4	10
cinnamon sticks	4	10
finely chopped onions	100 g (4 oz)	250 g (10 oz)
clove garlic, crushed	1	$1\frac{1}{2}$
finely chopped fresh ginger	12 g ($\frac{1}{2}$ oz)	30 g ($1\frac{1}{4}$ oz)
ground chilli	$\frac{1}{2}$ tsp	$1\frac{1}{4}$ tsp
salt to taste		
ginger, fresh coriander and roasted almonds		

1 Mix together the tikka paste and yoghurt in a suitable bowl.
2 Add the lamb and marinate for a minimum of 1 hour.
3 Heat the ghee or oil in a suitable frying pan.

4 Add the cumin seeds, cardamon, cloves and cinnamon and fry for 1 minute.
5 Add the onion, garlic and ginger. Fry for approximately 5 minutes until golden brown.
6 Add the lamb. Fry together for 10–15 minutes, adding a little water if necessary to prevent sticking.
7 Add salt and chilli. Cover and simmer for a further 15 minutes, or until the lamb is tender.
8 Serve garnished with coriander leaves and roasted almonds.

8 – Palak lamb   A medium spiced dish from the Punjab

	4 portions	10 portions
diced 2.5 cm (1 in) shoulder loin or leg of lamb	400 g (1 lb)	1 kg (2½ lb)
vegetable ghee or oil	62 ml (⅛ pt)	155 ml (⅜ pt)
cumin seeds	1 tsp	2½ tsp
finely chopped onion	50 g (2 oz)	125 g (5 oz)
finely chopped fresh ginger	12 g (½ oz)	30 g (1¼ oz)
clove garlic, crushed	1	3
hot curry paste	2 tsp	5 tsp
natural yoghurt	125 ml (¼ pt)	312 ml (⅝ pt)
tomato purée	25 g (1 oz)	62 g (2½ oz)
chopped spinach	200 g (8 oz)	500 g (1¼ lb)
salt to taste		
coriander lemon for garnish		

1 Heat the ghee or oil in a suitable frying pan.
2 Add the cumin seeds and fry for 1 minute.
3 Add the onion and fry until golden brown.
4 Add the ginger and garlic and stir fry until all is brown.
5 Add the lamb and simmer for 15–20 minutes.
6 Add curry paste, yoghurt and salt.
7 Cook for 5 minutes. Add water if necessary to prevent sticking.
8 Stir in the tomato purée and spinach. Cover and simmer for 10–15 minutes, until the lamb is tender.
9 Serve garnished with coriander leaves.

9 – Chemmeen Kari   A prawn curry from the south of India

	4 portions	10 portions
large king-size prawns (preferably raw)	400 g (1 lb)	1 kg (2½ lb)
malt vinegar	4 tsp	10 tsp
finely chopped onion	50 g (2 oz)	125 g (5 oz)
vegetable oil	4 tsp	10 tsp
red chillies	4	10
desiccated coconut	100 g (4 oz)	250 g (10 oz)
mustard seeds	1 tsp	2½ tsp
curry leaves	10	25
finely chopped fresh ginger	25 g (1 oz)	60 g (2½ oz)
cloves garlic, crushed	2	5
ground turmeric	1 tsp	2½ tsp
ground coriander	12 g (½ oz)	25 g (1 oz)
tomato flesh, deseeded and chopped	100 g (4 oz)	250 g (10 oz)
hot water	125 ml (¼ pt)	300 ml (⅜ pt)

1 Shell the prawns and remove the veins by slitting the back.
2 Rub the prawns with salt and two teaspoons of vinegar and keep aside.
3 Sweat the onions in a little of the oil until a light golden brown colour. Remove from heat, add the chillies, coconut and mustard seeds. Place in the oven stirring occasionally for approximately 8 minutes. or continue to sweat on top of the stove to extract the flavours. Remove from heat, place in a food processor and blend to a fine paste. This is the masala.
4 Heat the oil in a wok or other suitable pan, fry the curry leaves for 1 minute. Add the ginger and garlic and fry for a further 1 minute. Now add the turmeric, ground coriander and chilli powder and the masala. Stir-fry for 1–2 minutes.
5 Add the tomatoes, salt to taste add 125 ml (½ pt) of hot water. Bring to boil, simmer for 5 minutes.
6 Drain the prawns. Add them to the pan. Mix well, continue to cook until the prawns are tender (if you are using raw prawns this usually takes approximately 8–10 minutes). They will curl and turn a pinky/ orange colour. Add the remaining vinegar. Do not overcook the prawns otherwise they will become hard and dry.
7 Serve immediately garnished with coriander leaves.

| V | 10 – **Alu-Chloe**   A vegetarian curry from north India |

	4 portions	10 portions
vegetable ghee or oil	45 ml (3 tsp)	125 ml ($\frac{1}{4}$ pt)
small cinnamon sticks	4	10
bay leaves	4	10
cumin seeds	1 tsp	2$\frac{1}{2}$ tsp
finely chopped onion	100 g (4 oz)	250 g (10 oz)
cloves garlic, finely chopped	2	5
chopped plum tomatoes, canned	400 g (1 lb)	1 kg (2$\frac{1}{2}$ lb)
hot curry paste	3 tsp	7$\frac{1}{2}$ tsp
salt to taste		
chick peas (canned drained weight)	400 g (1 lb)	1 kg (2$\frac{1}{2}$ lb)
potato, 12 mm ($\frac{1}{2}$ in) dice	100 g (4 oz)	250 g (10 oz)
water	125 ml ($\frac{1}{4}$ pt)	300 ml ($\frac{5}{8}$ pt)
tamarind sauce or lemon juice	2 tsp	5 tsp
chopped coriander leaves	50 g (2 oz)	125 g (5 oz)

1 Heat the ghee in a suitable pan.
2 Add the cinnamon, bay leaves and cumin seeds. Fry for approximately 1 minute.
3 Add the onion and garlic. Fry until golden brown.
4 Add the chopped tomatoes, curry paste and salt. Fry for a further 2–3 minutes.
5 Stir in the potatoes and water. Bring to the boil. Cover and simmer until the potatoes are cooked.
6 Add the chick peas and allow to heat through.
7 Stir in the coriander and lemon juice. Serve immediately.

| V | 11 – **Onion Bhajias** |

	4 portions	10 portions
besan or gram flour	45 g (3 tsp)	112 g (7$\frac{1}{2}$ tsp)
hot curry powder	1 tsp	2$\frac{1}{2}$ tsp
salt		
water	75 ml (5 tsp)	187 ml (12$\frac{1}{2}$ tsp)
finely shredded onion	100 g (4 oz)	250 g (10 oz)

1 Mix together the flour, curry powder and salt.
2 Blend in the water carefully to form a smooth, thick batter.
3 Stir in the onion.
4 Drop the mixture off a tablespoon into deep oil at 200°C (400°F). Fry for approximately 5–10 minutes until golden brown.
5 Drain well and serve as a snack or an accompaniment, with mango chutney as a dip.

V 12 – Rajmah   A curried bean dish

	4 portions	10 portions
vegetable ghee or oil	45 ml (3 tsp)	125 ($\frac{1}{4}$ pt)
cumin seeds	1 tsp	2$\frac{1}{2}$ tsp
bay leaves	4	10
finely chopped onion	100 g (4 oz)	250 g (10 oz)
clove garlic, crushed	1	2$\frac{1}{2}$
freshly chopped ginger	1 tsp	2$\frac{1}{2}$ tsp
chopped plum tomatoes, canned	400 g (1 lb)	1 kg (2$\frac{1}{2}$ lb)
medium curry powder	2 tsp	5 tsp
salt to taste		
pinch of ground chilli		
cooked red kidney beans	400 g (1 lb)	1 kg (2$\frac{1}{2}$ lb)
butter	75 g (3 oz)	200 g ($\frac{1}{2}$ lb)
fresh coriander leaves		

1 Heat the ghee or oil in a suitable pan.
2 Add the cumin seeds and bay leaves. Fry for 1 minute.
3 Stir in the onion, garlic and ginger. Fry for 5–7 minutes until golden brown.
4 Cover with a suitable lid and simmer until the meat is tender (30–45 minutes).
5 Stir in the cream, ground almonds, salt and garam masala.
6 Bring back to the boil. Simmer for a further 5 minutes.
7 Serve garnished with fresh coriander leaves.

V 13 – Pepper Bhajee

	4 portions	10 portions
oil	45 ml (3 tsp)	112 ml (7½ tsp)
finely chopped onion	100 g (4 oz)	250 g (10 oz)
black mustard seeds	1 tsp	2½ tsp
hot curry powder	2 tsp	5 tsp
chopped plum tomatoes, canned	100 g (4 oz)	250 g (10 oz)
potatoes (½ in cubed)	200 g (8 oz)	500 g (1¼ lb)
mixed red and green peppers (cut in half, deseeded and finely shredded)	600 g (1½ lb)	1½ kg (3¼ lb)
salt to taste		

1 Heat oil in a suitable pan.
2 Fry the mustard seeds for 1 minute.
3 Add the onions and fry until golden brown in colour.
4 Stir in the curry powder and cook for 1 minute.
5 Add the canned tomatoes.
6 Add the potatoes, red and green peppers. Mix well.
7 Add a little water to prevent sticking. Cover the pan and cook for approximately 15 minutes. Season and serve.

14 – Samosas

	4 portions	10 portions
short pastry	400 g (1 lb)	1 kg (2½ lb)

1 Make the pastry from ghee fat and fairly strong flour as the dough should be fairly elastic. Brush the pastry with ghee or vegetable after rolling into a smooth ball.
2 Take a small piece of dough and roll into a ball (approximately 25 mm diameter). Keep the rest of the dough covered with either a wet cloth, cling film or plastic, otherwise a skin will form on the dough.
3 Roll the ball into a circle approximately 90 cm (3½ in) in diameter on a lightly floured surface. Cut the circle in half.
4 Moisten the straight edge with egg wash or water.
5 Shape the semi-circle into a cone. Fill the cone with approximately

$1\frac{1}{2}$ teaspoons of filling. Moisten the top edges and press them well together.

6 The samosas may be made in advance, covered with cling film or plastic and refrigerated before being deep fried.

7 Deep fry at 180°C (375°F) until golden brown. Remove from fryer and drain well.

8 Serve on a dish garnished with coriander leaves, with a suitable chutney served separately.

– *Potato filling*

	4 portions	10 portions
peeled potatoes	200 g (8 oz)	500 g (1¼ lb)
vegetable oil	1½ tsp	3¾ tsp
black mustard seeds	½ tsp	1¼ tsp
finely chopped onions	50 g (2 oz)	125 g (5 oz)
finely chopped fresh ginger	12 g (½ oz)	30 g (1¼ oz)
fennel seeds	1 tsp	2½ tsp
cumin seeds	¼ tsp	1 tsp
turmeric	¼ tsp	1 tsp
frozen peas	75 g (3 oz)	187 g (7½ oz)
salt to taste		
water	2½ tsp	6¼ tsp
finely chopped fresh coriander	1 tsp	2½ tsp
garam masala	½ tsp	2½ tsp
pinch of cayenne pepper		

1 Cut the potatoes into 6 mm (¼ in) dice. Cook in water until only just cooked.

2 Heat the oil in a suitable pan. Add the mustard seeds and cook until they burst.

3 Add the onions and ginger. Fry for 7–8 minutes, stirring continuously until golden brown.

4 Stir in the fennel, cumin and turmeric. Add the potatoes, peas, salt and water.

5 Reduce to a low heat, cover the pan and cook for 5 minutes.

6 Stir in the coriander and cook for a further 5 minutes.

7 Remove from the heat and stir in the garam masala and the cayenne season.

8 Remove from pan. Place into a suitable bowl for the filling to cool before using.

~ Lamb filling

	4 portions	10 portions
saffron	$\frac{1}{2}$ tsp	$1\frac{1}{4}$ tsp
boiling water	$2\frac{1}{2}$ tsp	$6\frac{1}{4}$ tsp
vegetable oil	3 tsp	$7\frac{1}{2}$ tsp
finely chopped fresh ginger	12 g ($\frac{1}{2}$ oz)	30 g ($1\frac{1}{4}$ oz)
cloves garlic, crushed	2	5
finely chopped onions	50 g (2 oz)	125 g (5 oz)
salt to taste		
lean minced lamb	400 g (1 lb)	1 kg ($2\frac{1}{2}$ lb)
pinch of cayenne pepper		
garam masala	1 tsp	$2\frac{1}{2}$ tsp

1 Infuse the saffron in the boiling water. Allow to stand for 10 minutes.
2 Heat the vegetable oil in a suitable pan. Add the ginger, garlic, onions and salt, stirring continuously. Fry for 7–8 minutes, until the onions are soft and golden brown.
3 Stir in the lamb and add the saffron with the water. Keep stirring the lamb until it is cooked.
4 Add the cayenne and garam masala. Reduce the heat and allow to cook gently for a further 10 minutes.
5 The mixture should be fairly tight with very little moisture.
6 Transfer to a bowl and allow to cool before using.

15 ~ Punjab Palak Paneer   A milk, spinach and paneer dish

	4 portions	10 portions
oil	45 ml (3 tsp)	125 ml ($\frac{1}{4}$ pt)
finely shredded onion	100 g (4 oz)	250 g (10 oz)
mild curry powder	3 tsp	$7\frac{1}{2}$ tsp
cloves garlic, crushed	2	5
fresh spinach	400 g (1 lb)	1 kg ($2\frac{1}{2}$ lb)
milk or cream	45 ml (3 tsp)	112 ml ($7\frac{1}{2}$ tsp)
paneer or fried tofu – cubed	100 g (4 oz)	250 g (10 oz)
salt		
coriander leaves for garnish		

1 Heat the oil in a suitable pan. Add the onions and fry until golden brown.

2 Add the curry powder and garlic. Fry for a further 5 minutes.
3 Add the picked leaf spinach with approximately 125 ml ($\frac{1}{4}$pt) water. Cook for 5 minutes.
4 Add the cream or milk.
5 In a separate pan, fry the paneer until the pieces are light brown.
6 Add the paneer to the spinach, heat through and serve garnished with coriander leaves.

Note Paneer is a special cheese for cooking. It is produced by draining soured milk.

—— *Indonesia* ——

16 – Sop bobor Spinach and coconut soup

	4 portions	10 portions
vegetable oil	75 ml ($\frac{1}{8}$pt)	150 ml ($\frac{1}{3}$pt)
onion, finely chopped	25 g (1 oz)	60 g (2$\frac{1}{2}$oz)
garlic, chopped	12 g ($\frac{1}{2}$oz)	30 g (1$\frac{1}{4}$oz)
lesser galangal, peeled and finely chopped	12 g ($\frac{1}{2}$oz)	30 g (1$\frac{1}{4}$oz)
salam leaf	1	2$\frac{1}{2}$–3
lemon grass stalk, crushed	1	2$\frac{1}{2}$–3
coriander powder	3 g ($\frac{1}{2}$tsp)	10 g (1$\frac{1}{2}$tsp)
brown sugar	12 g ($\frac{1}{2}$oz)	25 g (1$\frac{1}{4}$oz)
chicken stock	500 ml (1 pt)	1$\frac{1}{4}$ litre (2$\frac{1}{2}$pt)
coconut milk	250 ml ($\frac{1}{2}$pt)	600 ml (1$\frac{1}{4}$pt)
spinach leaves	100 g (4 oz)	250 g (10 oz)
coconut flesh, diced	100 g (4 oz)	250 g (10 oz)
Garnish		
spinach leaves, finely chopped	50 g (2 oz)	125 g (5 oz)
coconut flesh	50 g (2 oz)	125 g (5 oz)

1 Sauté the onions in the oil, add garlic and lesser galangal. Sweat for 2–3 minutes without colour.
2 Add the salam leaf, lemon grass, coriander powder and brown sugar. Sauté for a further 2–3 minutes.
3 Cover with chicken stock, add coconut milk, bring to the boil, stir frequently.

4 Add chopped spinach leaves and diced coconut flesh. Season with salt and pepper. Reduce the heat, simmer for 15 minutes.
5 Remove the salam leaf and lemon grass.
6 Purée the soup in a liquidiser.
7 Serve in individual soup bowls, garnished with finely shredded spinach and diced coconut flesh.

Notes
If fresh coconut flesh is not available, use dried coconut flakes, soaked in water for 10 minutes.

Lesser galangal (kencur) is a rhizome which originally came from India and is used sparingly. It has a hot, strong flavour. Fresh kencur can be found in Asian food stores, it can also be purchased in a powdered form (Kaempferia galanga).

Wood fungus (jamur kuping) is also called cloud ear fungus, because it swells to a curled shape when soaked in water. Sold in dried form and greyish black in colour, it turns brown and translucent when soaked.

17 – Sop pelangi pagi Clear prawn soup with lemon grass

	4 portions	10 portions
red snapper fillets, skinned	150 g (6 oz)	375 g (15 oz)
garlic, chopped	50 g (2 oz)	125 g (5 oz)
carrots, chopped – brunoise	50 g (2 oz)	125 g (5 oz)
leeks, chopped – brunoise	50 g (2 oz)	125 g (5 oz)
egg whites	2	5
lemon grass stalk, crushed	1	2–3
bay leaf	1	2–3
chilli juice	10 ml (2 tsp)	25 ml (5 tsp)
tamarind pulp	25 g (1 oz)	60 g (2½ oz)
clear fish stock	1 litre (2 pt)	2½ litre (5 pt)
tomatoes, cut into concasse	4	10
Garnish		
baby sweetcorn, cut into 1 cm (⅜ in) pieces	4	10
lemon grass stalk, finely chopped	1	2–3
sweet basil leaves (kemangi)	12	30
medium sized prawns, shelled, cleaned, and cooked in stock	12	30

1 Mince the snapper fillets with garlic, carrots and leeks. Place into a bowl and add the egg whites.
2 Mix in lemon grass, bay leaf, chilli juice and tamarind pulp; mix well.
3 Place two-thirds of the fish stock into a saucepan and bring to the boil.
4 Add the remaining one-third to the minced fish mixture. Mix well, add this to the boiling fish stock. Stir well.
5 Reduce heat and gently simmer; allow to clarify for approximately 15 minutes; strain through a muslin.
6 Divide the garnish into portions and place in suitable individual containers. Pour over the clarified stock. Serve immediately.

Note Pre-packaged chilli sauce may be used but it is not the same as fresh chilli juice.

~ *Fresh chilli juice*

	4 portions	10 portions
red or green chillis	500 g (1¼ lb)	1½ kg (3 lb)
water	½ litre (1 pt)	1¼ litre (2½ pt)
white vinegar	15 ml (3 tsp)	45 ml (8 tsp)
salt	15 g (½ oz)	25 g (1¼ oz)

1 Wash the chillies.
2 Add water, vinegar and salt, bring to boil, simmer for 20 minutes.
3 Drain off half the water.
4 Purée in a liquidiser, strain and store in a refrigerator.

Note The juice should be fairly thick.

18 ~ **Banyuwangi sauce**   Chilli sauce

	250 ml (½ pt)
peanut oil	15 ml ($\frac{1}{32}$ pt)
shallots, finely chopped	50 g (2 oz)
red chillies, seeded and finely chopped	12 g (½ oz)
green chillies, seeded and finely chopped	50 g (2 oz)
sweet basil leaves, finely chopped	15
coconut milk	250 ml (½ pt)
sweet basil leaves	12 g (½ oz)

1 Heat the peanut oil in a suitable pan. Sauté the shallots, garlic and chillies without colour for 3–5 minutes.
2 Add chopped basil leaves and coconut milk, bring to the boil and simmer for 10 minutes.
3 Liquidise until smooth; pass through a fine strainer.
4 Put back into saucepan, bring to the boil, add whole basil leaves.

V 19 – **Saus acar kuning**   Sour turmeric sauce

	500 ml (1 pt)
peanut oil	35 ml ($\frac{1}{16}$ pt)
fresh ginger, finely chopped	25 g (1 oz)
shallots, finely chopped	25 g (1 oz)
garlic, finely chopped	25 g (1 oz)
bay leaf	1
lemon grass stalk, crushed	1
turmeric powder	3 g ($\frac{1}{2}$ tsp)
candle nuts or brazil nuts or macedamia nuts	50 g (2 oz)
sugar	5 g (1 tsp)
coconut milk	500 ml (1 pt)
white vinegar	70 ml ($\frac{1}{8}$ pt)
seasoning	

1 Heat the oil in a suitable pan. Sauté the ginger, shallots, garlic, bay leaf and lemon grass for 2 minutes.
2 Add the turmeric, nuts and sugar, continue to sauté for 3–5 minutes.
3 Add coconut milk and vinegar. Simmer for 10 minutes, season.
4 Remove from heat, discard the bay leaf and lemon grass.
5 Liquidise and pass through a fine strainer.

20 – **Rendang**   Beef curry

	4 portions	10 portions
cooking oil	70 ml ($\frac{1}{8}$ pt)	150 ml ($\frac{3}{8}$ pt)
finely chopped onion	100 g (4 oz)	250 g (10 oz)
cloves garlic, crushed	2	5
finely chopped fresh ginger	12 g ($\frac{1}{2}$ oz)	30 g (1$\frac{1}{4}$ oz)
hot Thai curry blend	2 tsp	5 tsp
ground lemon grass	1 tsp	2$\frac{1}{2}$ tsp
desiccated coconut	100 g (4 oz)	250 g (10 oz)

rump or sirloin cut into thin strips	400 g (1 lb)	1 kg (2½ lb)
creamed coconut	100 g (4 oz)	250 g (10 oz)
hot water	¼ litre (½ pt)	¾ litre (1¼ pt)
salt to taste		

1 Heat the oil in a suitable pan. Fry the onions, garlic and ginger until lightly coloured.
2 Add the curry blend and lemon grass. Continue to fry for a further 2 minutes.
3 Add the desiccated coconut and fry for a further 1 minute.
4 Quickly fry the beef in a separate pan. Drain off excess oil.
5 Place the beef in a clean saucepan. Season and add the coconut milk (creamed coconut and hot water blended together).
6 Add the other prepared ingredients to the beef.
7 Bring to the boil, then simmer until the beef is tender and the liquid has evaporated. Stir occasionally.
8 This curry should be served quite dry.
9 Serve with prawn crackers.

21 – Rendang kambang kot baru   Lamb in spicy coconut sauce

	4 portions	10 portions
loin chops	4 × 150 g (6 oz)	10 × 150 g (6 oz)
peanut oil	35 ml (1/16 pt)	125 ml (¼ pt)
shallots	25 g (1 oz)	60 g (2½ oz)
garlic clove, finely chopped	1	2½
candlenuts, or brazils or macedamia nuts, ground	50 g (2 oz)	125 g (5 oz)
turmeric powder	5 g 1 tsp)	12 g (2½ tsp)
coriander powder	5 g (1 tsp)	12 g (2½ tsp)
lemon grass stalk, finely chopped	1	2–3
white cabbage leaves, blanched	4	10
spicy coconut sauce	500 ml (1 pt)	1¼ litre (2½ pt)

1 In a basin, place the peanut oil, shallots, garlic and ground nuts. Sprinkle with turmeric and coriander. Add the lemon grass and season. Mix to a thick paste. Add oil and ground nuts until a spreadable mixture is obtained.

2 Spread mixture on to the lamb, marinate for 2 hours in a refrigerator.
3 Quickly fry the lamb on both sides for 1 minute.
4 Wrap each chop in a blanched cabbage leaf.
5 Place the lamb in a suitable pan for braising, cover with hot spicy coconut sauce. Cover with a lid and braise in a moderate oven 180°C (350°F) for approximately 10 minutes.
6 Serve with stir-fry vegetables, flavoured with turmeric.

22 – Saus rendang   Spicy coconut sauce

	1 pint
peanut oil	35 ml ($\frac{1}{16}$ pt)
shallots, finely chopped	50 g (2 oz)
garlic clove, finely chopped	1
ginger, finely chopped	12 g ($\frac{1}{2}$ oz)
greater galangal, peeled and finely chopped	12 g ($\frac{1}{2}$ oz)
candlenuts, brazil nuts or macadamia nuts	25 g (1 oz)
lemon grass stalk, chopped	1
kaffir lime leaves	4
coriander powder	2 g ($\frac{1}{2}$ tsp)
red chilli juice	375 ml ($\frac{3}{4}$ pt)
coconut milk	250 ml ($\frac{1}{2}$ pt)
salt	

1 In a saucepan, heat the peanut oil, sauté the shallots, ginger, garlic and greater galangal for approximately 5 minutes, until they are a light brown colour.
2 Add the nuts, lemon grass, lime leaves, turmeric and coriander. Continue to sauté for a further 2 minutes.
3 Add chilli juice and coconut milk and season. Bring to the boil, simmer for approximately 6–10 minutes, stirring continuously.
4 Remove the lime leaves.
5 Liquidise and pass through a strainer, use as required.

Note   Greater galangal is less aromatic and pungent than lesser galangal. Always used fresh in Indonesia. If unavailable, use fresh ginger but double the amount.

23 – Kukus cumi cumi dengan saus mangga
Squid on mango coconut sauce

This dish can be served as a starter or as a main course.

	4 portions	10 portions
squid, body tube only, ink sac removed	4	10
diced snapper fillets or other suitable fish	150 g (6 oz)	375 g (15 oz)
double cream	140 ml ($\frac{1}{4}$ pt)	300 ml ($\frac{5}{8}$ pt)
black wood fungus, soaked in warm water for 1 hr (optional)	12 g ($\frac{1}{2}$ oz)	25 g ($1\frac{1}{4}$ oz)
red chilli, finely chopped	1	2–3
sweet basil leaves (kemangi)	10	25
egg white	1	2–3
fish stock	500 ml (1 pt)	$1\frac{1}{4}$ litre ($2\frac{1}{2}$ pt)
Garnish		
mango slices	16	40
wood fungus, soaked in water for 1 hour	4	10
quennelles of young coconut	125 g (5 oz)	325 g ($12\frac{1}{2}$ oz)

1 Purée the fish fillets in a food processor.
2 Place in a bowl over ice, add the wood fungus (cut into julienne), chilli and chopped sweet basil leaves. Mix in egg white. Season with salt and pepper.
3 Carefully beat in the cream taking care not to overmix.
4 Fill the prepared squid with this mixture. Secure the ends with a cocktail stick or truss with string.
5 Place in a suitable pan with the fish stock, cover with greased paper and lid.
6 Poach in a moderate oven 180°C (350°F) for approximately 10–12 minutes.
7 Keep the squid warm.
8 For service, slice squid neatly into 4–5 pieces. Serve on a mirror of mango coconut sauce. Garnish with mango, slices of wood fungus and young coconut.

– *Mango coconut sauce*

	4 portions	10 portions
mango flesh	250 g (10 oz)	600 g (1½ lb)
young coconut flesh	100 g (4 oz)	250 g (10 oz)
lime, juice of	1	2–3

1 Place all ingredients in a liquidiser and then pass through a fine strainer.
2 Season, heat sauce. Use immediately.

24 – Kukus ikan sebalah madura   Fillet of halibut madura

	4 portions	10 portions
pieces of halibut fillet	4 × 100 g (4 oz)	10 × 100 g (4 oz)
julienne of chillies	25 g (1 oz)	60 g (2½ oz)
sweet basil leaves (kemangi)	25 g (1 oz)	60 g (2½ oz)
fish stock	140 ml (¼ pt)	300 ml (⅝ pt)
seasoning		
shallots	50 g (2 oz)	125 g (5 oz)
potatoes, small cubes or balls	50 g (2 oz)	125 g (5 oz)
carrots, small cubes or balls	50 g (2 oz)	125 g (5 oz)
green beans, small pieces	50 g (2 oz)	125 g (5 oz)
peanut oil	15 ml (3 tsp)	60 ml (7½ tsp)
garlic, peeled and chopped	6 g (¼ oz)	15 g (⅝ oz)
banyumangi sauce	140 ml (¼ pt)	300 ml (⅝ pt)
sour turmeric sauce	70 ml (⅛ pt)	150 ml (⅓ pt)
whole green beans, blanched	4	10

1 Sprinkle the halibut with chillies and chopped basil leaves and season.
2 Place in a suitable pan with enough fish stock to come half way up the fish. Cover with greased paper, poach in a moderate oven for approximately 5–8 minutes.
3 Keep warm.
4 Blanch the finely chopped shallots, potatoes and carrots for 1 minute.
5 Blanch and refresh the French beans.
6 Heat the peanut oil in a suitable pan. Sauté the blanched vegetables and garlic for approximately 2–5 minutes until tender.
7 Remove the vegetables. Keep warm.

8 On plates, place the banyuwangi sauce with a little sour turmeric sauce on top.
9 Carefully place the halibut on top.
10 Garnish with sautéed vegetables and the blanched whole green beans, tied in a knot.

—— *Mexico* ——

25 – Asado antiguo a la venezolana mechado
Larded beef pot roast with capers

	4 portions	10 portions
top rump of beef (one piece)	800 g (1½ lb)	2 kg (4 lb)
strips of larding pork	3	8
capers	40 g (1½ oz)	100 g (4 oz)
white distilled vinegar	2 tsp	5 tsp
finely chopped onion	40 g (1½ oz)	100 g (4 oz)
clove of garlic crushed and chopped	½	1
seasoning		
olive oil	1¼ tbsp	3 tbsp
dark brown sugar	20 g (¾ oz)	50 g (2 oz)

1 Lard the beef in the normal way, and with the tip of a knife push the capers into the beef around the strips of pork.
2 Mix the vinegar, onion, garlic and seasoning together.
3 Press and rub this mixture into the outside of the beef.
4 Sprinkle the beef with brown sugar, press down into the meat.
5 Heat the oil in a suitable pan, place the meat into the pan, brown well all over.
6 Add water or brown stock to come three-quarters of the way up the meat.
7 Make sure all the residue is removed from the bottom of the pan and is captured in the sauce.
8 Bring to boil, reduce the heat and gently braise for 2 hours.
9 *Note*   50 g (2 oz) of tomato purée and a bouquet garni may be added to the meat before braising commences.
10 Remove meat from the pan once cooked.
11 Reduce the cooking liquor by half, lightly thicken with arrowroot, strain.

12 Correct the seasoning and consistency.
13 Serve the beef carved with the sauce over, garnished with a few capers.

26 – Chancho adobado
Pork in orange and lemon sauce with sweet potatoes

	4 portions	10 portions
distilled vinegar	250 ml ($\frac{1}{2}$ pt)	625 ml ($1\frac{1}{2}$ pt)
liquid annatto (colouring)	1 tsp	$2\frac{1}{2}$ tsp
ground cumin seeds	$1\frac{1}{2}$ tsp	4 tsp
garlic cloves, chopped and crushed	2	5
seasoning		
boneless pork (cut into $2\frac{1}{2}$ cm (1 in) cubes)	1 kg (2 lb)	$2\frac{1}{2}$ kg (5 lb)
olive oil	2 tbsp	5 tbsp
fresh orange juice	250 ml ($\frac{1}{2}$ pt)	625 ml ($1\frac{1}{2}$ pt)
lemon, juice of	1	2
sweet potatoes boiled (peeled and sliced 6 mm ($\frac{1}{4}$ in) thick)	4	10

1 Place the vinegar, annatto, cumin, garlic and seasoning into bowl, mix well.
2 Place in the pork, stir and marinade for 24 hours in a refrigerator.
3 Remove the pork from the marinade, *keep the marinade.*
4 Dry the pork quickly, fry in hot oil until golden brown.
5 Drain off the fat, add the marinade.
6 Bring to boil, remove the residue, cover with the lid, gently simmer until the pork is cooked.
7 Add the orange and lemon juice, simmer for 2–3 minutes.
8 Remove the pork, keep warm.
9 Reduce the sauce by one-third, lightly thicken if required with arrowroot. Correct seasoning.
10 Add back the pork.
11 Serve in a suitable dish, garnished with the slices of cooked sweet potato.

27 – Huachinango veracruzano
Red snapper with tomato sauce, olives and potatoes

	4 portions	10 portions
medium-sized potatoes	1 kg (2 lb)	2½ kg (5 lb)
medium-sized tomatoes, skinned, seeded and coarsely chopped or	10	25
drained plum tomatoes	1 kg (2 lb)	2 kg (4 lb)
olive oil	3 tbsp	7 tbsp
finely chopped onion	100 g (4 oz)	250 g (10 oz)
garlic cloves, crushed and chopped	2	5
chopped red chilli	1	3
stuffed pimento olives	50 g (2 oz)	125 g (5 oz)
lemons or limes, juice of	2	5
pinch of salt		
ground cinnamon	¼ tsp	¾ tsp
ground cloves	¼ tsp	¾ tsp
seasoning		
flour	50 g (2 oz)	125 g (5 oz)
red snapper fillets	4	10
butter or margarine	50 g (2 oz)	125 g (5 oz)
triangles of white bread	4	10
chopped parsley		

1 Cook the potatoes plain boiled.
2 In a food processor, place the tomatoes and garlic, mix to a purée.
3 Heat half the oil in a suitable pan, add the chopped onion, cook without a cover.
4 Add the tomatoes, garlic, chopped chillies, olives, lime or lemon juice sugar, cinnamon, cloves, seasoning and cook for 5 minutes to extract flavours.
5 Meanwhile, pass the fish fillets through the flour.
6 With the remainder of the oil, fry the fillets until golden brown on both sides.
7 Place fillets in a suitable serving dish.
8 Fry the bread triangles in the butter until crisp and brown.
9 To serve, mask the fish with the tomato sauce, garnished with the slices of boiled or steam potatoes, triangles of bread, sprinkle with chopped parsley.

28 ~ Pescado Yucateco   Baked fish with olive and pimento sauce

	4 portions	10 portions
olive oil	2 tbsp	5 tbsp
finely chopped onions	25 g (1 oz)	62 g (2½ oz)
pimento stuffed olives cut into quarters	50 g (2 oz)	125 g (5 oz)
chopped sweet red pepper	25 g (1 oz)	62 g (2½ oz)
chopped fresh coriander	2 tsp	5 tsp
liquid annatto	½ tsp	1½ tsp
large orange, juice of	1	3
large lemon, juice of	1	3
seasoning		
butter	12 g (½ oz)	30 g (1½ oz)
white fish fillets (cod, hake, sole, plaice or turbot)	1 kg (2 lb)	2½ kg (5 lb)

1 Lightly fry the onions in the olive oil for approximately 5 minutes.
2 Add the olives, red pepper, coriander and annatto. Cook for a further 3 minutes.
3 Add orange and lemon juice, season.
4 Butter a suitable dish. Place the fish in the dish.
5 Pour the sauce over the fish.
6 Bake in a moderate oven until the fish is cooked.
7 Serve the fish in the dish or in a suitable serving dish and sprinkle with chopped coriander.

Note   The fish may also be sprinkled with sieved hard boiled egg.

—— *Middle East* ——

29 ~ Borani   Spinach and yoghurt salad

	4 portions	10 portions
fresh spinach	200 g (½ lb)	500 g (1½ lb)
lemon, juice of	1	1½
finely chopped onion	50 g (2 oz)	125 g (5 oz)
seasoning		
plain yoghurt	250 ml (½ pt)	625 ml (1¼ pts)
finely chopped fresh mint	2½ tsp	5 tsp

1 Wash the spinach well. Drain, remove stalks.
2 Blanch the spinach in boiling salted water for approximately
    2 minutes, refresh and drain.
3 Chop spinach finely.
4 Place spinach in a basin, add lemon juice, mix and season.
5 Stir in yoghurt, mix thoroughly.
6 Refrigerate for 1 hour before serving, serve sprinkled with fresh mint.

30 – Mast va khiar   Yoghurt, vegetable and herb salad

	4 portions	10 portions
cucumber	1 medium	2 large
green pepper, finely chopped	$\frac{1}{2}$	$1\frac{1}{2}$
spring onions finely chopped		
including part of the green		
chopped fresh tarragon	$1\frac{1}{2}$ tbsp	4 tbsp
chopped fresh dill	$2\frac{1}{2}$ tbsp	6 tbsp
lemon, juice of	$\frac{1}{2}$	$1\frac{1}{2}$
seasoning		
plain yoghurt	250 ml ($\frac{1}{2}$ pt)	625 ml ($1\frac{1}{4}$ pt)

1 Peel the cucumber and chop finely.
2 Place in a bowl, with the green pepper, spring onions, lemon juice and
    fresh herbs. Mix well.
3 Add the yoghurt, mix well.
4 Chill for 1 hour before serving.

31 – Dajaj mahshi   Roast chicken with rice and pine kernel stuffing

	4 portions	10 portions
chicken	$1 \times 1\frac{1}{2}$ kg (3 lb)	$2\frac{1}{2} \times 1\frac{1}{2}$ kg (3 lb)
uncooked long grain rice	162 g ($6\frac{1}{2}$ oz)	$\frac{1}{2}$ kg (1 lb)
butter	50 g (2 oz)	125 g (5 oz)
finely chopped onions	50 g (2 oz)	125 g (5 oz)
chicken liver and heart		
pine kernels	$1\frac{1}{2}$ tbsp	3 tbsp
water	375 ml ($\frac{3}{4}$ pt)	1 litre (2 pt)
currants	50 g (2 oz)	125 g (5 oz)
seasoning		
melted butter	50 g (2 oz)	125 g (5 oz)
yoghurt	$2\frac{1}{2}$ tbsp	7 tbsp

1 Sweat the onions in butter with colour.
2 Add the finely chopped liver and heart and the pine kernels, cook for a further 2–3 minutes.
3 Add the washed rice, currants and seasoning.
4 Stir well, bring to boil, cook until the rice is cooked and all the moisture has been absorbed.
5 Remove from heat, stir in the melted butter.
6 Stuff the chicken with the rice, truss to secure the filling. Keep any remainder of rice to serve separately.
7 Place in a suitable roasting pan, season, smear with yoghurt.
8 Roast in a suitable oven in the normal way, baste constantly with yoghurt.
9 Serve the chicken whole or portioned with the rice.

32 – Fesenjan   Braised duck with walnut and pomegranate sauce

	4 portions	10 portions
duck	1 × 2.4 kg (4½ lb)	2½ × 2.4 kg (4½ lb)
olive oil	3 tbsp	7 tbsp
shredded onion	100 g (4 oz)	250 g (10 oz)
turmeric	½ tsp	1½ tsp
shelled walnuts (purée in a food processor)	400 g (1 lb)	1¼ kg (2½ lb)
water	750 ml (1½ pt)	2¼ litre (4½ pt)
seasoning		
ground black pepper		
fresh pomegranates	3	9
lemons	2	5
sugar	50 g (2 oz)	125 g (5 oz)

1 Heat the olive oil in a suitable pan, add the onions and turmeric, fry quickly, stirring continuously until brown.
2 Drain, add to a suitable casserole pan.
3 Add the walnuts and seasoning. Add the water, bring to boil, gently simmer for approximately 20 minutes.
4 Cut the duck into 8 (20 for 10 portions) even pieces (similar to chicken sauté).
5 Fry the duck in olive oil until brown
6 Add the duck pieces to the casserole.
7 Coat the duck with the walnut sauce.

8 Simmer the duck with casserole lid on in the oven for approximtely 1½–2 hours. The duck should be well cooked.

9 Remove the duck, skim the sauce (during the cooking, it may be necessary to add more water to prevent drying and burning).

10 Add to the sauce fresh pomegranate juice, lemon juice and sugar.

11 Continue to simmer for a further 30 minutes. Keep the duck warm and moist.

12 Serve the duck in a suitable dish masked with sauce and serve.

Serve with braised basmati rice flavoured with dried sumak (a Middle Eastern spice).

33 – Lubya khadra billahma   Lamb with French beans

	4 portions	10 portions
French beans, trimmed and cut into 5 cm (2 in) lengths	800 g (2 lb)	2 kg (4½ lb)
olive oil	2½ tbsp	6 tbsp
neck of lamb, boned, cut into 2½ cm (1 in) cubes	400 g (1 lb)	1 kg (2½ lb)
finely chopped onion	100 g (4 oz)	250 g (10 oz)
tomatoes, peeled, seeded, cut into concasseé	6	15
seasoning		
ground nutmeg	½ tsp	1½ tsp
ground allspice	½ tsp	1½ tsp

1 Place the beans in the bottom of a suitable pan.

2 Sauté the lamb in the olive oil until brown.

3 Place the lamb on top of the beans.

4 Fry the onions in the same pan until soft and slightly brown.

5 Place the onions over the lamb, add the tomato concassée. Add seasoning and spices.

6 Add a little water, cover with a lid, cook for approximately 1 hour until tender.

7 It is important to make sure that the casserole never boils dry, that the beans are well covered and that the meat and other ingredients leave sufficient but not excessive moisture during the cooking process.

8 Serve once the meat is tender with steamed or boiled rice.

Note   The tomatoes may be replaced with canned plum tomatoes. It is also advisable to add a little tomato purée during the cooking process.

34 – Bacalhau trás-os-montes
Baked cod with ham, tomato and black olives

	4 portions	10 portions
pieces salt cod	4 × 100 g (4 oz)	10 × 100 g (4 oz)
milk	375 ml ($\frac{3}{4}$ pt)	1 litre (2 pt)
olive oil	4 tbsp	6 tbsp
slices of smoked ham	12	30
slices of tomato	4	10
sieved hard boiled eggs	2	5
stoned black olives	50 g (2 oz)	125 g (5 oz)
chopped parsley		

1 Soak the salt cod in water for approximately 12 hours, change the water 2 or 3 times.
2 Drain the cod, rinse under cold water.
3 Arrange the cod into a suitable dish.
4 Boil the milk, pour over the cod.
5 Allow to stand for 1 hour.
6 Drain, discard the milk.
7 Pour the olive oil over the fish, place in a moderate oven 180°C (350°F) approximately, basting occasionally with the oil.
8 After 10 minutes, place on the slices of ham, and a slice of tomato on each fish portion.
9 Baste with the oil, cook for a further 5 minutes.
10 When the fish is cooked, sprinkle with egg yolks, and the olives cut neatly into small pieces.
11 Serve from the baking dish sprinkled with chopped parsley.

35 – Truchas a'la navarra
Marinated trout baked with red wine and herbs

	4 portions	10 portions
red wine	124 ml ($\frac{1}{4}$ pt)	375 ml ($\frac{3}{4}$ pt)
olive oil	3 tbsp	8 tbsp
finely chopped onion	50 g (2 oz)	125 g (5 oz)
chopped mint	2 tsp	3 tsp
chopped rosemary	$\frac{1}{2}$ tsp	$1\frac{1}{2}$ tsp
chopped thyme	$\frac{1}{2}$ tsp	$1\frac{1}{2}$ tsp

bay leaf chopped	$\frac{1}{2}$	1
black peppercorns	15–20	35–50
seasoning		
cleaned trout	4 × 200 g (8 oz)	10 × 200 g (8 oz)
yolks of egg, lightly beaten	3	8

1 Put the red wine, onions, peppercorns, herbs and salt into a suitable baking dish. Stir well.
2 Place the cleaned trout into this marinade, allow to stand for 1 hour turning once.
3 Place the dish in the stove, bring to boil, cover fish with a buttered greaseproof sheet and lid.
4 Place in a suitable oven, moderately hot, until the fish is just cooked.
5 Remove the trout and keep warm.
6 Strain the cooking liquor. Bring back to the boil.
7 Beat the egg yolks, add this slowly to the cooking liquor whisking continuously. *Do not allow to boil* otherwise it will curdle. Heat to 80°C (176°F).
8 Correct seasoning.
9 Place the trout in a suitable serving dish, mask with sauce.
10 Traditionally, the trout is accompanied by hot, fresh boiled potatoes.

36 – Calamares en su tinta   Squid in its own ink

	4 portions	10 portions
fresh whole squid with their ink sacs	4	10
olive oil	4 tbsp	10 tbsp
finely chopped onion	100 g (4 oz)	250 g (10 oz)
garlic clove, crushed and chopped	1	3
chopped parsley		
seasoning		
grated nutmeg		
cold water	250 ml ($\frac{1}{2}$ pt)	625 ml ($1\frac{1}{4}$ pt)
flour	12 g ($\frac{1}{2}$ oz)	62 g ($1\frac{1}{2}$ oz)

1 Prepare the squid in the following way:
  (a) Grasp the tail and head sections firmly in the hands and pull the fin and outer part of the tail away from the head and tentacles.
  (b) Now carefully lift the silvery grey ink sac, if there is one, from

the inner section of the tail, place to one side.

(c) Use a sharp knife to set the tentacles free, just beyond the eyes of the squid. Discard the entrails and eye section, pull out the small round cartilage from the core of the tentacle base.

(d) Pull the transparent icicle-shaped pen or tail skeleton from the inside of the tail cone and discard it.

(e) Pull the fins away from the cone-shaped tail and set aside.

(f) Peel the red, lacy outer membrane away from the fins and the cone with your fingers under cold running water and remove as much of the membrane as possible from the tentacles. Gently invert the cone and then wash it thoroughly.

2 Clean the squid and carefully reserve the ink sacs in a small fine sieve set over a bowl.

3 Wash the tail cone, fins and tentacles under cold running water and dry on a cloth or kitchen paper.

4 Then slice the tail crosswise into 13 mm (1 in) wide rings. Cut the tentacles from the base, cut the base and each tentacle into 2 or 3 pieces, and slice each fin in half.

5 Heat the olive oil in a suitable frying pan. Add the squid, onions, garlic and parsley and cook rapidly for 5–6 minutes stirring continuously.

6 Add the nutmeg, seasoning, reduce the heat and continue to cook until tender.

7 Meanwhile purée the ink sacs in a sieve. Press out as much of the ink as possible. Pour the water over the sacs and purée again to extract any remaining ink.

8 Beat the flour and the ink with a whisk and continue to beat until smooth.

9 When the squid is tender, pour over the ink, stir well but gently. Bring to the boil.

10 Immediately reduce the heat, simmer for 5 minutes.

11 Correct seasoning.

12 Serve with hot boiled rice.

— *Spain* —

37 – Canja   Chicken soup with lemon and mint

	4 portions	10 portions
good chicken stock	1 litre (2 pt)	2½ litre (5 pt)
finely chopped onions	100 g (4 oz)	250 g (10 oz)
julienne of cooked chicken	200 g (8 oz)	500 g (1¼ lb)
short grain rice	50 g (2 oz)	125 g (5 oz)
lemon, juice of	1	3
chopped mint	1 tbsp	2½ tbsp

1 Add the chopped onions to the boiling chicken stock.
2 Add the rice, cook until tender.
3 Add the chicken, lemon juice and mint.
4 Correct seasoning, serve immediately.

38 – Riñones al jerez   Sautéed kidneys with sherry sauce

	4 portions	10 portions
olive oil	4 tbsp	10 tbsp
finely chopped onion	75 g (3 oz)	200 g (8 oz)
small bay leaf	1	2
flour	12 g ($\frac{1}{2}$ oz)	30 g (1¼ oz)
beef or chicken stock	125 ml ($\frac{1}{4}$ pt)	310 ml ($\frac{5}{8}$ pt)
finely chopped parsley	1 tbsp	2 tbsp
calves kidneys	750 g (1½ lb)	1.8 kg (3¾ lb)
seasoning		
dry sherry	62 ml ($\frac{1}{8}$ pt)	186 ml ($\frac{3}{8}$ pt)

1 Heat 2 tablespoons of olive oil in a suitable frying pan.
2 Add the onions, garlic and bay leaf. Gently fry to a light golden brown colour.
3 Add the flour and mix well.
4 Pour in the stock and stir continuously until boiling point.
5 Add the parsley.
6 Season the kidneys (trimmed and cut into regular dice), fry quickly in the remainder of the olive oil. Remove kidneys and keep warm.
7 Deglaze the pan with sherry. Remove from heat.

8 Return kidneys to the sherry pan. Add the onion sauce.

9 Correct seasoning and consistency.

10 Serve at once with saffron rice garnished with chopped red pimento.

Note Lambs' or pigs' kidney may be used in place of calves' kidney. In the case of lambs' kidney, cut in half and remove the inner white core.

39 – Porco con ameijuas a alentejaru
Marinated pork with clams, tomatoes and coriander

	4 portions	10 portions
dry white wine	250 ml ($\frac{1}{2}$ pt)	725 ml (1$\frac{1}{4}$ pt)
paprika	2 tsp	4$\frac{1}{2}$ tsp
seasoning		
cloves of garlic	2	4$\frac{1}{2}$
small bay leaf	1	2$\frac{1}{2}$
lean boneless pork	1 kg (2 lb)	2$\frac{1}{2}$ kg (5 lb)
lard	75 g (1$\frac{1}{2}$ oz)	187 g (3$\frac{3}{8}$ oz)
shredded onion	200 g (8 oz)	500 g (1$\frac{1}{4}$ lb)
large red pepper, seeded and cut into 13 mm ($\frac{1}{2}$ in) strips	1	2
cloves of garlic	2	5
medium tomatoes, peeled, deseeded and finely chopped	2	5
small clams, washed and thoroughly scrubbed	12	30
finely chopped fresh coriander	3 tbsp	8 tbsp

1 Mix the white wine, paprika and seasonings.

2 Add garlic cloves cut in half and the bay leaf.

3 Place the diced pork into this marinade, mix well and allow to stand for 3 hours, turning occasionally.

4 Remove the pork from the marinade. Pass the marinade through a fine strainer, reserve.

5 Melt half the lard in a suitable frying pan. Quickly fry the pork until golden brown and cooked through.

6 Remove pork, pour off excess fat, deglaze with the marinade, reduce by half.

7 Melt the remainder of the lard in a suitable casserole, gently fry the onion, red pepper, cook for 5 minutes until soft but not coloured.

8 Add the chopped and crushed garlic, tomatoes. Correct seasoning. Cook for 5 minutes.

9 Spread the clams, hinge side down, over the sauce. Cover the casserole and cook over a high heat for about 8–10 minutes, until the clams open. (Discard any clams that remain closed.)

10 Stir in the reserved pork and all its juices, simmer for 5 minutes. Sprinkle the top with coriander, garnish with lemon wedges. Serve at once.

Note The number of clams maybe doubled if costs allow. Oysters could also be used.

40 – Rojoes cominho Braised pork with cumin, coriander and lemon

	4 portions	10 portions
lean boneless pork cut into 2½ cm (1 in) cubes	1 kg (2 lb)	2½ kg (5 lb)
lard	14 g (½ oz)	35 g (1½ oz)
white wine	125 ml (¼ pt)	300 ml (⅝ pt)
ground cumin seed	1½ tsp	3 tsp
clove crushed and chopped garlic	1	2
seasoning		
lemons cut into segments	2	5
finely chopped coriander	2 tbsp	3 tbsp

1 Heat the lard in a suitable frying pan. Quickly fry the pork until brown and evenly coloured.

2 Add white wine, cumin, garlic, seasoning. Bring to boil. Reduce heat, allow to simmer until pork is cooked.

3 Add lemon segments, stir in coriander, correct seasoning.

4 *Note* The sauce may be thickened with a little arrowroot or cornflour.

5 Serve with sauté potatoes fried in olive oil.

—— *Thailand* ——

41 – Dom yam nua   Beef soup with chives

	4 portions	10 portions
beef, cut into strips	200 g (8 oz)	500 g (1¼ lb)
chopped chives	60 g (2 oz)	125 g (5 oz)
good brown stock	1 litre (2 pt)	2½ litre (5 pt)
cloves of garlic, crushed and chopped	2	5
lemon grass stalk, crushed	1	2½
lime, juice of	½ tsp	1 tsp
nam pla (fish sauce)	1 tsp	2½ tsp
seasoning		

1 Place the beef, stock, garlic, lemon grass, lime juice and *nam pla* in a suitable saucepan.
2 Bring to the boil and simmer for approximately 1 hour.
3 Serve in individual bowls, garnished with chopped chives.
4 Season liberally with salt and pepper to taste.

Notes   *Nam pla* is a fish sauce, which is a characteristic of several Thai dishes. This is a brown salty sauce made from fermented fish. It can be purchased from specialised shops.

As an alternative, grill 1 teaspoon of dried shrimp paste for 5 minutes each side, crush with 125 ml (¼ pt) of soy sauce.

42 – Mi krob   Fried crispy vermicelli

	4 portions	10 portions
rice vermicelli	200 g (8 oz)	500 g (1¼ lb)
vegetable oil	3 tbsp	7 tbsp
cloves of garlic, crushed and chopped	4	10
onions, finely chopped	50 g (2 oz)	125 g (5 oz)
pork, cut into strips	150 g (6 oz)	375 g (15 oz)
white crab meat (cooked)	100 g (4 oz)	250 g (10 oz)
dried mushrooms, soaked, drained and sliced	12 g (½ oz)	25 g (1 oz)
shelled prawns	200 g (8 oz)	500 g (1¼ lb)

breast of chicken, cut into strips	200 g (8 oz)	500 g (1¼ lb)
firm bean curd, diced	100 g (4 oz)	250 g (10 oz)
wood fungus, soaked	12 g (½ oz)	25 g (1 oz)
eggs	4	10
bean sprouts	100 g (4 oz)	250 g (10 oz)
chopped chives	75 g (3 oz)	180 g (7½ oz)
pickled garlic cloves	4–5	10–12
fresh coriander stalk	1	2–3
red chillies, finely chopped	2	5

Seasoning ingredients, accompaniments

soya sauce	4 tbsp	10 tbsp
sugar	4 tbsp	10 tbsp
vinegar	4 tbsp	10 tbsp
nam pla (fish sauce)	3 tbsp	7 tbsp
chopped chillies		

1 Deep fry vermicelli at 140°C (380°F) until it puffs and swells up. Drain well and reserve.
2 Heat oil in the wok, lightly fry the garlic and onion until brown.
3 Add the pork, chicken and mushrooms. Stir fry until all is cooked.
4 Add the prawns, crab meat, bean curd and diced wood fungus.
5 Break in the eggs and stir until they are set.
6 Add all seasonings, vermicelli and bean sprouts, toss to mix.
7 Serve in individual dishes. Serve with accompaniments.

43 – Phat priu wan   Sweet and sour pork and snow peas

	4 portions	10 portions
loin of pork, free from bone and excess fat	400 g (1 lb)	1¼ kg (2½ lb)
mange tout	300 g (12 oz)	1 kg (2 lb)
vegetable oil	62 ml (⅛ pt)	150 ml (⅓ pt)
garlic cloves, chopped and crushed	4	10
prawns	300 g (12 oz)	1 kg (2 lb)
soya sauce	62 ml (⅛ pt)	150 ml (⅓ pt)
monosodium glutamate (optional)		

1 Heat the oil in suitable wok and brown the garlic.
2 Add the thinly sliced pork and stir fry until lightly browned.
3 Add the prawns and stir fry for 1 minute.
4 Add all seasoning and stir fry for another 2 minutes.
5 Add the mange tout, stir fry for another 2–3 minutes.
6 Serve immediately.

44 – Pla nergn   Steamed fish, Thai style

	4 portions	10 portions
white fish (sole, plaice, cod) cut into scallops/slices	400 g (1 lb)	1¼ kg (2½ lb)
dried chillies, soaked, drained and seeded	2	5
onion, chopped	100 g (4 oz)	250 g (10 oz)
garlic cloves, crushed	3	7–8
lemon grass stalk	1	2–3
nam pla (fish sauce)	2 tbsp	5 tbsp
thick coconut milk	125 ml (¼ pt)	300 ml (⅝ pt)
egg, beaten	1	2–3
large cabbage leaves	4	10
rice flour	12 g (½ oz)	25 g (1¼ oz)
spring onions	2	5
coriander stalk	1	2–3
chilli	1	2–3

1 Purée the chillies, onion, garlic cloves and lemon grass in a food processor. Season the purée, with salt, pepper and fish sauce.
2 Add the fish and half of the coconut milk.
3 Mix in the beaten egg.
4 Line a suitable dish with the cabbage leaves and spread the fish mixture on top.
5 Mix the rice flour with the remaining coconut milk and pour over the fish.
6 Sprinkle with finely chopped spring onions, coriander and chilli.
7 Cover with aluminium foil, lightly greased. Either steam over boiling water in a suitable steamer or in a combination oven for approximately 20–30 minutes.
8 Serve in portions with boiled white rice.

45 – Pla cian   Fried fish, Thai-style

	4 portions	10 portions
whole sole, lemon sole or plaice	$1 \times 600\,g$–1 kg $(1\frac{1}{2}$–2 lb)	$2\frac{1}{2} \times 600\,g$–1 kg $(1\frac{1}{2}$–2 lb)
oil for frying		
spring onions, cut into julienne	2	5
garlic cloves, crushed	4	10
fresh ginger, shredded	50 g (2 oz)	125 g (5 oz)
red chillies, sliced	2	5
soya sauce	2 tbsp	5 tbsp
palm sugar or brown sugar	1 tbsp	2–3 tbsp
tamarind	25 g (1 oz)	60 g ($2\frac{1}{2}$ oz)
water	62 ml ($\frac{1}{8}$ pt)	150 ml ($\frac{1}{5}$ pt)
nam pla (fish sauce)	1 tbsp	2–3 tbsp

1 Heat the oil in a suitable pan, fry the fish on both sides, until crispy and brown. Place in a suitable dish.
2 In fresh oil, fry the spring onion, garlic and ginger, until lightly brown.
3 Add the chillies and seasoning to all other ingredients.
4 There should be sufficient liquor in the pan to mask the fish, if not add a little more water or fish stock.
5 Mask over the fried fish.
6 Served with boiled white rice.

Note   Palm sugar is sugar from the sap of the coconut palm. Tamarind is a tropical fruit with an acid taste.

46 – Kung khao plat   Fried prawn rice

	4 portions	10 portions
cooked rice	200 g (8 oz)	500 g ($1\frac{1}{4}$ lb)
shelled prawns	200 g (8 oz)	500 g ($1\frac{1}{4}$ lb)
eggs	2	5
seasoning		
vegetable oil	2 tbsp	5 tbsp
onions, finely chopped	150 g (6 oz)	375 g (15 oz)
dried mushrooms, soaked, drained and sliced	25 g (1 oz)	60 g ($2\frac{1}{2}$ oz)
nam pla (fish sauce)	1 tbsp	$2\frac{1}{2}$ tbsp

sugar	1 tsp	2½ tsp
soya sauce	1 tbsp	2½ tbsp
sprigs of coriander		

1 Heat the oil in pan. Using beaten eggs and seasonings, make two thin, flat omelettes.
2 Cool and cut into julienne.
3 Heat the oil in a wok, add onions and mushrooms, cook until onions are soft and highly coloured.
4 Add prawns and cook for 2 minutes.
5 Add the rice, season with *nam pla*, sugar and soya sauce, mix well.
6 Serve on individual plates, garnished with omelette cut into julienne, chilli and coriander leaves.

47 – Fan taeng   Stuffed marrow

	4 portions	10 portions
medium size marrow	1	2½
cooking oil	1 tbsp	2½ tbsp
garlic cloves, sliced	3	7
loin of pork, minced	200 g (8 oz)	500 g (1¼ lb)
prawns	150 g (6 oz)	375 g (15 oz)
garlic cloves, crushed and chopped	2	5
nam pla (fish sauce)	½ tsp	1 tsp
white crab meat, cooked	100 g (4 oz)	250 g (10 g)
a few sprigs of coriander		
seasoning and black pepper		
vegetable stock	500 ml (1 pt)	1¼ litre (2½ pt)

1 Heat the oil in a suitable pan, add the sliced garlic and brown. Then reserve to one side.
2 Remove the ends of the marrow and carefully remove the pith and seeds. Slice into 2½ cm (1 in) rings.
3 Mix the minced pork, prawns, chopped garlic, seasoning and *nam pla*. Use this to stuff the marrow rings.
4 Steam for approximately 15–20 minutes.
5 Drain the marrow, place on serving plate.
6 Bring the vegetable stock to the boil, add flaked crab meat and season.
7 Ladle the crab meat and vegetable stock over the marrow, sprinkle with fried garlic, garnish with coriander leaves.

VEGETARIAN FOOD

Prepare, cook and finish complex vegetable dishes

1   Select the type, quantity and quality of vegetables in accordance with recipe specifications.
2   Identify that the products not for immediate consumption are stored in accordance with recipe specification and current legislation.
3   Demonstrate that the nutritional value of the vegetables is adequately retained during the preparation and cooking.
4   Demonstrate that the cooking, regeneration and finished dishes must fully meet the recipe specification.

—— *Vegetarian and Vegan Catering* ——

This information has been adapted from the technical brief on vegetarian and vegan catering prepared by HCIMA, 1993.

1. INTRODUCTION

1.1   People choose to eat vegetarian or vegan food for a variety of reasons.

Vegetarians
religious beliefs, ethical and ecological views against meat eating, Jews and Muslims without access to Kosher or Halal meat and for "Health" reasons.

"Demi-Vegetarians"
are people who choose to exclude red meat from their diet.

Vegans
will not eat any animal food or product because they consider it cruel to do so. Veganism is living entirely on the products of the plant kingdom.

1.2   Within the above groups, the foods which are avoided by each sector are:

Lacto Vegetarians
eat milk and cheese but not eggs, whey or

ANYTHING which has been produced as a result of an animal being slaughtered, that is: meat, poultry, fish or any by-products such as fish oils, rennet, cochineal.

Ovo-Lacto Vegetarians
include eggs, otherwise as for lacto vegetarian.

"Demi-Vegetarians"
usually choose to exclude red meat, though they may occasionally eat it. White poultry and fish are generally acceptable

Vegans
avoid ALL animal products including milk, cheese, yoghurt, eggs, fish, poultry, meat and honey. They eat only items or products from the plant kingdom.

1.3   These groups of people are generally more interested in a diet lower in fat and higher in fibre

2. SPECIAL POINTS FOR CONSIDERATION

2.1 **Protein**

In a meat eater's diet, meat, poultry and fish provide a considerable amount of the daily protein intake. Protein cannot be destroyed by cooking but, more importantly, it CANNOT be stored in the body. Any vegetarian or vegan meal must therefore contain an adequate source of protein to replace meat protein.

2.2 **Amino Acids**

Protein is made up of amino acids. Human protein tissue and animal proteins contain all the "essential" amino acids (the body can manufacture the non-essential amino acids). Vegetable proteins however contain fewer of the essential amino acids. The lack of some amino acids in one plant is compensated for by another.

2.3 **Protein Complementing**

Means combining various plant proteins in one dish or meal to provide the equivalent amino acid profile of animal protein. Putting together 60% beans (or other pulses) or nuts with 30% grains or seeds and grains and 10% green salad or vegetables, makes the ideal combination.

2.4 **The best sources of vegetarian protein are** cheese, eggs, milk, textured vegetable protein (T.V.P.) followed by Tofu, soya beans, all other pulses and nuts. Seeds: sesame, sunflower and pumpkin. Cereals: (preferably wholegrain) millet, wheat, barley and oats. Vegans exclude cheese, eggs and milk as a source of protein. Substitute soya milk, soya cheese and soya yoghurt. All other items above are acceptable.

2.5 In protein equivalent terms (all cooked weights)
2 oz meat = 3 oz fish
2 oz (hard) cheese
4 oz soft or cottage cheese
2 eggs
4 oz nuts
2 oz peanut butter
6 oz pulses (lentils, peas, beans)
3 oz seeds

2.6 Pulses, nuts, seeds and to a lesser extent tubers and roots contain significant protein. Leaves, stems, buds and flowers are almost all water and have an insignificant protein content.

2.7 A dish such as ratatouille, made from "water" vegetables is only suitable as a side dish. "Vegetable" curries, hotpots and similar dishes should all include a recognisable and good vegetable protein source.

3. ITEMS WHICH MUST BE EXCLUDED OR CONSIDERED IN A VEGETARIAN MENU

3.1 Rennet or pepsin based cheeses (rennet is an enzyme from the stomach of a newly killed calf, pepsin is from pigs' stomachs).

replace with approved "vegetarian" cheeses or non-rennet cheeses such as cottage and cream cheese (not for vegans, unless made with soya milk). Check to ensure ready made vegetarian dishes include vegetarian cheese.

Battery farm eggs (hens may have been fed fish meal, also strict vegetarians consider battery rearing of hens is cruel).

replace with free range eggs Strict vegetarians will only eat free range eggs, this is impractical for most manufacturers and caterers, so clear labelling is important so as not to mislead.

Whey is a by-product of cheese making and therefore may contain rennet. Can be found in biscuits.	–	Check all product labels of items bought in and used in the production of a vegetarian choice.
Cochineal or E120 is made from the cochineal beetle.	–	Often present in glacé cherries and mincemeat. Choose an alternative red colouring.
Alcohol – some wines or beers may be refined using isinglass (a fish product) or dried blood. Some ciders contain pork to enhance the flavour.	–	Check with the wholesaler or manufacturer where possible if in any doubt before use in cooking or serving to a vegetarian.
Crisps may contain whey as a processing aid, this need not be stated on the label. Some Muesli may also contain whey.	–	Check with the manufacturer before using in a vegetarian dish.
Meat or bone stock for soups or sauces. Animal based flavourings for savoury dishes.	replace with	stock made from vegetables or yeast extracts (Tastex, Barmene, Marmite), or bought vegetable stock cubes/bouillon; soya sauce, miso, Holbrook's Worcester Sauce (which is anchovy free).
Animal fats (suet, lard or dripping) ordinary white cooking fats or margarine. (Some contain fish oil). Bought in pastry may contain lard or fish oil margarine.	replace with	Trex and Pura white vegetable fats. 100% vegetable oil margarines. Suenut or Nutter. (Available from health food stores) White Flora.
Oils containing fish oil	replace with	100% vegetable oil (sunflower, corn, soya, groundnut, walnut, sesame, olive) or mixed vegetable oil.

N.B. Fish oils may well be "hidden" in margarine and products such as biscuits, cakes and bought in pastry items. Check suitability before using.

Gelatine, aspic, block or jelly crystals (for glazing, moulding, in cheesecakes and desserts). Some yoghurts are set with gelatine also some sweets, particularly nougat and mints.	replace with	agar agar (a fine, white odourless powder), gelozone. Apple pectin.
Animal-fat ice cream.	replace with	vegetable-fat ice cream.

N.B. Many additives contain meat products, look on the label for: "edible fats", "emulsifiers", "fatty acids" and the preservative E471. The safest course is to ask the manufacturer of any bought in product you wish to use.

4. CLAIMS

4.1 Never claim that a food or dish is vegetarian if you have used a non-vegetarian ingredient.

4.2 If you knowingly mislead a customer into believing you have a suitable vegetarian choice on offer, you can be prosecuted under the Trade Descriptions Act (1968) and/or the Food Safety Act (1990).

RECIPES

1 – White vegetable stock

1 litre (2 pt)

onion	} mirepoix	100 g (4 oz)
carrots		100 g (4 oz)
celery		100 g (4 oz)
leeks		100 g (4 oz)
water		1½ litre (3 pt)
water		

Place all the ingredients into a saucepan, bring to the boil and allow to simmer for approximately 1 hour, skim if necessary. Strain and use.

2 – Brown vegetable stock

1 litre (2 pt)

onions	} mirepoix	100 g (4 oz)
carrots		100 g (4 oz)
celery		100 g (4 oz)
leeks		100 g (4 oz)
sunflower oil		60 ml ($\frac{1}{8}$ pt)
tomatoes		50 g (2 oz)
mushroom trimmings		50 g (2 oz)
peppercorns		6
water		1½ litre (3 pt)
yeast extract		5 g ($\frac{1}{4}$ oz)

1 Fry the mirepoix in the oil until golden brown.
2 Drain and place into a suitable saucepan. Add all the other ingredients except the yeast extract.
3 Cover with the water, bring to the boil.
4 Add the yeast extract, simmer gently for approximately 1 hour. Then skim if necessary and use.

3 – Clear vegetable soup

	1 litre (2 pt)
chopped mixed vegetables (onion, leek, carrot, celery)	400 g (1 lb)
vegetable oil	60 ml ($\frac{1}{8}$ pt)
egg whites	1–2
water	1 litre (2 pt)
tomatoes	100 g (4 oz)
mushroom trimmings	50 g (2 oz)
peppercorns	6
bouquet garni	
yeast extract	5 g ($\frac{1}{4}$ oz)
salt	

1 Fry the vegetables in the oil until golden brown.
2 Drain off all the fat, place vegetables in a saucepan.
3 Deglaze the frying pan with a little water and add to the saucepan.
4 Lightly beat the egg whites with the remaining water and add to the pan.
5 Add remainder of ingredients, bring to the boil stirring occasionally.
6 Allow to simmer without stirring for 45 minutes to 1 hour.
7 Strain through a double muslin, skim off all fat, correct seasoning and serve.

I 4 – Aubergine pasta bake

(R Priddy)

	4 portions	10 portions
aubergine	1 large	3 medium
salt		
olive oil	60 ml ($\frac{1}{8}$ pt)	100 ml ($\frac{1}{3}$ pt)
garlic clove, crushed	1	2
onion, chopped	1	2–3
green or red pepper	1	3
can of tomatoes (chopped)	2 × 500 g (1$\frac{1}{4}$ lb)	4 × 500 g (1$\frac{1}{4}$ lb)
red wine	75 ml (3 fl oz)	200 ml (7$\frac{1}{2}$ fl oz)
tomato purée	2 tsp	5 tsp
sugar	$\frac{1}{2}$ tsp	1$\frac{1}{2}$ tsp

> Using processed cheese
> 1 portion provides:
>
> 509 kcals
> 27.5 g fat
> (of which 11.1 g saturated)
> 42.9 g carbohydrate
> (of which 11.6 g sugars)
> 21.8 g protein
> 6.0 g fibre

finely chopped basil *or* dried basil	1 tbsp	3 tbsp
freshly ground black pepper		
dried tagliatelle	175 g (7 oz)	400 g (1 lb)
processed cheese or vegetarian Cheddar	10 slices	25 slices
Parmesan cheese (grated)	25 g (1 oz)	50 g (2½ oz)
coriander sprigs to garnish		

1 Wash and trim off the stalk of the aubergine. Slice the aubergine into ½cm (¼in) thick slices and put them in a colander in layers, sprinkling salt between each layer. Cover with a plate and place a heavy weight on top. Leave for 1 hour to draw out the bitter juice, then rinse the slices and put to dry on absorbent paper.
2 Heat the oven to 180°C (350°F).
3 Heat 1 tablespoon (2½ tablespoons for 10 portions) of the oil in a saucepan, add the garlic, onion, finely chopped pepper and fry gently for about 5 minutes until the onion is soft and light coloured. Stir in tomatoes with juice, wine and tomato purée. Bring to boil. Stir in the sugar, basil and season with salt and pepper. Let the sauce boil gently to reduce and thicken.
4 Meanwhile, bring a pan of salted water to the boil and add 1 teaspoon (2½ teaspoons for 10 portions) of oil. Cook the tagliatelle for 6–7 minutes, until tender yet firm to the bite, then drain thoroughly.
5 Heat the remaining oil in a frying pan, add the aubergine slices and fry gently until they are lightly coloured on both sides. Remove with a slotted spoon and drain well on absorbent paper.
6 Spread a third of tomato sauce over the bottom of a lightly oiled ovenproof dish. Place half the pasta on top, followed by half the aubergine slices and half the cheese. Cover with another third of the tomato sauce and then the remaining pasta, aubergine slices and cheese. Spread the remaining tomato sauce over the cheese and sprinkle the Parmesan cheese on top.
7 Cook the pasta bake in the oven for about 20 minutes, until heated through.
8 Garnish with coriander sprigs, if liked, and serve immediately straight from the dish.

I 5 – Asparagus and wild mushroom bouchée served with a lime hollandaise

	4 portions	10 portions
asparagus tips	600 g (1½ lb)	1½ kg (3¾ lb)
puff pastry	450 g (18 oz)	1⅛ kg (2¼ lb)
mixed wild mushrooms	125 g (5 oz)	300 g (12 oz)
button mushrooms	60 g (2½ oz)	150 g (5 oz)
shallots	50 g (2 oz)	125 g (5 oz)
double cream	½ litre (1 pt)	1½ litre (3 pt)
dill		
tarragon	25 g (1 oz)	60 g (2½ oz)
chervil		
paprika	pinch	
salt, pepper		
julienne zest of lime	1	2–3

Hollandaise sauce		
butter	200 g (8 oz)	500 g (1¼ lb)
egg yolks	2	5
white wine vinegar	1 tbsp	2–3 tbsp
white wine	1 tbsp	2–3 tbsp
crushed white peppercorns	6	15
lime, juice of	½	1½

1 Peel and trim the asparagus.
2 Cook in an asparagus kettle and refresh in ice water.
3 Roll out pastry and cut 4 or 10 vol-au-vent cases 9 × 6 cm (3½ × 2¼ in) with lids.
4 Melt butter for hollandaise, skim and keep in a bain-marie.
5 Reduce the wine, vinegar and peppercorns until almost dry.
6 Allow to cool and add 2 tablespoons water (5 tablespoons for 10 portions).
7 Add the yolks and whisk to a sabayon over gentle heat.
8 Gradually whisk in the butter.
9 Season, strain and finish with lime juice.
10 Sweat off shallots in 25 g (1 oz) butter (60 g (2½ oz) for 10 portions), add mushrooms and sweat.
11 Cover with a cartouche and place in a hot oven for approximately 25 minutes until almost dry.
12 Add cream, chopped herbs and season.

13 Egg wash the vol-au-vent cases and cook in a hot oven till golden brown.
14 Keep warm.
15 Reheat the asparagus in seasoned water.
16 Melt the butter in a pan.
17 Add the chanterelles, season and sauté quickly.
18 Place the duxelle mixture in the vol-au-vent cases.
19 Arrange the asparagus in cases and place lids on top.
20 Arrange the sautéed mushrooms and asparagus tips around the plate.
21 Add hollandaise, lime juice, paprika and chervil and serve.

Note   It is advisable to use pasteurised egg yolks.

V 6 – Tofu pâté with raw vegetables

	4 portions	10 portions
small cauliflower	1	$2\frac{1}{2}$
small head celery	1	$2\frac{1}{2}$
large carrots	2	5
Pâté		
sunflower seeds	100 g (4 oz)	250 g (10 oz)
tofu	275 g (10 oz)	750 g ($1\frac{1}{2}$ lb)
sunflower oil	1 tbsp	2–3 tbsp
wheatgerm	75 g (3 oz)	180 g ($7\frac{1}{2}$ oz)
finely grated carrot	100 g (4 oz)	250 g (10 oz)
dill weed	10 g ($\frac{1}{2}$ oz)	25 g (1 oz)
paprika	5 g ($\frac{1}{4}$ oz)	12 g ($\frac{5}{8}$ oz)

1 Prepare and wash the vegetables: cut the cauliflower into bite-sized florets and the celery and carrots into batons.
2 Grind half of the sunflower seeds into a fine powder.
3 Add tofu, sunflower oil, wheatgerm and liquidise until smooth.
4 Place into a basin and add grated carrot, remaining whole sunflower seeds, seasoning, chopped dill and paprika.
5 Place into a suitable serving dish, surrounded by the raw vegetables.

Note   Tofu is a bean curd available in 3 types:

(a) Silken – soft like junket.
(b) Firm – like firm cheese.
(c) Soft – between silken and firm.

7 – Vegetarian terrine

	4 portions	10 portions
fresh washed spinach	300 g (12 oz)	750 g (1¾ lb)
salt and pepper		
ground allspice	1 tsp	2½ tsp
chopped chives	25 g (1 oz)	60 g (2½ oz)
carrots ⎫ washed and peeled	400 g (1 lb)	1 kg (2½ lb)
celeriac ⎭	400 g (1 lb)	1 kg (2½ lb)
choux pastry	375 ml (¾ pt)	1 litre (2 pt)
double cream or crème fraîche	190 ml (⅜ pt)	475 ml (1 pt)

1 Cook, refresh and drain spinach, purée in food processor and season with salt, pepper, allspice and chopped chives.
2 Cut carrots and celeriac into even pieces, cook and purée separately.
3 To each purée add 125 ml (¼ pt) of choux pastry and 60 ml (⅛ pt) of double cream (×2½ for 10 portions). Mix well.
4 Take a large well greased loaf tin, preferably aluminium foil (disposable).
5 Layer carrot purée over the base. Next layer with celeriac and finish with the spinach.
6 Cover with foil. Cook in a bain-marie in the oven at 180°C (350°F) for approximately 1¼ hours.
7 Remove from oven, cool and serve cold, sliced with a suitable sauce, e.g. green peppercorn and paprika (see below).

– Green peppercorn and paprika sauce

	4 portions	10 portions
plum tomatoes	200 g (8 oz)	500 g (1¼ lb)
green peppercorns (crushed)	25 g (1 oz)	60 g (2½ oz)
paprika	12 g (½ oz)	25 g (1¼ oz)
double cream or unsweetened vegetable creamer	250 ml (½ pt)	600 ml (1¼ pt)
lemon, juice of	½	1–2

1 Purée the plum tomatoes, place in a suitable pan with the peppercorns and bring to the boil. Simmer for 5 minutes.

2 Add paprika, simmer for a further 5 minutes.
3 Finish with cream, bring back to boil. (If using unsweetened vegetable creamer check if product is heat-stable.)
4 Add lemon juice, pass through a fine strainer, cool and serve chilled.

8 – Stuffed avocado pears garnished with asparagus

	4 portions	10 portions
ripe avocado pears	2	5
lemon, juice of	1	2–3
butter or margarine	50 g (2 oz)	125 g (5 oz)
finely chopped onion	25 g (1 oz)	60 g (2½ oz)
tomato, skinned, deseeded and diced	50 g (2 oz)	125 g (5 oz)
chopped mushrooms	50 g (2 oz)	125 g (5 oz)
chopped hazelnuts	100 g (4 oz)	250 g (10 oz)
grated Cheddar cheese	100 g (4 oz)	250 g (10 oz)
seasoning		
dry sherry or white wine	125 ml (¼ pt)	300 ml (⅝ pt)
cooked asparagus tips	12	30
cheese sauce	250 ml (½ pt)	600 ml (1¼ pt)

1 Cut the avocado pears in half, remove stones and skin, taking particular care that they do not break up.
2 Place on a suitable lightly greased tray and brush all over with lemon juice.
3 Heat the butter or margarine in a small sauté pan, add the finely chopped onion and sweat without colour.
4 Add the tomato and mushrooms and sweat also. Remove from heat.
5 Add the chopped hazelnuts and grated Cheddar cheese, season with salt and pepper. Mix in the sherry or white wine.
6 Fill the avocado pears with this mixture, garnish with asparagus tips and mask with cheese sauce.
7 Place avocado pears in the oven and glaze slowly until golden brown, serve immediately.

Note   To hold the avocado pears in shape they may be placed in china avocado pear dishes, filled and then glazed.

With imagination, avocado pears may be served hot with a variety of vegetable fillings. For example:

(a) Spinach and mushrooms in a yoghurt, cream or cheese sauce.
(b) Carrot purée flavoured with fresh ginger.
(c) Stir-fry vegetables cut small.
(d) Pilaff rice with chopped dates, nuts and peppers.
(e) Small pasta shells in a light cream sauce using fromage frais.

Remember that for healthy eating cheese sauce may be made with wholemeal flour, sunflower oil and skimmed milk, natural yoghurt, or fromage frais.

9 – Carrot and ginger soufflé

	4 portions	10 portions
grated Parmesan cheese	50 g (2 oz)	125 g (5 oz)
carrots	300 g (12 oz)	1 kg (2 lb)
seasoning		
béchamel sauce	125 ml ($\frac{1}{4}$ pt)	300 ml ($\frac{5}{8}$ pt)
root ginger (grated)	25 g (1 oz)	60 g (2$\frac{1}{2}$ oz)
egg yolks	3	7
egg whites	4	10

1 Well grease soufflé dishes and sprinkle with grated Parmesan.
2 Peel the carrots, cut into regular-sized pieces and place into a saucepan. Cover with water, bring to the boil and simmer until tender.
3 Drain, purée, place into a suitable basin and season.
4 Add remainder of cheese. Bind with the béchamel sauce. Mix well.
5 Add grated ginger, allow to cool. Add the egg yolks, mix well.
6 Whisk egg whites to soft peak, beat one-third of the whites into the carrot purée, then carefully fold in the remainder.
7 Pour into the soufflé mould, clean the edges.
8 Bake in a preheated oven at 200°C (400°F) for approximately 20–25 minutes. Serve with a suitable sauce, e.g. broccoli, asparagus.

Note Alternatively this soufflé may be served in individual soufflé dishes.

10 – Brazil nut roast in pastry

	4 portions	10 portions
chick peas, soaked for 24 hr	100 g (4 oz)	250 g (10 oz)
yeast extract	5 g ($\frac{1}{4}$oz)	12 g ($\frac{5}{8}$oz)
brazil nuts	100 g (4 oz)	250 g (10 oz)
wholemeal breadcrumbs	100 g (4 oz)	250 g (10 oz)
butter or margarine	25 g (1 oz)	60 g (2$\frac{1}{2}$oz)
finely chopped onion	50 g (2 oz)	125 g (5 oz)
clove of garlic, crushed and chopped	1	2–3
button mushrooms	150 g (6 oz)	375 g (15 oz)
mixed herbs	5 g ($\frac{1}{4}$oz)	12 g (1$\frac{1}{4}$oz)
seasoning		
egg, beaten	1	2–3
brioche pastry	200 g (8 oz)	500 g (1$\frac{1}{4}$lb)

> 1 portion provides:
>
> 599 kcals/2501 kJ
> 38.2 g fat
> (of which 15.6 g saturated)
> 47.4 g carbohydrate
> (of which 4.8 g sugars)
> 19.6 g protein
> 6.6 g fibre

1 Drain the chick peas, cover with fresh cold water, bring to the boil and gently simmer until tender.
2 Drain the chick peas when cooked, place into a clean basin and mix in the yeast extract.
3 Chop the brazil nuts in a food processor, mix in with the chick peas, add the breadcrumbs and mix well.
4 Heat the fat in a small sauté pan, sweat the onion and the garlic without colour, add the mushrooms and cook for a few minutes then mix with the other ingredients.
5 Add mixed herbs and season, then bind with the egg.
6 Line well-greased 400 g (1 lb) bread tin(s) with brioche pastry.
7 Fill with the chick pea and nut mixture. Lightly egg wash the top and cover with brioche. Make a small hole in the centre.
8 Allow to prove.
9 Bake in a moderately hot oven (200°C, 400°F, Reg. 6) for approximately 10 minutes. Turn the oven down to 180°C (350°F, Reg. 4) and bake for a further 30 minutes approximately. If the top of the brioche colours too much cover with either a sheet of wetted greaseproof or aluminium foil.
10 When cooked, allow to cool slightly and serve sliced or on individual plates with tomato, asparagus or broccoli sauce (see opposite).

Note For healthy eating, the brioche paste may be made from 25%, 50% or 95% wholemeal flour, using hardened sunflower margarine.

~ Asparagus sauce

	4 portions	10 portions
cooked asparagus	300 g (12 oz)	750 g (1¾ lb)
vegetable stock	125 ml (¼ pt)	300 ml (⅝ pt)
white wine	125 ml (¼ pt)	300 ml (⅝ pt)
seasoning		
smetana or double cream	4 tbsp	10 tbsp

1 Liquidise asparagus, stock and wine until a smooth sauce is obtained.
2 Gently bring to the boil.
3 Strain through a coarse strainer into a clean saucepan. Season.
4 Add smetana or double cream. *Do not boil.*
5 Correct seasoning and consistency, use as required.

Note This sauce is suitable for serving cold with other dishes.

11 ~ Gratin of nuts with a tomato and red wine sauce flavoured with basil

	4 portions	10 portions
finely chopped onion	100 g (4 oz)	250 g (10 oz)
green pepper, in brunoise	50 g (2 oz)	125 g (5 oz)
celery, in brunoise	50 g (2 oz)	125 g (5 oz)
butter or margarine	25 g (1 oz)	60 g (2½ oz)
cloves garlic	2	5
cooked fresh or canned chestnuts	200 g (8 oz)	500 g (1¼ lb)
or dried chestnuts (well soaked then cooked in vegetable stock)	75 g (3 oz)	180 g (7½ oz)
cashew nuts	200 g (8 oz)	500 g (1¼ lb)
walnuts	50 g (2 oz)	125 g (5 oz)
Cheddar cheese	100 g (4 oz)	250 g (10 oz)
red wine	60 ml (⅛ pt)	150 ml (⅓ pt)
brandy	60 ml (⅛ pt)	150 ml (⅓ pt)
paprika	10 g (½ oz)	25 g (1¼ oz)
thyme (dried)	5 g (¼ oz)	12 g (⅝ oz)
egg	1	2–3

1 Sweat the onion, green pepper and celery in the butter or margarine without colour.
2 Add the crushed and chopped garlic, continue to sweat for 1 minute.
3 Add the finely chopped nuts and grated Cheddar cheese, mix well.
4 Add the red wine, brandy and herbs, season well and bind with an egg.
5 Place mixture into a well-greased and silicone paper-lined 400 g (1 lb) loaf tin.
6 Cover with aluminium foil and bake at 190°C (375°F, Reg. 5) for approximately 45 minutes. (Alternatively, bake in a bain-marie in the oven.)
7 When cooked turn out and carefully portion into individual plates on to a red wine and tomato sauce with basil (see below). Decorate with fresh basil and a little tomato concassée.

– *Tomato and red wine sauce flavoured with basil*

	4 portions	10 portions
fresh tomato coulis	125 ml ($\frac{1}{4}$ pt)	300 ml ($\frac{5}{8}$ pt)
red wine	125 ml ($\frac{1}{4}$ pt)	300 ml ($\frac{5}{8}$ pt)
sprigs chopped basil	2	5
natural yoghurt or single cream	60 ml ($\frac{1}{8}$ pt)	150 ml ($\frac{1}{3}$ pt)
seasoning		

1 Bring the tomato coulis to the boil, add the red wine and chopped basil. Simmer for 2 minutes.
2 Finish with natural yoghurt or single cream, and correct seasoning and consistency. Pass through a fine strainer if necessary before use.

Note   This dish is suitable for vegans if the cheese is omitted.

12 – Crown of brioche filled with leaf spinach, fennel and pine kernels

	4 portions	10 portions
brioche pastry	150 g (6 oz)	375 g (15 oz)
leaf spinach	400 g (1 lb)	1¼ kg (2½ lb)
margarine or butter	50 g (2 oz)	125 g (5 oz)
finely chopped onion	25 g (1 oz)	60 g (2½ oz)
clove of crushed garlic	1	2–3
julienne of fennel	100 g (4 oz)	250 g (10 oz)
velouté, made with vegetable stock	250 ml (½ pt)	600 ml (1¼ pt)
English mustard	10 g (½ oz)	25 g (1¼ oz)
seasoning		
single cream or natural yoghurt	60 ml (⅛ pt)	150 ml (⅓ pt)
pine kernels	25 g (1 oz)	60 g (2½ oz)

With yoghurt
1 portion provides:

406 kcals/1 685 kJ
29.8 g fat
(of which 12.6 g saturated)
26 g carbohydrate
(of which 5.6 g sugars)
9.8 g protein
3.6 g fibre

1 Divide the brioche dough into portions and place into well-greased individual savarin moulds, prove and bake in a moderately hot oven at 200°C (400°F, Reg. 6) for approximately 10 minutes.
2 When cooked, remove from oven and unmould. Keep warm.
3 Blanch the spinach in boiling salted water, refresh and drain well. Squeeze lightly to remove excess water.
4 Add some butter or margarine to a sauté pan, or sauteuse, and sweat the chopped onion and garlic without colour.
5 Separately sweat the julienne of fennel in the remaining butter or margarine, without colour.
6 Add the leaf spinach to the chopped onion and garlic, and allow to reheat through.
7 Bind with the vegetable velouté, add the diluted mustard and season well.
8 Add the fennel and mix gently. Finish with single cream or natural yoghurt.
9 Place the brioches on suitable plates and fill with the spinach and fennel mixture.
10 Sprinkle with lightly roasted pine kernels and serve.

Note Many variations to this basic recipe may be adopted. Different combinations of cooked vegetables may be used to fill the brioche, e.g. mushrooms, chiffonade of lettuce, salsify in tomato sauce or ratatouille.

13 – Gratin of spinach, mushrooms, nuts and cheese

This dish is prepared in 3 layers: (a) spinach, (b) mushrooms, (c) cheese.

	4 portions	10 portions
Spinach		
leaf spinach, cooked and puréed	600 g (1½ lb)	2 kg (4 lb)
fresh double or non-dairy cream	3 tbsp	7 tbsp
grated Parmesan cheese	50 g (2 oz)	125 g (5 oz)
egg yolks	3	7
salt, pepper, grated nutmeg		
Mushroom		
sunflower margarine	50 g (2 oz)	125 g (5 oz)
button mushrooms	150 g (6 oz)	375 g (15 oz)
double or non-dairy cream	2 tbsp	5 tbsp
seasoning		
Cheese		
cottage cheese	150 g (6 oz)	375 g (15 oz)
ground cashew nuts	50 g (2 oz)	125 g (5 oz)
ground blanched almonds	50 g (2 oz)	125 g (5 oz)
chopped chives	25 g (1 oz)	60 g (2½ oz)
seasoning		
egg whites	4	10

1 Mix together the spinach, cream and half the Parmesan cheese, and add the egg yolks and seasoning.
2 Heat the sunflower margarine in a sauteuse, add the sliced mushrooms and sweat for 1–2 minutes. Stir in the cream, season.
3 Mix cottage cheese with nuts and chives – season.
4 Place one-third of the spinach in the bottom of 18 cm (7 in) well-greased soufflé dish(es).
5 Place the mushrooms on top, followed by a second spinach layer.
6 Next place on the cottage cheese and finally the rest of the spinach.
7 Bake in a preheated oven at 180°C (350°F, Reg. 4) for approximately 15 minutes and remove.
8 Beat the egg whites until full peak, season and carefully fold in remainder of the grated Parmesan cheese.
9 Using a forcing bag and 1 cm (⅜ in) star tube, pipe on top of the layered mixture and cook for a further 10 minutes at 200°C (400°F, Reg. 6), then serve immediately.

14 – Vegetable, bean and saffron risotto

	4 portions	10 portions
vegetable stock	185 ml ($\frac{3}{8}$ pt)	1 litre (2 pt)
saffron	5 g ($\frac{1}{4}$ oz)	12 g ($\frac{5}{8}$ oz)
sunflower margarine	50 g (2 oz)	125 g (5 oz)
chopped onion	25 g (1 oz)	60 g (2$\frac{1}{2}$ oz)
celery	50 g (2 oz)	125 g (5 oz)
short-grain rice	100 g (4 oz)	250 g (10 oz)
small cauliflower	1	2–3
sunflower oil	4 tbsp	10 tbsp
large aubergine	1	2–3
cooked haricot beans	100 g (4 oz)	250 g (10 oz)
cooked peas	50 g (2 oz)	125 g (5 oz)
cooked French beans	50 g (2 oz)	125 g (5 oz)
tomato sauce made with sunflower margarine and vegetable stock	250 ml ($\frac{1}{2}$ pt)	600 ml (1$\frac{1}{4}$ pt)
grated Parmesan cheese	25 g (1 oz)	60 g (2$\frac{1}{2}$ oz)

> 1 portion provides:
>
> 440 kcals/1831 kJ
> 29.7 g fat
> (of which 5.9 g saturated)
> 32.6 g carbohydrate
> (of which 6 g sugars)
> 10.8 g protein
> 5.3 g fibre

1 Infuse the vegetable stock with saffron for approximately 5 minutes by simmering gently, whilst maintaining the quantity of stock.
2 Melt the margarine, add the onion and celery and cook without colour for 2–3 minutes. Add the rice.
3 Cook for a further 2–3 minutes. Add the infused stock and season lightly. Cover with a lid and simmer on the side of the stove.
4 While rice is cooking prepare the rest of the vegetables. Cut the cauliflower into small florets, wash, blanch and refresh, quickly fry in the sunflower oil in a sauté pan. Add the aubergines cut into $\frac{1}{2}$ cm ($\frac{1}{4}$ in) dice and fry with the cauliflower. Add the cooked haricot beans, peas and French beans.
5 Stir all the vegetables together and bind with tomato sauce.
6 When the risotto is cooked, serve in a suitable dish, make a well in the centre. Fill the centre with the vegetables and haricot beans in tomato sauce.
7 Sprinkle the edge of the risotto with grated Parmesan cheese to serve.

Note This dish is suitable for vegans if the Parmesan cheese is omitted.

I 15 – Spinach, riccotta and artichoke filo bake with cranberries

(Gary Thompson)

	4 portions	10 portions
spinach	400 g (1 lb)	1 kg (2½ lb)
riccotta	500 g (1¼ lb)	1¼ kg (3 lb)
tinned artichokes, drained	200 g (8 oz)	500 g (1¼ lb)
filo pastry	275 g (11 oz)	700 g (1¾ lb)
frozen cranberries	500 g (1¼ lb)	1¼ kg (3 lb)
butter	25 g (1 oz)	60 g (2½ oz)
olive oil	1 tbsp	2–3 tbsp
onion, sliced	100 g (4 oz)	250 g (10 oz)
salt, freshly ground black pepper		
chopped fresh parsley to taste		

> 1 portion provides:
>
> 499 kcals/2091 kJ
> 23.7 g fat
> (of which 12.4 g saturated)
> 51.0 g carbohydrate
> (of which 8.2 g sugars)
> 21.8 g protein
> 5.5 g fibre

1 Cook, refresh and drain the spinach, then chop finely.
2 Break down the riccotta and mix with the spinach.
3 Sauté the onion in the olive oil without colour. Add to the riccotta and spinach with the chopped parsley. Season to taste.
4 Line a lightly buttered flan dish with 3 layers of filo pastry, leaving overhang.
5 Fill with spinach mixture and press drained artichokes evenly around the dish.
6 Top with cranberries.
7 Gather in the overhanging filo pastry, adding more layers to cover centre.
8 Russe up pastry, brush with butter and bake at 180°C (350°F, Reg. 4) for 35 minutes approximately.

V 16 – Spaghetti with lentil bolognese

	4 portions	10 portions
wholemeal spaghetti	300 g (12 oz)	1 kg (2 lb)
brown lentils	150 g (6 oz)	375 g (15 oz)
sunflower oil	4 tbsp	10 tbsp
finely chopped onion	50 g (2 oz)	125 g (5 oz)
clove garlic, chopped	1	2–3
diced mushrooms	300 g (12 oz)	1 kg (2 lb)

dried mixed herbs	5 g ($\frac{1}{4}$ oz)	12 g ($\frac{5}{8}$ oz)
tomatoes, skinned, deseeded and diced	400 g (1 lb)	1$\frac{1}{4}$ kg (2$\frac{1}{2}$ lb)
tomato purée	25 g (1 oz)	60 g (2$\frac{1}{2}$ oz)
vegetable stock	125 ml ($\frac{1}{4}$ pt)	300 ml ($\frac{5}{8}$ pt)
yeast extract	10 g ($\frac{1}{2}$ oz)	25 g (1$\frac{1}{4}$ oz)
sunflower margarine	25 g (1 oz)	60 g (2$\frac{1}{2}$ oz)
seasoning		
grated Parmesan cheese	50 g (2 oz)	125 g (5 oz)

1 Cook the spaghetti in boiling salted water, stirring occasionally, until *al dente*, refresh and drain.
2 Place the lentils in a saucepan of cold water, bring to the boil, skim and simmer until tender. Drain.
3 Heat the oil and sweat the onion and garlic until soft, for 4–5 minutes.
4 Add the diced mushrooms and mixed herbs, cook for 5 minutes.
5 Add the lentils, tomatoes and tomato purée.
6 Add vegetable stock, stir well and add yeast extract. The consistecy of the sauce should be thick.
7 Reheat the spaghetti in sunflower margarine, season with salt, pepper and nutmeg.
8 Serve the spaghetti in a suitable dish, make a well in the centre and place in the bolognese sauce. Sprinkle with grated Parmesan cheese.

Note This dish is suitable for vegans if the Parmesan cheese is omitted.

17 – Tofu and vegetable flan with walnut sauce

	4 portions	10 portions
shortcrust pastry	150 g (6 oz)	375 g (15 oz)
sunflower oil	4 tbsp	10 tbsp
carrots, diced	50 g (2 oz)	125 g (5 oz)
sliced mushrooms	50 g (2 oz)	125 g (5 oz)
celery, diced	50 g (2 oz)	125 g (5 oz)
broccoli florets, blanched and refreshed	100 g (4 oz)	250 g (10 oz)
fresh chopped basil	3 g ($\frac{1}{8}$ oz)	7$\frac{1}{2}$ g ($\frac{1}{3}$ oz)
chopped dill weed	3 g ($\frac{1}{8}$ oz)	7$\frac{1}{2}$ g ($\frac{1}{3}$ oz)
skimmed milk	125 ml ($\frac{1}{4}$ pt)	300 ml ($\frac{5}{8}$ oz)
egg	1	2–3
tofu	200 g (8 oz)	500 g (1$\frac{1}{4}$ lb)
seasoning		

I portion provides:

568 kcals/2359 kJ
45.8 g fat
(of which 9.3 g is saturated)
25.8 g carbohydrate
(of which 5.6 g sugars)
15 g protein
2.5 g fibre

1 Line 18 cm (7 in) flan ring(s) with shortcrust pastry and bake blind for approximately 8 minutes in a preheated oven at 180°C (350°F, Reg. 4).
2 Heat the sunflower oil in a sauté-pan, add the carrots, mushrooms and celery, gently cook for 5 minutes without colouring.
3 Add the broccoli, cover and cook gently until just crisp, stirring frequently and adding a little water if the mixture begins to dry.
4 Sprinkle over the herbs. Cook for 1 minute. Drain vegetables and allow to cool.
5 Warm the milk to blood heat. Whisk the egg and tofu in a basin, add seasoning then gradually incorporate milk. Whisk well.
6 Fill the flan case with the drained vegetables and add the tofu and milk mixture.
7 Bake for 20 minutes approximately at 180°C (350°F, Reg. 4). Serve with walnut sauce.

— Walnut sauce

	4 portions	10 portions
finely chopped onion	100 g (4 oz)	250 g (10 oz)
clove garlic, chopped	1	2–3
walnut oil	50 g (2 oz)	125 g (5 oz)
brown sugar	10 g ($\frac{1}{2}$ oz)	25 g (1 oz)
curry powder	25 g (1 oz)	60 g (2$\frac{1}{2}$ oz)
lemon, grated zest and juice	1	2–3
peanut butter	25 g (1 oz)	60 g (2$\frac{1}{2}$ oz)
soy sauce	1 tsp	2–3 tsp
tomato purée	25 g (1 oz)	60 g (2$\frac{1}{2}$ oz)
vegetable stock	375 ml ($\frac{3}{4}$ pt)	900 ml (1$\frac{3}{4}$ pt)
seasoning		
very finely chopped walnuts	100 g (4 oz)	250 g (10 oz)
arrowroot	10 g ($\frac{1}{2}$ oz)	25 g (1 oz)

1 Fry the onion and garlic in the walnut oil, add the sugar and cook to a golden brown colour.
2 Add the curry powder, cook for 2 minutes.
3 Add zest and juice of lemon, peanut butter, soy sauce and tomato purée. Mix well.
4 Add vegetable stock, bring to boil, simmer for 2 minutes, season.
5 Add chopped walnuts.
6 Dilute arrowroot with a little water and gradually stir into sauce. Bring back to the boil stirring continuously. Simmer for 5 minutes.
7 Correct seasoning and consistency.

V **18 — Oriental vegetable kebabs with herb sauce**

	4 portions	10 portions
small cauliflower	1	2–3
red pepper	1	2–3
green pepper	1	2–3
button mushrooms	100 g (4 oz)	250 g (10 oz)
small courgettes	4	10
small tomatoes (very firm)	4	10
sticks celery	2	5
large aubergine	1	2–3
large leek	1	2–3
Marinade		
sunflower oil	125 ml ($\frac{1}{4}$ pt)	300 ml ($\frac{5}{8}$ pt)
red wine	250 ml ($\frac{1}{2}$ pt)	600 ml ($1\frac{1}{4}$ pt)
dried mixed herbs	5 g ($\frac{1}{4}$ oz)	12 g ($\frac{5}{8}$ oz)
bay leaves	4–8	10–16
seasoning		

1 Prepare the vegetables as follows: cut cauliflower into small florets; wash peppers, remove seeds and cut into $1\frac{1}{2}$–2 cm ($\frac{3}{4}$–1 in) dice; wash button mushrooms, trim stalks; wash courgettes and cut into $1\frac{1}{2}$–2 cm ($\frac{3}{4}$–1 in) sections; blanch and peel tomatoes; cut into quarters; trim and wash celery, cut into $1\frac{1}{2}$–2 cm ($\frac{3}{4}$–1 in); wash aubergine, cut in half then into 2×1 cm ($1 \times \frac{1}{2}$ in) batons; split leeks, wash, cut into 2 cm (1 in) lengths.
2 Marinade the vegetables in the sunflower oil, red wine and dried herbs, seasoning and bay leaves for approximately 2 hours. Turn occasionally.
3 Neatly arrange vegetables on skewers.
4 Place on a greased tray, brush with oil and grill under salamander for approximately 10–15 minutes turning occassionally.
5 The vegetables will have different textures, they should, however, be slightly firm. The cauliflower, courgettes, and leek may also be blanched and refreshed before marinading to achieve different textures.
6 Serve kebabs on a bed of pilaff rice garnished with cooked peas.
7 Separately serve a sauceboat of herb sauce made from the marinade (see overleaf).

– Herb sauce

	4 portions	10 portions
marinade (from kebabs)	375 ml ($\frac{3}{4}$ pt)	1 litre (2 pt)
vegetable stock	125 ml ($\frac{1}{4}$ pt)	500 ml ($\frac{5}{8}$ pt)
yeast extract	10 g ($\frac{1}{2}$ oz)	25 g ($1\frac{1}{4}$ oz)
tomato purée	50 g (2 oz)	125 g (5 oz)
finely chopped onion	50 g (2 oz)	125 g (5 oz)
clove garlic, chopped	1	2–3
sunflower margarine	10 g ($\frac{1}{2}$ oz)	25 g ($1\frac{1}{4}$ oz)
sunflower margarine	10 g ($\frac{1}{2}$ oz)	25 g ($1\frac{1}{4}$ oz)
arrowroot	10 g ($\frac{1}{2}$ oz)	25 g ($1\frac{1}{4}$ oz)
seasoning		

1 Place marinade, vegetable stock, yeast extract and tomato purée into a suitable saucepan and bring to boil.
2 Sweat the onion and garlic in the margarine for 2–3 minutes without colour.
3 Add the marinade and stock liquid from stage 1. Bring to boil.
4 Dilute the arrowroot in a little cold water.
5 Stir the arrowroot into the liquid and bring back to boil, stirring continuously. Simmer for 2 minutes, correct consistency. Season, strain and use as above.

19 – Lentil and mushroom burgers with groundnut and sesame sauce

	4 portions	10 portions
lentils	200 g (8 oz)	500 g ($1\frac{1}{4}$ lb)
finely chopped onion	50 g (2 oz)	125 g (5 oz)
cloves of garlic, chopped	2	5
sunflower margarine	25 g (1 oz)	60 g ($2\frac{1}{2}$ oz)
finely chopped mushrooms	400 g (1 lb)	1 kg ($2\frac{1}{2}$ lb)
wholemeal breadcrumbs	75 g (3 oz)	180 g ($7\frac{1}{2}$ oz)
chopped parsley		
egg	1	2–3
seasoned flour for coating		
oil for shallow frying		

> Without sauce
> I portion provides:
>
> 361 kcals/1515kJ
> 18.3 g fat
> (of which 2.9 g saturated)
> 33.8 g carbohydrate
> (of which 1.9 g sugars)
> 17.7 g protein
> 6.9 g fibre

1 Place the lentils in a saucepan of cold water. Bring to boil and simmer until cooked.

2 Sweat the onion and garlic in the margarine until soft. Add mushrooms.

3 Cook over a moderate heat for approximately 15–20 minutes until all the liquid has been evaporated and the mushrooms are in a thick purée.

4 Allow to cool and mix in the drained, cooked lentils.

5 Add breadcrumbs and parsley, bind with beaten egg and mix well.

6 If the mixture is too slack bind with a little more breadcrumbs. If too dry, add a little more beaten egg.

7 Mould into burgers on a floured board.

8 Pass through seasoned flour and quickly fry in a little hot oil, taking care that the burgers do not break up.

9 Alternatively, place on a lightly greased baking sheet, brush with oil and bake in a preheated oven at 180°C (350°F, Reg. 4) for approximately 20 minutes, turning them over half way during cooking.

10 When cooked serve on individual plates on a bed of groundnut and sesame sauce (see below).

– *Groundnut and sesame sauce*

	4 portions	10 portions
raisins	100 g (4 oz)	250 g (10 oz)
tahini (sesame seed paste)	2 tbsp	5 tbsp
peanut butter	100 g (4 oz)	250 g (10 oz)
sesame oil	2 tbsp	5 tbsp
red wine vinegar	2 tbsp	5 tbsp
concentrated apple juice	4 tbsp	10 tbsp
pinch of ground cinnamon		
water	375 ml ($\frac{3}{4}$ pt)	1 litre (2 pt)
seasoning		

1 Place the raisins in a saucepan of cold water. Bring to the boil. Refresh and drain.

2 Liquidise all ingredients together until a smooth sauce is obtained.

3 Correct seasoning and consistency. Pass through a coarse strainer and use as required.

I 20 – Vegetable olives

(GARY THOMPSON, NEIL YULE)

	4 portions	10 portions
crêpes	8 × 15 cm	20 × 15 cm
basil leaves, bunch		
mushrooms	100 g (4 oz)	250 g (10 oz)
carrots	100 g (4 oz)	250 g (10 oz)
onions	100 g (4 oz)	250 g (10 oz)
leeks	100 g (4 oz)	250 g (10 oz)
capsicums	100 g (4 oz)	250 g (10 oz)
aubergine	100 g (4 oz)	250 g (10 oz)
mozzarella cheese	150 g (6 oz)	375 g (1 lb)
béchamel	250 ml ($\frac{1}{2}$ pt)	600 g (1$\frac{1}{4}$ pt)
tomato sauce	1.2 litre (2 pt)	3 litre (5 pt)
seasoning		

> 1 portion provides:
>
> 554 kcals/2321 kJ
> 29.5 g fat
> (of which 10.2 g saturated)
> 48.4 g carbohydrate
> (of which 24.3 g sugars)
> 26.7 g protein
> 6.7 g fibre

1 Cut the vegetables into a paysanne and sweat.
2 Place a basil leaf on a crêpe, add the vegetable mixture and roll up.
3 Place in an earthenware dish on a little tomato sauce.
4 Cover completely with the remaining tomato sauce, cover with foil and bake to heat thoroughly at 150°C (300°F, Reg. 2) for approximately 15 minutes.
5 Remove from the oven, remove the foil, coat the centre with a little béchamel, top with cheese and grill.
6 Sprinkle with chopped basil and serve with Italian garlic bread or French bread.

I 21 – Baby aubergine soufflé with salsa sauce

(MARK HANCOCK)

	4 portions	10 portions
baby aubergines	4	10
finely chopped onions	50 g (2 oz)	125 g (5 oz)
garlic cloves	1	2
Parmesan cheese	50 g (2 oz)	125 g (5 oz)
butter	25 g (1 oz)	65 g (2$\frac{1}{2}$ oz)
flour	15 g ($\frac{3}{4}$ oz)	50 g (2 oz)
double cream	125 ml ($\frac{1}{4}$ pt)	250 ml ($\frac{1}{2}$ pt)
egg yolks	3	8

1 Cut the aubergines in half lengthways and remove the inside. Finely chop the flesh and keep the shells of aubergines.
2 Fry the onion, garlic and aubergine in oil till golden brown and cool.
3 Melt the butter in a pan and add flour, cook out slightly. Add the double cream and mix to a smooth mixture, simmer gently.
4 Add the egg yolks and season, add cheese.
5 Whisk the egg whites with a pinch of salt until stiff.
6 Gently fold in the egg whites slightly mixing.
7 Place into the seasoned aubergine shells and bake in oven 220°C (428°F) for 5–10 minutes till golden brown.

~ *Salsa sauce*

	4 portions	10 portions
plum tomatoes	200 g (8 oz)	450 g (16 oz)
coriander	25 g (1 oz)	50 g (2 oz)
onions	100 g (4 oz)	125 g (5 oz)
garlic cloves	2	4
fresh chillies	10 g ($\frac{1}{2}$ oz)	25 g (1 oz)
oil	50 ml ($\frac{1}{8}$ pt)	100 ml ($\frac{1}{4}$ pt)
fresh parsley		

1 Finely chop the onions, chillies and garlic. Sweat down in oil without colour.
2 Add the chopped plum tomatoes and cook gently.
3 Add the chopped fresh coriander.
4 Season to taste and garnish with a parsley sprig.

I 22 ~ **Caraway and carrot rösti roulade with ginger filling**

(MARK HANCOCK)

	4 portions	10 portions
grated potato	300 g (12 oz)	800 g (2 lb)
caraway seeds	12 g ($\frac{1}{2}$ oz)	25 g (1 oz)
grated carrots	150 g (6 oz)	400 g (1 lb)
fresh ginger	10 g ($\frac{1}{2}$ oz)	35 g (1$\frac{1}{2}$ oz)
cream cheese	300 g (12 oz)	800 g (2 lb)
leaf salad		
salt and pepper		

1 Mix the grated potatoes and caraway seeds together and season.
2 Heat the oil in a small frying pan. Add the mixture and spread thick and evenly over the pan. Fry till golden brown then turn over and cook the other side.
3 Remove from the pan when cooked and place on absorbent paper to remove excess oil. Allow to cool.
4 Mix the cream cheese and grated carrots. Add finely chopped fresh ginger. Season to taste.
5 Spread the carrot mixture evenly over the rösti and roll into a roulade.
6 Reheat the rösti through oven when at the correct temperature, carve into slices. Place on a plate and garnish with leaf salad.

I 23 – Savoury bread and butter pudding with tomato and basil sauce

(IAN PERKINS)

	4 portions	10 portions
garlic clove	1	2
mushrooms	100 g (4 oz)	250 g (10 oz)
large onions	1	2½
wholemeal bread	8 slices	20 slices
softened butter	100 g (4 oz)	250 g (10 oz)
Cheddar cheese (grated)	150 g (6 oz)	375 g (15 oz)
eggs	2	5
milk	250 ml (½ pt)	625 ml (1¼ pt)
seasoning		
tomato sauce with basil	250 ml (½ pt)	625 ml (1¼ pt)

1 Sweat the mushrooms and onions, add crushed garlic.
2 Spread butter on to bread, trim crusts and cut to size.
3 Lay bread on the base of an ovenproof dish, cover with a layer of mushrooms and onions, then a layer of cheese, repeat again. Top this with a layer of bread, finish with remaining cheese.
4 Make up custard using eggs and milk, season well. Pour into dish.
5 Bake for approximately 40 minutes in a bain-marie at 160°C (moderate oven).
6 Portion and serve with a tomato sauce flavoured with basil.

I V 24 ~ Baked babagnough and aubergine charlotte

(MARK McCANN)

	4 portions	10 portions
medium aubergines	2	5
chillies	2	5
chopped coriander	¼ bunch	1½ bunches
lime, juice and zest	1	2
onion, halved and peeled	1	2 large
cloves garlic	6	15
olive oil	2 tsp	5 tsp
sea salt	½ tsp	1¼ tsp
ground black pepper	1 pinch	2 pinch
butter	12 g (½ oz)	30 g (1¼ oz)

1 Remove skin from aubergine lengthways, leaving ½ cm of flesh on the skin.
2 Boil in boiling salt water till soft and then refresh in cold water.
3 Place the aubergine on a baking tray with the chillies, onion and garlic.
4 Season well with salt and spoon over the olive oil.
5 Bake in a hot oven at 160°C for approximately 15 minutes, or until a deep golden brown.
6 Remove from the oven and allow to cool.
7 When cold, finely dice the aubergine, garlic, onion and chilli.
8 Add the zest and juice of the lime and chopped coriander.
9 Correct the seasoning to taste.
10 Grease 4 ramekin moulds with melted butter and line the moulds with the aubergine skins ensuring that you overlap the edges.
11 Fill the ramekins with the aubergine mix and fold over the overlapping skins to the centre.
12 Bake in a moderate oven at 140°C for 8–10 minutes.
13 Take the dish out of the oven, turn out on to a plate and serve.

Suggested Sauces
Serve a fresh tomato coulis or make a sauce from a purée of cooked lentils, thinned with a little roasted pepper oil and vegetable stock, and garnished with a fine dice of sautéed red peppers.

VEGETABLE DISHES

Prepare, cook and finish complex vegetable dishes

1   Select the type, quantity and quality of vegetables in accordance with recipe specifications.
2   Identify that the products not for immediate consumption are stored in accordance with recipe specification and current legislation.
3   Demonstrate that the nutritional value of the vegetables is adequately retained during the preparation and cooking.
4   Demonstrate that the cooking, regeneration and finished dishes must fully meet the recipe specification.

—— Vegetables ——

As people are becoming more conscious of healthy eating, the serving of a variety of correctly cooked, colourful, attractively presented vegetables becomes increasingly important.

This can be achieved in a variety of ways: a small selection of vegetables served on a separate plate to the main course is popular when appropriate, as is the practice of placing dishes of vegetables on the table for customers to help themselves. There are also people who would welcome a small selection of vegetables served as a separate course.

As fast world-wide transport is now the norm, the more exotic vegetables – which were previously unknown – are now available and caterers should learn how to prepare, cook and serve them.

However, these should not replace but, rather, supplement freshly picked and cooked local produce, which will always be popular if correctly cooked, of good colour and attractively presented.

RECIPES

1 – Artichokes with spinach and cheese sauce

Prepared and cooked artichoke bottoms are filled with leaf spinach, coated with Mornay sauce, browned and served.

Variations   Other vegetables that can be substituted for spinach include asparagus points, cooked peas, and a mixture of peas and carrots; also, a duxelle-based stuffing with various additions, which may be finished either with Mornay sauce or au gratin.

2 – Sautéed artichoke bottoms

1 Remove the leaves and chokes from the artichokes.
2 Trim the bottoms and cut into slices.
3 Cook in a blanc, drain well then sauté in butter, margarine or oil until lightly browned.
4 Season lightly and serve sprinkled with chopped parsley.

Note   Alternatively the artichoke bottoms may be fried from raw, but they must first be rubbed with lemon to prevent discoloration.

3 – Aubergine soufflé

	4 portions	10 portions
egg plants (aubergines)	2	5
thick béchamel	250 ml ($\frac{1}{2}$ pt)	600 ml ($1\frac{1}{4}$ pt)
grated Parmesan cheese	50 g (2 oz)	125 g (5 oz)
eggs, separated	3	7
salt and pepper		

> I portion provides:
>
> 278 kcals/1160 kJ
> 18.5 g fat
> (of which 9.9 g saturated)
> 13.9 g carbohydrate
> (of which 7.7 g sugars)
> 15.2 g protein
> 4 g fibre

1 Cut egg plants in halves.
2 Slash the flesh criss-cross and deep fry for a few minutes.
3 Drain well, scoop out the flesh and finely chop.
4 Lay the skins in a buttered gratin dish.
5 Mix the egg plant flesh with an equal quantity of béchamel.
6 Heat this mixture through, then mix in the cheese and yolks, and season.

7 Fold in the stiffly beaten whites.
8 Fill the skins with this mixture, bake at 230°C (450°F, Reg. 8) for
   approximately 15 minutes and serve immediately.

Note   For extra lightness use 4 egg whites to 3 yolks (10 egg whites to 7
yolks for 10 portions).

4 – Baby sweetcorn

These are cobs of corn which are harvested when very young. They are
widely used in oriental cookery and are available from December to
March.

Always select cobs that look fresh and are undamaged. Baby corns are
removed from their protective husks, cooked for a few minutes in
unsalted water and may then be served whole or cut in slices and coated
with butter or margarine. Unlike fully grown sweetcorn, baby corn are
not removed from the cob before eating – when cooked the vegetable is
tender enough to eat whole.

Baby sweetcorns are used in stir-fry dishes, e.g. with chicken, crab or
prawns, and may also be served cold with vinaigrette. Baby corn looks
attractive when served as one of a selection of plated vegetables.

5 – Bamboo shoots

These are the shoots of young edible bamboo, stripped of the tough
outer brown skin, so that the insides are eaten. They have a texture
similar to celery and a flavour rather like that of globe artichokes. They
are also obtainable preserved in brine.

Methods of cooking: chopped bamboo shoots are used in a number of
stir-fry dishes, meat and poultry casseroles and as a soup garnish. They
can also be served hot with a hollandaise-type sauce or beurre blanc.

6 – Bean sprouts

These are the tender young sprouts of the germinating soya or mung
bean. As they are a highly perishable vegetable, it is best to select white,
plump, crisp sprouts with a fresh appearance.

Methods of cooking: first, rinse well and drain, they may then be stir-fried and served as a vegetable, mixed in with other ingredients in stir-fry dishes, used in omelets and also served as a crisp salad item.

Bean sprouts are available all year round. It is essential that they are very thoroughly washed before being cooked.

7 – Stir-fried bean sprouts

	4 portions	10 portions
bean sprouts	400 g (1 lb)	$1\frac{1}{4}$ kg ($2\frac{1}{2}$ lb)
oil	1 tbsp	$2\frac{1}{2}$ tbsp
spring onions	4–6	10–18
chopped ginger	1 tsp	2–3 tsp
soy sauce	2 tsp	5 tsp
salt		

1 Wash, dry and trim the bean sprouts.
2 Heat the oil in a frying pan or wok and add the spring onions (cut in 2 cm (1 in) pieces) and ginger.
3 Fry for a few seconds, then add the sprouts.
4 Stir continuously and add salt.
5 Keeping the sprouts crisp, add soy sauce and serve.

8 – Bean sprout sauté

	4 portions	10 portions
sunflower oil or butter or margarine	1 tbsp	2–3 tbsp
bean sprouts	125 g (4 oz)	250 g (10 oz)
salt and pepper		
carrots	125 g (4 oz)	250 g (10 oz)
courgettes	125 g (4 oz)	250 g (10 oz)
spring onions	2	5

1 Begin by preparing the vegetable. Wash, dry and trim the bean sprouts. Cut the carrots, courgettes and onions in coarse julienne.
2 Heat the oil or butter in a frying pan, add the bean sprouts and sauté for 1 minute.
3 Season, add the carrots and spring onions, and sauté for 1 minute.
4 Add the courgettes, sauté for 1 minute, correct seasoning and serve.

9 – Broad beans with tomato and coriander

	4 portions	10 portions
shelled broad beans	300 g (12 oz)	1 kg (2 lb)
oil or butter	1 tbsp	2½ tbsp
tomatoes, skinned, deseeded and diced	2	5
salt and pepper		
freshly chopped coriander	1 tbsp	2½ tbsp

1 Cook the broad beans, keeping them slightly firm, and drain.
2 Heat the oil in a pan and add the tomatoes.
3 Add the broad beans and correct the seasoning.
4 Add the coriander and toss lightly to mix. Correct seasoning and serve.

10 – Braised red cabbage with apples, red wine and juniper

	4 portions	10 portions
red cabbage, shredded	400 g (1 lb)	1¼ kg (2½ lb)
oil	2 tbsp	5 tbsp
cooking apples, peeled, cored and diced	200 g (8 oz)	500 g (1¼ lb)
red wine	250 ml (½ pt)	600 ml (1¼ pt)
salt and pepper		
juniper berries (optional)	12	30

1 Blanch and refresh the cabbage.
2 Heat the oil in a casserole, add the cabbage and apples, and stir.
3 Add the wine, seasoning and juniper berries.
4 Bring to the boil, cover and braise for approximately 40–45 minutes until tender.
5 If any liquid remains when cooked, continue cooking uncovered to evaporate the liquid.

11 – Braised red cabbage with chestnuts

	4 portions	10 portions
red cabbage, shredded	400 g (1 lb)	1¼ kg (2½ lb)
good beef stock	250 g (10 oz)	600 g (1½ lb)
shelled raw chestnut pieces	200 g (8 oz)	500 g (1¼ lb)
oil or pork dripping	2 tbsp	5 tbsp
salt and pepper		

<table>
<tr><td>Oil used not dripping
1 portion provides:

168 kcals/709 kJ
8.2 g fat
(of which 1 g saturated)
22.4 g carbohydrate
(of which 7.5 g sugars)
2.7 g protein
4.5 g fibre</td></tr>
</table>

1 Mix all the ingredients, cover with buttered paper and a tight-fitting lid.
2 Braise in a covered pan (not aluminium or iron) until tender.

12 – Cardoons

These are a long plant, similar to celery, with an aroma and flavour like that of the globe artichoke. Select cardoons with bright leaves, crisp stems and a fresh-looking appearance.

Method of cooking: remove leaves, stalks and tough parts and cut into small pieces; cook in acidulated water for approximately 30–40 minutes.

Cardoons may be used as a plain vegetable, in other vegetable dishes or served raw as an appetiser.

13 – Cardoons with onions and cheese

	4 portions	10 portions
cardoons	400 g (1 lb)	1¼ kg (2½ lb)
lemon, juice of	1	2–3
finely sliced onion	100 g (4 oz)	250 g (10 oz)
butter	25 g (1 oz)	60 g (2½ oz)
salt		
grated Parmesan	50 g (2 oz)	125 g (5 oz)

1 Trim and wash the cardoons, rub with lemon juice and cut into 8 cm (3 in) pieces.
2 Cook in salted lemon water for approximately 30 minutes, drain.
3 Gently cook the onion in the butter until light brown.

4 Add the cardoons and a little of the cooking liquid and simmer gently until tender.

5 Correct seasoning and serve sprinkled with cheese.

14 – Cardoon fritters

	4 portions	10 portions
cardoons	400 g (1 lb)	1¼ kg (2½ lb)
Marinade		
lemon, juice of	1	2–3
chopped onion	100 g (4 oz)	250 g (10 oz)
vegetable oil	60 ml (⅛ pt)	150 ml (⅓ pt)
chopped parsley	1 tbsp	2–3 tbsp
salt		
frying batter		

1 Prepare and cook cardoons as in recipe 13, stages 1–2.
2 Drain well and place while hot in the marinade for 1 hour.
3 Drain and dry the cardoon pieces thoroughly.
4 Dip in the batter and deep fry at 185°C (360°F) until golden brown.
5 Serve with quarters of lemon.

15 – Celery moulds

	4 portions	10 portions
head celery, braised	1	2–3
dry celery purée (cooked)	200 g (8 oz)	500 g (1¼ lb)
thick béchamel	60 ml (⅛ pt)	150 ml (⅓ pt)
egg yolks	2	5
salt and pepper		
jus-lié, to serve		

1 Butter dariole moulds and line with strips of braised celery.
2 Thoroughly heat the celery purée, mix in béchamel and egg yolks, and correct seasoning. Use to fill the prepared moulds.
3 Poach in a bain-marie in a moderate oven (200°C, 400°F, Reg. 6) for approximately 1 hour, covered with buttered greaseproof paper or foil.

4 When cooked, allow to stand for a few minutes before turning out.

5 Serve with a cordon of jus-lié.

16 – Mousse of vegetables

Almost any vegetables can be made into a mousse if required (see page 72). A vegetable mousse with a suitable sauce can be offered as a first or main course, e.g. carrot and ginger mousse served with spicy tomato, asparagus or broccoli sauce.

17 – Vegetable royals

These are prepared and cooked in buttered moulds such as darioles. When thoroughly cold they can be cut into shapes and used as garnish for soups. They can also be served whole hot or cold as a first course accompaniment by a suitable sauce or salad or as a garnish to many main course dishes of meat, poultry or game.

18 – Carrot royal

	4 portions	10 portions
carrot, peeled and sliced	200 g ($\frac{1}{2}$ lb)	500 g ($1\frac{1}{4}$ lb)
butter	25 g (1 oz)	60 g ($2\frac{1}{2}$ oz)
béchamel	30 ml ($\frac{1}{16}$ pt)	75 ml ($\frac{3}{16}$ pt)
cream	125 ml ($\frac{1}{4}$ pt)	300 ml ($\frac{5}{8}$ pt)
eggs beaten	3	7
salt and pepper		

1 Gently cook the carrot in the butter in a covered pan without colouring.

2 Mix in the cold béchamel, cream, season, liquidise and pass through a fine sieve.

3 Strain on the beaten eggs, place in buttered dariole moulds and slowly cook in a bain-marie in a moderate oven until set.

Note Many other vegetables can be made into royals, e.g. celery, asparagus, leek, green pea and mushroom.

19 – Chinese cabbage

A wide variety of Chinese cabbage – or Chinese leaves – is grown in China, but the one generally seen in Britain is similar in appearance to a large pale cos lettuce. It is crisp and delicate, with a faint cabbage flavour.

Always select fresh looking, crisp cabbage.

Method of cooking: the hard centre stems are removed from outer leaves and they can then be stir-fried, braised, boiled or steamed like cabbage. The inner leaves can be used for salads in place of lettuce.

20 – Stir-fried Chinese cabbage

	4 portions	10 portions
oil	25 g (1 oz)	50 g (2½ oz)
Chinese leaves	600 g (1½ lb)	2 kg (4 lb)
soy sauce, optional	25 g (1 oz)	60 g (2½ oz)
salt		
chicken stock or water	30 ml ($\frac{1}{16}$ pt)	75 ml ($\frac{1}{4}$ pt)

1 Heat the oil in a frying pan or wok, add the roughly chopped leaves and stir-fry for 3–4 minutes.
2 Add the remainder of the ingredients and stir-fry until the leaves are cooked but still slightly crisp.

21 – Spicy stir-fry Chinese cabbage

	4 portions	10 portions
oil	25 g (1 oz)	60 g (2½ oz)
finely chopped ginger	25 g (1 oz)	60 g (2½ oz)
cloves garlic, finely chopped	2	5
curry powder	5 g ($\frac{1}{4}$ oz)	12 g ($\frac{5}{8}$ oz)
soy sauce	25 g (1 oz)	60 g (2½ oz)
sugar	10 g ($\frac{1}{2}$ oz)	60 g (2½ oz)
stock or water	2 tbsp	5 tbsp
Chinese cabbage, chopped	600 g (1½ lb)	2 kg (4 lb)

1 Heat the oil in a frying pan or wok, add ginger, garlic and curry powder, and toss for a few seconds.
2 Add soy sauce, sugar and stock, and bring to the boil.
3 Add the cabbage and boil for 5 minutes, stirring occasionally, and serve at once.

22 – Christophine

Christophine, also known as chow-chow, chayotte, or vegetable pear, looks rather like a ridged green pear and is available in several varieties including white and green, spiny and smooth-skinned, rounded and ridged, or more or less pear-shaped. Christophines usually weigh between 150–250 g (6–8 oz), the inside flesh is firm and white with a flavour and texture resembling a combination of marrow and cucumber.

Christophines are peeled and the stones removed in preparation and they can be cooked in similar ways to courgettes. They are also suitable for being stuffed and braised.

23 – Colcannon

This is an Irish dish for which there are many variations.

	4 portions	10 portions	
cabbage	300 g (12 oz)	1 kg (2 lb)	Using milk 1 portion provides:
peeled potatoes	200 g (8 oz)	500 g (1¼ lb)	
leeks	100 g (4 oz)	250 g (10 oz)	150 kcals/625 kJ
milk or single cream	250 ml (½ pt)	600 ml (1¼ pt)	8.1 g fat
salt, pepper and nutmeg			(of which 5 g saturated) 15.4 g carbohydrate
butter	25 g (1 oz)	60 g (2½ oz)	(of which 6.9 g sugars) 4.8 g protein 3 g fibre

1 Shred the cabbage, cook and drain well.
2 Cook and mash the potatoes.
3 Chop the leeks and simmer in the milk until tender.
4 Mix the leeks in with the potatoes, cabbage and seasoning.
5 Place in a serving dish, make a well in the centre, pour in the melted butter and serve.

24 – Fennel gratinated

		4 portions	10 portions
fennel bulbs		2	5
Mornay sauce		500 ml (1 pt)	1¼ litres (2½ pt)
chopped mushrooms		100 g (4 oz)	250 g (10 oz)
chopped shallot	duxelle	25 g (1 oz)	60 g (2⅓ oz)
butter or oil		25 g (1 oz)	60 g (2⅓ oz)
grated cheese		50 g (2 oz)	125 g (5 oz)
fresh breadcrumbs		25 g (1 oz)	60 g (2⅓ oz)
melted butter		50 g (2 oz)	125 g 5 oz)

> 1 portion provides:
>
> 564 kcals/2340 kJ
> 46.4 g fat
> (of which 25.8 g saturated)
> 20.5 g carbohydrate
> (of which 7.9 g sugars)
> 17.5 g protein
> 2.3 g fibre

1 Boil or steam the fennel until tender, approximately 30–35 minutes.
2 Drain, cut into 5 cm (2 in) pieces.
3 Mix the Mornay sauce with duxelle and place half in an ovenproof dish.
4 Add the fennel and cover with remainder of the sauce.
5 Sprinkle with cheese, crumbs and melted butter.
6 Heat through and brown in a moderate oven.

T 25 – Fennel casserole

(ROBERT JONES)

	4 portions	10 portions
fennel	450 g (1 lb)	1¼ kg (2½ lb)
olive oil	2 tbsp	5 tbsp
finely diced onion	200 g (8 oz)	500 g (1¼ lb)
cloves garlic, crushed	2	5
tomato concassée	400 g (1 lb)	1¼ kg (2½ lb)
salt		
freshly ground black pepper		
wholemeal breadcrumbs	50 g (2 oz)	125 g (5 oz)
grated Cheddar cheese	50 g (2 oz)	125 g (5 oz)

1 Prepare the fennel by removing the outer leaves and trimming the root base. Slice the bulbs thinly, reserving the green ends for decoration.
2 Heat the oil and gently fry the chopped onions and garlic in a frying pan without colour for a few minutes.
3 Add the slices of fennel and cook for a few minutes.

4 Add the tomatoes, season well, cover the pan and slowly cook for about 15 minutes.
5 Transfer the mixture to an ovenproof dish, mix the breadcrumbs and cheese together and sprinkle over the fennel mixture.
6 Bake in a preheated oven at 200°C (400°F, Reg. 6) for about 15–20 minutes until the top is golden brown and crisp. Serve immediately.

26 – French beans in cream sauce with garlic

	4 portions	10 portions
French beans	400 g (1 lb)	1¼ kg (2½ lb)
butter or margarine	50 g (2 oz)	125 g (5 oz)
crushed clove garlic	1	2–3
salt and pepper		
thin cream sauce	250 ml (½ pt)	600 g (1¼ pt)

1 Prepare, blanch and drain the beans.
2 Melt the butter and sweat the garlic for 20 seconds.
3 Add the beans, season and sweat gently for 1–2 minutes.
4 Add the cream sauce and simmer gently until tender.
5 Correct seasoning and consistency and serve.

27 – Hop shoots

Only the young shoots of hops can be used as a vegetable, and they must be fresh and green.

Method of cooking: wash well, tie in bundles and cook in boiling salted water for the minimum time until just tender. They can be served hot with a hollandaise or butter-type sauce and cold with mayonnaise or vinaigrette. They may also be used in egg dishes, e.g. omelets, scrambled eggs.

28 – Kohlrabi

This is a stem which swells to a turnip shape above the ground. When grown under glass it is pale green in colour, when grown outdoors it is purplish. Select kohlrabi with tops that are green, young and fresh. If the globes are too large they may be woody and tough.

Methods of cooking: trim off stems and leaves (which may be used for soups), peel thickly at the root end, thinly at top end, wash and cut into even-sized pieces. Young kohlrabi can be cooked whole. Simmer in well-flavoured stock until tender. Kohlrabi may be served with cream sauce, baked, or stuffed, and added to casseroles (meat and vegetarian) and stews.

29 – Stuffed kohlrabi

	4 portions	10 portions
kohlrabi, peeled	4 × 150–200 g (6–8 oz)	10 × 150–200 g (6–8 oz)
finely chopped onion	100 g (4 oz)	250 g (10 oz)
butter or oil	50 g (2 oz)	125 g (5 oz)
chopped mushrooms	100 g (4 oz)	250 g (10 oz)
chopped lean ham	100 g (4 oz)	250 g (10 oz)
tomatoes skinned, deseeded and diced	100 g (4 oz)	250 g (10 oz)
salt, pepper and rosemary		
fresh breadcrumbs		

> Oil used
> 1 portion provides:
>
> 170 kcals/711 kJ
> 14.3 g fat
> (of which 1.8 g saturated)
> 4.6 g carbohydrate
> (of which 3.5 g sugars)
> 6.5 g protein
> 3.6 g fibre

1 Cook the kohlrabi in salted water, drain.
2 Cut a slice from the top of each and hollow out centres with a spoon.
3 Cook the onion in butter without colour.
4 Add the mushrooms and cook for 2–3 minutes.
5 Add the ham, tomatoes and season.
6 Cook for 2–3 minutes, correct seasoning. Adjust the consistency with breadcrumbs if necessary.
7 Stuff the kohlrabis, replace the lids and brush with butter or oil. Heat through in a hot oven and serve.

30 – Mooli

Mooli or white radish – or rettiche as it is sometimes known – is a parsnip-shaped member of the radish family and is available all year round. Mooli does not have a hot taste like radishes but is slightly bitter and is pleasant to eat cooked as a vegetable. Mooli should have smooth flesh, white in appearance and be a regular shape.

Mooli has a high water content which can be reduced before cooking or serving raw by peeling and slicing, sprinkling with salt and leaving to stand for 30 minutes. Otherwise, the preparation is to wash well and grate, shred or slice before adding to salads or cooking as a vegetable.

Mooli may be used as a substitute for turnips.

31 – Okra

Okra are also known as gumbo or ladies' fingers. The flavour is slightly bitter and mild. Select pods that are firm, bright green and fresh looking.

Methods of cooking: cut off the conical cap at the stalk end, scrape the skin lightly, using a small knife, to remove any surface fuzz and the tips, then wash well. Okra can be served as a plain vegetable, tossed in butter or with tomato sauce and may be prepared in a similar fashion to a ratatouille. Okra are also used in soups, stews, curries, pilaf rice and fried as fritters.

Okra contain a high proportion of sticky glue-like carbohydrate which, when they are used in stews, gives body to the dish.

32 – Stewed okra

	4 portions	10 portions
okra	400 g (1 lb)	1¼ kg (2½ lb)
butter or oil	25 g (1 oz)	60 g (2½ oz)
finely chopped onion	100 g (4 oz)	250 g (10 oz)
clove of finely chopped garlic	1	2–3
tomatoes, skinned, deseeded and diced	400 g (1 lb)	1¼ kg (2½ lb)
salt and mill pepper		

1 Top and tail the okra, clean, wash and drain.
2 Melt the butter in a thick-based pan, add the onions and cook gently without colour for 5 minutes.
3 Add the garlic and tomatoes, cover with a lid and simmer for 5 minutes.
4 Add the okra, season, reduce heat and cook gently on top of stove or in the oven until the okra is tender, approximately 15–20 minutes, and serve.

33 – Palm hearts

Palm hearts are the tender young shoots or buds of palm trees and are generally available tinned or bottled in brine. Fresh palm hearts have a bitter flavour and need to be blanched before being used.

Methods of cooking: palm hearts can be boiled, steamed or braised and are served hot or cold, usually cut in halves lengthwise. When hot they are accompanied by a hollandaise-type of sauce or beurre blanc, when cold by mayonnaise or a herb-flavoured vinaigrette.

34 – Stewed palm hearts

	4 portions	10 portions
oil	1 tbsp	2–3 tbsp
lean cooked ham	50 g (2 oz)	125 g (5 oz)
finely chopped garlic	25 g (1 oz)	60 g (2½ oz)
tomatoes, skinned, deseeded and diced	200 g (8 oz)	500 g (1¼ lb)
tomato purée	1 tbsp	2–3 tbsp
chopped onion or chives	25 g (1 oz)	60 g (2½ oz)
chopped parsley	5 g (¼ oz)	12 g (⅝ oz)
tinned palm hearts	400 g (1 lb)	1¼ kg (2½ lb)

1 Heat the oil in a thick-bottomed pan, add the ham and garlic and cook without colour for 2–3 minutes.
2 Add the tomatoes, tomato purée, onion, parsley and seasoning.
3 Simmer gently until of a thickened consistency.
4 Add the palm hearts, mix in, simmer for 3–5 minutes and serve.

35 – Scorzonera

Scorzonera, also known as black-skinned salsify or oyster plant, has a white flesh when skinned, with a slight flavour of asparagus and oysters. Select salsify with fresh looking leaves at the top.

Methods of cooking: wash well, boil or steam in the skin, then peel using a potato peeler and immediately place in a blanc to prevent discoloration. Cut into suitable length pieces and serve plain, with butter, with cream or as for any cauliflower recipe. If peeling salsify raw, immediately place into cold water and lemon juice and cook in a blanc to prevent discoloration. Salsify requires approximately 20–30 minutes cooking; test by pressing a piece between the fingers, if cooked it will crush easily.

36 – Salsify with onion, tomato and garlic

	4 portions	10 portions
salsify	400 g (1 lb)	1¼ kg (2½ lb)
margarine, oil or butter	50 g (2 oz)	125 g (5 oz)
chopped onions	50 g (2 oz)	125 g (5 oz)
clove of garlic, crushed and chopped	1	2–3
tomatoes, skinned, deseeded and diced	100 g (4 oz)	250 g (10 oz)
tomato purée	25 g (1 oz)	60 g (2½ oz)
white stock	250 ml (½ pt)	600 ml (1¼ pt)
seasoning		
chopped parsley		

> With oil
> 1 portion provides:
>
> 151 kcals/636 kJ
> 12.9 g fat
> (of which 1.3 g saturated)
> 12.9 g carbohydrate
> (of which 3.7 g sugars)
> 2 g protein
> 3.8 g fibre

1 Wash and peel the salsify, cut into 5 cm (2 in) lengths. Place immediately into acidulated water to prevent discoloration.
2 Place salsify into a boiling blanc or acidulated water with a little oil and simmer until tender, approximately 10–40 minutes. Drain well.
3 Melt the margarine, oil or butter, add the onion and garlic. Sweat without colour.
4 Add the tomatoes and tomato purée, cook for 5 minutes.
5 Moisten with white stock, correct seasoning.
6 Place the cooked and well-drained salsify into the tomato sauce.
7 Serve in a suitable dish, sprinkled with chopped parsley.

37 – Salsify sautéed in butter

	4 portions	10 portions
salsify, peeled and cooked in a blanc	400 g (1 lb)	1¼ kg (2½ lb)
butter	50 g (2 oz)	125 g (5 oz)
salt and pepper		
chopped parsley		

1 Cut the salsify in 8 cm (3 in) pieces, dry well.
2 Heat the butter in a pan until foaming.
3 Add the salsify and sauté until lightly brown.
4 Season, finish with chopped parsley and serve.

Note   A little chopped garlic may be mixed with the parsley if desired.

38 – Salsify with onions

Proceed as for previous recipe, adding 100 g (4 oz) finely sliced, lightly browned onion (250 g (10 oz) for 10 portions).

39 – Salsify fritters

Mix 400 g (1 lb) cooked salsify in 2 tablespoons olive oil, salt, pepper, chopped parsley and lemon juice, and leave for 30–45 minutes. Dip in a light batter, deep fry to a golden brown and serve. (Increase the proportions $2\frac{1}{2}$ times for 10 portions).

40 – Shallow-fried spinach cakes (subrics)

	4 portions	10 portions
spinach, picked and washed	600 g ($1\frac{1}{2}$ lb)	$2\frac{1}{2}$ kg ($4\frac{1}{2}$ lb)
salt, pepper and nutmeg		
thick béchamel	60 ml ($\frac{1}{8}$ pt)	150 ml ($\frac{1}{3}$ pt)
double cream	1 tbsp	2–3 tbsp
egg yolks	2	5
egg	1	2–3
clarified butter, margarine, or oil for frying		

1 Lightly cook the spinach, dry well, season and coarsely chop.
2 Thoroughly mix over gentle heat, adding béchamel, cream and yolks plus egg. Allow to cool.
3 Lift the mixture out in tablespoons and shallow fry.
4 Colour on both sides, drain well and serve.

Notes   Alternatively, in place of béchamel, cream and yolks, the spinach cakes can be passed through a light batter.

A cream sauce may be offered separately.

41 ~ Spinach with cheese sauce and croûtons

1 Prepare a mixture as in the previous recipe.
2 Add diced croûtons, fried in butter.
3 Shape the cakes but do not fry them.
4 Wrap the cakes in large blanched spinach leaves and place in a buttered ovenproof dish.
5 Coat with Mornay sauce, grated cheese and melted butter.
6 Gratinate in a hot oven or under the salamander and serve.

42 ~ Leaf spinach with pine nuts and garlic

	4 portions	10 portions
spinach	1 kg (2 lb)	2½ kg (5 lb)
pine nuts	50 g (2 oz)	125 g (5 oz)
oil or butter	1 tbsp	2–3 tbsp
garlic clove, chopped	1	2–3
salt and pepper		

1 Cook the spinach for 2–3 minutes and drain well.
2 Lightly brown the pine nuts in oil, add garlic and sweat for 2 minutes.
3 Add coarsely chopped spinach and heat through over a medium heat.
4 Correct seasoning and serve.

43 ~ Spinach moulds

	4 portions	10 portions
carrot, cooked	50 g (2 oz)	125 g (5 oz)
spinach	600 g (1½ lb)	2¼ g (4½ lb)
thick béchamel	125 ml (¼ pt)	300 ml (⅝ pt)
eggs, separated	2	5
salt, pepper and nutmeg		

1 Butter dariole moulds and place in the bottom of each a slice of fluted cooked carrot.
2 Line the moulds with blanched spinach leaves.
3 Prepare a dry spinach purée and heat it through thoroughly.
4 Mix in the béchamel and yolks, season and allow to cool.

5 Fold in the stiffly beaten whites and use to three-quarters fill the moulds.
6 Poach in a bain-marie in moderate oven (200°C, 400°F, Reg. 6) for approximately 15–20 minutes.
7 Test by finger pressure to ensure that the moulds are cooked before turning out to serve.

Note Using this recipe as a basis, many variations can be produced using other vegetables.

T 44 – Spinach soufflé with anchovy sauce

(RICHARD SHEPHERD)

	6 portions	10–12 portions
butter	100 g (4½ oz)	150 g (6 oz)
flour	100 g (4½ oz)	150 g (6 oz)
warm milk, infused with onion, bay leaf and clove	¾ litre (1½ pt)	1 litre (2 pt)
washed spinach	150 g (6 oz)	200 g (8 oz)
eggs, separated	6	8
cayenne, ground nutmeg		
salt		

1 Make a roux from the butter and flour. Cook gently without colour, add the infused milk slowly and, stirring constantly, allow to cook out slowly.
2 Cook the spinach in a little boiling salted water and refresh in cold water. Squeeze thoroughly and chop finely.
3 Add a pinch of salt to the egg whites and beat until very stiff.
4 Season the sauce with cayenne, nutmeg and salt. Add egg yolks and mix thoroughly, then add spinach, continuing to mix, and fold in little by little the beaten egg whites.
5 Fill well-buttered soufflé moulds and cook in a pre-heated oven at 220°C (425°F, Reg. 7) for about 20 minutes. Serve with anchovy sauce (see opposite).

Note This is served as a first course.

– Anchovy sauce

	6 portions	10–12 portions
egg yolks	3	4–5
clarified butter	200 g (8 oz)	300 g (12 oz)
cayenne, salt and lemon juice		
small tin anchovy fillets	1	$1\frac{1}{2}$

1 Add 1 tablespoon water to the egg yolks and cook over a gentle heat, whisking continuously to a sabayon.
2 Allow to cool slightly and slowly add the warm clarified butter. When combined add a little cayenne, salt and squeeze of lemon juice.
3 Squeeze the anchovy fillets free from oil and blend with a drop of water to a smooth paste. Place into a bowl and add sauce, whisking continuously until thoroughly mixed.
4 Pass through a fine chinois and use to accompany spinach soufflé.

45 – Squash

There are many different varieties of squash, which is a relative of the pumpkin. Squash should be firm with a blemish-free skin; summer squash should have a more yielding skin than winter squash, which are allowed to harden before harvesting.

The most usual variety sold is the custard squash, which is best when eaten young and can be cooked in similar ways to courgettes – sliced and lightly boiled, stewed or fried with the skins on and served with butter. Winter squash have the skin removed before cooking and can then be cooked like marrow, e.g. stuffed.

46 – Swiss chard

Swiss chard or seakale beet have large, ribbed, slightly curly leaves. The flavour is similar to spinach, although it is milder, and it can be prepared in the same way as any of the spinach recipes.

It can also be served *au gratin* and made into a savoury flan or quiche, using half lean cooked ham or bacon, flavoured with onion, garlic and chopped parsley.

47 – Stuffed vegetables

Certain vegetables can be stuffed and served as a first course, as a vegetable course and as an accompaniment to a main course.

The majority of vegetables used for this purpose are the bland, gourd types, such as aubergines, courgettes and cucumbers, in which case the stuffing should be delicately flavoured so as not to overpower the vegetable. Below are some of the more popular types of vegetable used for this purpose and the usual type of stuffing in each case. There is, however, considerable scope for variation and experimentation in any of the stuffings.

Artichoke bottoms
Duxelle stuffing, cordon of thin demi-glace or jus-lié flavoured with tomato.

Aubergine
The cooked chopped flesh is mixed with cooked chopped onion, sliced tomatoes and chopped parsley.

The cooked chopped flesh is mixed with duxelle, sprinkled with fresh breadcrumbs, grated cheese and gratinated. Served with a cordon of light tomato sauce or tomato cullis.

The cooked chopped flesh is mixed with cooked chopped onion, garlic, tomato concassé, parsley, breadcrumbs and gratinated. Served with a cordon of light tomato sauce or cullis.

The cooked chopped flesh is mixed with diced or minced cooked mutton, cooked chopped onion, tomato concassé, cooked rice and chopped parsley. Served with a cordon of tomato sauce or cullis.

Mushrooms and ceps
Duxelle stuffing.

Stuffed ceps, forest style: equal quantities of duxelle stuffing and sausagemeat.

Stuffed cabbage
Veal stuffing and pilaff rice.

Cucumber
This can be prepared in two ways:

1 Peeled, cut into 2 cm (1 in) pieces, the centres hollowed out with a parisienne spoon and then boiled, steamed or cooked in butter.
2 The peeled whole cucumber is cut in halves lengthwise, the seed pocket scooped out and the cucumber cooked by boiling, steaming or in butter.

Suitable stuffings can be made from a base of duxelle, pilaff rice or chicken forcemeat, or any combination of these three.

To stuff the cucumber pieces, pipe the stuffing from a piping bag and complete the cooking in the oven. When the whole cucumber is stuffed, rejoin the two halves, wrap in pig's caul and muslin and braise.

Lettuce
Stuff with two parts chicken forcemeat, one part duxelle and braise.

Turnips
Peel the turnips, remove the centre almost to the root and blanch the turnips. Cook and purée the scooped-out centre and mix with an equal quantity of potato purée. Refill the cavities and gently cook the turnips in butter in the oven, basting frequently. Turnips may also be stuffed with cooked spinach, chicory or rice.

Pimentos
Pilaff rice, varied if required with other ingredients, e.g. mushrooms, tomatoes or duxelle.

Duxelle stuffing with garlic and diced ham. Served with a cordon of demi-glace flavoured with tomato.

Chopped hard-boiled egg bound with thick béchamel, grated cheese and gratinated. Served with a cordon of light tomato sauce.

Scrambled egg, mushrooms and diced ham, sprinkled with breadcrumbs fried in butter.

Risotto with tomato concassé. Coat with thin tomato sauce.

Cooked tomato concassé, chopped onion, garlic and parsley, bound with fresh breadcrumbs and gratinated. May be served hot or cold.

Pilaff rice in which has been cooked dice of tomato and red pimento. Cook gently in oven and sprinkle with chopped parsley.

48 – Wild mushrooms

Ceps, morels, chanterelles and oyster mushrooms are four of the most popular of the wide variety of wild mushrooms that may be gathered.

Ceps are bun-shaped fungi with a smooth surface and a strong, distinctive flavour. Ceps are also available dried and should be soaked in warm water for approximately 30 minutes before use. The soaking liquid should be used as it contains a good flavour.

Methods of cooking: ceps hold an amount of water and need to be sweated gently in oil or butter and then drained, utilising the liquid. Ceps may be used in soups, egg dishes, particularly omelets, fish, meat, game and poultry dishes. They may also be: sautéed in oil or butter with garlic and parsley and served as a vegetable; stuffed with chopped ham, cheese, tomato and parsley; or sliced, passed through batter and deep fried.

Morels appear in spring. They vary in colour from light to dark brown and have a meaty flavour. Morels are obtainable dried, and then require soaking for 10 minutes, are squeezed dry and used as required.

Methods of cooking: morels can be used in soups, egg dishes, meat, poultry and game dishes and as a vegetable, first course or as an accompaniment.

Chanterelles are common, trumpet-shaped and frilly. They are generally bright yellow with a delicate flavour, slightly resembling apricots, and are obtainable in summer and autumn. There are many varieties and they can be obtained dried, when they require about 25 minutes soaking in warm water before cooking.

Methods of cooking: because of their pleated gills, chanterelles must be carefully washed under running cold water then well dried. As they have a rubbery texture they require lengthly gentle cooking in butter or oil. They can be served with egg, chicken or veal dishes.

Oyster mushrooms are 'ear' shaped, grey or greyish brown in colour, and have an excellent flavour. They can be tough in texture and therefore need careful cooking.

Method of cooking: cook in butter or oil with parsley and garlic, or flour, egg and breadcrumbs, then deep fry.

49 – Yams

Yams may be white or yellow, with a texture similar to potatoes. In certain parts of the world orange-fleshed sweet potatoes are known as yams, but the true yam is sweeter and moister than the sweet potato. However, they may both be prepared and cooked in the same way.

50 – Fried yam cakes

	4 portions	10 portions
yams	400 g (1 lb)	1¼ kg (2½ lb)
butter	10 g (½ oz)	25 g (1¼ lb)
onion	50 g (2 oz)	125 g (5 oz)
chopped parsley	5 g (¼ oz)	12 g (⅝ oz)
salt and pepper		
egg yolks	2	5
oil		

1 Wash, peel and finely grate the yams.
2 Add the melted butter, finely chopped onion, parsley, salt and pepper.
3 Add the egg yolks, mix well, form into a roll and cut into an even number of cakes.
4 Neaten the shapes, using a little flour only if necessary, and shallow fry for 3–4 minutes on each side, then drain and serve.

51 – Yam soufflé

	4 portions	10 portions
yams	400 g (1 lb)	1¼ kg (2½ lb)
butter or margarine	50 g (2 oz)	125 g (5 oz)
milk or cream	125 ml (¼ pt)	300 ml (⅝ pt)
grated Parmesan cheese	25 g (1 oz)	60 g (2½ oz)
salt and pepper		
egg yolks	3	7
egg whites	4	10

1 Wash, peel and cut the yams into even-sized pieces.
2 Boil or steam until tender, drain well.
3 Purée the yams, return to a clean pan and dry out thoroughly over a

gentle heat, stirring continuously with a wooden spoon.

4 Mix in the butter and then gradually add the milk.
5 Mix in half the cheese, seasoning and the egg yolks.
6 Allow the mixture to cool, and butter and flour a soufflé dish.
7 Carefully fold in the stiffly beaten egg whites, and place mixture in soufflé dish.
8 Carefully smooth the surface, add remainder of cheese and bake at 220°C (425°F, Reg. 7) for approximately 20 minutes. Serve immediately.

52 – Grilled vegetables

Tender young vegetables can be cooked from raw and are best cooked on an under-fired grill or barbecue.

4 portions

leeks	8
carrots	8
turnips	8
sweetcorn	8

1 Wash, peel and trim the vegetables.
2 Dry well, brush with olive oil, season lightly.
3 Grill the vegetables with the tenderest last, e.g. turnips, carrots, leeks, sweetcorn.
4 Serve as a first course accompanied by a suitable sauce, e.g. spicy tomato sauce, or as a vegetable accompaniment to a main course.

Notes Slices of aubergine, courgette and red and/or yellow peppers can also be used (discard the pith and seeds of the peppers).

If vegetables other than baby ones, e.g. carrot, turnip, parsnip, are grilled, then they need to be cut into thickish slices and par-boiled until half-cooked, drained well, dried, then brushed with oil and grilled.

They can be served plain, sprinkled with chopped mixed herbs, or with an accompanying sauce.

53 – Vegetables as a garnish

Vegetables, e.g. carrot, turnip, celeriac and parsnip, cut in fine julienne and deep-fried until crisp can be used as a garnish or sprinkled over many dishes of fish, meat or poultry.

Parsnip, beetroot, carrot and celeriac, thinly sliced on a mandoline, can also be deep fried and used as an alternative to potato crisps, both as a garnish or a snack.

Cucumber can also be used, peeled and cut into 16 cm (6 in) strips on a mandoline. Trim off and discard the seeds and cut the strips into spaghetti-like lengths. Lightly sprinkle with salt and drain in a colander. Wash off, blanch in boiling water for 2 seconds and use as required, e.g. as a garnish for poached fish dishes. The cucumber spaghetti can also be quickly tossed in hot butter or oil if required.

—— *Potatoes* ——

Varieties of potato fall into four categories: floury, firm, waxy or salad. As certain varieties are best suited for specific cooking purposes, potatoes should always be sold by name, e.g. King Edward, Desirée, Marin Piper and Binje.

When using potatoes as a vegetable dish, for 4 portions allow 400 g (1 lb) for new potatoes and 500 g (1 lb 4 oz) for old potatoes (increase $2\frac{1}{2}$ times for 10 portions). The actual quantity required will vary according to the number of courses and how many other vegetables are served. As a garnish, allow approximatly 50 g (2 oz) potatoes per head.

Traditionally potatoes have been served as a vegetable in a separate dish; however, small new potatoes can give a pleasing appearance by being served with other vegetables.

Small young carrots, turnips and peas mixed with small potatoes, finished in butter and chopped mint bring both potatoes and vegetables together. Other additions could be button mushrooms, button onions and cauliflower florets. Lightly sautéeing the vegetables to a golden colour lends variation to the presentation.

RECIPES

54 – Duchess potato – variations

Additions to the basic duchess potato mixture can include chopped herbs, such as parsley or mint, tomato purée or a purée of peas, chopped nuts or truffle.

The mixture may be cylinder-shaped, round cake, ball-shaped, or piped in rounds or in nests. When piped like a nest, as for marquise potatoes, in place of tomatoes, any of the following could be used: peas, peas and mushrooms, purée of spinach, purée of carrots and macédoine of vegetables.

55 – Fried croquette potatoes with ham

	4 portions	10 portions
potatoes	500 g (1¼ lb)	1½ kg (3 lb)
butter	25–50 g (1–2 oz)	60–125 g (2½–5 oz)
egg yolk	1	2–3
chopped ham	50 g (2 oz)	125 g (5 oz)
flour, eggwash and crumbs		
seasoning		

1 Prepare a duchess potato mixture from the potatoes, butter and yolk.
2 Mix in the ham.
3 Mould into croquette shapes.
4 Flour, egg and crumb and deep fry. Drain well and serve.

56 – Fried croquette potatoes with ham and vermicelli

1 Prepare the potatoes as in the previous recipe.
2 Flour, egg wash and roll the potatoes in cooked vermicelli which has been broken into small pieces.
3 Mould into rectangular shapes and deep fry.

57 – Potato cakes stuffed with spinach

	4 portions	10 portions
choux paste (without sugar)	125 ml ($\frac{1}{4}$ pt)	300 ml ($\frac{5}{8}$ pt)
duchess potato mixture	400 g (1 lb)	1$\frac{1}{4}$ kg (2$\frac{1}{2}$ lb)
cooked leaf spinach	400 g (1 lb)	1$\frac{1}{4}$ kg (2$\frac{1}{2}$ lb)

1 Combine the choux paste with the potato mixture.
2 Mould carefully into croquette shapes, stuff with well-drained, seasoned, cooked spinach by cutting a line in the top, opening out gently, laying the spinach in the opening then carefully remoulding.
3 Carefully place on to oiled greaseproof paper.
4 Allow to slide off the paper into hot deep fat and fry at 185°C (370°F) until golden brown.
5 Drain well and serve.

58 – Fried potato balls with almonds

1 Prepare the duchess potato mixture.
2 Shape into rounds the size of apricots.
3 Flour, egg wash and roll in sliced or nibbed almonds.
4 Deep fry to a golden colour, drain well and serve.

59 – Potato cakes with chives

	4 portions	10 portions
large potatoes	4	10
egg yolks	2	5
butter	50 g (2 oz)	125 g (5 oz)
chopped chives	50 g (2 oz)	125 g (5 oz)
salt and pepper		

1 Bake the potatoes in their jackets.
2 Halve and remove the centres from the skins.
3 Mash with the yolks and butter.
4 Mix in the chopped chives and season.
5 Mould into round cakes 2 cm (1 in) diameter.
6 Lightly flour and shallow fry to a golden colour on both sides.

60 – Braised potatoes with thyme

	4 portions	10 portions
potatoes	500 g (1¼ lb)	1½ kg (3 lb)
white stock	375 ml (¾ pt)	1 litre (2 pt)
pinch of powdered thyme		
butter or margarine	50 g (2 oz)	125 g (5 oz)
salt and pepper		

1 Trim and cut the potatoes to an even size.
2 Place in a dish, half cover with the stock to which has been added the thyme.
3 Brush with melted butter and season.
4 Cook in a hot oven (230°C, 450°F, Reg. 8), brushing occasionally with melted butter.
5 When ready the potatoes should have absorbed the stock and be golden brown in colour and cooked through.

Note As thyme is a strong, pungent herb, it should not be used in excess.

61 – Potatoes baked in stock with cheese and garlic

	4 portions	10 portions
potatoes, peeled	400 g (1 lb)	1¼ kg (2½ lb)
stock	375 ml (¾ pt)	1 litre (2 pt)
egg	1	2–3
grated cheese	50 g (2 oz)	125 g (5 oz)
clove garlic, crushed and chopped	1	2–3
butter or margarine	50 g (2 oz)	125 g (5 oz)

1 Thinly slice the potatoes.
2 Mix the stock, egg and grated cheese in a basin.
3 Butter an earthenware dish and add the potatoes, stock and garlic.
4 Sprinkle with more grated cheese and a little melted butter.
5 Bake in a moderate oven (190°C, 375°F, Reg. 5) until the potatoes are cooked and golden brown.

62 – Potatoes cooked with button onions and tomatoes

	4 portions	10 portions
peeled potatoes	400 g (1 lb)	1¼ kg (2½ lb)
button onions	100 g (4 oz)	250 g (10 oz)
clove garlic	1	2–3
stock	375 ml (¾ pt)	1 litre (2 pt)
salt and pepper		
tomatoes, skinned, deseeded and diced	100 g (4 oz)	250 g (10 oz)

1 Trim and dice the potatoes into 2 cm (1 in) pieces.
2 Add to the peeled onions, crushed garlic and stock.
3 Season and cook gently in a suitable pan in the oven or on the stove until the potatoes are just cooked.
4 Add the tomatoes and cook for a few more minutes then serve.

63 – Potatoes cooked in milk with cheese

	4 portions	10 portions
potatoes	500 g (1¼ lb)	1¼ kg (3 lb)
milk	250 ml (½ pt)	600 ml (1¼ pt)
salt and pepper		
grated cheese	50 g (2 oz)	125 g (5 oz)

1 Slice the peeled potatoes ½ cm (¼ in) thick.
2 Place in an ovenproof dish and just cover with milk.
3 Season, sprinkle with grated cheese and cook in a moderate oven (190°C, 375°F, Reg. 5) until the potatoes are cooked and golden brown.

64 – Soufflé potatoes

Success with this dish depends on the type of potato used and the care taken in the handling of the potato. A waxy type of potato is required and experimentation is needed to find one that is suitable.

1 Cut peeled potatoes into rectangles approximately 5 cm (2 in) by 2½ cm (1 in) and then into ¼ cm (⅛ in) slices lengthwise.

2 Wash and dry on a cloth.
3 Fry a small number at a time in deep fat at 180°C (360°F).
4 Add each piece separately, stirring carefully with a spider.
5 Turn down the heat and allow to cook for about 5 minutes.
6 Carefully lift out the soufflé potatoes with a spider and arrange on absorbent paper or a thick cloth.
7 When required, place into hot fat at 190°C (380°F).
8 Fry until the potatoes are golden brown and puff up, stir with a spider to ensure even colouring.
9 Drain, season lightly and serve.

65 – Sweet potatoes

Also known as boniato, sweet potatoes have a sticky texture; they are slightly aromatic and sweet. Small or medium-sized potatoes with firm, fresh-looking skins should be selected.

Sweet potatoes can be steamed, boiled or baked in their skins, with the centre removed and puréed or creamed. They can be made into vegetarian dishes with the addition of other ingredients, and they may also be fried or made into bread or sweet pudding.

66 – Candied sweet potatoes

	4 portions	10 portions
oil or butter	1 tbsp	2½ tbsp
sweet potatoes, in 1 cm (1½ in) dice	400 g (1 lb)	1¼ kg (2½ lb)
chopped onion	100 g (4 oz)	250 g (10 oz)
honey	2 tbsp	5 tbsp
cider vinegar	2 tbsp	5 tbsp
cinnamon	¼ tsp	½ tsp
salt		

1 Heat the oil in a frying pan and add the potatoes.
2 Cook for 10 minutes, stirring occasionally.
3 Add the onion and cook until brown.
4 Mix the honey, cider vinegar, cinnamon and salt in a bowl. Pour the honey mixture on to the potatoes, heat through, season and serve.

67 – Swiss potato cakes (rösti)

In Switzerland the potatoes for this dish would be grated on a rösti grater, however, a grater which produces large flakes can be used. Each Canton district has its own variations, which include Gruyère or Emmental cheese, grated raw apple, chopped onion, chives and parsley. Cumin or nutmeg may also be used to flavour and the potato can be coated with cream and glazed.

	4 portions	10 portions
lardons of bacon	50 g (2 oz)	125 g (5 oz)
chopped onion	50 g (2 oz)	125 g (5 oz)
oil, butter or margarine	50 g (2 oz)	125 g (5 oz)
grated raw potatoes	500 g (1¼ lb)	1½ kg (3 lb)
salt and pepper		

1 Sweat the lardons and onions in the fat or oil in a frying pan.
2 Add the potatoes and mix well, season.
3 Press together and cook on both sides until cooked and golden brown.

68 – Anna potatoes

oil	
peeled potatoes	600 g (1½ lb)
butter	25 g (1 oz)

1 Grease an anna mould using hot oil.
2 Trim the potatoes to an even cylindrical shape.
3 Cut into slices 2 mm ($\frac{1}{12}$ in) thick.
4 Place a layer of slices neatly overlapping in the bottom of the mould, season lightly with salt and pepper.
5 Continue arranging the slices of potato in layers, seasoning in between.
6 Add the butter to the top layer.
7 Cook in a hot oven (230–250°C, Reg. 8–9) for $\frac{3}{4}$–1 hour, occasionally pressing the potatoes flat.
8 To serve, turn out of the mould and leave whole or cut into four portions.

PASTRY

Patisserie and confectionery

1   Demonstrate cleanliness of preparation areas and equipment throughout production periods according to relevant legislation.
2   Identify appropriate recipe adjustments to meet customers' expressed requirements.
3   Process and finish products to meet recipe specifications.
4   Identify storage requirements for each product in accordance with recipe specifications and relevant legislation.
5   Identify type, quantity and quality of ingredients according to recipe specifications.

—— Preparation and materials ——

All baking times and temperatures stated are approximate, as a pastry cook learns through experience how raw materials bake differently in various types of ovens. When using forced air convection ovens it is often necessary to reduce the stated temperatures in accordance with manufacturers' recommendations. Also, certain ovens produce severe bottom heat and to counteract this the use of double baking sheets (one sheet on top of another) is necessary.

When using vanilla pods, infuse the pod in the heated milk for approximately 30 minutes, remove, rinse, dry and store for further use in a jar of castor sugar. For dry mixes add a few grains of vanilla from inside the pod.

TYPES OF FLOUR IN PASTRY WORK

- **White flour** is heavily milled and sieved to remove the outer skins and germ. It will store better without the germ, which contains fat and enzymes. About 70 per cent of the wheat is extracted to produce white flour. It is usually fortified by added calcium, iron, vitamin B_1 and nicotinic acid.
- **Wholemeal flour** is the whole grain crushed into flour. (The bran is not digested by humans – this acts as roughage.) Stoneground flour is ground by stones, and is said to have a superior flavour.

- **Germ flour** (Hovis-type flour) is a mixture of 75 per cent white flour plus 25 per cent cooked germ. The germ is cooked to delay the onset of rancidity in the fat. Cooking gives a malted flavour.
- **Starch-reduced flour** is prepared for commercial products. Much of the starch is washed out, leaving the gluten and other proteins.
- **Self-raising flour** is white flour, usually of medium to soft strength, with the correct proportion of raising agent to give sufficient raising action for cake making.
- **High ratio flour** is flour which has been finely milled in order that it is able to absorb more liquid and sugar.

Flour contains two main proteins, gliadin and glutenin which, when combined with water, produce gluten which is elastic and as a result will stretch. When cake, pastry or bread doughs are formed, the gluten is able to give the mixture its structure.

Wheat contains a large quantity of this protein, a substance other cereals do not contain so much, so they are not so suitable for making cakes, bread, etc. Canadian type hard wheat contains more gluten than British and Australian wheats.

- **Strong flours** are milled from a mixture of wheat, in which spring wheat predominates, and contains 10–16 per cent strong glutens used for bread, yeast doughs, puff pastry.
- **Medium general purpose** contains less strong and elastic gluten; it is used for plain cakes, scones and rich-yeast mixtures.
- **Soft flour (cake flour)** contains a small percentage of gluten to give a soft structure to a cake. Uses: sponge cakes and biscuits.

EGGS IN PASTRY WORK

Egg albumen (protein) is soluble in cold liquid; it begins to coagulate immediately on application of heat, becoming opaque and firm. The degree of firmness depends on the degree of heat and length of cooking time. Egg yolk does not harden to the same extent or as quickly as the white, due to the high percentage of fat. If egg is over-cooked or added too quickly to hot liquid, curdling will result.

- **Thickening.** The coagulation of protein on heating to 68°C (155°F) is responsible for the thickening properties.
- **Lightening.** By means of whisking either egg white or whole egg, air is entangled and lightness given to a mixture. There they will:

(a) act as a raising agent in cakes;
(b) produce light dishes, e.g. soufflés and meringues.
- **Glazing.** Beaten egg used as a glaze (egg wash).
- **Binding.** The coagulating properties of the egg will give cohesiveness to a mixture containing dry ingredients.
- **Emulsifying.** The lecithin contained in the yolk will assist in the emulsification (mixing) of products.
- **Coating.** Beaten egg forms a protective coating for foods.
- **Enriching.** The addition of whole eggs or yolks to a mixture is a means of adding protein and fat. Eggs improve nutritive value and flavour.

FATS USED IN PASTRY WORK

Fats and oils are composed of fatty acids and glycerine. Fatty acids may be saturated or unsaturated.

- **Saturated fatty acids.** A saturated fat has each carbon atom in the fatty acids combined with two hydrogen atoms, e.g. palmitic and stearic acid. Saturated fats are solid at room temperature and predominate in fats of animal origin, e.g. butter, cream, lard, hard cheese, egg yolks, lard and suet. They are also present in hard margarines.
- **Unsaturated fatty acids**
  (a) *Monounsaturated fatty acids.* These have an adjacent pair of carbon atoms, each with only one hydrogen atom attached, so they are capable of taking up more hydrogen atoms. Monounsaturated fats are soft at room temperature but will solidify when in the coolest part of the refrigerator. They are present in many animal and vegetable fats. Oleic acid found in olive oil is an example of a monounsaturated fatty acid.
  (b) *Polyunsaturated fatty acids* have two or more pairs of carbon atoms which are capable of taking up more hydrogen atoms. Polyunsaturated fats are very soft or oily at room temperature and will not solidify even in a refrigerator. They are present in soya bean, corn and sunflower seed oils.
- **Butter** is composed of the fat of milk, traces of curd (casein) and milk sugar lactose, water and mineral matter which includes salt added to improve flavour and help preservation. A good butter adds flavour to cakes, biscuits and pastry.
- **Lard** is derived from pig fat. Good lard is a pure white fat. It is a tough, plastic fat, with no creaming properties but excellent

shortening properties. Usually mixed with butter or margarine for cakes and pastry to add colour and flavour.

- **Suet** is obtained from around the kidneys of beef cattle. Suet is a hard fat and cannot be rubbed into flour or creamed. It is added by chopping finely or shredding finely into the mixture. Suet is used to make suet pastry which is usually steamed. Baking gives a hard, dry result. Commercial suet is purified fat which has been shredded and mixed with wheat or rice flour to stop the pieces of fat sticking together.
- **Vegetable fats and oils.** Soya beans, sunflower seeds, cotton seeds, groundnuts, sesame seeds, coconuts, palm kernel, olives all yield oils which are used in cooking fats and oils, margarine and creams.
- **Margarine**
  (a) *Table margarine.* This is blended to give the best possible flavour.
  (b) *Cake margarine.* This is developed to have good creaming properties.
  (c) *Pastry margarine.* It is blended to produce a tough plastic margarine which has a fairly high melting point. It may contain a high percentage of stearin (a type of fat) or may be hydrogenated to harden it.
- **High ratio fat** is hydrogenated edible oil, to which a quantity of a very pure and refined quality emulsifying agent has been added, e.g. glyceryl monostearate (GMS), although other emulsifiers may be used. By the use of such special fats, cakes can be made containing higher than normal quantities of liquid. Combining the use of this special type of emulsifying shortening with high ratio flour, it is possible to make successfully cakes with abnormal percentages of both sugar and liquid; high ratio cakes are so called because of the high percentages of sugar and liquid.
- **Compounds fats and oils** are practically 100 per cent salt free and have no flavour. They are made by refining extracted vegetable oils. The blend of oils is hydrogenated to produce the consistency desired, processed by creaming and chilling and then packed.

Creaming properties

Fats for some types of pastry work must cream well. To do this they must possess a 'plastic', waxy consistency and have a good flavour. Fats may be purchased which have had their chemistry altered so that they cream well. These are known as plasticised or precreamed fats.

QUALITY REQUIREMENTS OF FRUIT

Fresh fruit used for desserts and in pastry work should be:

- Whole and of fresh appearance. (For maximum flavour the fruit must be ripe but not overripe.)
- Firm according to the type and variety.
- Clean, free from traces of pesticides and fungicides.
- Free from external moisture.
- Free from an unpleasant foreign smell or taste.
- Free from pests or disease.
- Sufficiently mature. It must be capable of being handled and travelling without damage.
- Free of any defects characteristic of the variety in shape, size and colour.
- Free of bruising and any other damage due to weather conditions.

—— *Hot sweets* ——

I **1 ~ Apple cake with Wensleydale**

(Paul A. Nicholas)

	4 portions	10 portions
bramley apples, peeled, cored and diced	300 g (12 oz)	750 g (1¾ lb)
castor sugar	50 g (2 oz)	125 g (5 oz)
self-raising flour, sifted	75 g (3 oz)	190 g (7½ oz)
baking powder	½ tsp	1 tsp
salt, pinch		
chopped hazelnuts	25 g (1 oz)	60 g (2½ oz)
sultanas	50 g (2 oz)	125 g (5 oz)
egg, beaten	1	3
sunflower oil	60 ml (⅛ pt)	150 ml (⅓ pt)
Wensleydale, sliced thick	150 g (6 oz)	375 g (15 oz)

> I portion provides:
>
> 455 kcals
> 26.9 g fat
> (of which 9.4 g saturated)
> 43.1 g carbohydrate
> (of which 28.7 g sugars)
> 13.1 g protein
> 3.8 g fibre

1 Preheat oven to 180°C (350°F).
2 Lightly grease and base line 18 cm (7 in) round loose-bottom cake tin(s).
3 Mix together the apples, sugar, flour, baking powder, salt, hazelnuts and sultanas.

4 Combine the egg and oil and stir into the dry ingredients.
5 Spoon half the mixture into the prepared cake tin.
6 Arrange the cheese on top, spoon over the remaining cake mixture and level the surface.
7 Bake for 1½ hours until firm to the touch.
8 Leave to cool before removing from the tin.

Note This cake may be served with a selection of summer fruits and vanilla yoghurt.

2 – Apple strudel

	4–5 portions	8–10 portions
Paste		
strong flour	100 g (4 oz)	200 g (8 oz)
pinch of salt		
egg	1	1
butter, margarine or oil	12 g (½ oz)	25 g (1 oz)
hot water	40 ml (⅟₁₆ pt)	85 ml (³⁄₁₆ pt)
Filling		
cooking apples	500 g (1 lb)	1 kg (2 lb)
breadcrumbs	25 g (1 oz)	50 g (2 oz)
butter, margarine or oil	12 g (½ oz)	25 g (1 oz)
brown sugar	50 g (2 oz)	100 g (4 oz)
sultanas	50 g (2 oz)	100 g (4 oz)
raisins	50 g (2 oz)	100 g (4 oz)
ground almonds	25 g (1 oz)	50 g (2 oz)
nibbed almonds	25 g (1 oz)	50 g (2 oz)
grated lemon zest and juice	1	2½
mixed spice	1½ g (⅟₁₆ oz)	3 g (⅛ oz)
ground cinnamon	1½ g (⅟₁₆ oz)	3 g (⅛ oz)

Using butter
1 portion provides:

393 kcals/1657 kJ
13.5 g fat
(of which 4.3 g saturated)
64.1 g carbohydrate
(of which 42.7 g sugars)
8 g protein
4.4 g fibre

If 50 per cent wholemeal flour is used for the pastry, this increases fibre to 5.2 g.

1 First, make the paste: sieve together flour and salt and make a well.
2 Place the egg, fat and water in the centre and work until it is a smooth dough.
3 Cover with a damp cloth and relax for 20 minutes.
4 For the filling: peel and core the apples. Cut into thin, small slices and place in a basin.
5 Fry the breadcrumbs (white or brown) in the butter, margarine or oil.
6 Add to the apples and mix well with all the other ingredients.

7 Roll out the dough into a square $\frac{1}{4}$cm ($\frac{1}{8}$in) thick, place on a cloth and brush with melted fat or oil.

8 Stretch the dough on the backs of the hands until it is very thin.

9 Spread the filling on to the paste to within 1 cm ($\frac{1}{2}$in) from the edge.

10 With the aid of a cloth, roll up tightly and seal the ends.

11 Place on a lightly greased baking sheet and brush with melted fat or oil.

12 Bake in a moderate oven (approximately 190°C, 375°F, Reg. 5) for 35–40 minutes.

13 When baked, dust with icing sugar and serve as required.

Note Alternatively, the strudel paste may be made with: 50 per cent wholemeal and 50 per cent strong flour, or 70 per cent wholemeal and 30 per cent strong flour. With the increased proportion of wholemeal flour a little more water is required to achieve a smooth elastic dough.

Variation

(a) Proceed as for apple strudel, replacing the apples with stoned cherries – fresh, canned or frozen.

(b) Proceed as for apple strudel, but replace 50 per cent of the apples with stoned cherries (fresh, canned or frozen).

T 3 ~ Apple charlotte and cinnamon ice-cream

(DAVID ADLARD)

	4 portions	10 portions
bramley apples	400 g (1 lb)	1$\frac{1}{4}$kg (2$\frac{1}{2}$lb)
sugar		
lemon juice		
nutmeg/cinnamon		
white bread or preferably brioche (the bread must be firm)		
butter for sautéeing		
clarified butter to soak the bread		

1 Peel and cut the apples in 12 mm ($\frac{1}{2}$in) cubes.

2 Sauté quickly in butter so the apples will not go brown.

3 Add sugar, cinnamon/nutmeg, sugar to taste. Leave the apples undercooked. They will cook more when you cook the charlotte.

4 Line the base of a pudding mould with greaseproof paper.

5 Cut the bread up into 3 mm ($\frac{1}{8}$ in) thickness, soak in butter and line the mould.
6 Press the apple in firmly, press down hard.
7 Cover the apple with bread and then cover the pudding mould with foil.
8 Cook in a very hot oven for 20 minutes. After 15 minutes, examine the side of the charlotte to see if the bread is brown.
9 Demould it on to a plate which has a pool of *crème anglaise* on the base and serve it with cinnamon ice-cream.

– Crème anglaise

	4 portions	10 portions
double cream	250 ml ($\frac{1}{2}$ pt)	600 ml (1$\frac{1}{4}$ pt)
milk	250 ml ($\frac{1}{2}$ pt)	600 ml ($\frac{1}{4}$ pt)
vanilla pod	$\frac{1}{2}$	1–2
sugar	75 g (3 oz)	180 g (7$\frac{1}{2}$ oz)
egg yolks	6	15

1 Infuse the milk and cream with vanilla.
2 Make crème anglaise with the infused milk and cream.
3 Pass through a sieve.

– Cinnamon ice-cream

	4 portions	10 portions
double cream	250 ml ($\frac{1}{2}$ pt)	600 ml (1$\frac{1}{4}$ pt)
milk	250 ml ($\frac{1}{2}$ pt)	600 ml (1$\frac{1}{4}$ pt)
cinnamon stick, broken up	1	2–3
vanilla pod	$\frac{1}{2}$	1
sugar	75 g (3 oz)	180 g (7$\frac{1}{2}$ g)
egg yolks	6	15

1 Infuse the milk and cream with cinnamon and vanilla.
2 Make crème anglaise with the infused milk and cream.
3 Pass through a sieve. When it is cool, churn in ice-cream machine.

4 – French rice pudding

	4 portions	10 portions
milk (whole or skimmed)	500 ml (1 pt)	1¼ litre (2½ pt)
short grain rice (white or brown)	50 g (2 oz)	125 g (5 oz)
eggs, separated	2	5
castor or unrefined sugar	50 g (2 oz)	125 g (5 oz)
butter or margarine	25 g (1 oz)	60 g (2½ oz)
natural vanilla essence or pod		

> 1 portion provides:
>
> 225 kcals/944 kJ
> 8.82 g fat
> (of which 4.43 g saturated)
> 29.6 g carbohydrate
> 8.74 g protein
> 0.24 g fibre

1 Boil the milk in a thick-bottomed saucepan, add the rice and simmer until almost cooked.
2 Prepare the liaison by creaming together the egg yolks, sugar and the butter or margarine.
3 Add the liaison carefully by stirring in one-third of the milk with the rice. Add vanilla essence.
4 Return all to the main saucepan and stir on the side of the stove until the mixture thickens but *do not boil*. Remove from the stove.
5 Stiffly beat the egg whites and carefully fold into the cooked rice.
6 Three-quarters fill a buttered pie dish.
7 Place in a bain-marie of warm water, bake at approximately 200°C (400°F, Reg. 6) for 20–30 minutes and serve.

Note   Semolina, sago or tapioca may also be prepared in this way.

I 5 – Sopaipillas

(PAUL BURTON)

	4 portions	10 portions
flour (plain)	90 g (3 oz)	225 g (8 oz)
baking powder	5 g (¼ oz)	12.5 g (½ oz)
salt	¼ tsp	½ tsp
unsaturated margarine	20 g (¾ oz)	50 g (2 oz)
lukewarm water	70 ml (2½ fl oz)	175 ml (6 fl oz)
oil for frying		
maple syrup or honey		
cinnamon and castor sugar		
dried eating apricots	120 g (4 oz)	300 g (10 oz)

1 Sift the flour, baking powder and salt into a bowl.
2 Cut in the fat and bind to a dough with lukewarm water.
3 Knead until smooth.
4 Cover and leave to stand at room temperature for 20 minutes.
5 Roll out the dough on a lightly floured surface to 6 mm ($\frac{1}{4}$ in) thick.
6 Cut into 7$\frac{1}{2}$ cm (3 in) squares.
7 Deep fry in small batches until puffed up and golden, turning once. Drain on paper towels.
8 Tear off one corner and pour in the warm, cinnamon-flavoured honey or maple syrup and diced dried apricots.
9 Sprinkle with castor sugar.

Note Roll out, cut into larger squares, egg wash the edges, fill with your choice of fruit. Fold to form a turnover before deep frying.

6 – Soufflé pudding

	4 portions	10 portions
milk, whole or skimmed	185 ml ($\frac{3}{8}$ pt)	500 ml (1 pt)
flour, white or wholemeal	25 g (1 oz)	60 g (2$\frac{1}{2}$ oz)
butter or margarine	25 g (1 oz)	60 g (2$\frac{1}{2}$ oz)
castor or unrefined sugar	25 g (1 oz)	60 g (2$\frac{1}{2}$ oz)
eggs, separated	3	8

1 Boil the milk in a sauteuse.
2 Combine the flour, butter and sugar.
3 Whisk into the milk and reboil.
4 Remove from heat, add yolks one at a time, whisking continuously.
5 Stiffly beat the whites and carefully fold into the mixture.
6 Three-quarters fill buttered and sugared dariole moulds.
7 Place in a roasting tin, half full of water.
8 Bring to the boil and place in a hot oven (approximately 230–250°C, 450–500°F, Reg. 8–9) for 12–15 minutes.
9 Turn out on to a flat dish and serve with a suitable hot sauce, e.g. custard or sabayon sauce.

7 – Royal soufflé pudding

1 Prepare a soufflé pudding mix as in the previous recipe, adding vanilla.
2 Liberally grease the moulds and line with thin slices of jam swiss roll.

3 Add the soufflé pudding mix and cook as in the previous recipe.
4 Serve with apricot sauce flavoured with Marsala or sherry.

8 – Soufflé pudding with cherries

1 Prepare a vanilla soufflé pudding.
2 Add fresh or preserved cherries macerated in kirsch.
3 Cook as in recipe 6.
4 Serve with raspberry or redcurrant sauce.

9 – Vanilla soufflé

	4 portions	10 portions
milk	125 ml ($\frac{1}{4}$ pt)	300 ml ($\frac{5}{8}$ pt)
natural vanilla or pod		
eggs, separated	4	10
flour	10 g ($\frac{1}{2}$ oz)	25 g ($1\frac{1}{4}$ oz)
castor sugar	50 g (2 oz)	125 g (5 oz)
butter	10 g ($\frac{1}{2}$ oz)	25 g ($1\frac{1}{4}$ oz)

1 Coat the inside of a soufflé case/dish with fresh butter (as thinly as possible).
2 Coat the butter in the soufflé case with castor sugar, tap out surplus.
3 Boil the milk and vanilla in a thick-bottomed pan.
4 Mix half the egg yolks, the flour and sugar to a smooth consistency in a basin.
5 Add the boiling milk to the mixture, stir vigorously until completely mixed.
6 Return this mixture to a *clean* thick-bottomed pan and stir continuously with a wooden spoon over gentle heat until the mixture thickens, then remove from heat.
7 Allow to cool slightly.
8 Add the remaining egg yolks and the butter, mix thoroughly.
9 Stiffly whip the egg whites and *carefully* fold into the mixture, which should be just warm. (An extra egg white can be added for extra lightness.)
10 Place the mixture into the prepared mould and level it off with a palette knife, do not allow it to come above the level of the soufflé case.

11 Place on a baking sheet and cook in a moderately hot oven, approximately 200–230°C (400–450°F, Reg. 6–8) until the soufflé is well risen and is firm to touch, approximately 15–20 minutes.
12 Remove carefully from oven, dredge with icing sugar and serve at once. A hot soufflé *cannot* be allowed to stand or it will sink.

10 – Chocolate soufflé

1 Proceed as for vanilla soufflé, dissolving 50 g (2 oz) (125 g, 5 oz for 10 portions) grated couverture or powdered chocolate in the milk.
2 If the mixture is found to be too stiff an extra beaten egg white may be added.

11 – Chocolate and vanilla soufflé

1 This is half vanilla, half chocolate.
2 The mixtures should be carefully placed side by side in the mould.

12 – Grand Marnier soufflé

(René Pauvert)

	4 portions
egg yolk	1
whole egg	1
sugar	100 g (4 oz)
French flour	75 g (3 oz)
milk	25 cl ($\frac{1}{2}$ pt)
split vanilla pod	$\frac{1}{4}$
egg yolks	5
Soufflé	
egg whites	7
sugar	100 g (4 oz)
Grand Marnier	10 cl ($\frac{1}{8}$ pt)
biscuit cuillère	4

1 Whisk the egg yolk and the egg together, add the sugar and flour.
2 Boil the milk with the vanilla pod.
3 Add the boiled milk to the mixture and return to the heat. Cook until it thickens.

4 Place in a mixer, whisk the lumps out, then add the egg yolks.
5 Take four soufflé moulds and 'chemise' with soft butter and sugar.
6 Whisk the egg whites with a touch of salt until stiff.
7 Soak the biscuit cuillère in Grand Marnier.
8 Mix some Grand Marnier into the sweet basic.
9 Add a small amount of egg white into the basic, incorporate well, then gently fold the rest of the egg into the mixture.
10 Pour a spoonful of the mixture into the mould, then add the soaked biscuit and then the rest of the mixture up to the rim.
11 Cook for about 14 minutes at 200°C (390°F) in the oven.

Note This soufflé could be accompanied with a sauce boat of whipped cream with chocolate chips folded in it.

T 13 – Cinnamon soufflé with Drambuie cream

(CHRIS OAKES)

	4 portions	10 portions
Panada		
pears, roughly chopped	550 g (1 lb 6 oz)	2 kg (4 lb)
water	500 ml (1 pt)	1¼ litre (2½ pt)
cornflour	1 level tsp	2½ level tsp
water	1 level tbsp	2½ level tsb
cinnamon	3 level tbsp	9 level tbsp
whipping cream	250 ml (½ pt)	600 ml (1¼ pt)
sugar	10 g (½ oz)	25 g (1¼ oz)
Drambuie	½ measure	1½ measure
egg whites	5	12
sugar	75 g (3 oz)	180 g (7½ oz)

1 To make the panada: place the pears in a saucepan, barely cover with water and cook until soft.
2 Liquidise and pass. Reheat in a clean pan and simmer until thick, stirring occasionally (approximately 10 minutes).
3 Mix the cornflour and water together. Whisk into pear mixture and leave on a low heat for approximately 10 minutes.
4 Add ground cinnamon and whisk. This mixture can now be used immediately or kept in the fridge for later use.
5 Whisk the cream until it peaks. Add sugar and Drambuie to taste.
6 To make the soufflé: warm the panada gently in a bain-marie.

7 Whisk the egg whites in a suitable bowl until they peak, adding the sugar a little at a time.

8 Mix a spoonful of the egg whites into the panada, then fold in the rest.

9 Spoon soufflé mixture into buttered and sugared ramekin moulds. Smooth off around the edge at an angle with a palette knife, finishing with a flat top.

10 Place on a baking sheet in a preheated oven at 220°C (425°F, Reg. 7) for approximately 10–12 minutes.

11 Serve *immediately*, dusted with icing sugar and a sauceboat of cream.

Note Any fruit can be used in the soufflé but omit the cinnamon if not using pears.

—— *Cold sweets* ——

14 – Biscuit viennoise

This is now becoming a classical recipe developed in France for almond roulade, cold sweets and gâteaux. This recipe may also be used as a base. Spread the mixture on to small baking sheets and bake at 220°C (430°F) for 4–6 minutes.

A suitable size baking sheet would be 60 cm × 40 cm for a base. This mixture would make two baking sheets.

ground almonds	100 g (4 oz)
icing sugar	100 g (4 oz)
flour	80 g (3⅛ oz)
whole egg	120 g (4½ oz)
egg yolk	30 g (1⅛ oz)
melted butter	30 g (1⅛ oz)
egg white	180 g (7⅛ oz)
castor sugar	65 g (2⅜ oz)

1 Sieve the ground almonds, icing sugar and flour together well.

2 Add half the beaten whole egg and egg yolk, add the remainder gradually.

3 Add the melted butter.

4 Stiffly beat the egg white and the castor sugar, fold into the above mixture.

5 If required for jaconde base, the mixture will need to be knocked back.
6 Bake at 220°C (430°F) for 4–6 minutes.

15 – Chocolate décor paste

butter or margarine	80 g ($3\frac{1}{8}$ oz)
icing sugar	80 g ($3\frac{1}{8}$ oz)
egg whites	2–3
flour	60 g (2 oz)
cocoa powder	20 g ($\frac{2}{3}$ oz)

1 Lightly cream the butter and sugar.
2 Add egg whites one by one, mixing well, being careful not to curdle the mixture.
3 Gently fold in the sifted flour and cocoa powder.
4 Spread on 2 Silpat trays, mark with a comb and allow to freeze.
5 When frozen, spread on the jaconde biscuit mixture and bake at 220–240°C (400–420°F) for approximately 3–5 minutes.

Notes These mixtures allow the pastry cook to be both creative and versatile. There is also a variety of specialised equipment available for this work in the form of scrapers, combs, moulds and frames.

Cornstarch and colour may be used as a substitute for cocoa powder.

16 – Biscuit jaconde

Decorative sponge/biscuit for sweets and gâteaux. This mixture is sufficient for two Silpat trays.

icing sugar	$187\frac{1}{2}$ g ($7\frac{1}{2}$ oz)
ground almonds	$187\frac{1}{2}$ g ($7\frac{1}{2}$ oz)
flour, soft	50 g (2 oz)
egg	140 g (5 oz)
water if required	
egg	160 g ($6\frac{1}{4}$ oz)
melted butter or margarine	40 g ($1\frac{1}{2}$ oz)
egg whites	190 g ($7\frac{1}{2}$ oz)
castor sugar	100 g (4 oz)
egg white powder	small pinch
squeeze of lemon juice	

1 Sieve the icing sugar and ground almonds with the flour.
2 Mix in the 140 g (5 oz) beaten egg and water for a total mixing time of 8–10 minutes.
3 Now add the 160 g (6¼ oz) of beaten egg in 3–4 stages.
4 Gradually add the melted butter.
5 Stiffly beat the egg whites with the lemon juice and egg white powder and castor sugar. The mixture must be stiff. Fold this mixture into the base and knock back well (this is only done for the two-coloured sponge).
6 Bake at 220–240°C (400–420°F) for approximately 5–7 minutes.

Note The egg white powder and the lemon juice strengthens the egg white.

17 – Chocolate leaves

(Mark McCann)

dark chocolate	150 g (6 oz)
milk	1 litre (2 pt)
egg yolks	10
castor sugar	100 g

1 Make pastry cream as follows. Add the chocolate to the boiling milk. Mix the egg yolks and sugar together. Pour ⅓ of the milk on to the yolks and sugar. Mix well. Return to the saucepan. Heat to just under boiling point. Leave the mixture to cool.
2 Cut a circle measuring 7½ cm (3 in) in diameter from a thin piece of card.
3 Grease and flour a tray.
4 Place the card with the centre cut out on to a tray.
5 Spread the pastry cream evenly into the centre using a palette knife.
6 When completed, lift off the card.
7 Cook in the oven at 150°C for about 10–15 minutes.
8 Take out and store in a dry place until required. A hot cupboard is the best for this.

These leaves are used to decorate cold sweets.

18 – Charlotte russe

A charlotte russe is a vanilla bavarois (see below) set in a charlotte mould which has been lined with sponge fingers (recipe 88, page 518). The bottom of the charlotte mould should be lined with fan-shaped pieces of finger biscuit. If, in place of fan shaped biscuit, $\frac{1}{2}$cm ($\frac{1}{4}$in) of red jelly is used, the charlotte is called charlotte moscovite.

1 Prepare and cook the finger biscuits.
2 Remove on to a cooling grid.
3 Prepare the bavarois.
4 While the bavarois is setting line the bottom of the charlotte mould by either method described below in point 5.
5 Trim sufficient biscuits into fan shaped pieces of a length half the diameter of the base of the mould and neatly arrange in the bottom of the mould round side down, *or* pour in sufficient red jelly for a thickness of $\frac{1}{2}$cm ($\frac{1}{4}$in).
6 Neatly line the sides of the mould with trimmed finger biscuits, round sides facing outwards (if using a red jelly base, allow this to set first).
7 Pour the bavarois mixture into the lined mould at the last possible moment before setting point is reached.
8 Place the charlotte in the refrigerator to set.
9 To serve, trim off any ends of the biscuit which may project above the mould.
10 Carefully turn the charlotte out on to a serving dish (if red jelly base is used dip the bottom of the mould into boiling water for 2–3 seconds, wipe dry and turn out).
11 Decorate the charlotte with whipped sweetened cream (crème Chantilly).

– *Vanilla bavarois*

	6–8 portions
gelatine	10 g ($\frac{1}{2}$oz)
eggs, separated	2
castor sugar	50 g (2 oz)
milk, whole or skimmed, flavoured with vanilla	250 ml ($\frac{1}{2}$pt)
whipping or double cream or non-dairy cream	250 ml ($\frac{1}{2}$pt)

1 If using leaf gelatine, soak in cold water.
2 Cream the yolks and sugar in a bowl until almost white.
3 Whisk on the milk which has been brought to the boil, mix well.
4 Clean the milk saucepan (which should be a thick-bottomed one) and return the mixture to it.
5 Return to a low heat and stir continuously with a wooden spoon until the mixture coats the back of the spoon. The mixture must not boil.
6 Remove from the heat, add the gelatine, stir until dissolved.
7 Pass through a fine strainer into a clean bowl, leave in a cool place, stirring occasionally until almost setting point.
8 Then fold in the lightly beaten cream.
9 Fold in the stiffly beaten whites.
10 Pour the mixture into a mould (may be very lightly greased with oil).
11 Allow to set in the refrigerator.

19 – Kirsch-flavoured peach charlotte

	4 portions	10 portions
orange jelly		
sponge fingers		
vanilla bavarois	250 ml ($\frac{1}{2}$ pt)	600 ml ($1\frac{1}{4}$ pt)
peach purée	125 ml ($\frac{1}{4}$ pt)	300 ml ($\frac{5}{8}$ pt)
diced peaches	50 g (2 oz)	125 g (5 oz)
kirsch, to taste		

1 Line the bottom of a charlotte mould with orange jelly.
2 Line with sponge fingers.
3 Fill with vanilla bavarois (see recipe 18) mixed with peach purée and a small dice of peaches, soaked in kirsch.

20 – Harlequin charlotte

Glaze sponge fingers with white, pink and chocolate fondant. Allow to dry well. Line a suitable timbale mould with silicone paper and the glazed sponge fingers, alternating the colours. Fill the centre with vanilla bavarois and allow to set. Turn out on a flat salver, decorate with whipped cream and serve.

T 21 ~ Drambuie chocolate charlotte with coffee bean sauce

(David Miller)

	4 portions	10 portions
plain eating chocolate	60 g (2½ oz)	180 g (½ lb)
egg yolks	4	10
castor sugar	100 g (4 oz)	250 g (10 oz)
unsalted butter, softened	125 g (5 oz)	300 g (12½ oz)
cocoa powder	60 g (2½ oz)	180 g (½ lb)
miniature bottle Drambuie	1	2
double cream	250 ml (½ pt)	600 ml (1¼ pt)
icing sugar	25 g (1 oz)	60 g (2½ oz)
sponge fingers	12–18	30–40
cold black coffee (not instant)	25 ml (1 fl oz)	125 ml (¼ pt)

Decoration

double cream	125 ml (¼ pt)	300 ml (⅝ pt)
icing sugar	10 g (½ oz)	60 g (2½ oz)
plain eating chocolate, grated	35 g (1½ oz)	85 g (4 oz)
mould, refrigerated	1 × 10 cm	3 × 10 cm

1 Place the plain chocolate in a bain-marie to melt slowly.
2 Whisk the egg yolks and castor sugar together until light and thick.
3 Add the melted chocolate to the eggs slowly, keeping warm and not allowing the chocolate to set.
4 In a separate bowl, cream the unsalted butter and cocoa powder until light and creamy. Add half the Drambuie.
5 Fold together the eggs and butter, mixing until smooth. Fold in the whipped cream.
6 Use the mixture to half-fill the mould.
7 Soak half sponge fingers with the remaining Drambuie and a little black coffee.
8 Cover the mixture evenly with the sponge fingers. Add the rest of the mixture and refrigerate for 2 hours.
9 To remove, run the mould under hot water and turn out on to a plate. Cut the remaining sponge fingers to size and place round the sides. Decorate the top of the charlotte with whipped cream and grated chocolate, and serve with coffee bean sauce (see overleaf).

– Coffee bean sauce

	4 portions	10 portions
milk	125 ml ($\frac{1}{4}$ pt)	300 ml ($\frac{5}{8}$ pt)
double cream	125 ml ($\frac{1}{4}$ pt)	300 ml ($\frac{5}{8}$ pt)
castor sugar	35 g ($1\frac{1}{2}$ oz)	85 g (4 oz)
freshly ground fine coffee	1 tsp	2–3 tsp
egg yolks	3	8
castor sugar	25 g (1 oz)	60 g ($2\frac{1}{2}$ oz)

1 Bring the milk, cream and sugar to boil.
2 Remove, add ground coffee and cover to infuse for 15 minutes.
3 Meanwhile, whisk the egg yolks and remaining sugar until light.
4 Bring the coffee infusion to the boil, add to eggs and whisk. Then return to the pan and cook slowly on a low heat for 5 minutes without boiling.
5 Transfer coffee cream to cool bowl and allow to cool, stirring occasionally.

Note If necessary, in order to speed up cooling, place bowl into cold water with ice cubes.

22 – Chocolate mousse

	4 portions	10 portions
plain chocolate	100 g (4 oz)	250 g (10 oz)
butter	25 g (1 oz)	60 g ($2\frac{1}{2}$ oz)
eggs, separated	4	10
castor sugar	100 g (4 oz)	250 g (10 oz)
whipped cream	125 ml ($\frac{1}{4}$ pt)	300 ml ($\frac{5}{8}$ pt)

1 Break the chocolate into small pieces, place in a basin, stand in a bain-marie and allow to melt with the butter.
2 Whisk the egg yolks and sugar until almost white and thoroughly mix in the melted chocolate.
3 Carefully fold in the stiffly beaten egg whites, pour into a suitable dish or individual dishes and refrigerate until set.
4 Decorate with whipped cream and serve.

23 – Chocolate and orange mousse

Add the lightly grated zest of 2 oranges (5 for 10 portions).

24 – Chocolate rum mousse

Add 1–2 tablespoons rum ($2\frac{1}{2}$–5 tablespoons for 10 portions).

25 – Chocolate brandy mousse

Add 1–2 tablespoons brandy ($2\frac{1}{2}$–5 tablespoons for 10 portions).

26 – Chocolate and almond mousse

Add 50 g (2 oz) lightly toasted sliced almonds (125 g, 5 oz for 10 portions).

T 27 – Mango mousse with fresh coconut sauce

(ANTHONY BLAKE)

	4 portions	10 portions
egg yolks	2	5
castor sugar	75 g (3 oz)	180 g ($7\frac{1}{2}$ oz)
milk	250 ml ($\frac{1}{2}$ pt)	600 ml ($1\frac{1}{4}$ pt)
gelatine (dissolved)	10 g ($\frac{1}{2}$ oz)	25 g ($1\frac{1}{4}$ oz)
mango (peeled and puréed)	1	$2\frac{1}{2}$
double cream, whipped	250 ml ($\frac{1}{2}$ pt)	600 ml ($1\frac{1}{4}$ pt)
coconut	1	2–3
castor sugar	50 g (2 oz)	125 g (5 oz)
milk ⎫ sauce	125 ml ($\frac{1}{4}$ pt)	300 ml ($\frac{5}{8}$ pt)
coconut cream	50 g (2 oz)	125 g (5 oz)
whipped cream ⎭	250 ml ($\frac{1}{2}$ pt)	600 ml ($1\frac{1}{4}$ pt)
marshmallows dipped in coconut	12	30

1 Whisk the egg yolks and sugar together until very light and fluffy.
2 Heat the milk to just below boiling point in a heavy-based pan then slowly pour on to the egg yolks, whisking constantly.

3 Return the mixture to a clean pan and cook gently until thick enough to coat the back of a spoon, but do not allow mixture to boil.

4 Whisk in the gelatine and mango purée then pass through a fine sieve. Leave to cool, then chill until it just begins to set.

5 Gently fold in the whipped cream then pour into moulds (timbales or ramekins) and chill for about 4 hours.

6 Make the sauce by first cracking open the coconut, scraping out the flesh and reserving the milk. Cut the flesh into small pieces and cook with the sugar, coconut milk, milk and coconut cream until slightly soft.

7 Pass through a fine sieve and fold in the whipped cream.

8 To serve: unmould the mousse on to cold plates, spoon some of the sauce around and add marshmallows which have been dipped in toasted coconut.

28 ~ Burned, caramelised or browned cream (crème brulée)

	4 portions	10 portions
milk	125 ml ($\frac{1}{4}$ pt)	300 ml ($\frac{5}{8}$ pt)
double cream	125 ml ($\frac{1}{4}$ pt)	300 ml ($\frac{5}{8}$ pt)
natural vanilla essence or pod		
eggs	2	5
yolk	1	2–3
castor sugar	25 g (1 oz)	60 g ($2\frac{1}{2}$ oz)
demerara sugar		

1 Warm the milk, cream and vanilla essence in a pan.

2 Mix the eggs, egg yolk and sugar in a basin and add the warm milk. Stir well and pass through a fine strainer.

3 Pour the cream into individual dishes and place them into a tray half-filled with warm water.

4 Place in the oven at approximately 160°C (325°F, Reg. 3) for about 30–40 minutes, until set.

5 Sprinkle the tops with demerara sugar and glaze under the salamander to a golden brown.

6 Clean the dishes and serve.

Variations Sliced strawberries, raspberries or other fruits, e.g. peaches, apricots, may be placed in the bottom of the dish before adding the cream mixture or placed on top after the creams are caramelised.

29 ~ Pumpkin crème brulée with tarragon

(SEAN O'BRIAN)

	4 portions	10 portions
peeled seeded pumpkin	500 g (1 lb)	1.2 kg (2 lb 8 oz)
castor sugar	150 g (5 oz)	350 g (12 oz)
double cream	500 ml (1 pt)	1¼ litre (2½ pt)
egg yolks	6	14
tarragon leaves	½ tsp	1 tsp

1 Cook the pumpkin and sugar until soft, drain in a conical sieve, return to heat and cook until dry and pass through a drum sieve.
2 Mix the pumpkin purée with the eggs and cream.
3 Blanch the tarragon in boiling water for 10 seconds to remove the bitterness, chop coarsely and add to the brulée mix.
4 Carefully pour the mix into suitable dishes and cook in a bain-marie for approximately 45 minutes at 150°C (300°F) until lightly set in the centre.
5 Remove from oven, leave to cool, dust with ground demarara sugar and glaze under a hot salamander until the sugar is caramelised.

30 ~ Chestnut meringue nests

It is best to use canned marrons glacé for this recipe.

1 Pass the chestnuts through a sieve and flavour with rum.
2 Dust individual savarin moulds with icing sugar. Place the chestnut purée in a forcing bag with a 1 cm (½ in) plain tube and fill the moulds but do not press down.
3 Turn out on to individual rounds of meringue and fill the centres with whipped cream using a star tube. Sprinkle with chocolate shavings.

Note In place of meringue nests (vacherins) individual rounds of cooked sablé paste may be used.

31 – Sugar-topped choux buns filled with rum-flavoured pastry cream on chocolate sauce (salambos)

	4 portions	10 portions
choux pastry	125 ml (¼ pt)	300 ml (⅝ pt)
rum-flavoured pastry cream*	250 ml (½ pt)	600 ml (1¼ pt)
cube sugar	200 g (8 oz)	500 g (1¼ lb)
water	60 ml (⅛ pt)	150 ml (⅓ pt)
pinch of cream of tartar		
chocolate	250 ml (½ pt)	600 ml (1¼ pt)

> 1 portion provides:
>
> 664 kcals/2776 kJ
> 21.8 g fat
> (of which 12.2 g saturated)
> 111.9 g carbohydrate
> (of which 92.5 sugars)
> 12.2 g protein
> 0.7 g fibre
>
> Note   Use of wholemeal flour in pastry cream and 50 per cent wholemeal pastry increase fibre to 1.5 g.

* Pastry cream may be made in the traditional way or using skimmed milk, unrefined sugar and wholemeal flour.

1 Pipe large choux buns approximately 4 cm (1½ in) diameter using a 1 cm (½ in) star tube on a lightly greased baking sheet.
2 Egg wash lightly and bake in a moderately hot oven (approximately 220°C, 425°F, Reg. 7) for approximately 20–25 minutes.
3 When cooked, split and allow to cool and fill with rum-flavoured pastry cream.
4 Place the cube sugar, water and cream of tartar into a suitable saucepan and cook to hard crack (155°C).
5 Dip the tops of the buns in hard crack sugar.
6 Serve individually on plates on a layer of chocolate sauce.

– Choux paste

	4 portions	10 portions
water	250 ml (½ pt)	600 ml (1¼ pt)
pinch of sugar and salt		
butter, margarine or oil	100 g (4 oz)	250 g (10 oz)
flour (strong)	125 g (5 oz)	300 g (12½ oz)
eggs	4	10

1 Bring the water, sugar and fat to the boil in a saucepan.
2 Remove from heat.
3 Add the sieved flour and mix in with a wooden spoon.

4 Return to a moderate heat and stir continuously until the mixture leaves the sides of the pan.
5 Remove from the heat and allow to cool.
6 Gradually add the beaten eggs, mixing well.
7 The paste should be of dropping consistency.

Note 50 per cent, 70 per cent or 100 per cent wholemeal flour may be used.

32 – Cream beau rivage

	4–6 portions	10–12 portions
butter	25 g (1 oz)	60 g (2½ oz)
praline	50 g (2 oz)	125 g (5 oz)
milk	500 ml (1 pt)	1¼ litre (2½ pt)
eggs	4	10
sugar	50 g (2 oz)	125 g (5 oz)
natural vanilla essence or pod		
vanilla cornets		
cream	250 ml ½ pt)	625 ml (1¼ pt)

1 Liberally butter savarin mould(s).
2 Evenly coat the buttered mould(s) with the praline.
3 Warm the milk.
4 Pour the warm milk on to the beaten eggs, sugar and vanilla and mix well.
5 Pass the mixture through a fine strainer into a basin.
6 Carefully pour the mixture into the savarin mould(s).
7 Place the mould(s) into a bain-marie in a moderate oven (approximately 180°C, 350°F, Reg. 4) to cook and set for approximately 30–40 minutes.
8 When cooked, remove from the oven, allow to cool, then place in the refrigerator.
9 To serve, turn the mould(s) out carefully on to a suitable dish.
10 Fill the cornets (see recipe 90) with the whipped sweetened cream and pipe the remainder into the centre of the ring.
11 Neatly arrange the cornets on top of the cream, points to the centre.
12 Place a crystallised violet or rose in the centre of the cream in cornets.

33 – Sablé paste

egg	1
castor sugar	75 g (3 oz)
butter or margarine	150 g (6 oz)
soft flour	200 g (8 oz)
pinch of salt	
ground almonds	75 g (3 oz)

1 Lightly cream egg and sugar without over-softening.
2 Lightly mix in butter, do not over-soften.
3 Incorporate sieved flour, salt and the ground almonds.
4 Mix lightly to a smooth paste.
5 Rest in refrigerator before use.

Note Alternatively, 50 per cent wholemeal and 50 per cent white flour may be used, or 70 per cent wholemeal and 30 per cent white flour.

Sablé paste may be used for petits fours, pastries and as a base for other desserts.

34 – Strawberry cream biscuits (strawberry sablé)

	4 portions	10 portions
sablé paste	200 g (8 oz)	500 g (1¼ lb)
ripe strawberries, washed and sliced	200–300 g (8–12 oz)	500–750 g (1¼–1¾ lb)
whipped cream	125 ml (¼ pt)	300 ml (⅝ pt)
strawberry sauce	125 ml (¼ pt)	300 ml (⅝ pt)
icing sugar		

1 Pin out the sablé paste, ¼ cm (⅛ in) thick.
2 Cut into rounds, 8 cm (3 in) diameter, and bake in a cool oven (approximately 160°C, 325°F, Reg. 3) until light golden brown.
3 When cooked, remove from baking sheet on to a cooling grid.
4 Place a layer of cream on to half the biscuits, then a layer of strawberries, a second layer of cream and top with the remaining biscuits.
5 Dust with icing sugar and serve with the strawberry sauce.

35 – Raspberry cream biscuits (raspberry sablé)

As recipe 34 but substitute raspberries for strawberries, keeping the raspberries whole.

Note If required, the fruit may be macerated (after slicing) in a little castor sugar and a suitable liqueur, e.g. Grand Marnier, Cointreau.

These sweets can also be made up in two layers using three biscuits instead of two.

36 – Snow eggs

	4 portions	10 portions
Poaching liquid		
milk, whole or skimmed	500 ml (1 pt)	1¼ litre (2½ pt)
castor or unrefined sugar	50 g (2 oz)	125 g (5 oz)
natural vanilla essence or pod		
Meringue		
egg whites	4	10
castor sugar	50 g (2 oz)	125 g (5 oz)
Sauce anglaise		
milk from poaching		
egg yolks	4	10
castor or unrefined sugar	25 g (1 oz)	60 g (2½ oz)
Caramel		
granulated or cube sugar	50 g (2 oz)	125 g (5 oz)
water	30 ml ($\frac{1}{16}$ pt)	75 g ($\frac{1}{4}$ pt)

1 Place the milk, sugar and vanilla essence in a shallow pan and bring to boil. Draw to side of the stove and simmer.
2 Whisk the egg whites stiffly, add sugar and make meringue.
3 Using two large spoons, drop balls of the meringue into the milk, poach for 3–4 minutes, turn over and poach for another 3–4 minutes. Drain on a cloth.
4 Make the milk up to 500 ml (1 pt) (1¼ litre, 2½ pt) and use to prepare a sauce anglaise with the egg yolks and the sugar. Strain and stir until cold, on ice.
5 Place a little sauce anglaise in a glass bowl, or in individual dishes, and place the snow eggs on top.
6 Mask over with sauce anglaise and decorate with a criss cross of caramel sugar.

37 – Tiramisu

There are many different recipes for tiramisu. This may be served as a chocolate sponge moistened with coffee liqueur and sandwiched together with mascarpone cream cheese covered with cream and chocolate. The gâteau may then stand on an almond biscuit base, such as an amaretto or macaroon. Alternatively, tiramisu may be served in a glass as tiramisu if translated means 'pick me up' or 'lift me up'. The following recipe is an example:

	4 portions	10 portions
egg chocolate sponge	1 × 3	1 × 8
amaretto biscuits	100 g (4 oz)	250 g (10 oz)
mascarpone cheese	250 g (6 oz)	375 g (1½ lb)
whipping cream	250 ml (½ pt)	625 ml (1¼ pt)
coffee liqueur	62 ml (⅛ pt)	155 ml (⅜ pt)
orange, juice and zest of	1	2

1 Cream the mascarpone cheese with the juice and grated zest of orange.
2 Sandwich the sponge liberally with mascarpone cheese.
3 Dice the sponge into ½ cm (¼ in) cubes, place in the bottom of individual suitable glasses.
4 Moisten with coffee liqueur.
5 Sprinkle with crushed amaretto biscuits.
6 Decorate the top with whipped cream, top with an armaretto biscuit.

Note   To add variety to the dish, the sponge may be topped with coffee mousse sprinkled with crushed amaretto biscuit, finished with piped mascarpone cheese and whipped cream. Finally, decorate with piped chocolate and serve.

38 – Strawberry mousse (1)

	4 portions	10 portions	1 portion provides:
ripe strawberries	400 g (1 lb)	1¼ kg (2½ lb)	481 kcals/2000 kJ
icing sugar	50 g (2 oz)	125 g (5 oz)	29.42 g fat
eggs, separated	3	7–8	(of which 16.77 g saturated)
castor sugar	100 g (4 oz)	250 g (10 oz)	47.5 g carbohydrate
gelatine, melted	10 g (½ oz)	25 g (1 oz)	9.59 g protein
whipping cream	250 ml (½ pt)	600 ml (1¼ pt)	1.40 g fibre

1 Retain 4 (10 for 10 portions) strawberries for decoration and purée the remainder with the icing sugar.
2 Whisk the egg yolks and castor sugar until almost white.
3 Whisk in the strawberry purée and the gelatine and strain.
4 Fold in three-quarters of the whipped cream and the stiffly whisked egg whites.
5 Pour into a suitable serving bowl or individual bowls or glasses.
6 Refrigerate until set, then decorate with whipped cream and a strawberry and serve accompanied by a suitable biscuit, e.g. sablé, shortbread, palmier.

Variations
(a) Proceed as above, adding the lightly grated zest and juice of 1–2 oranges (2½–5 for 10 portions). Also increase the gelatine by 5 g (¼ oz) (12 g, ⅝ oz for 10 portions).
(b) Proceed as above, substituting raspberries for strawberries.

39 – Strawberry mousse (2)

	4 portions	10 portions
strawberry purée	375 ml (¾ pt)	1 litre (2 pt)
water	125 ml (¼ pt)	300 ml (⅝ pt)
castor sugar	75 g (3 oz)	180 g (7½ oz)
soaked leaf gelatine	25 g (1 oz)	60 g (2½ oz)
lemon, juice of	½	1–2
whipped cream	250 ml (½ pt)	600 ml (1¼ pt)
egg whites	4	10

1 Place the strawberry purée into a suitable basin.
2 Boil the water with the sugar, then add the soaked gelatine and the lemon juice.
3 Whisk this syrup into the purée.
4 When the mixture is on setting point, fold in the whipped cream and whipped egg whites and place into a suitable mould or individual moulds. Place in refrigerator to set.
5 When set, turn out on to suitable dish or individual plates, decorated with whipped cream and a fresh strawberry.

40 – Summer pudding

	4 portions	10 portions
redcurrants, raspberries, blackcurrants (fully ripe)	400 g (1 lb)	1¼ kg (2½ lb)
sugar	150 g (6 oz)	375 g (15 oz)
thinly sliced white bread, crusts removed	200 g (8 oz)	500 g (1¼ lb)

1 Prepare and wash the fruits.
2 Boil the sugar in 125 ml (¼ pt) water (300 ml, ⅝ pt for 10 portions) until dissolved.
3 Add the fruit and simmer gently until cooked, allowing the fruits to retain their shape and not cook to a mush.
4 Line the bottom and sides of either individual pudding basins or individual moulds, with the bread, packing the slices tightly so that no spaces are left in between.
5 Add the completely cold fruit and cover with more slices of bread.
6 Place a flat dish or plate with a weight on top and refrigerate overnight.
7 Turn out on to a flat plate or dish and serve with cream, clotted cream, ice-cream or yoghurt.

41 – Fruit terrine

	4 portions	10 portions
Sponge		
eggs	3	8
castor sugar	85 g (3½ oz)	200 g (8 oz)
soft flour	60 g (2½ oz)	150 g (6 oz)
Filling		
soft butter	200 g (8 oz)	500 g (1¼ lb)
icing sugar	200 g (8 oz)	500 g (1¼ lb)
fine ground almonds	150 g (6 oz)	375 g (15 oz)
Cointreau	60 ml (⅛ pt)	150 ml (⅓ pt)
whipping cream	250 ml (½ pt)	600 ml (1¼ pt)
kiwifruit	2	5
strawberries	150 g (6 oz)	375 g (15 oz)
peaches	100 g (4 oz)	250 g (10 oz)

1 Prepare the sponge by whisking the eggs and sugar to ribbon stage over a bain-marie of warm water.

2 Carefully fold in the sifted flour.
3 Pour into a prepared swiss roll tin lined with greasepaper and lightly greased.
4 Cook sponge in a hot oven (approximately 220–230°C, 425–450°F, Reg. 7–8) for approximately 4 minutes. Turn out on to a wire rack and allow to cool.
5 When cold, cut a layer of sponge to line suitable terrine(s) approximately 8 cm (3 in) deep and 15–20 cm (6–8 in) wide.
6 Place the sponge in the deep freeze to harden for easier handling.
7 Prepare the filling by creaming the butter and the icing sugar on a machine until soft, light and white.
8 Add the ground almonds and the Cointreau and mix well.
9 Carefully fold in the whipped cream taking care *not to over mix*.
10 Line suitable terrine(s) with greaseproof or silicone paper.
11 Arrange the layers of thin sponge in the bottom and sides.
12 Place a layer of the filling in the base, on top of the sponge, and arrange pieces of fruit over this.
13 Continue with the filling and the fruit to achieve approximately 3 layers. Finish with a thin layer of sponge.
14 Place the terrine(s) in the refrigerator to set for approximately 3–4 hours before serving.
15 Turn out, remove paper and cut into approximately 1 cm ($\frac{1}{2}$in) slices.
16 Serve on individual plates with a cordon of fresh raspberry sauce.

42 – English trifle

	4 portions	10 portions
milk	500 ml (1 pt)	$1\frac{1}{4}$ litre ($2\frac{1}{2}$pt)
vanilla pod *or*	1	2–3
natural vanilla essence	2–3 drops	5–7 drops
eggs *plus* egg yolks	2 (each)	5 (each)
or egg yolks	8	20
castor sugar	50 g (2 oz)	125 g (5 oz)
sponge cake	200 g (8 oz)	500 g ($1\frac{1}{4}$lb)
raspberry or strawberry jam	150 g (6 oz)	375 g (15 oz)
medium or sweet sherry	60 ml ($\frac{1}{8}$pt)	150 ml ($\frac{1}{3}$pt)
double cream, whipped	250 ml ($\frac{1}{2}$pt)	600 ml ($1\frac{1}{4}$pt)
flaked, sliced or nibbed almonds (toasted)	50 g (2 oz)	125 g (5 oz)
glacé cherries	4 or 8	10 or 20

1 Heat the milk with the vanilla pod, cover with a lid, then remove from heat and stand for 15 minutes. Remove the vanilla pod.
2 Thoroughly whisk the eggs and sugar in a basin.
3 Boil the milk, add a quarter to the eggs whisking continuously.
4 Add the remainder of the milk and clean the saucepan.
5 Return the eggs and milk to the clean pan and cook over a gentle heat, stirring continuously with a wooden spoon, until the mixture thickens.
6 Immediately remove from the heat. Strain the mixture into a clean basin and allow to cool, stirring occasionally.
7 Spread the sponge cake with jam, cut into small squares and place in a trifle bowl or individual dishes.
8 Sprinkle on the sherry, allow to soak in.
9 Pour the custard over the sponge cake and allow to set.
10 Decorate with whipped cream, almonds and halves of cherries.

Notes 100 g (4 oz) lightly crushed macaroon biscuits can be added with the sponge cake (250 g, 10 oz for 10 portions).

If whipping cream is available, use this in place of double cream as more volume can be achieved.

A layer of fresh soft fruit, e.g. raspberries or sliced strawberries, which may be macerated in a little sugar and Cointreau or Grand Marnier, can be used in place of jam.

The egg custard can be given a chocolate flavour.

The final decoration can include angelica or chocolate – grated, in curls or in piped shapes.

T 43 – Summer fruit trifle

(SALLY CLARKE)

	4 portions	8–10 portions
Genoise sponge cake, cubes	48	120
double cream, lightly whipped	60 ml ($\frac{1}{8}$ pt)	125 ml ($\frac{1}{4}$ pt)
selection of summer berries	2–3 punnets	4–6 punnets
sugar syrup	60 ml ($\frac{1}{8}$ pt)	150 ml ($\frac{1}{3}$ pt)
chopped pistachio nuts	1 tbsp	2 tbsp

Crème anglaise

egg yolks	4	8
vanilla pod	1	2–3
sugar	25 g (1 oz)	50–75 g (2–3 oz)
milk	500 ml (1 pt)	1 litre (2 pt)

1 Mix the crème anglaise with whipped cream.
2 In chilled soup plates arrange cubes of Genoise, cut the size of large sugar lumps, around the outside.
3 Purée the sugar syrup with one quarter of the mixed fruit, pass it through a fine sieve and toss gently with the remaining fruits. Fill the centre with the fruit mixture and carefully pour cream over the Genoise.
4 Sprinkle the cream with roughly chopped raw pistachio nuts and serve immediately.

Ice-creams and sorbets

SUGAR SYRUPS

BAUMÉ	DENSITY	BAUMÉ	DENSITY	BAUMÉ	DENSITY	BAUMÉ	DENSITY
5	= 1.0359	13	= 1.0989	21	= 1.1699	29	= 1.2515
6	= 1.0434	14	= 1.1074	22	= 1.1799	30	= 1.2624
7	= 1.0509	15	= 1.1159	23	= 1.1896	31	= 1.2736
8	= 1.0587	16	= 1.1247	24	= 1.1995	32	= 1.2850
9	= 1.0665	17	= 1.1335	25	= 1.2095	33	= 1.2964
10	= 1.0745	18	= 1.1425	26	= 1.2197	34	= 1.3082
11	= 1.0825	19	= 1.1515	27	= 1.2301	35	= 1.3199
12	= 1.0907	20	= 1.1609	28	= 1.2407	36	= 1.3319

For many pastry dishes, for example, ice-cream and sorbets, sugar syrups of a definite density are required. This density is measured by a hydrometer known as a saccharometer. The saccharometer may be calibrated in either Brix or degrees baumé. The instrument is a hollow glass tube sealed at each end. One end is weighted with lead shot so that when it is placed in the solution it floats upright. The scale marked in either brix or baumé indicates the depth at which the tube floats. This is influenced by the density of the sugar which in turn is controlled by the ratio of sugar to water used for the solution. The instrument thus measures the amount of sugar in the solution.

ICE-CREAMS

The Ice-cream Regulations 1959 and 1963 require ice-cream to be pasteurised by heating to:

65°C (150°F) for 30 minutes or
71°C (160°F) for 10 minutes or
80°C (175°F) for 15 seconds or
149°C (300°F) for 2 seconds (sterilised).

After heat treatment the mixture is reduced to 7.1°C (45°F) within $1\frac{1}{2}$ hours and kept at this temperature until the freezing process begins. Ice-cream needs this treatment so as to kill harmful bacteria. Freezing without correct heat treatment does not kill bacteria, it allows them to remain dormant. The storage temperature for ice-cream should not exceed −2°C (28°F). All establishments making ice-cream for sale must be licensed by the local authority Environmental Health Officer.

44 – Vanilla ice-cream

	4 portions	10 portions
egg yolks	4	5
castor or unrefined sugar	50 g (2 oz)	125 g (5 oz)
vanilla pod or essence		
milk, whole or skimmed	190 ml ($\frac{1}{3}$ pt)	500 ml ($\frac{3}{4}$ pt)
cream or non-dairy cream	60 ml ($\frac{1}{8}$ pt)	150 ml ($\frac{1}{3}$ pt)

Using whole milk, single cream
1 portion provides:

147 kcals/616 kJ
8.1 g fat
(of which 4.2 g saturated)
15.8 g carbohydrate
(of which 15.8 g sugars)
3.5 g protein
0.0 g fibre

1 Whisk the yolks and sugar in a bowl until almost white.
2 Boil the milk with the vanilla pod or essence in a thick-bottomed pan.
3 Whisk on to the eggs, add sugar, mix well.
4 Return to the cleaned saucepan, place on a low heat.
5 Stir continuously with a wooden spoon until the mixture coats the back of the spoon.
6 Pass through a fine strainer into a bowl.
7 Freeze in an ice-cream machine, gradually adding the cream.

45 – Coffee ice-cream

Add coffee essence to taste to the custard after it is cooked.

46 – Chocolate ice-cream

Add 50–100 g (2–4 oz) of chopped couverture to the milk before boiling.

47 – Strawberry ice-cream

Add 125 ml ($\frac{1}{4}$ pt) of strawberry pulp in place of 125 ml ($\frac{1}{4}$ pt) of milk (increase amounts by $2\frac{1}{2}$ times for 10 portions). The pulp is added after the custard is cooked.

SORBETS

48 – Lemon sorbet

	4 portions	8–10 portions
sugar	100 g (4 oz)	200 g (8 oz)
water	250 ml ($\frac{1}{2}$ pt)	$\frac{1}{2}$ litre (1 pt)
lemons	1	2
egg white	$\frac{1}{2}$	1

> 1 portion provides:
>
> 100 kcals/421 kJ
> 0.0 g fat
> (of which 0.0 g saturated)
> 26.3 g carbohydrate
> (of which 26.3 g sugars)
> 0.4 g protein
> 0.0 g fibre

1 Bring the sugar, water and peeled zest of lemons to the boil.
2 Remove from the heat and cool. The saccharometer reading for the syrup should be 18–20° baumé.
3 Add the juice of the lemon.
4 Add the white and mix well.
5 Pass through a fine strainer and freeze.

49 – Orange sorbet

	4 portions	8–10 portions
sugar	100 g (4 oz)	200 g (8 oz)
water	250 ml ($\frac{1}{2}$ pt)	$\frac{1}{2}$ litre (1 pt)
large oranges	1	2
lemon	$\frac{1}{2}$	1
egg white	$\frac{1}{2}$	1

Prepare and freeze as for lemon ice, 18–20° baumé.

50 – Strawberry sorbet

	4 portions	8–10 portions
sugar	100 g (4 oz)	200 g (8 oz)
water	180 ml ($\frac{1}{3}$ pt)	375 ml ($\frac{3}{4}$ pt)
lemon	$\frac{1}{2}$	1
strawberry purée	60 ml ($\frac{1}{2}$ pt)	125 ml ($\frac{1}{4}$ pt)
egg white	$\frac{1}{2}$	1

Prepare and freeze as for lemon ice, 18–20° baumé.

51 – Raspberry sorbet

	4 portions	8–10 portions
sugar	100 g (4 oz)	200 g (8 oz)
water	180 ml ($\frac{1}{3}$ pt)	375 ml ($\frac{3}{4}$ pt)
lemon	$\frac{1}{2}$	1
raspberry purée	60 ml ($\frac{1}{2}$ pt)	125 ml ($\frac{1}{4}$ pt)
egg white	$\frac{1}{2}$	1

Prepare and freeze as for lemon ice, 18–20° baumé.

52 – Tutti frutti sorbet

Lemon and strawberry ice with candied fruits.

—— Gâteaux, flans and slices ——

53 – Baked cheesecake

	8 portions
Paste	
margarine or butter	75 g (3 oz)
castor sugar	25 g (1 oz)
water	60 ml ($\frac{1}{8}$ pt)
soft flour	100 g (4 oz)
crushed digestive biscuits	25 g (1 oz)

Filling

margarine or butter	50 g (2 oz)
castor sugar	100 g (4 oz)
egg	50 g (2 oz)
lemon, zest and juice	$\frac{1}{2}$
pinch of salt	
cornflour	25 g (1 oz)
low-fat curd cheese	300 g (12 oz)
washed sultanas	50 g (2 oz)

Paste of lattice

margarine or butter	100 g (4 oz)
castor sugar	50 g (2 oz)
egg	50 g (2 oz)
soft flour	125 g (5 oz)

1 Prepare the filling by creaming together the fat and sugar until light and creamy.
2 Beat in the egg and add the lemon juice and zest. Mix well.
3 Add the salt. Mix in the cornflour and curd cheese.
4 Fold in the sultanas.
5 For the paste, cream together the fat and sugar and add the water. Mix well.
6 Fold in the flour and crushed digestive biscuits. Relax the paste for 10 minutes.
7 Roll out the paste to approximately $\frac{1}{2}$cm ($\frac{1}{4}$in) thick into a circle and use to line a lightly greased 20 cm (8 in) shallow baking tin.
8 Add the filling to come to the top of the tin.
9 Prepare the lattice by creaming together the fat and sugar, beating in the egg and carefully folding in the flour. Mix to a smooth paste.
10 Roll out the paste into a rectangle approximately $\frac{1}{2}$cm ($\frac{1}{4}$in) thick and cut into 1 cm ($\frac{1}{2}$in) strips.
11 Egg wash the edge of the cheesecake, lay a lattice work over the top using strips.
12 Bake in a moderate oven (approximately 200°C, 400°F, Reg. 6) for about 30 minutes.

54 – Black cherry cheesecake

8–10 portions

eggs		3
castor sugar	} sponge	85 g (3½ oz)
soft flour		60 g (2½ oz)
egg yolks		6
castor sugar		300 g (12 oz)
orange, zest of		1
lemon, zest of		1
cream cheese		400 g (1 lb)
gelatine		25 g (1 oz)
egg whites		3
castor sugar		75 g (3 oz)
whipped cream		750 ml (1½ pt)
natural vanilla essence or pod		
20 cm (8 in) disc sweet pastry		1
black cherries (stoned)		200 g (8 oz)

Total recipe provides:

8349 kcals/34636 kJ
592.2 g fat
(of which 341.7 g saturated)
679.9 g carbohydrate
(of which 557.9 g sugars)
117.3 g protein
6.8 g fibre

1 Prepare the sponge in the normal way (recipe 41, stages 1–4) using a swiss roll tin.
2 Beat together the yolks, sugar and orange and lemon zest.
3 Mix the cream cheese until smooth.
4 Blend the egg mixture into the cheese.
5 Stir in the gelatine which has been soaked in cold water and melted, add while still warm.
6 Whisk the egg whites, adding 75 g (3 oz) castor sugar.
7 When the cheese mixture is on setting point, fold in the cream and egg whites and flavour with vanilla essence.
8 Line a 20 cm (8 in) cake tin with a disc of cooked sweet pastry and line the sides with greaseproof paper.
9 Half-fill the mould with half the cheese mixture. Place on top a layer of well-drained black cherries.
10 Cover with a second layer of cheese mixture and finish with a layer of thinly sliced genoise.
11 Allow to set in the refrigerator for 3 hours.
12 Turn out of the tin and remove the greaseproof paper. Dust the sponge with icing sugar and mark trellis fashion with a hot poker.

Variations Blackcurrants, strawberries, apricots, peaches and raspberries may also be used in place of black cherries.

55 – Apricot and almond cream flan

6 portions
1 Line a flan ring with sweet paste and place on a baking sheet.
2 Spread the base with a thin layer of almond cream (frangipane) (see below).
3 Half-fill with well-drained, cooked apricots.
4 Cover with almond cream.
5 Cook at approximately 190°C (375°F, Reg. 5) for 20–25 minutes.
6 When cooked brush with hot apricot glaze and water icing.
7 Return to oven for 30 seconds to glaze.

Note   Other fruits may be used in the same way.

– *Frangipane*

butter	100 g (4 oz)
castor sugar	100 g (4 oz)
eggs	2
ground almonds	100 g (4 oz)
flour	10 g ($\frac{1}{2}$ oz)

Cream the butter and sugar, gradually beat in the eggs. Mix in the almonds and flour, mix lightly.

56 – Fruit and pastry cream flan

6 portions
1 Line a flan ring with sweet paste and place on a baking sheet.
2 Fill with desired fruit, e.g. apple, gooseberries, apricots. Sprinkle with sugar.
3 Cook at approximately 200°C (400°F, Reg. 6) for 20–25 minutes.
4 Carefully mask fruit with hot pastry cream.
5 Sprinkle with crushed macaroons. Dust with icing sugar and glaze under a salamander.

Note   This flan can also be cooked blind and filled with poached or tinned fruit and finished as above.

57 – Apple and custard flan

6 portions
1 Line a flan ring with short paste and place on a baking sheet.
2 Half-fill with sections of apple and sprinkle with brown sugar.
3 Cook at approximately 200°C (400°F, Reg. 6) for 20–25 minutes.
4 Fill with a raw egg custard (see below) and carefully replace in the oven.
5 Cook at 190°C (275°F, Reg. 5) until custard is cooked and set.
6 Remove flan ring and allow to cool.
7 Dust with a mixture of icing sugar and cinnamon.

Note   Other types of fruit may be used in the same way.

– *Raw egg custard*

milk	125 ml ($\frac{1}{4}$ pt)
egg	1
castor sugar	25 g (1 oz)
natural vanilla essence or pod	

Mix all ingredients together, strain and use as required.

T 58 – Burnt lemon tart

(BRIAN TURNER)

8–10 portions

Flan pastry
sugar	100 g (4 oz)
butter	200 g (8 oz)
orange, zest of	1
flour	300 g (12 oz)

Filling
eggs	16
sugar	350 g (14 oz)
lemons, juice of	4
double cream	300 g (12 fl oz)
icing sugar	

1 To make pastry: cream the sugar, butter and orange zest. Fold in the flour and leave to rest.

2 Use the pastry to line a 30 cm (12 in) flan case, bake blind and cool.
3 Mix together the eggs and sugar. Add the lemon juice, then double cream and pass.
4 Pour the mixture into a cooked flan case. Bake at 160°C (325°F, Reg. 3) for 40 minutes until set.
5 Sprinkle the flan with icing sugar and burn in a pattern to caramelise the sugar. Remove and cool.

Note Do not refrigerate. This flan must be eaten fresh.

59 – Fruit meringue torte

	4 portions	10 portions
Sweet paste		
butter or margarine	5 g (2¼oz)	140 g (5½oz)
castor sugar	25 g (1 oz)	60 g (2½oz)
whole egg	5 g (¼oz)	12 g (½oz)
soft flour	50 g (2 oz)	125 g (5 oz)
Piped shortbread		
butter or margarine	55 g (2¼oz)	140 g (5½oz)
icing sugar	37 g (1½oz)	90 g (3¾oz)
egg	1	1–2
soft flour	88 g (3½oz)	220 g (8¾oz)
natural vanilla essence or pod		
egg whites	50 g (2 oz)	125 g (5 oz)
granulated sugar	100 g (4 oz)	250 g (10 oz)
water	30 ml (1/16 pt)	75 ml (⅓pt)
blackcurrants, strawberries or raspberries (frozen or fresh)	62 g (2½oz)	155 g (6¼oz)

> 1 portion provides:
>
> 509 kcals/2123 kJ
> 24.4 g fat
> (of which 15.4 g saturated)
> 70.4 g carbohydrate
> (of which 44.2 g sugars)
> 6.3 g protein
> 1.6 g fibre

1 Prepare the sweet paste by creaming together the fat and sugar, beating in the egg and gradually working in the flour to a smooth paste – but do *not* over-work.
2 Prepare the piped biscuits in the same way as for sweet paste.
3 Roll out the sweet paste into a base approximately ½cm (¼in) thick.
4 Pipe the shortbread into the base, using a forcing bag and 1 cm (½in) star tube.
5 Bake together for about 20 minutes at approximately 200°C (400°F).
6 Meanwhile, prepare an Italian meringue (see page 521).
7 To assemble: coat the base with Italian meringue, add the soft fruit

and completely decorate with more meringue. Dust with castor sugar and flash in a very hot oven for 2–3 minutes.

60 – Gâteau japonaise

6–8 portions

whites of egg	10
ground almonds	200 g (8 oz)
castor sugar	400 g (1 lb)
cornflour	25 g (1 oz)
praline buttercream	200 g (8 oz)
chocolate fondant	50 g (2 oz)

1 Beat the whites to full peak and whisk in 100 g (4 oz) of sugar.
2 Carefully fold in the almonds, sugar and cornflour, well sifted together.
3 Pipe the mixture on to baking sheets lined with rice paper or silicone paper in circles of about 20–22 cm (8–9 in) diameter using a 1 cm (½ in) plain tube.
4 Dust with icing sugar and cook in a very cool oven at approximately. 140–150°C (250–275°F, Reg. 1–2) for approximately 1 hour, until a light biscuit colour and crisp.
5 Remove silicone paper or, if using rice paper, leave on the rounds but trim the edges. Allow to cool.
6 Trim all rounds to the same size with the aid of a suitable round flan ring, and pass the trimmings through a sieve.
7 Sandwich 2 or 4 rounds together with praline buttercream, the bottom layer flat surface up and the top layer also.
8 Spread the top and sides with praline buttercream.
9 Cover the top trellis fashion. Pipe a disc of chocolate fondant in the centre.

– *Boiled buttercream (praline flavour)*

eggs	125 ml (¼ pt)
icing sugar	50 g (2 oz)
granulated or cube sugar	300 g (12 oz)
water	100 g (4 oz)
glucose	50 g (2 oz)
unsalted butter	400 g (1 lb)

1 Beat eggs and icing sugar until ribbon stage (sponge).
2 Boil granulated or cube sugar with water and glucose to 118°C (245°F).
3 Gradually add the sugar at 118°C (245°F) to the eggs and icing sugar at ribbon stage, whisk continuously and allow to cool to 26°C (80°F).
4 Gradually add the unsalted butter, while continuing to whisk, until a smooth cream is obtained.
5 Mix with praline (recipe 93, page 521) to make praline buttercream as required.

61 – Gâteau St. Honoré

6 portions

puff or short pastry	125 g (5 oz)
choux pastry	125 ml ($\frac{1}{4}$ pt)
cube sugar	150 g (6 oz)
water	60 ml ($\frac{1}{8}$ pt)
pinch of cream of tartar	
glacé cherries	50 g (2 oz)
angelica	50 g (2 oz)
crème St. Honoré or chibouste (see overleaf)	250 ml ($\frac{1}{2}$ pt)

1 Roll out the pastry $\frac{1}{4}$ cm ($\frac{1}{8}$ in) thick and cut out a circle approximately 23 cm (9 in) in diameter, place on a slightly greased baking sheet.
2 Prick with a fork and egg wash the edge and centre.
3 Pipe on a ring of choux paste, approximately $\frac{3}{4}$ cm ($\frac{3}{8}$ in) from the edge of the pastry and pipe on a choux bun in the centre, using 1 cm ($\frac{1}{2}$ in) plain tube.
4 On a separate baking sheet, pipe out approximately 16–20 small choux buns.
5 Egg wash the choux ring and buns and cook in a fairly hot oven (approximately 230°C, 450°F, Reg. 8) for about 20–25 minutes.
6 Place the cube sugar, water and cream of tartar into a suitable saucepan and cook to hard crack, 155°C (312°F).
7 Dip the buns in hard crack sugar and decorate alternatively with half a glacé cherry on one and a diamond of angelica on the other. As they are dipped and decorated place on the large ring. Make sure the buns match those on either side and that there is an even number.
8 Fill the finished case with rochers of crème St. Honoré or chibouste,

forming a dome shape in the centre. The finished item may be decorated with spun sugar (page 525).

Note A *rocher* is a quenelle shape formed by taking a dessert or tablespoon of the mixture, dipping a second spoon in boiling water, drying it and using it whilst warm to remove the mixture from the first spoon.

~ Crème St. Honoré

cube sugar	200 g (8 oz)
eggs, separated	3
milk, whole or skimmed	125 ml ($\frac{1}{4}$ pt)
leaf gelatine, soaked and squeezed dry	6 g ($\frac{1}{4}$ oz)

1 Boil the sugar with a little water to soft ball stage, 118°C (245°F).
2 Whisk the egg whites, pour on the sugar as for Italienne meringue (see page 521).
3 Cook the egg yolks and milk as for sauce anglaise and add the gelatine.
4 Add to the meringue.

~ Crème chibouste

leaf gelatine	6 g ($\frac{1}{4}$ oz)
pastry cream	250 ml ($\frac{1}{2}$ pt)
egg whites	5
castor sugar	100 g (4 oz)

1 Add the soaked gelatine to the hot pastry cream.
2 Make a meringue with the egg whites and sugar.
3 Fold in the pastry cream, taking care not to overmix, and use as required.

Note The pastry cream may be made from skimmed milk, unrefined sugar and wholemeal flour, or in the traditional way.

62 – Choux pastry ring with toffee almond cream

	4 portions	10 portions
choux pastry	125 ml ($\frac{1}{4}$ pt)	300 ml ($\frac{5}{8}$ pt)
flaked almonds	50 g (2 oz)	125 g (5 oz)
whipped cream, flavoured with praline *or* use non-dairy creamer flavoured with praline	250 ml ($\frac{1}{2}$ pt)	600 ml ($1\frac{1}{4}$ pt)
icing sugar	50 g (2 oz)	125 g (5 oz)

1 Pipe out a large ring of choux pastry, using a 1 cm ($\frac{1}{2}$ in) star tube.
2 Egg wash and decorate with flaked almonds.
3 Cook at approximately 220°C (425°F, Reg. 7) for about 25–30 minutes.
4 Split through the ring crossways and allow to cool.
5 Fill with cream flavoured with praline.
6 Replace the top and dust with icing sugar.

Note Alternatively, the ring may be filled with soft fruit and ice-cream, e.g. strawberries and raspberries.

63 – Lucerne fruit and pastry cream

	10 portions
Plain russe	
yolks of egg	8
castor sugar	250 g (10 oz)
cornflour	25 g (1 oz)
milk	700 ml ($1\frac{1}{4}$ pt)
soaked gelatine	6 g ($\frac{1}{4}$ oz)
Sponge	
soft flour	60 g ($2\frac{1}{2}$ oz)
castor sugar	35 g ($3\frac{1}{2}$ oz)
eggs	3
Filling	
diced, cooked apple, sprinkled with lemon juice	200 g (8 oz)
seedless raisins, boiled, cooled and soaked in rum	50 g (2 oz)
whipped cream	250 g (10 oz)

1 Make a plain russe: mix together the egg yolks, sugar and cornflour. Boil the milk, add to the egg yolks and continue to stir for 1 minute. Bring back to the boil.
2 Add the soaked gelatine and strain through a fine strainer.
3 Make the sponge as recipe 41 (page 486) stages 1–4. Pour into a lined swiss roll tin and bake at 230–250°C (450–500°F, Reg. 8–9) for approximately 3–4 minutes.
4 Allow the sponge to cool and use to line a half pudding sleeve.
5 Prepare the filling: add the apple and raisins to the cream, and fold in carefully 40 g ($\frac{1}{2}$oz) of plain russe on setting point.
6 Place this mixture into the prepared pudding sleeve lined with sponge.
7 Set in the refrigerator for 3–4 hours.
8 Turn out, dust with icing sugar and mark a trellis with hot pokers to caramelise the sugar.
9 Decorate with whipped cream along the top in a rope fashion. This may be served on individual plates with a suitable sauce, e.g. raspberry or orange, or whole on a sweet trolley.

Note   Other fruits may also be used, e.g. pears, raspberries, strawberries, peaches, apricots, kiwis.

64 – Slices (tranches)

There are three ways of making a tranche:

(a) The tranche mould can be lined the same as for a flan ring, the ingredients and methods for flans can be used.
(b) Roll out short paste to $\frac{1}{2}$cm ($\frac{1}{4}$in) thick and cut a strip the length of the baking sheet and 10 cm (4 in) wide. Place on a greased baking sheet and dock. Egg wash both sides. Prepare 2 strips of puff paste $\frac{1}{2}$cm ($\frac{1}{4}$in) thick and 1 cm ($\frac{1}{2}$in) wide. Place on the egg washed sides. Notch along the edges with the back of a small knife and egg wash. Cook at 220°C (425°F, Reg. 7) for approximately 20 minutes. When cold spread centre with crème Chantilly or pastry cream. Arrange suitable fruits neatly on this e.g. strawberries, raspberries, grapes, bananas, kiwi or poached or tinned fruits. Glaze with a suitable glaze and decorate sides with whipped cream.
(c) Roll out sweet paste $\frac{1}{2}$cm ($\frac{1}{4}$in) thick and cut into a strip 12 cm (5 in) wide and the length of a baking sheet. Place on to a greased baking sheet and egg wash the edges. Turn the edges in by 1 cm ($\frac{1}{2}$in), thumb

up and decorate with pastry pincers. Cook at approximately 200°C (400°F, Reg. 6) for 15–20 minutes.

65 – Parisian slice

This is a mixed fruit slice, using method (b).

66 – Almond slice

1 Prepare a slice using methods (c) or (a), but do not cook.
2 Spread the centre with raspberry jam.
3 Pipe frangipane (page 520) over the jam.
4 Sprinkle with flaked or filleted almonds.
5 Cook at approximately 200°C (400°F, Reg. 6) for about 20–25 minutes.
6 Brush with hot apricot glaze and lemon water icing.

67 – Belgian slice

1 Prepare a slice using method (a).
2 Spread the bottom with raspberry jam.
3 Two-thirds fill with frangipane (page 520).
4 Decorate with a trellis of thin strips of sweet paste and egg wash.
5 Cook at approximately 200°C (400°F, Reg. 6) for 20–25 minutes.
6 Brush with apricot glaze and lemon water icing.
7 Replace in oven for 30 seconds to set the glaze.

68 – Viennese slice

	6–8 portions
Filling	
cooking apples	200 g (8 oz)
mixed dried fruit	50 g (2 oz)
brown sugar	25 g (1 oz)
mixed spice and apricot jam to bind	

1 Prepare a slice using method (a).
2 Prepare the filling by peeling, coring and dicing the apple ($\frac{1}{4}$ cm, $\frac{1}{8}$ in, dice) and mixing with the remainder of the ingredients.
3 Place the filling down the centre of the slice.

4 Decorate with a trellis of sweet paste and egg wash.
5 Cook at approximately 225°C (425°F, Reg. 7) for about 15–20 minutes.
6 Dust with icing sugar and glaze under a salamander.

— *Yeast goods* —
YEAST

Yeast is a living organism – it is a plant of the fungi group. Yeast produces the gas carbon dioxide by fermentation. This occurs when it is given food in the form of sugar, warmth 25–29°C (77–84°F) and moisture, water or milk.

Types of yeast

- **Compressed yeast** is the most widely used. It is a very pure form of yeast packed and sold in cakes. It crumbles easily and has a fresh smell. It will keep in a cold place for 2–3 days.
- **Dried yeast** can be stored indefinitely if dry and well sealed. It takes longer to cream and is more concentrated.
- **Fresh yeast** has a pleasant characteristic smell, is a putty colour, will crumble easily and will cream readily.

Conditions for the fermentation of yeast

Yeast requires food, warmth and moisture. Yeast is destroyed at temperatures higher than those given above, and its activity is retarded at lower temperatures. Yeast can be destroyed during the mixing or rising processes if it is put in a very hot place.

Fermentation is brought about by a number of enzymes present in yeast – maltase, which acts upon maltose to form glucose, and invertase, which acts upon sucrose, producing glucose and fructose – but before these can be effective a substance called diastase present in the flour converts some of the starch to dextrin and maltose.

The zymase group of enzymes changes simple sugars – glucose and fructose – to carbon dioxide and alcohol.

69 – Brioche

yield approx. 20

milk	125 ml ($\frac{1}{4}$ pt)
yeast	25 g (1 oz)
strong flour	450 g (1 lb 2 oz)
castor sugar	25 g (1 oz)
pinch of salt	
butter or margarine	50 g (2 oz)
eggs	4
malt extract	2 g (1 dram)
zest of lemon	
butter or margarine, softened	150 g (6 oz)

1 Warm the milk to 26°C (80°F), disperse the yeast in the milk, add a little flour and all of the sugar. Sprinkle a little flour on the surface.
2 Stand in a basin of warm water covered with a damp cloth for 15 minutes to ferment.
3 Take the rest of the flour, salt and 50 g (2 oz) of butter or margarine, rub together well.
4 Make a well and add the eggs, malt, lemon zest and the ferment, when it has broken through the surface flour.
5 Mix to a smooth dough.
6 Place on a machine with a dough hook and add 150 g (6 oz) of softened butter or margarine on low speed.
7 When all the butter or margarine has been incorporated, turn out of the bowl, cover with a damp cloth and allow to prove in a warm place for approximately 1 hour.
8 Knock back the dough and place it in the refrigerator until ready for use.
9 Divide into approximately 50 g (2 oz) pieces, mould into a brioche shape (i.e. small cottage loaf shapes) and place into deep individual fluted moulds which have been well greased.
10 Egg wash, prove and bake at approximately 230°C (450°F, Reg. 8) for approximately 10 minutes.

70 – Croissants

yield approx. 20–24

bread flour	600 g (1 lb 8 oz)
butter or margarine	100 g (4 oz)
milk	125 ml ($\frac{1}{4}$ pt)
water	125 ml ($\frac{1}{4}$ pt)
yeast	60 g (1$\frac{1}{2}$ oz)
egg	125 ml ($\frac{1}{4}$ pt)
castor sugar	60 g (1$\frac{1}{2}$ oz)
salt	10 g ($\frac{1}{2}$ oz)
butter, margarine or pastry margarine	200 g (8 oz)

1 Sieve the flour into a suitable basin and rub in the 100 g (4 oz) butter or margarine.
2 Warm the milk and water to 32°C (90°F) and disperse the yeast in the milk and water. Add to the flour and fat.
3 Blend in all the rest of the ingredients except the 200 g (8 oz) fat. Mix lightly but do not develop or toughen up the dough.
4 Rest for 10 minutes. Keep covered with a damp cloth or polythene in order to prevent skinning.
5 Roll into the dough, as in making of puff pastry, the 200 g (8 oz) fat and give the dough 4 single turns, resting for 15–20 minutes between turns.
6 When the fat is incorporated, roll out dough to about $\frac{1}{2}$ cm ($\frac{1}{4}$ in) thick and 22 cm (9 in) wide.
7 Cut down the middle of the dough lengthways. Place one strip on another and cut into triangles approximately 10 cm (4 in) wide.
8 Roll each triangle up from the widest end, pulling and stretching into a crescent.
9 Egg wash and prove in a little steam for 15 minutes. Then bake at approximately 230°C (450°F, Reg. 8) for 20–25 minutes.

Note Double baking sheets may be required if the oven gives out a fierce bottom heat.

71 – Danish pastry dough

yield approx. 10–12

medium strength flour	300 g (12 oz)
salt	3 g ($\frac{1}{8}$ oz)
margarine	35 g ($1\frac{1}{2}$ oz)
milk	100 g (4 oz)
yeast	30 g ($1\frac{1}{4}$ oz)
egg	75 g (3 oz)
castor sugar	25 g (1 oz)
butter, margarine or pastry margarine	200 g (8 oz)

1 Sieve the flour and salt, rub in the 35 g ($1\frac{1}{2}$ oz) margarine.
2 Warm the milk to 26°C (80°F) and disperse the yeast in the milk. Add this to the flour.
3 Add the egg and sugar to make into a slack dough. Do *not* toughen by over-working.
4 Fold into the dough 200 g (8 oz) fat, giving it two single turns and one double turn. Rest for 10 minutes between turns.
5 Work the pieces into desired shapes and egg wash. Prove in a little steam and bake as indicated in the following recipes.

Note Double baking sheets may be required if the oven gives out a fierce bottom heat.

72 – Danish pastries with almond fruit filling

10–12 pastries

Almond fruit filling

raw marzipan (commercial product)	125 g (5 oz)
egg	25 g (1 oz)
melted butter	35 g ($1\frac{1}{2}$ oz)
chopped apple	35 g ($1\frac{1}{2}$ oz)
cake crumbs	50 g (2 oz)
water	50 g (2 oz)
glacé cherries	35 g ($1\frac{1}{2}$ oz)
currants	35 g ($1\frac{1}{2}$ oz)
sultanas	35 g ($1\frac{1}{2}$ oz)
orange, zest and juice	$\frac{1}{2}$

Based on a yield of 12
1 portion provides:

366 kcals/1528 kJ
23.3 g fat
(of which 12.7 g saturated)
35.2 g carbohydrate
(of which 15.1 g sugars)
5.9 g protein
0.6 g fibre

1 Soften marzipan with egg and melted butter to a smooth paste.
2 Add all remaining ingredients and mix well.

Triangles
Roll out the dough ½cm (¼in) thick, cut into 8cm (3in) squares and place a small amount of almond fruit filling into the centre. Fold over, egg wash. Prove at 29–32°C (85–90°F) without steam. Bake at 220°C (425°F, Reg.7) for approximately 10 minutes. Mask with hot apricot jam and lemon water icing, sprinkle with roasted flaked almonds.

Round buns
Roll out the dough into an oblong ½cm (¼in) thick. Spread the surface thinly with almond fruit filling. Roll up as for swiss roll and cut into 1cm (½in) pieces. Place on a lightly greased baking sheet with the cut side up, prove at 29–32°C (85–90°F) without steam. Bake at approximately 220°C (425°F, Reg.7). Mask with hot apricot jam and water icing, sprinkle with roasted flaked almonds.

Crescents
Roll out dough ¼cm (⅛in) thick and cut into 8cm (3in) squares. Pipe almond fruit filling in the centre. Egg wash, fold over and press down. Cut the edge with a knife, making incisions right through, approximately 1cm (½in) apart. Prove at 29–32°C (85–90°F) without steam. Bake at approximately 220°C (425°F, Reg.7).

73 – Danish pastries with custard filling

10–12 pastries

Custard

milk	500ml (1pt)
eggs	50g (2oz)
castor sugar	60g (2½oz)
cornflour	40g (1¼oz)
colour and flavour as desired	

1 Boil the milk in a suitable saucepan.
2 Mix the eggs, sugar and cornflour together to a smooth paste.
3 When milk is boiling, add half to the egg, sugar and cornflour, mix well to a smooth consistency.
4 Return to the rest of the milk, bring back to the boil and add flavour and colour as desired.

Maultaschen

1 Roll out the dough ½cm (¼in) thick and cut into 10 cm (4 in) squares.
2 Egg wash and pipe in the centre of each a little lemon-flavoured custard filling (recipe above plus zest and juice of 1 lemon).
3 Bring the four corners to the centre, seal lightly, egg wash and place on a greased baking sheet.
4 Roll a strip of dough ¼cm (⅛in) thick and cut 8 cm (3 in) strips.
5 Press two strips on to each pastry, crosswise (these will help to retain the shape during cooking and proving).
6 Prove and cook at approximately 200–220°C (400–425°F, Reg. 6–7) for about 20 minutes.
7 Brush with hot apricot glaze and warm thin fondant.

Croquante rolls

1 Roll out the dough as for Chelsea buns and egg wash the sides.
2 Spread with cold custard filling and sprinkle generously with fine croquante (see below).
3 Roll up and cut as for Chelsea buns, arrange in rows in a 2 cm (1 in) deep tin. Egg wash the tops and prove.
4 Cook at approximately 200–220°C (400–425°F, Reg. 6–7) for 20 minutes.
5 Brush tops with hot apricot glaze and sprinkle with coarse croquante (see below).

~ Croquante

granulated sugar	200 g (8 oz)
juice of lemon *or* pinch of cream of tartar	
nibbed almonds	150 g (6 oz)

1 Place sugar and lemon juice or cream of tartar in a suitable pan and stir over a gentle heat until all the sugar has melted.
2 Cook until of a pale amber colour.
3 Warm the almonds, stir into the sugar and remove from the heat.
4 Turn out on to an oiled tray and allow to cool.
5 When set, crush into a fine powder with a rolling pin. Pass through a sieve to remove any large particles and crush and sieve these.

Envelopes

1 Roll out the dough ½cm (¼in) thick and cut into 10 cm (4 in) squares, and lightly egg wash.

2 Bring 2 opposite corners to the centre and seal.
3 Lay the pastries on a greased baking sheet, egg wash and prove.
4 Pipe custard filling in the 2 open ends and egg wash again.
5 Cook at approximately 200–220°C (400–425°F, Reg. 6–7) for about
   20 minutes and brush with hot apricot glaze.

Fruit rings
1 After giving the dough a second turn, sprinkle with washed chopped
   dried fruit then give the final turn. Relax.
2 Roll out ½ cm (¼ in) thick, in a strip approximately 24 cm (10 in) wide.
3 Cut into 2 cm (1 in) wide pieces.
4 Twist each strip fairly tightly then form into a ring.
5 Lay on to a greased baking sheet, egg wash and prove.
6 Fill the centres with custard filling, sprinkle on a few split almonds
   and cook at approximately 200–220°C (400–425°F, Reg. 6–7) for about
   20 minutes and brush with hot apricot glaze.

Hazelnut custards
1 Roll out the dough ½ cm (¼ in) thick and cut into 7 cm (3 in) strips.
2 Lay one strip on a greased baking sheet and egg wash the edges.
3 Spread with custard filling, cover with a strip of dough and egg wash.
4 Sprinkle well with chopped roasted hazelnuts, cover with a third strip
   of dough, seal and cut into portions. (Do not separate the pieces at
   this stage.)
5 Egg wash, prove and cook at approximately 200–220°C (400–425°F,
   Reg. 6–7) for about 20 minutes.
6 Brush with hot apricot glaze and warm thin fondant then divide into
   portions.

74 – Burgomeister rolls

1 Roll out the paste ½ cm (¼ in) thick in a large rectangle.
2 Cut out as for croissants, making the triangles longer and narrower at
   the bases.
3 Egg wash lightly and pipe in the centre a little burgomeistermasse (see
   opposite).
4 Roll up the pastries from the base to the point and lay on a greased
   baking sheet. Do not curve them.
5 Egg wash, prove and cook at approximately 200–220°C (400–425°F,
   Reg. 6–7) for about 20 minutes.
6 Brush with hot apricot glaze and warm thin fondant.

– *Burgomeistermasse*

castor sugar	150 g (6 oz)
butter or margarine	350 g (14 oz)
raw marzipan	400 g (1 lb)

Mix all ingredients but do not aerate.

75 – Schnecken

1 Roll out dough $\frac{1}{2}$ cm ($\frac{1}{4}$ in) thick in a large rectangle and egg wash the edges.
2 Spread with 'copenhagenmasse' (see below) and roll up tightly.
3 Lightly egg wash the outside and roll in maw seeds.
4 Cut into individual pieces and lay them on a greased baking sheet with the closing of the seam underneath. (This will help keep them in shape.)
5 Egg wash, prove and cook at approximately 200–220°C (400–425°F, Reg. 6–7) for about 20 minutes, then brush with hot apricot glaze.

– *Copenhagenmasse*

granulated sugar	300 g (12 oz)
butter or margarine	300 g (12 oz)
raw marzipan	200 g (8 oz)
nibbed almonds	50 g (2 oz)

Mix all ingredients together, rub down well.

76 – Cherry rolls

yield approx. 40 pieces

soft flour	300 g (12 oz)
butter or margarine	200 g (8 oz)
natural vanilla essence or pod	
glacé cherries (chopped)	100 g (4 oz)
icing sugar	35 g (1$\frac{1}{2}$ oz)

1 Sift the flour, cream the butter and icing sugar, add the flour and vanilla and mix lightly.

2 Fraiser* the paste and add the chopped glacé cherries.
3 Roll into a sausage shape, 2 cm (1 in) diameter, and place into the
   refrigerator to harden.
4 When firm, cut into rounds 1½ cm (¾ in) thick.
5 Place on to a lightly greased baking sheet and bake at approximately
   200°C (400°F, Reg. 6) for 10–12 minutes.

* *Fraiser* means to rub or scrape down, using either a palette knife or the
heel of the hand.

—— Sweetmeats (petits fours) and biscuits ——

77 – Chocolate fudge

yield: approx. 60–70 pieces

granulated sugar ⎫	200 g (8 oz)
glucose ⎬ syrup	75 g (3 oz)
water ⎭	60 ml (⅛ pt)
evaporated milk	25 g (1 oz)
fondant	200 g (8 oz)
butter, melted	30 g (1¼ oz)
plain chocolate, melted	250 g (10 oz)
natural vanilla essence	

1 Place the granulated sugar, glucose and water into a thick-bottomed
   pan, place on the stove and cook to 115°C (240°F).
2 Add the evaporated milk and again cook to 115°C (240°F).
3 Place into a machine bowl the fondant, melted butter and melted
   chocolate. Add a few drops of vanilla essence and mix for 1 minute at
   low speed.
4 Add the sugar syrup at 115°C (240°F) and mix well.
5 Place on to a suitable lightly oiled tray and allow to set.
6 When set, cut into pieces and place into paper cases.

78 – Chocolate caramel

yield: approx. 50–60 pieces

glucose	150 g (6 oz)
castor sugar	200 g (8 oz)
plain chocolate	100 g (4 oz)
single cream	250 ml ($\frac{1}{2}$ pt)

1 Boil together the glucose, sugar and chocolate with half the cream to 118°C (245°F).
2 Once this temperature has been reached add the remaining cream and bring back to 118°C (245°F).
3 Pour on to an oiled marble slab or on to a suitable oiled tray and cut into pieces while still warm.
4 Place into paper cases.

79 – Florentines

yield: 70–80 pieces

butter	200 g (8 oz)
castor sugar	200 g (8 oz)
fresh cream	50 g (2 oz)
chopped cherries	50 g (2 oz)
cut mixed peel	100 g (4 oz)
sultanas	75 g (3 oz)
nibbed almonds	200 g (8 oz)
flaked almonds	200 g (8 oz)
soft flour	25 g (1 oz)
chocolate couverture or baker's chocolate	

1 Place the butter, sugar and cream in a saucepan and bring to the boil to 115°C (240°F).
2 Remove from heat and add all the remaining ingredients, except the chocolate. Allow to cool.
3 Prepare the baking sheets, lined with silicone paper.
4 Spoon the mixture on to the lined baking sheets into rounds approximately 10 g ($\frac{1}{2}$ oz) in weight, not too close together.
5 Bake at 200°C (400°F, Reg. 6) for approximately 10–12 minutes.
6 When cooked the florentines will spread over the baking sheet, bring

back to form a neat round with a plain cutter as soon as they are removed from the oven.

7 Remove from baking sheets and allow to cool.
8 Coat the backs of each florentine with couverture or baker's chocolate and mark with a comb scraper.

80 – Coconut biscuits

yield: approx. 40 pieces

butter or margarine	250 g (10 oz)
castor sugar	375 g (14 oz)
eggs	2
soft flour	375 g (14 oz)
desiccated coconut	250 g (10 oz)

1 Cream together the fat and sugar.
2 Add the eggs, one at a time, beating well between additions.
3 Sieve the flour, add it and the coconut into the butter and sugar, mixing to form a dough.
4 Roll out to $\frac{1}{2}$ cm ($\frac{1}{4}$ in) thick and cut out rounds using a small plain or fancy cutter, 2 cm (1 in) diameter.
5 Place on a lightly greased baking sheet and bake at 150°C (275°F, Reg. 2) for about 15 minutes, until a light biscuit colour.

81 – Coconut macaroons

yield: approx. 30–40 pieces

egg whites	250 ml ($\frac{1}{2}$ pt)
ground rice or semolina	75 g (3 oz)
granulated sugar	625 g (1 lb 10 oz)
fine coconut	150 g (6 oz)
coarse coconut	150 g (6 oz)

1 Mix in a basin the egg whites, ground rice or semolina and the granulated sugar.
2 Add the fine and coarse coconut and mix well.
3 Heat over a bain-marie of warm water to 48°C (120°F).
4 Place into a forcing bag with a 1 cm ($\frac{1}{2}$ in) plain tube and pipe on to a

baking sheet on rice paper to the required size, approximately 2 cm (1 in) diameter.

5 Place half a glacé cherry on each one and bake at 180°C (350°F, Reg. 4) for approximately 15 minutes.

82 – Marshmallows

yield: approx. 50 pieces

granulated or cube sugar	600 g (1 lb 8 oz)
egg whites	3
leaf gelatine, soaked in cold water	35 g (1½ oz)

1 Place sugar in a suitable saucepan with 125 ml (¼ pt) water and boil to soft ball stage 140°C (245°F).
2 When sugar is nearly ready whisk egg whites to a firm peak.
3 Pour in boiling sugar and continue to whisk.
4 Squeeze the water from the gelatine and add.
5 Add colour and flavour if desired.
6 Turn out on to a tray dusted with cornflour and dust with more cornflour.
7 Cut into sections and roll in a mixture of icing sugar and cornflour.

83 – Nougat Montelimar

yield: approx. 50–60 pieces

granulated sugar	350 g (14 oz)
water	100 g (4 oz)
honey	100 g (4 oz)
glucose	100 g (4 oz)
egg white	35 g (1½ oz)
glacé cherries	50 g (2 oz)
pistachio nuts	50 g (2 oz)
nibbed almonds	25 g (1 oz)
flaked almonds or flaked hazelnuts	25 g (1 oz)

1 Place the sugar and water into a suitable pan, bring to the boil and cook to 107°C (225°F).

2 When the temperature has been reached, add the honey and glucose and cook to 137°C (280°F).
3 Meanwhile whisk the egg whites to full peak in a machine, then add the syrup at 137°C (280°F) slowly, while whisking on full speed.
4 Reduce speed, add the glacé cherries cut into quarters, chopped pistachio nuts, and the nibbed and flaked almonds.
5 Turn out on to a lightly oiled tray or rice paper and mark into pieces while still warm.
6 When cold cut into pieces and place into paper cases to serve.

84 – Piped ganache

yield: approx. 20–30 pieces

single cream	125 ml ($\frac{1}{4}$ pt)
chocolate couverture, cut into pieces	225 g (9 oz)
rum, to flavour	

1 Bring the cream to the boil, remove from the stove and add the couverture.
2 Flavour with rum.
3 Stir to a piping consistency over a bain-marie of cold water.
4 Using a piping bag and $\frac{1}{2}$ cm ($\frac{1}{4}$ in) tube, pipe ganache into small paper cases and decorate with crystallised violets or mimosa.

85 – Turkish delight

yield: approx. 60–70 pieces

granulated or cube sugar	600 g (1 lb 8 oz)
glucose	200 g (8 oz)
lemon, zest and juice	4
water	750 ml ($1\frac{3}{4}$ pt)
sherry or rose water (optional)	
cornflour	150 g (6 oz)
leaf gelatine (soaked)	50 g (2 oz)

1 Boil together the sugar, glucose, lemon zest and juice with 625 ml ($1\frac{1}{4}$ pt) water in a suitable saucepan.

2 Flavour with sherry or rose water.
3 Thicken with the cornflour diluted with 250 ml ($\frac{1}{2}$ pt) water. Add soaked gelatine and stir well.
4 Pour into shallow trays and allow to set, then cut into sections and roll in cornflour.

86 – Snowballs

yield: approx. 30–35 pieces

egg whites	4
castor sugar	200 g (8 oz)
ground almonds	200 g (8 oz)
nibbed almonds	100 g (4 oz)
apricot jam	50 g (2 oz)
icing sugar	50 g (2 oz)

1 Whisk egg whites to full peak.
2 Add approximately 100 g (4 oz) castor sugar and whisk to a meringue.
3 Carefully fold in the rest of the castor sugar with the ground almonds into the meringue.
4 Prepare lightly greased and floured baking sheets, or baking sheets lined with silicone paper, and pipe the mixture into bulbs, with a forcing bag and $\frac{1}{2}$ cm ($\frac{1}{4}$ in) plain tube.
5 Sprinkle with nibbed almonds and dredge lightly with icing sugar.
6 Bake at 140°C (275°F, Reg. 1) for approximately 30 minutes.
7 Remove from baking sheets, stick together in pairs with hot apricot jam and dredge lightly with icing sugar.

87 – Viennese biscuits

yield: approx. 40 pieces

butter or margarine	350 g (14 oz)
castor sugar	350 g (14 oz)
eggs	2
natural vanilla essence	2 drops
soft flour	450 g (1 lb 2 oz)
melted chocolate, to finish	

1 Cream the butter and sugar in a basin until white and light.
2 Add the eggs, one at a time, and cream well.
3 Add the vanilla essence and then the flour carefully by gradually incorporating into the butter, sugar and egg mixture.
4 Pipe on to lightly greased baking sheets, using a 1 cm ($\frac{1}{2}$in) star tube.
5 Allow to stand for 2 hours or longer if possible.
6 Cook at 200°C (400°F, Reg. 6) for approximately 15 minutes and allow to cool.
7 To finish, dip the points into melted chocolate.

—— *Miscellaneous* ——

88 – Sponge fingers

yield: approx. 32 pieces

eggs, separated	4
castor sugar	100 g (4 oz)
flour	100 g (4 oz)

1 Cream the egg yolks and sugar in a bowl until creamy and almost white.
2 Whip the egg whites stiffly.
3 Add a little of the whites to the mixture and cut in.
4 Gradually add the sieved flour and remainder of the whites alternately, mixing as lightly as possible.
5 Place in a piping bag with 1 cm ($\frac{1}{2}$in) plain tube and pipe in 8 cm (3 in) lengths on to baking sheets lined with greaseproof or silicone paper.
6 Sprinkle liberally with icing sugar. Rest for 15 minutes.
7 Bake in a moderately hot oven (approximately 200–220°C, 425–450°F, Reg. 6–7) for about 10 minutes.
8 Remove from the oven, lift the paper on which the biscuits are piped and place upside down on the table.
9 Sprinkle liberally with water. This will assist the removal of the biscuits from the paper. (No water is needed if using silicone paper.)

89 – Chocolate fudge sauce

yield: 16 portions

water	250 ml ($\frac{1}{2}$ pt)
golden syrup	60 ml ($\frac{1}{8}$ pt)
dark brown sugar	150 g (6 oz)
granulated sugar	50 g (2 oz)
dark cooking chocolate	200 g (8 oz)
condensed milk	350 g (14 oz)
evaporated milk	175 g (7 oz)
vanilla essence	

1 Place the water in a suitable saucepan, add the golden syrup, brown and white sugar, bring to boil and simmer for 3 minutes.
2 Melt the chocolate carefully in a basin over a bain-marie of hot water.
3 Add the chocolate to the sugar and water mix. *Do not boil.*
4 Heat the condensed and evaporated milk gently in a saucepan over a low heat; when warmed to simmering point add to the chocolate mixture.
5 Finish with vanilla essence.

90 – Cornets

yield: approx. 10–12 pieces

icing sugar	150 g (6 oz)
butter	100 g (4 oz)
natural vanilla essence	
egg whites	4
soft flour	100 g (4 oz)

1 Lightly cream the sugar and butter, add 3–4 drops of vanilla.
2 Add the egg whites one by one mixing continuously, taking care not to allow the mixture to curdle.
3 Gently fold in the sifted flour and mix lightly.
4 Using a 3 mm ($\frac{1}{8}$ in) plain tube, pipe out the mixture on to a lightly greased baking sheet into rounds approximately 2$\frac{1}{2}$ cm (1$\frac{1}{4}$ in) in diameter.
5 Bake in a hot oven (approximately 230–250°C, 450–500°F, Reg. 8–9) until the edges turn brown and the centre remains uncoloured.
6 Remove the tray from the oven.

7 Work quickly while the cornets are hot and twist them into a cornet shape using the point of a cream horn mould. (For a tight cornet shape it will be found best to set the pieces tightly inside the cream horn moulds and to leave them until set.)

91 – Frangipane

yield: approx. 600 g (1 lb 8 oz)

milk	250 ml ($\frac{1}{2}$ pt)
natural vanilla essence or pod	
eggs	2
castor sugar or brown sugar	100 g (4 oz)
strong or wholemeal flour	25 g (1 oz)
butter or margarine	100 g (4 oz)
ground almonds	100 g (4 oz)
rum	1 tbsp

1 Boil the milk and vanilla in a saucepan.
2 In a basin, mix together the eggs, sugar and flour, whisk on the boiling milk, return to the boil, then allow to cool.
3 Cream the butter or margarine and mix in with the pastry cream, ground almonds and rum. Use as required – for filling gâteaux, hot sweets, etc.

92 – Brandy snaps

yield: approx. 10 pieces

margarine or butter	75 g (3 oz)
castor sugar	200 g (8 oz)
golden syrup	200 g (8 oz)
plain flour	100 g (4 oz)
ground ginger	6 g ($\frac{1}{4}$ oz)

1 Cream the margarine and sugar until light and fluffy.
2 Add the golden syrup and cream well.
3 Gradually fold in the sieved flour and ground ginger.
4 Place mixture into a piping bag with a $\frac{1}{2}$ cm ($\frac{1}{4}$ in) plain tube.
5 Pipe on to a silicone lined baking sheet into 1 cm ($\frac{1}{2}$ in) diameter rounds.

6 Bake in a hot oven (approximately 220°C, 425°F, Reg. 7) for approximately 5 min until golden brown on the edges.
7 Allow to cool until slightly firm. Roll round a suitable wooden rod and allow to cool until crisp.
8 Remove from rod and use as required.

Uses   Brandy snaps can be offered as sweetmeats and pastries. The mixture can be shaped as required, e.g. tartlets, barquettes, and can be used as containers for sweets, e.g. filled with lemon syllabub, raspberries and cream.

93 – Praline

Praline is a basic preparation used for flavouring items such as gâteaux, soufflés and ice-creams.

		4 portions	10 portions
almonds	peeled	100 g (4 oz)	250 g (10 oz)
hazelnuts		100 g (4 oz)	250 g (10 oz)
water		60 ml ($\frac{1}{8}$ pt)	150 ml ($\frac{1}{3}$ pt)
sugar		200 g (8 oz)	500 g (1$\frac{1}{4}$ lb)

1 Lightly brown the almonds and hazelnuts in an oven.
2 Cook the water and sugar in a copper or thick-bottomed pan until the caramel stage is reached.
3 Remove the pan from the heat and mix in the nuts.
4 Turn out the mixture on to a lightly oiled marble slab.
5 Allow to become quite cold.
6 Crush to a coarse texture using a rolling pin and store in an airtight container.

94 – Italian meringue

	4 portions	10 portions
granulated or cube sugar	200 g (8 oz)	500 g (1$\frac{1}{4}$ lb)
water	60 ml ($\frac{1}{8}$ pt)	150 ml ($\frac{1}{3}$ pt)
pinch of cream of tartar		
egg whites	4	10

1 Boil the sugar, water and cream of tartar to hard ball stage (121°C, 250°F).
2 Beat the egg whites to full peak and while stiff, beating slowly, pour in the boiling sugar.
3 Use as required for fillings, covering certain gâteaux, tartlets, etc.

95 ~ Swiss meringue

	4 portions	10 portions
egg whites	4	10
icing sugar	200 g (8 oz)	500 g (1¼ lb)

1 Place the ingredients into a suitable bowl in a bain-marie and beat to ribbon stage.
2 When it stands its own weight, use as required for vacherins, petits fours and nests.

—— *Sugar* ——

Further information on pastillage, marzipan, chocolate and sugar products is also available in *Complete Confectionery Techniques* by Ildo Nicolello and Rowland Foote.

BOILED SUGAR

Sugar is boiled for a number of purposes – in pastry work, bakery and sweet-making. Loaf (lump) sugar is generally used, placed in a copper saucepan or sugar boiler and moistened with sufficient cold water to melt the sugar (approximately 125 ml (¼ pt) per 250 g (12 oz)) and allowed to boil steadily without being stirred. Any scum on the surface should be carefully removed, otherwise the sugar is liable to granulate. Once the water has evaporated the sugar begins to cook and it will be noticed that the bubbling in the pan will be slower. It is now necessary to keep the sides of the pan free from crystallised sugar; this can be done either with the fingers or a piece of damp linen. In either case the fingers or linen should be dipped in ice water or cold water, rubbed round the inside of the pan and then quickly dipped back into the water.

The cooking of the sugar then passes through several stages which may be tested with a special sugar thermometer or by the fingers (dip the fingers into ice water, then into the sugar and quickly back into the ice water).

Note To prevent the granulation of sugar a tablespoon of glucose or a few drops of lemon juice per 400 g (1 lb) may be added before boiling. If using cream of tartar it is advisable to add this to the sugar three-quarters of the way through the cooking.

Degrees of cooking sugar

- **Small thread (104°C, 220°F).** When a drop of sugar held between thumb and forefinger forms small threads when the finger and thumb are drawn apart. Used for stock syrup.
- **Large thread (110°C, 230°F).** When proceeding as for small thread the threads are more numerous and stronger. Used for crystallising fruits.
- **Soft ball (116°C, 240°F).** Proceeding as above, the sugar rolls into a soft ball. Used for making fondant.
- **Hard ball (121°C, 250°F).** As for soft ball, but the sugar rolls into a firmer ball. Used for making sweets.
- **Small crack (140°C, 285°F).** The sugar lying on the finger peels off in the form of a thin pliable film which sticks to the teeth when chewed. Used for meringue.
- **Large crack (153°C, 307°F).** The sugar taken from the end of the fingers when chewed breaks clean in between the teeth, like glass. Used for dipping fruits.
- **Caramel (176°C, 349°F).** Cooking is continued until the sugar is a golden brown colour. Used for cream caramels.
- **Black-jack.** Cooking is continued until the sugar is deeply coloured and almost black. Water is then added and the black sugar is allowed to dissolve over a gentle heat. Used for colouring.

Points to note

1 Never attempt to cook sugar in a damp atmosphere, when the humidity is high. The sugar will absorb water from the air and will render it impossible to handle.
2 Never work in a draught as this will prevent it from becoming elastic and will be difficult to mould.
3 Work in clean conditions as any dirt or grease can adversely affect the sugar.

4 The choice of equipment is also important – copper sugar boilers are better suited as these conduct heat rapidly.

5 Never use wooden implements for working with or stirring the sugar. Wood absorbs grease which can in turn ruin the sugar.

6 The amount of glucose you add to the sugar and water will vary depending on the effect you wish to achieve. You may add 10–20 per cent more glucose for blown sugar – this will make it more elastic and, in doing so, increase the cooking temperature by 1–2°C ($\frac{1}{2}$–1°F).

7 The precise cooking temperature varies according to the weight of the sugar being cooked.

8 If you are colouring the sugar, it is advisable to use powdered food colourings as these tend to be brighter. Before using, dilute with a few drops of 90 per cent proof alcohol. Add the colourings to the boiling sugar when the sugar reaches 140°C (284°F). For poured sugar, if you want a transparent effect, add the colour while the sugar is cooking.

9 Once the sugar is poured on to marble and it becomes pliable, it should be transferred to a special, very thick and heat-resistant plastic sheet.

10 To keep the sugar pliable, it should be kept under infra-red or radiant heat lamps.

11 For a good result with poured sugar, use a small gas jet to eliminate any air bubbles while you pour the sugar.

12 Ten per cent calcium carbonate (chalk) may be added to sugar for pouring to give an opaque effect and to improve its shelf-life. This should be added as a slurry at 140°C (280°F).

13 To keep completed sugar work, place in airtight containers, the bottom of which should be lined with a dehydrating compound, such as silica gel, carbide or quicklime.

14 If you are using a weak acid, such as cream of tartar, to prevent crystal formation, it is advisable to add the small amount of acid towards the end of the cooking. Too much acid will over-invert the sugar, producing a sticky, unworkable product.

96 – Poured sugar

sugar cubes	1 kg (2 lb)
water	400 ml ($\frac{3}{4}$ pt)
glucose	250 g (10 oz)
peanut oil	
or pure vaseline for greasing	

1 Prepare templates from cardboard or metal.
2 Roll out plasticine to a thickness of 5–7 mm ($\frac{1}{4}$–$\frac{1}{3}$ in). The larger the model, the thicker the plasticine.
3 Using the template, cut out the shape.
4 Place the plasticine with the model cut out on to aluminium foil.
5 Grease the inside of the shape.
6 Boil the sugar and water. When it forms into a slurry, skim off any white foam.
7 Add the glucose, cook to 140°C (248°F), add any colouring or calcium carbonate.
8 Cook to 136°C (312°F), take off the heat.
9 Stand for 2 minutes, allow any air bubbles to escape.
10 Pour the sugar carefully in a continuous stream into the plasticine template until it reaches the surface.
11 Gently blow any air bubbles away with a gas jet or prick them with the point of a knife.
12 Leave to cook for approximately 20 minutes until it hardens.
13 Lift off the plasticine, leave to cool for 3–4 hours. Peel off the foil. Attach the model to a sugar base made from poured sugar.
14 Dip the base of the model in hard crack sugar, immediately stick it to the base.
15 Using a small paper cone, pipe a fine line of hard crack sugar around the perimeter of the base.
16 For transparent models, spray a thin film of clear, varnish over the models when they are cold. Confectioners' varnish will protect them from damp, dust and fingerprints and act as a preservative.

97 – Spun sugar

Spun sugar is used for decoration.

cube sugar	500 g (1 lb 4 oz)
water	180 ml ($\frac{3}{8}$ pt)
glucose	125 g (5 oz)
pure peanut oil	
or vaseline for greasing	

1 Place the water into a pan, add the sugar, stir gently with a metal spoon.
2 Place over a gentle heat, stir until the sugar begins to boil.

3 Once the sugar starts to foam, skim off the white foam.
4 Clean around the inside of the pan with a clean brush dipped in clean water. This will help to prevent crystallisation.
5 Add the glucose, cook over a high heat.
6 When the sugar reaches 152°C (305°F), take off the heat and allow to cool for 2–5 minutes.
7 The sugar will not spin if it is too hot.
8 Dip the prongs of a fork or whisk into the sugar and flick the fork or whisk rapidly backward and forwards over an oiled wooden rod or rods. The sugar will run down and form fine threads. Continue until a web or mesh of sugar is formed.
9 Carefully collect the spun sugar, place on a tray of silicone paper.
10 Use as required.

Notes Spun sugar very easily picks up moisture from the atmosphere and will soften.

Spun sugar is also used to make the stamens of sugar flowers. Gently roll a handful into an oblong shape approximately 2 cm (1 in) diameter with a heated knife and cut off about 3–4 cm ($1\frac{1}{2}$ in), taking care that the other end remains open. Dip the opened end into crystallised sugar tinted with colour.

98 – Rock sugar

As the name implies this give a rocky effect and is used to decorate cakes and centrepieces.

sugar cubes	500 g (1 lb)
water	200 ml ($\frac{3}{8}$ pt)
royal icing	25–50 g (1–2 oz)

1 Preheat an oven to 120°C (250°F). Line a suitable bowl with foil.
2 Place water into a suitable pan, add sugar, stir with a metal spoon.
3 Gently heat the pan, stir until the sugar has dissolved completely and begins to boil.
4 When the white foam appears skim it off.
5 Clean the inside of a pan with a pastry brush dipped in cold water.
6 Cook the sugar over a high heat.
7 Add colouring at 120°C (248°F).
8 Cook until 138°C (280°F), remove from heat.

9 With a suitable metal spoon, stir in the royal icing quickly.
10 The sugar should rise and double in volume.
11 Pour quickly on to the prepared dish where it will finish rising.
12 Place in the preheated oven for 10 minutes, it will then harden.
13 Store in a cool, dry place for 12 hours.
14 Turn the sugar out and remove the foil.
15 Use as required.

Note The sugar may be sprayed with colour to give a number of different effects. Assemble pieces with royal icing.

99 – Blown sugar

sugar cubes	1 kg (2 lb)
water	400 ml (¾ pt)
glucose	250 g (10 oz)
peanut oil	
or pure vaseline for greasing	

1 Pour the water into a suitable pan, add the sugar.
2 Proceed as for poured sugar.
3 Cook until it reaches 150°C (302°F). Allow to stand for 30 seconds.
4 During the cooking process (up to 140°C, 280°F), the sugar will take on a yellowish tint – this is sometimes used for a base colour for painting models.
5 Pour the cooked sugar on to a marble slab, work with a palette knife.
6 Pull 5–6 times.
7 When the sugar is cool enough to handle, place one hand on one end of the mass and pull it out. Then fold it back on itself. Do this 20–30 times, alternating the direction each time, until the sugar becomes glassy and smooth.
8 Place the sugar on a plastic sheet under a lamp.
9 Cut off a large ball enough to make your designed shape.
10 The ball must be elastic and uniform in temperature.
11 Dig your thumbs into the centre to make a cavity. Heat the end of the aluminium tube of the nozzle of a sugar pump, so that the sugar will stick to it, then insert it halfway into the cavity. With your fingertips firmly press the edges of the sugar around the end of the tube so that it sticks.
12 Blow in air gently and regularly so that the sugar ball swells. Make

sure that the thickness remains constant and even throughout the operation.

13 Use your hands to manipulate and control the bubble as it enlarges and begins to form desired shapes.
14 To maintain the air pressure inside the sugar ball, blow constantly while you shape.
15 When you have achieved your desired shape, mark it as you wish with a knife, grater or hard brush.
16 Place the finished object in a cold place.
17 Remove the sugar cord between the model and the tube with a hot knife or hot scissors.

Notes   The finished objects may be painted with food colour.

Once the sugar has been sanitized (cooked and cooled) it may be kept in air-tight tins with quicklime, carbide or silica gel, covered with foil. When required reheat under a lamp.

Lacquer may be used to give a high-gloss finish to models.

100 – Pulled sugar

cube sugar	1 kg (2 lb)
water	500 ml ($\frac{1}{2}$ pt)
cream of tartar	1.5 kg ($\frac{1}{2}$ tsp)
peanut oil	
or pure vaseline for greasing	

1 Cook the sugar as in previous recipes, removing the white foam when it appears.
2 Add colouring when the temperature reaches 140°C (284°F).
3 When the temperature reaches 156°C (312°F), remove from heat and allow to stand for 30 seconds.
4 Pour sugar on to a clean, lightly greased marble slab or on to a tefal sheet.
5 Using a lightly oiled palette knife or metal scraper, fold the edges back on themselves for 3 or 4 minutes until the sugar almost stops spreading.
6 Fold the mass of sugar back on to itself, with your fingertips or using a palette knife. Pull 5–6 times.
7 With your hands pull the sugar in and out using a folding action. Do this approximately 35–40 times. The sugar will begin to shine and will

become quite smooth. It it starts to crack, it is ready for moulding.

8 Place the sugar in a plastic sheet under a lamp.

9 Cut off the amount you require and mould the sugar into a shape.

Note Once the sugar has become a mass and is sanitised, any left-over pieces may be stored in airtight tins, lined with silica gel, carbide or quicklime covered with aluminium foil. When required, the sugar is reheated under the infrared or radiant lamps.

—— *Marzipan* ——

Most marzipan which is used today for culinary use is produced by large manufacturers. Much of this is of high quality made from sweet and bitter almonds.

There are two distinct types of almond: hard or soft shelled. The hard-shelled types are grown in Italy, Sicily, Spain, Majorca and other European countries. Their kernels are more sweet and tender than those of the soft-shelled type, which are grown in California.

Sugar and water is added to the almonds and this is refined to a smooth paste through granite rollers and then roasted. The paste is then cooled before packing ready for use. Almond pastes are made from this marzipan by the addition of using sugar and glucose.

Hard granulated sugar and white of egg is added to the almond paste to produce commercial macaroon paste.

101 – Marzipan wafers

yield: approx. 24

marzipan	400 g (1 lb)
icing sugar	200 g (8 oz)
cornflour	50 g (2 oz)
milk	50 g (2 oz)
egg white	5–6 oz
vanilla essence	

1 Work down the marzipan with half the egg white until pliable and smooth.

2 Add icing sugar, cornflour, milk and the remaining whites.
3 Allow the mixture to stand for 24 hours, covered well. This is an essential maturing process, which will add to the plasticity of the marzipan when it comes to rolling up the hot shapes.
4 The baking sheet must be heavy duty, best lined with silicone or 100 per cent fat, then dusted with flour.
5 Use stencils to acquire the desired shapes.
6 Bake at 210°C (420°F) for approximately 5–8 minutes.

102 – Almond drops and fingers

yield: approx. 24

marzipan	400 g (1 lb)
caster sugar	400 g (1 lb)
egg white	150 g (6½ oz)

1 Break the marzipan down with a little egg white in a suitable mixing bowl.
2 When the mixture is smooth, add the remaining egg white and the castor sugar. The mixture must be smooth and free from lumps.
3 Pipe the mixture into a baking sheet lined with silicone paper with various shapes. Bake at 180°C (375°F) for approximately 8–10 minutes.
4 The mixture may be piped into small fingers, rounds and ovals.
5 To finish, the biscuits may be sandwiched together with chocolate, apricot jam, butter cream or nougat and, if desired, partially dipped in chocolate.

103 – English rout biscuits

yield: approx. 24

marzipan	800 g (2 lb)
icing sugar	200 g (8 oz)
egg whites	3

1 Work down the marzipan with the egg white to a smooth, pliable paste.
2 Divide into 6 pieces. Leaving 1 plain, colour and flavour, each piece

with raspberry, orange, pistachio, lemon and chocolate.
3 Cut into small pieces and make into various shapes (using icing sugar for dusting).
4 Place on silicone-lined baking sheets, decorate as desired with almonds, glacé cherries and allow to stand for 24 hours.
5 Brush with egg wash, flash in a very hot oven (220°C, 450°F) for approximately 2–5 minutes.
6 Finally, glaze with a solution of hot gum arabic.

104 – Marzipan shortcake fingers

yield: approx. 36

marzipan	600 g (1½ lb)
castor sugar	200 g (8 oz)
butter or margarine	400 g (1 lb)
flour	500 g (1¼ lb)
milk	125 g (5 oz)

1 Cream the butter and sugar together.
2 Work the marzipan down with 100 g (4 oz) of the milk to a smooth, pliable dough. Carefully add this to the butter and sugar.
3 Stir in the flour and milk.
4 Pipe on to silicone-lined baking sheets with a star tube 9 mm (⅜ in). Bake at 190°C (375°F) for approximately 8–10 minutes.
5 After baking, dip the end in melted chocolate.
6 *Note* Fingers may also be sandwiched together with apricot jam, butter cream or chocolate. The mixture may also be flavoured with the zest of lemon, lime or orange or, alternatively, vanilla.
7 If you require cups, cornets or baskets, shape while still warm.

—— *Chocolate* ——

Chocolate must be treated with great care. If chocolate is over-heated it will taste strong and burnt. Water will change the characteristics of chocolate causing it to thicken, affecting the texture, taste and appearance.

PREPARING AND USING CHOCOLATE

Equipment and types of chocolate

- thermometer
- double boiler or porringer
- dipping fork and ring
- moulds preferably plastic
- paint brushes

Cooking chocolate is very often a chocolate substitute and is unsuitable for moulding and for luxury chocolate work.

Real chocolate is produced from cocoa beans, roasted and ground to produce a cocoa mass. Cocoa butter and chocolate liquor form the basis of all chocolate products; the higher the percentage of cocoa solids contained in the chocolate, the richer the chocolate.

Couverture is very high in cocoa butter and requires careful handling.

Dipping chocolate is sold by specialist suppliers – it gives a crisp, hard coat.

Chocolate is available in bars, buttons or drops. Buttons and drops have the advantage that they melt quickly and easily.

The melting process

Break the chocolate into small pieces and melt slowly in a bowl standing in hot water. If the chocolate is allowed to become too hot, the fats will not combine, the chocolate will lose stability, and its flavour and texture will be spoilt. Stir the chocolate gently until smooth; the temperature should never go above 50–55°C (122–131°F). Workable consistency is around 40–45°C (104–113°F).

Microwave melting

Break the chocolate into small pieces and place into a non-metallic bowl. Put the microwave on full power for about 30 seconds. After each 30 seconds, stir the chocolate. Do not allow too long before stirring, otherwise hot spots develop in the bowl, resulting in burnt chocolate.

Tempering

It is essential that a thermometer is used for this process. Tempering is necessary because of the high proportion of cocoa butter and other fats in the chocolate. This stabilises the fats in the chocolate to give a crisp, glossy finish when dry.

The following temperatures are for most dark or plain couverture; for milk couverture, the temperatures at all the stages should be reduced by about 2°C (4°F).

1 Break the couverture into even-sized pieces. Begin the melting process, stir until it melts. Check the temperature.
2 Allow the chocolate to reach a temperature of between 48°C (113°F) and 50°C (122°F). Remove the bowl from the pan. Cool the chocolate quickly by plunging the bowl into cold water. Do not allow the water to come into contact with the chocolate.
3 When the temperature of the couverture reaches 25–27°C (77–81–88°F) return the bowl to the pan of hot water.
4 Raise the temperature, this time to 31–32°C (88–90°F).
5 Remove from the heat. The chocolate is now ready to use.

Points to remember:
- Do not attempt to melt chocolate over direct heat.
- Chocolate burns easily.
- Never allow water or steam to come into contact with the chocolate.

Ingredient additions to chocolate
- **Butter.** Always use unsalted butter as salt can taste and therefore produce an inferior product.
- **Sugar.** Generally castor and icing sugars are used.
- **Milk.** Use whole milk rather than skimmed or semi-skimmed, as this give more body to finished sweets.
- **Glucose.** Liquid glucose is easier to measure if you warm the syrup. Use warm spoons and knives to measure and scrape with.

Moulding

Many different types of moulds are available for use in making confectionery. Moulds must always be scrupulously clean. Several days before you intend to use the moulds, they should be washed thoroughly, rinsed well and dried. Keep in a dry place. Immediately before use, polish the inside with cotton wool. Do not touch the inside with your fingers as this may tend to leave a mark on the finished item. Even the smallest amount of oil from the skin may cause problems when removing the chocolate from the mould. It is not necessary to wash the mould after each use, but you must not touch the inside of the mould between fillings.

Protect finished goods from damp and humidity. It is advisable when decorating moulded items to wear cotton gloves to avoid marking the surface.

Moulded baskets

Baskets and bowls can be filled with chocolate or other sweets or marzipan fruits. They may also be served with fresh fruit and cream or ice-cream to offer as a sweet. After having moulded the basket, make a handle from moulding chocolate. Attach the handle with a little melted chocolate.

– Chocolate for hand moulding

plain chocolate	125 g (5 oz)
liquid glucose	90 ml (4 fl oz)

1 Melt the chocolate in a bowl over a pan of hot water.
2 Add the liquid glucose and stir the mixture well.
3 Form into a bowl and wrap in cling film. Allow to rest for 3 hours in the refrigerator.
4 When ready to use, uncover, allow to come to room temperature but do not allow it to become too soft, otherwise it will be difficult to handle. It should be solid but pliable, slightly oily and tacky.

Dipping chocolates

In order to dip centres in chocolate successfully it is important that sufficient chocolate is melted to cover them completely when dipped. It is easier to dip chocolates if you have a set of dipping forks. As you become proficient at dipping centres, you will soon develop the skills to make and decorate finished chocolates with the dipping tools.

Dipping hard centres

1 Drop the sweet into the chocolate and turn it over using the fork. When completely covered, lift out of the chocolate with a fork.
2 Tap the fork on the side of the bowl so that the excess chocolate falls away, then draw the bottom of the fork across the lip of the bowl to remove any accumulation underneath the sweet.
3 Place the dipped chocolate on to a sheet of parchment paper to dry.

If the chocolate is difficult to remove, gently ease if off using a flat-bladed knife.

4 For round sweets, use a dipping ring. The metal ring is usually thicker than the prongs of the dipping fork and will not so readily penetrate the sweet as you proceed to dip.

5 Leave the dipped chocolates in a cool dry place for several hours to set completely.

Finishes

As in all forms of food preparation the finishing of chocolates and truffles is very important. The finish can sometimes help to identify the flavour or content of the chocolate. They may be finished by piping designs on each chocolate or dipping in a different type of chocolate to the filling using a contrast of flavours and finishes i.e., white, dark or milk. Chocolates may also be personalised, particularly if they are for a gift. Tiny chocolate or sugar flowers may be used. Crystallised or glacé fruits may be used alongside marzipan flowers and fruits. Rose and crystallised violet petals are sometimes used.

Using chocolate
Chocolate can also be used for finishing other foods. Chocolate coats are used for decorating cakes and gâteaux. Chocolate shapes cut with specialised cutters are impressive finishing touches to sweet dishes.

Chocolate leaves
The leaves from any non-poisonous plant may be used. Leaf moulds can be purchased.

When using fresh leaves, such as bay leaves, wash and dry thoroughly. Paint the underside of each leaf with melted chocolate taking care to go to the edge. Allow to cool until set. When dry, carefully remove the leaf. If the chocolate is too thin and starts to break, paint another thin coat over the first and again allow to dry. It is not advisable to set them in the refrigerator as the cold temperature makes the leaves brittle and so they will not peel from the chocolate.

Chocolate marbling
Using tempered chocolate and white chocolate a marbled or combed effect may be created by spreading the chocolate on to acetate or polythene sheets. The flexibility of the acetate or polythene allows you to 'shape' the chocolate as it sets.

105 – Truffles

yield: approx. 30

single cream	125 ml ($\frac{1}{4}$ pt)
couverture	225 g (9 oz)
rum to taste	

1 Break the couverture into small pieces. Bring the cream to the boil, then remove from heat and stir in the couverture.
2 Flavour with rum and allow to set in a refrigerator.
3 Turn out on to a tray and dust with icing sugar.
4 Form into rolls, 1½ cm (¾ in) in diameter and cut into sections.
5 Roll on to a mixture of icing sugar and cocoa powder, or grated couverture, and place into paper cases.

106 – White chocolate truffles

yield: approx. 20–25 truffles

white chocolate	200 g (8 oz)
unsalted butter	50 g (2 oz)
single cream	3 tbsp

1 Break the chocolate into small pieces and melt gently in a suitable double pan.
2 Stir the chocolate away from the heat.
3 Add the softened butter, slowly add the cream.
4 Cover the mixture, allow to cool until it is firm enough to handle.
5 Mould the mixture into small balls.
6 Roll the truffles in desiccated coconut to cover completely.

Variations, add:

brandy	4 tbsp
sloe gin	6 tbsp
Malibu	4 tbsp
Cointreau	4 tbsp
whisky	4 tbsp

107 – Champagne truffles

Champagne is very difficult to transfer from the bottle into chocolates. The addition of champagne or sparkling wine will produce a light and delicate texture to the truffle. The liquid must be added gradually. If the mixture starts to separate or curdle, do not add any more liquid. Allow to cool until set and stir gently. Leave the mixture to set completely before further handling.

35–40 truffles

milk chocolate	300 g (12 oz)
unsalted butter, softened	100 g (4 oz)
champagne	150 ml (5 fl oz)
milk chocolate to coat	100 g (4 oz)

1 Break the chocolate into small pieces and melt in a double pan. Stir gently until the chocolate is melted.
2 Remove the top saucepan, leave the chocolate to cool.
3 Stir the chocolate thoroughly. Gradually add the butter, the mixture must be thick and creamy and slightly grainy in appearance.
4 Slowly add the champagne, stirring gently. Cover and leave to set.
5 Mould into small balls, chill down until firm.
6 Dip in melted white chocolate.

—— *Pastillage* ——

108 – Gum paste (pastillage)

icing sugar	500 g ($1\frac{1}{4}$ lb)
cornflour	100 g (4 oz)
leaves gelatine	2
lemon, juice of	$\frac{1}{2}$
egg whites	2
or using gum tragacanth	
royal icing no acid or glycerine added	800 g (2 lb)
gum tragacanth added to 500 g ($1\frac{1}{4}$ lb) icing sugar	12 g ($\frac{1}{2}$ oz)

1 Soak the leaf gelatine in water and drain. Melt with lemon juice. Sieve the icing sugar and cornflour. Mix the egg whites in carefully, then

carefully pour in the melted gelatine which must not exceed a temperature of 48°C (120°F). Mix well, knead until a smooth dough is obtained.

2 Using gum tragacanth, this gives a better pastillage. Disperse the gum tragacanth in the icing sugar. Gradually add to the royal icing on slow speed. Cover with a damp cloth, allow to rest for 20 minutes. Remove from the mixing bowl, work to a smooth dough with additional icing sugar if required.

Notes   Pastillage should be allowed to relax for 24 hours covered with polythene or a plastic bag to prevent crusting – this allows the paste to roll out better and prevents excess shrinkage during the drying process.

Pastillage is used for modelling centrepieces and caskets with the aid of templates.

Always use a mixture of icing sugar and cornflour for dusting. Allow cut pieces to dry on glass, although wooden trays may be used, turn once in the drying process. Drying may also be carried out by laying the pieces on silicone or good-quality wax paper.

The sugar pieces are assembled together with royal icing which should not contain glycerine.

GLOSSARY

A blanc	To keep white, without colour
A brun	To colour brown
Agar agar	Gelatine substitute, obtained from dried seaweed
Aiguillettes	Small strips of cooked meat, poultry or fish
Akee	A Caribbean fruit
Al dente	Pasta or vegetables slightly underdone so that there is some resistance to the bite
Attereaux	Cooked small pieces of food (meat, fish or vegetables) coated with a thick sauce, crumbed and deep fried
Ballottine	Boned stuffed leg of poultry
Bamboo shoots	The inner shoots of the bamboo plant, used extensively in Chinese cooking
Barding	To cover breasts of birds with slices of fat bacon
Beurre blanc	Sauce of finely chopped shallots, white wine and melted butter
Blanc de volaille	White flesh of poultry, breast or wing (or suprême)
Bitok	A type of hamburger
Bouillabaisse	A fish stew
Bourbon	An American whisky
Bortsch	Russian or Polish duck and beetroot-flavoured soup
Brioche	Yeast dough, enriched with eggs
Calvados	Apple brandy from Normandy
Carapace	The shell of, for example crabs, lobster
Cartouche	A buttered paper for covering foods
Cassolettes	Individual dishes, ramekins in which foods are cooked or served
Ceps	An edible mushroom
Ceviche	Fish marinaded in lime and lemon juice, of Spanish Peruvian origin
Chanterelle	Small yellow mushroom with a frilly edge

Chantilly cream	Whipped cream, flavoured with vanilla and sweetened
Chapati	Crisp wholemeal pancake
Chiffonade	Shredded
Chowder	Unpassed shellfish or sweetcorn soup from the USA
Clafoutis	Fruit baked in batter
Clam	A type of shellfish
Cointreau	Orange-flavoured liqueur
Colcannon	Irish dish containing cabbage and potato
Coulibiac	Russian fish pie
Coulis (Fr)	A purée in liquid form, e.g. tomato, raspberry,
Cullis (Eng)	used as a sauce
Couscous	Arabic dish made using a fine type of semolina
Couverture	Covering chocolate
Craquelins	Small, filled, pancakes crumbed and deep fried
Crepinette	Thin pig's caul (membrane)
Croustade	Baked pastry cases in or on which cooked foods are served
Cru	Raw, not cooked, or from the raw state
Crudités	Raw vegetables cut in bite-size pieces, e.g. celery, carrot
Curaçao	Liqueur made from bitter oranges. Originally from the West Indies
Dahl	Indian dish using lentils
Demi-glace	Refined brown sauce
Dipping	Immersing into, for example, chocolate
Dock	Pierce pastry with numerous small holes
Drambuie	Whisky-based liqueur flavoured with honey and herbs
Dulse	Edible red seaweed
Duxelle	Chopped shallot and chopped mushrooms cooked together
Emulsify	To mix oil and liquid together
En-croûte	Wrapped in pastry
Enrobing	Coating with, for example, chocolate
En papillote	Oiled greaseproof paper or foil in which raw food is cooked in the oven
Eviscerating	Removing the innards or guts

File powder	An American spice
Filo paste	Very thin paste of Greek origin, usually purchased prepared
Fleurons	Small, crescent-shaped pieces of puff pastry
Fraiser	The action of scraping sweet paste to make smooth and to mix before use
Fricadelles	Chopped raw or cooked veal or beef steaks like hamburgers
Fricassé	A white stew in which the main ingredient is cooked in the sauce, e.g. veal, chicken
Fritots	Savoury fritters of meat, fish or vegetables, battered and deep fried
Forcemeat	Savoury stuffings of meat or poultry
Fromage frais	Fat-free, skimmed milk fresh cheese
Fruits de mer	Seafoods: shellfish, crustaceans and molluscs
Fumet	Concentrated essence of fish, meat or poultry
Galette	Small flat cake, e.g. sweetcorn, potato
Ganache	Rich chocolate cream filling for gâteaux or petits fours
Garam masala	A mixture of spices
Gazpacho	Spanish cold soup of cucumber, tomato and garlic
Ghee	Clarified butter, used in Indian cooking
Gosling	Baby goose
Gravlax	Swedish dish of raw salmon, marinaded with dill
Grenadins	Small thick larded slices of veal which are pot roasted
Guacamole	An avocado and chilli sauce used with meat, as a filling for tortillas or as a dip
Gum arabic	A type of edible gum
Gum paste or gum tragacanth	A type of dough used for modelling
Haunch	For example, of venison, the leg and rump (hip, buttock and thigh)
Hummus	Paste of chick peas and sesame seeds
Ignite	To light (to flame, e.g. brandy)
Infuse	To extract flavour and aroma by covering an ingredient with liquid and allowing it to stand

Jus-lié	Thickened gravy made from veal stock
Kemangi	Sweet basil leaves
Kirsch	Distilled white spirit made from wild cherries, mainly from France and Switzerland
Larding	Inserting fat bacon into meat
Lea and Perrins	Worcester sauce (a commercial product)
Lemon grass	A herb of lemon-flavour
Lesser galangal	A spice similar to ginger used in SE Asian dishes
Liaison	A thickening of yolks and cream used to finish certain soups and sauces
Macerating	Steeping to soften or to absorb, e.g. fruit in a liqueur
Maigret	Type of duck, menu term to describe breast of certain duck
Mange-tout	Type of pea (sugar pea), the pod of which is also eaten
Marinating	Steeping in a marinade to tenderise, e.g. venison
Mascapone	An Italian cream cheese
Maw seeds	Type of seed similar to poppy seeds
Monosodium glutamate	A flavour enhancer
Monté au beurre	The adding of small pieces of butter to thicken a reduced cooking liquid to make a sauce
Morels	Type of edible fungi, brown, irregular and cone shape
Mozzarella	Cheese originally made from the milk of water buffalo
Nam pla	A Thai fish sauce
Noilly Prat	A dry vermouth
Oak leaf	A type of lettuce
Okra	Type of vegetable, also known as gumbo and ladies fingers
Oyster mushrooms	Ear-shaped, grey or greenish-brown wild mushroom
Panada or panade	Thick base mixture, e.g. choux paste before eggs are added
Pastillage	Gum paste for modelling

Paupiette	Stuffed, rolled strip of fish or meat
Paw-paw	Tropical fruit
Pecorino	Ewe's milk cheese with peppercorns
Perdrix	Older pheasant suitable for braising
Pimentos	Green, red or yellow coloured vegetables, also known as peppers
Pitta bread	Type of Middle Eastern unleavened bread
Physalis	Cape gooseberry used for petits fours
Plain russe	Mixture of milk, egg yolks and sugar, set with gelatine and cornflour
Plantains	A type of large banana
Pluche	Small spray, e.g. of chervil, used as a garnish
Polyunsaturated fat	A healthier product than saturated fat as it produces less cholesterol
Porringer	A double saucepan used in chocolate work
Praline	Sugar and nuts cooked to hard boil stage, crushed and used for gâteaux and ice-cream
Prosciutto	A type of smoked ham
Quenelles	'Dumplings' of fish, poultry or game. Made by finely mincing the flesh, beating in egg white and cream and poaching
Quark	Salt-free soft cheese, made from semi-skimmed milk
Râble	Saddle, e.g. of hare, râble de lièvre
Rack of lamb	Best-end of lamb
Radicchio	A red-leaved type of lettuce
Ramekins	Small dishes for serving individual portions of food
Riccotta	Cheese made from the discarded whey of other cheeses
Saccharometer	An instrument to measure sugar density
Saffron	Stamens from a species of crocus used for flavour and yellow colour
Sake	Japanese wine made from rice
Salmis	A brown stew of game
Salsa	A sauce
Sauternes	Sweet white wine from Bordeaux region of France

Scorzonera	Type of vegetable, also known as oyster plant
Sec	Dry, not sweet
Sear	To very quickly seal the outside of food
Serrano ham	A smoked ham
Shitake	A type of mushroom
Shiso	A herb of basil-like flavour
Silicone paper	Paper to which foods do not stick
Silpat tray	A baking sheet for jaconde mixture
Smetana	A low-fat product – a cross between sour cream and yoghurt
Smoke box	Equipment to smoke food items
Smoking	The use of smoke to cook or partially cook meat, fish or game
Socle	A base of rice, wax or ice on which to place cold buffet items
Sorrel	A bright green leaf with sharp taste
Subric	A basic sweet or savoury shallow fried, e.g. spinach
Sweet potato	Potato with a chestnut flavour
Tahini	Paste of sesame seed
Tandoor	Indian clay oven
Tempering	A process in chocolate work
Tiramisu	An Italian trifle-like sweet
Tofu	Soya bean curd
Torten	A type of gâteau
Tortillas	Type of unleavened bread served with Mexican dishes
Tranche	A slice
Tresse	Plaited, e.g. sole
Ve-tsin	Chinese flavouring with a monosodium glutamate base
Vesiga	The marrow of the spinal column of the sturgeon
Water chestnuts	A white, crunchy, sweet root vegetable, about the size of a walnut
Yam	Type of vegetable
Yoghurt	An easily digested fermented milk product

Index